A
Doric
Dictionary

Two-way Lexicon of North-East Scots
Doric – English, English – Doric
New Enlarged Edition

Compiled and edited by
DOUGLAS KYNOCH M.A. (Abdn.)

Luath Press Limited
EDINBURGH
www.luath.co.uk

DOUGLAS KYNOCH was born, brought up and educated in Aberdeen. He spent most of his life in broadcasting: with Grampian Television from its opening, then with the BBC in Glasgow. A second career in writing began in the 1990s, his first book *Teach Yourself Doric* (a spoof language primer) becoming an immediate Scottish best-seller.

This dictionary was first published by the Scottish Cultural Press in 1996. A revised edition was published in 2004. This new enlarged edition was first published by Luath Press in 2019. Reprinted 2020

ISBN: 978-1-912147-68-7
The paper used in this book is recyclable. It is made from low chlorine pulps produced in a low energy, low emission manner from renewable forests.
Typeset in 10.5 point Sabon by Lapiz
Printed and bound by iPrint Global, Ely

Preface

DORIC IS A NAME given to broad and rustic dialect. Deriving from that spoken by the Dorians in ancient Greece, it has been applied in more recent times to the dialects of England and of Scotland, while in Scotland itself the term refers pre-eminently to the dialect of the Scots language which is spoken in the north-eastern corner of the country. The Doric of north-east Scotland meets both the traditional qualifications. On the one hand, its broadness can present difficulty even for Scots in other parts of Scotland, while on the other, its richest manifestation has always been found in the rural hinterland, where the language has recorded and labelled all the trappings of everyday life in what was a largely farming and fishing community.

It may be useful to establish what we mean in the present context by the term, north-east. For the purposes of this dictionary, it has been taken to include the old counties of Moray, Banffshire and Aberdeenshire, along with the former Kincardineshire, where there are language differences between north and south. Additionally, as the north-east has always claimed as its own such writers as Violet Jacob, Helen Cruickshank and Sir Alexander Gray, their home county of Angus has been included, or at least the northern part of it, which has strong linguistic ties with Kincardine. Certain forms appear in Angus which are unknown in, even alien to the rest of the north-east (*no* for *nae* for example); but similarities are strong and argue for inclusion.

It should come as no surprise to anyone that over so extensive an area there should be a considerable number of linguistic differences. If language can change slightly from village to village, as it does, then changes from county to county may be even greater. Only a rash man would say that this or that expression was not Doric simply because it was not his Doric. The truth is that there is not one monolithic form of Doric but a multiplicity of forms, differing to a greater or lesser degree here and there. Not only is there a northern and southern Doric, a Banffshire and a Mearns Doric, there is a farming and a fishing Doric and a now somewhat diluted (and often debased) urban Doric. It is interesting to note how the word for a scarecrow changes from county to county and that for a seagull from town to town.

A north-east born journalist has taken me to task for using the word *gae* in a Doric context, protesting that *gyang* was the only allowable rendering of the English verb, *to go*. This is, quite simply, untrue. It may have been the form used in the area my critic was brought up in; but as is clear from the ensuing text, there are other widely used and acceptable forms such as *ging* (Aberdeen city) and *gang*, gaan (coastal) and *gae*. Individual Doric speakers appear to use more than one.

The vocabulary in this dictionary has been drawn from the works of north-east writers published between 1871 and the present day, while Helen Beaton's book, *At the Back of Benachie* attempts to reproduce the speech of 100 years before, taking us back approximately to 1815. Some may question the value of including words long obsolete; but they are part of the Doric heritage and are useful for reading older Doric texts. The list of writers is far from exhaustive but contains as many as could be conveniently referred to by one individual over the six and a half month period allowed for the compilation of the dictionary.

Of especial value has been the work of writers of prose or dialogue, of which, sadly, there have been few. Into this category come not only Helen Beaton but the creator of *Johnny Gibb of Gushetneuk*, Wm. Alexander; the author of the dialogues, *Mains and Hilly*, James Alexander; several newspaper contributors from Wm. Donaldson's Victorian prose collection, *The Language of the People* and the autobiographical work of the Rev. David Ogston. Alexander Smith's work was of invaluable service in pointing to the linguistic variants to be found in Kincardineshire; and, although he spent the latter half of his life in Buchan and his Doric could conceivably have got a little *throwder*, I was never myself aware of any confusion.

Doric poetry, though more readily available than prose, can be something of a minefield for someone in search of purity of language, since purity of language need not be the poet's first concern. For one thing, a poet uses language creatively and moves it on from its original sense to mean something imaginatively different. For another, he or she may borrow terms used in other parts of Scotland, believing any Scots word to be fair game for the writer. Hugh MacDiarmid certainly subscribed to this view and various other writers were to follow his example in the Scottish Renaissance of the early 1920s. For this reason, at an early stage, I had to abandon the work of Helen Cruickshank, a devotee of MacDiarmid, as a reliable example of Angus dialect, when I found several intrusions of the kind described (although a few cullings from Miss Cruickshank's verse survive to confirm some of the more basic differences of Angus speech). The work of other well-known poets has, for similar reasons, been avoided or used with circumspection.

In using the dictionary, readers will occasionally find a word marked with an initial letter. This points to the writer in whose work the word was found and is an indication of the part of the north-east he or she comes from and the period in which the word was used. A list of authors and appropriate code signs is provided. This system of word identification is rudimentary but may prove useful as a general guide for writers and readers alike.

It may fairly be pointed out that some of the vocabulary listed here is not, strictly speaking, Doric at all but merely a Doric form of English. *Suppersteeshun* for *superstition* for example. Yet if this is or was the way in which the word was commonly spoken in the north-east, then it is right that it should be recorded and preserved rather than that the pure English form should be used in the speaking of Doric. As for what is pure Doric and what counts as slang, it is not within my competence to distinguish between the two any more than I can point categorically to obsolete usages.

A Doric Dictionary is offered to the people of the north-east, wherever they may be, in gratitude for having been nurtured by our shared culture.

Douglas Kynoch
Glasgow, 1996.

Preface to the Enlarged Edition

THIS ENLARGED EDITION of *A Doric Dictionary* benefits greatly from the inclusion of vocabulary drawn from the work of Prof W. P. Milne, whose novel, *Eppie Elrick*, written in his native Buchan dialect, was published in 1955.

Douglas Kynoch
Aberdeen, 2019.

Spelling

DESPITE SIGNS OF increasing standardisation, there is no universally recognised way of spelling Scots; and readers of the language will find considerable variation. This will become apparent in the first part of the dictionary, where, with a few exceptions, spelling is generally as found in the text from which the word was culled. In turning the dictionary around, however, and compiling the English to Doric section I have thought it sensible to review the orthography to some extent and to reduce the number of spelling options. It is not uncommon, therefore, for a word to be spelt one way in Part One and in another in Part Two, the latter being considered preferable for one reason or another.

There may, in fact, be more than one acceptable spelling in Part Two; and, as I have not eradicated the orthographical forms used in other parts of Scotland, a north-east Doric form may be followed by a more common all-Scotland form (eg, *daad* and *daud*; *meen* and *mune*; *stoor* and *stour*). Both spelling forms are capable of being spoken in the Doric way, while the latter (eg, *daud* and *mune*) may also be spoken using a vowel sound alien to the north-east but heard in other parts of Scotland. In writing, then, one has the choice of appealing to an exclusively north-east readership on the one hand or a wider Scots readership on the other. Charles Murray adopted the latter course and, perhaps in consequence, won himself a national following. Few other north-east poets have followed suit.

Modern practice is to eradicate the apostrophe as far as possible and certainly in common words such as *an* meaning *and* and *amo* meaning *among*. This is understood by some to indicate that the word in question exists in its own right and is not a mere corruption of English. Whatever the validity of that view, I am happy to respect the convention and apostrophes have been eliminated as far as possible, surviving only occasionally in Part Two, where the meaning of a word would otherwise be unclear.

Pronunciation

Vowels and Diphthongs

a, *aa* and *aw* are pronounced as in the English *car*.

a before *bb*, *m*, *mp* and *nk*, however is pronounced *u* as in
   cup in both English and Scots words (eg, *cabbage*, *crabbit*,
   stamp and *bank*). Before *g*, *a* may be pronounced *u* (eg,
   bag, *baggie*) or *a* as in *car* (eg, *stag*).

ai and *ae* are pronounced as in the English *hate* (eg, *mait*, *maet*).

a-e as in the English *seen* (eg, *ane*, *bane*, *stane*, more usually
   rendered *een*, *been*, *steen*).

ee and *ei* (sometimes also *ie*) as in the English *feet*.

i is pronounced somewhere between the English *i* and *e*.

ie is sometimes pronounced as in *feet* and sometimes as in *fit*.
   Several words are spelt now *ie*, now *ei*. To attempt to
   clarify the situation, I have classified those in Part Two
   according to pronunciation, so that *speil*, *speir*, *sheilin*,
   deil and *neist* are spelt *ei*, the first letter indicating the
   pronunciation, while *fient* and *nieve* are spelt *ie*, the
   first letter pointing once more to pronunciation. As the
   diphthong in *chiel*, *brier*, *chief*, *feish*, *neiper*, *remeid* and
   sheil appears to be spelt only one way, I have left these
   as they stand, though there is obviously room for further
   standardisation.

oi is said as *y*, being rendered this way in Part Two, eg, *dytit*, *doitit*.

oo as in *moon*.

ou may be pronounced either as in *moon* or as in *cow*. With a few words like *clout*, both pronunciations are possible, though generally with different meanings. For this reason, I have eliminated the *ou* spelling as far as possible in Part Two, replacing it either with *oo* or *ow* according to pronunciation. Where this was uncertain, I left *ou* untouched.

u is pronounced as in the English *jug*.

u-e as in *mune* is generally pronounced *ee*. Hence *meen* and *sheen*.

ui is problematic, being susceptible to different pronunciations in different areas. In the words *buird* and *buirdly*, for example, *boord(ly)* would appear to apply to Angus and the former South Kincardineshire, with *beerdly* or *byoordly* applying in the rest of the north-east. The *ui* division line, according to Chambers Scots Dictionary, is said to run from Mount Battock to Skateraw on the Kincardineshire coast.

Consonants

ch is pronounced as in the Scots *loch*.

g and *k* should be pronounced before *n* (eg, *knowe* and *gnap*).

ng in the middle of a word implies no *g* sound, so that the *g* in the Doric *hunger* is spoken like the *ng* in the English *singer*.

s or the *s* sound is sometimes replaced by *sh* in such words as *vessel*, *officer* and *sew (shoo)*.

wh at the start of a word is, with the exception of Angus,
   pronounced *f*, the words *whaar*, *whan* and *what* being
   rendered *faar*, *faan* and *fat*.

Diminutives

North-east Scots is much given to the use of diminutives. *Bairn*
can become *bairnikie*; *babbie*, *babbitie*; *lass* may be rendered
lassock or lassockie. The most popular of the diminutive forms,
however, is the simple *ie* ending which appears most commonly in
one-syllable words such as *loon(ie)*, though it can also be found
in words of two syllables, eg *bourach(ie)* and, exceptionally, in
longer words. Diminutives appear rarely in this dictionary, but,
by using the *ie* ending, can be created from appropriate nouns.

Bibliography & Key to Code Symbols

THE CODE SYMBOLS shown here indicate the writer in whose work the word was found, the home area and dates of the writer being given where known. They may also point either to the part of the north-east where the word came from or to the period in which use of the word was current. The symbol usually indicates an unusual word or an unusual variant of a word. A commonplace word is coded, where it is one of several having the same meaning. The system offers no more than a rough guide to the provenance of the word.

Code letter

A   **George Abel of Aberdeenshire** (1856–1916): brought up on farms in the parish of Kintore; minister of Udny Free Church for 35 years; author of the verse collection *Wylins fae My Wallet*, published 1916.

A1   **James Alexander of Ythan Wells, Aberdeenshire:** author of Mains and Hilly, a collection of dialogues in the Aberdeenshire dialect, originally published in the *Aberdeen Weekly Free Press* and brought out in book form in 1929.

A2   **William Alexander of Aberdeenshire** (1826–94): author of *Johnny Gibb of Gushetneuk*, published 1871 and *Life Among My Ain Folk*, published 1882; ploughman, journalist and editor of the *Aberdeen Free Press*, in which *Johnny Gibb* was serialised.

B   **Peter Buchan of Peterhead** (1917–1991): a fisherman like his father; author of a collection of poems, *Mount Pleasant* and a collection of north-east tales, *Fisher Blue*. What has been drawn on here is his contribution to *Buchan Claik*, a compendium of north-east words and phrases which he compiled in collaboration with David Toulmin.

B1   **Helen Beaton of Aberdeenshire.** Mrs Beaton's account of life in the Garioch in the 19th century is based in particular on the parish of Rayne and relies on the stories and language of her grandmother. Entitled *At the Back o' Benachie*, it was published in 1915.

C   **J. M. Caie of Banffshire** (1879–1949). John Morrison Caie was born in Banchory-Devenick, the son of a Banffshire minister. He was brought up on a farm in the parish of Enzie. Trained both in law and agriculture, he spent much of his working life with the Board of Agriculture for Scotland. Of his two volumes of verse, it is *'Twixt Hills and Sea* which helps give the dictionary its Banffshire flavour.

C1   **Helen B. Cruickshank of Angus** (1886–1975). Helen Burness Cruickshank was reared at Hillside between Montrose and the North Esk. The greater part of her working life with the civil service was spent in the Department of Health in Edinburgh. A devotee of Hugh MacDiarmid, her Scots vocabulary tends to be eclectic, so only the most basic terms are quoted as examples of Angus speech.

F   **Alexander Fenton of Aberdeenshire** (1929–2012). Director of the European Ethnological Research Centre in

Edinburgh, Prof Fenton, a native of the Howe of Pitglassie
in Auchterless, has used a farm in that parish as the basis
of a study of the words and expressions describing farm
equipment and techniques in the second quarter of the
20th century. This invaluable record of north-east farm
practice is contained in his book, *Wirds an' Wark 'e
Seasons Roon*, published in 1987.

G   **Flora Garry of Aberdeenshire** (1900–2000). Of farming
stock, Mrs Garry was brought up at Mains of Auchmunziel,
New Deer. Trained as a teacher, she taught at Dumfries
and Strichen, was married to R. Campbell Garry, Regius
Professor Physiology at Glasgow University and retired
to Comrie. Her verse collection, *Bennygoak* was first
published in 1974.

GI   **Sir Alexander Gray of Angus** (1882–1968). Gray was
first Jeffrey Professor of Political Economy at Aberdeen
University from 1921-34, to which period much of his
Scots verse belongs. The linguistic variants of Angus
become apparent in his verse collection, *Any Man's Life*
which appeared in 1924.

J   **Violet Jacob of Angus** (1863–1946). Mrs Jacob (née
Kennedy-Erskine) was a sister of the 19th laird of Dun, the
family having owned for centuries the Dun estate between
Brechin and Montrose. Author of four books of verse, her
Scottish Poems were published in 1944.

K   **William Knight** (1825–1866) was born and brought
up in Banffshire before settling in Aberdeen. Of a
brilliant turn of mind, he won a bursary to St Andrews
University, devoting himself largely thereafter to

shoemaking and the writing of verse. His collection,
Auld Yule and Other Poems was published in 1869
after his early death.

M   **Charles Murray of Aberdeenshire** (1864–1941). Born in
      Alford, Dr Murray was a civil engineer who spent most
      of his professional life in South Africa, where he was
      ultimately appointed the Union's Secretary for Public
      Works. He retired to the north-east, where several books
      of verse were published in his lifetime, *Hamewith: the
      Complete Poems* not appearing until 1979.

M1   **J.C. Milne of Aberdeenshire** (1897–1962). Another writer
      of farming stock, John Milne was born at Memsie near
      Fraserburgh. After a brilliant academic career at Aberdeen
      University, he turned to teaching, later becoming Master of
      Method at Aberdeen College of Education. Though much
      of his verse is devoted to school teaching, Milne will be
      no less well remembered for his humorous exposé of the
      trials of farming life laid bare in his first collection, the
      Orra Loon (1946). His collected *Poems* were published
      posthumously in 1963.

M2   **G. K. Murray of Banffshire** (1910–1985). Born in Keith,
      Gordon Murray was a land agent with the Forestry
      Commission. His little book of prose pieces, *Tales o a
      Gamie*, published in 1978, was specially written for use in
      schools and colleges.

M3   **William P. Milne** (1881–1967) was born at Longside and
      schooled at Peterhead and Aberdeen Grammar School.
      Graduating from Aberdeen University with first class
      honours in maths and natural philosophy, he was later

appointed to the chair of Mathematics at Leeds University. On retirement, he completed and published his novel of the 1715 rebellion, *Eppie Elrick*, written in his native Buchan dialect. It appeared in 1955.

O   **David D. Ogston of Aberdeenshire** (1945–2008). In two volumes of autobiography, *White Stone Country* and *Dry-stone Days*, David Ogston, minister at St John's, Perth, described in Doric his upbringing on farms in Buchan and the Garioch.

R   **Elsie S. Rae of Banffshire.** Elsie Rae was the wife of the Rev. Robert Wilson. Her verse collections include *Private John McPherson* (1917) and *Hansel Fae Hame and other Scots Poems* (1927), the latter forming part of this bibliography.

S   **Alexander Smith of Kincardineshire** (1911–1993). Alex Smith is remarkable for having, in the years before his death, written three substantial books in Doric. Two of them, *Forty Years in Kincardineshire* and *Forty Years in Buchan and Banff*, are autobiographical; the third, *Fairmin the Wey It Wis* records farm life over the period of a year. As well as having what appears to be total recall, Smith had a keen ear, which discerned the differences between the Doric of Kincardineshire and that of Buchan and Banff.

T   **David Toulmin of Aberdeenshire.** This was the pen-name of John Reid (1913–1998) born at Rathen in Buchan, the son of a farm-worker. He himself spent his working life in farm labour but turned, in due course, to the writing of novels. He contributed the farming data to *Buchan Claik*, while his collaborator, Peter Buchan provided the fishing material.

Additional Bibliography

Sheena Blackhall of Aberdeen and Deeside: *The Cyard's Kist* (1984)

George Bruce of Fraserburgh and Edinburgh: *Perspectives* (1984)

A.M. Davidson of Midmar: *Tinkler's Whussel* (1981)

Joyce Everill of Torry, Aberdeen and Fife: *Granny's Button Box* (1989)

Donald Gordon of Aberdeen: *The Low Road Hame* (1987)

William Imray of Tarland: *Langstene Nou and Syne* (1991)

M.S. Lumsden of Rothiemurchus and Aberdeen: *Affirmations* (1990)

Alastair Mackie of Aberdeen: *Ingaitherins* (1987)

Lilianne Grant Rich of Genlivet: *White Rose of Druminnor* (1969)

Alexander Scott of Aberdeen: *Collected Poems* (1994)

Robbie Shepherd of Dunecht: the weekly Doric column in *The Press and Journal*

Margaret Smith of Gardenstown and Banff: *Hard Graft* (unpub. dialogue)

Wm. Thom of Inverurie: *Rhymes and Recollections of a Hand-Loom Weaver* (1845)

Rev. James Wood of Portnockie and Aberdeen: *The Wind on the Hill* (1988)

The Living Doric verse anthology (1985)

The Language of the People: Scots Prose from the Victorian Revival edited by William Donaldson (1989)

Acknowledgements

FURTHER VOCABULARY WAS provided by the late Mrs Bella Sandison of Adendale, Strachan and Ronald W. McDonald of Longside and Aberdeen. To these, to the writers of all published work listed, to the compilers of the *Scottish National Dictionary*, the *Concise Scots Dictionary* and *Chambers Scots Dictionary*, the author is indebted. For kindnesses rendered, thanks are due too to the Aberdeenshire Library and Information Service, to James Slater of Portsoy and the late Bill Middleton of Ardlair, Strachan.

Abbreviations

Abdn.	Aberdeen	*n.*	noun
adj.	adjective, -ival	*naut.*	nautical
adv.	adverb	*neg.*	negative
aux.	auxiliary	*n. pl.*	noun plural
cf.	compare with	*obs.*	obsolete
chf.	chiefly	*orig.*	originally
conj.	conjunction	*perf.*	perfect
contempt.	contemptuous	*perh.*	perhaps
corr.	corruption	*phr.*	phrase
def. art.	definite article	*pl.*	plural
deriv.	derivative of, deriving from	*ppl.*	participle (present/past)
dim.	diminutive	*pred. adj.*	predicative adjective
eg	for example		
Eng.	English	*pr. n.*	proper noun
excl.	exclamation	*prep. phr.*	prepositional phrase
f.	female		
fig.	figuratively	*pro.*	pronounced
gen.	generally	*pron.*	pronoun
imp.	imperative	*ref.*	reference
incl.	including	*rel. pron.*	relative pronoun
indef.	indefinite article	*v.*	verb
		var.	variant
int.	interjection	*verb. n.*	verbal noun
interrog.	interrogative	*v. pr.*	verb present tense
lit.	literary	*v. pt.*	verb past tense
liter.	literally	*v. tr.*	verb transitive
m.	male	*v. intr.*	verb intransitive

Part One

Doric – English

A

A *pron.* I. *cf.* Aw, I
a *indef. art.* a
'a' *v. (in perf. tense with
    aux. v.)* have *eg,* mith 'a'
    been might have been
aa, a' *adj.* all, every; ~body *n.*,
    pron. everybody; ~ come
    in one's right mind; ~ gate
    everywhere; ~ his lane all
    on his own; ~ itherbody
    everyone else; ~ the airts
    in all directions; ~thing
    n. everything; ~wye
    adv. everywhere;
    an ~ also, too
aacre *n.* acre. *cf.* awcre
aafa, aafu *adj., adv.* awful;
    an ~ *with pl.* an awful lot
    of *eg,* an ~ midgies
aagent *n.* agent
Aagist *n.* August
aal(d), Aal(d) *adj.* old; ~er
    older; ~est oldest; Aal
    Eel *pr. n.* Old Yule; Aal(d)
    Hornie, Aal(d) Nick *pr.
    n.* the Devil. *cf.* aul(d)
aam *v.* thrash. *cf.* aum
aat, 'at *adj., pron., conj.* that
abee *adv.* alone; lat weel ~ let
    well alone
abeech, abeich *adv.* at a
    distance, aloof
abeen *adv., prep.* above.
    cf. abune

ablach *n.* dwarf;
    insignificant person
ablins *adv.* perhaps (B1)
ablo(w) *prep.* below (S)
abody *n., pron.* everybody
aboot *prep.* about
abreist *adv.* abreast
abune *prep., adv.* above.
    cf. abeen
Abyne *pr. n.* Aboyne village
accep *v.* accept; *ppl.* acceppit
accommodat *v.* accommodate
accoont *n., v.* account;
    ~able *adj.* accountable
acht *adj.* eight; *cf.* aicht,
    echt; ~een *adj.* eighteen;
    cf. auchteen
acht *n.* ownership; *v.* own;
    owe. *cf.* aucht, yacht
ack *n.* action; *v.* act; ~ir
    n. actor
acquaint *ppl.* acquainted (B)
acquant *ppl.* acquainted (G);
    ~ance *n.* acquaintance
acquint *ppl.* acquainted (S)
actiwal *adj.* actual
adap *v.* adapt; *pt.* ~pit
    adapted
adaya *n.* idea
addiscence *See* audiscence
adee *n.* a to-do; *v.* to do;
    muckle ~ much to do
ae *adj.* one, single
aefaul(d) *adj.* sincere (B1, O)
aenoo *adv.* now. *cf.* ivnoo,
    eyvnoo

aet *n.* a feed; **a gweed ~** a good feed; *v. inf. and pr.* eat; **~en** *ppl.* eaten; **~meat** *n.* one who eats without working

afen *adv.* often. *cf.* **aft, aften**

aff *adv., prep.* off; **~ his eggs** ill at ease; **~ his stotter** losing the thread of his thought; **~-cast** *n.* anything cast off; **~come** *n.* apology; excuse; **~-go** *n.* start; **~-han** *adj.* blunt, plain; without warning or preparation; *adv.* beforehand; **tae be ~-han wi** *phr.* to forestall; **~int** *prep. phr.* off it; from it (s); **~lat** *n.* time off, leave of absence; **~-pittin** *ppl., adj.* procrastinating

affa *adj., adv.* awful. *cf.* **aafa, yafa**

affeckit *adj.* moved, touched; **sair ~** deeply moved; **weel ~ tae** well disposed to

affhan *phr.* **tae be ~ wi** to forestall

affint *adj.* upset (s)

afflickit *adj.* afflicted

affoord *v.* afford

affrontit *ppl., adj.* ashamed; embarrassed; **black ~** deeply embarrassed

afore *adv.* in front; *prep., conj.* before, in front of

aft, aften *adv.* often. *cf.* **afen**

agane *prep.* against (K). *cf.* **agin**

agee *adj.* awry; in a disordered state, out of order; crooked

aggravation *n.* irritation

agin *prep.* against

agley *adv.* off the straight, obliquely

a-gyaun *ppl.* going about; going on

aheid *prep., adv.* ahead

ahin *prep.* behind; *adv.* late

ahint *adv.* behind

Aiberdeen *pr. n.* Aberdeen

Aiberdour *pr. n.* Aberdour

aiblins *adv.* perhaps (K, MI). *cf.* **ablins**

aicht *adj.* eight (s); **~y** *adj.* eighty. *cf.* **eichty**

aidder *n.* udder

aifter *prep., conj.* after; *adv.* afterwards; **~hin** *adv.* afterwards; **~neen** *n.* afternoon; **~nin** *n.* afternoon (s). *cf.* **efter**

aig *n.* egg

aik *n.* oak

ail *v.* to be unwell, to be amiss; **~ at** to be dissatisfied with

ain *adj.* own

aince *adv.* once (s). *cf.* **eence**

aipple *n.* apple

air *adv.* early (A); **~ an late** all the time

airch *n.* arch; *adj.* (ch *gutteral*)
anxious (A2); timorous.
cf. **arch**

airels *n. pl.* musical tones

airish *adj.* chilly

airly *adv.* early. *cf.* **air**

airm *n.* arm; **~-cheer**
n. armchair

airmy *n.* army

airn *n.* iron; *v.* earn

airse *n.* arse; **~pooch** *n.* back
pocket

airt *n.* direction; art

airth *n.* earth. *cf.* **yird**

aise *n.* ease. *cf.* **aiss**

aishan *n.* generation; family
connection (A2). *cf.* **ation**

aisp *n.* asp, serpent

aiss *n.* ash, ashes; **~-backet**
n. ash-can; **~-midden**
n. ash-heap; **~-cairt**
n. dustcart. *cf.* **aise**

aisy *adj., adv.* easy (s)

ait, aits *n.* oats; **~ kyaaks** oat
cakes (A1); **~meal** oatmeal;
~en *adj.* oaten

aith *n.* oath

aiven *adv.* even

aiv(e)rin *n.* cloudberry

aivis *n.* trick; fad (B1)

aix *n.* axe

aixle *n.* axle

aizle *See* **eyzle**

ajee *adv.* to one side, off the
straight; (of a door) ajar.
cf. **agee**

Ake, Akie *pr. n.* Alexander

alaft *adv.* above, aloft

alairm *n.* alarm

alane *adj., adv.* alone.
cf. **aleen**

alang *prep.* along

ale *n.* ale; lemonade etc; **~berry**
n. oatmeal boiled in ale,
sweetened with sugar (A2)

aleen *adj., adv.* alone. *cf.* **alane**

aleyven *adj.* eleven

alis(s) *excl.* (sudden cry of
pain) alas!

alist *adj.* alive; **come ~** recover
consciousness

alloo, allou *n.* approval;
v. allow, *pt.* **alloot**

Almichty *adj.* Almighty

alow, in alow *prep.* below (s)

alowe *adv.* on fire, ablaze

alunt *adv.* ablaze. *cf.* **alow**

amaist *adv.* almost

amang *prep.* among.
cf. **amin, amo**

ameesement *n.* amusement

amens *n. pl.* amends

amin *prep.* among (s).
cf. **amo**

amint, oot *prep. phr.* out of
things (s)

ammuneetion *n.* ammunition

amnin *v.* am not; **~ aw** am I
not? (A2)

amo, amon *prep.* among.
cf. **amin**

amous *n.* alms. *cf.* **amus**

amshach *n.* accident, mishap (B1)

amunt *n.* amount

amus *See* **amous**

an *conj.* and

ance *adv.* once (C, G1);
~ **eeran** on a special errand, specially. *cf.* **aince, eence**

Andra *pr. n.* deriv. of Andrew

ane *adj. n.* one. *cf.* **een**

anent *prep.* opposite; in front of; over against; concerning

Anersmas *pr. n.* Andrewmas

aneth *adv., prep.* beneath (A, M, M1). *cf.* **ablow, alow**

aneu, aneuch *adj.* enough

angersome *adj.* annoying, provoking

anidder *adj., pron.* another. *cf.* **anither, anodder**

anint *prep.* opposite. *cf.* **anent**

anither *adj., pron.* another;
~ **kind** much improved (B)

annwal *adj.* annual

anodder *adj., pron.* another (A2). *cf.* **anidder, anither**

anse *adv.* else (C)

anter *v.* saunter; wander (M3)

anterin, antrin *adj.* occasional

antic *n.* oddity; eccentric

anyntit *ppl.* anointed

anyoo *See* **aneu**

anyooch *See* **aneugh**

apairt *adv.* apart

apen *v.* open

apothec *n.* lot; collection. *cf.* **hypothec**

appale *n., v.* appeal

appearandly *adv.* apparently

appint *v.* appoint

appruv *v.* approve

aquent *See* **acquant**

arch (**ch** *guttural*) *adj.* timorous; anxious (A2)

aready *adv.* already

argie *v.* argue

argie-bargie; argle-bargle *n.* argument (A2); *v.* to argue, contend

argiement *n.* argument

arles *n.* earnest given on striking a bargain

arn-tree *n.* alder (J)

arnut *n.* earth-nut; pignut

aroon *adv., prep.* around

arreenge *v.* arrange

as *in phr.* ~ **much** so much

ashet *n.* large serving dish

aside *adv.* close by; present; *prep.* beside

asklent *adv.* askance

asseer (asser) *v.* assure (B1)

asteer *adv.* astir

astonisher *n.* a big surprise (A1)

astonishment, an *n.* shock (A1)

atheen *prep.* above (B1). *cf.* **abeen**

athin(g) *n.* everything

Athole brose *n.* honey or meal mixed with whisky

athoot *conj., prep.* without

athort *adv.* all over; *prep.*
  across
attlin *pr., ppl.* eager (M3).
  cf. **ettlin**
ation *n.* generation; family
  connection (A2). *cf.* **aishan**
atomie *n.* skeleton
atour *prep.* across; beyond
atten *v.* attend; *ppl.* ~**t**
attrack *v.* attract
atween *adv., prep.* between;
  ~ **hans** *adv.* between times (B)
atweesh *prep. See* **atween**
au *adj.* old (A1). *cf.* **aul**
Auchmacoy bummer *n.* the
  Buchan bumble bee
aucht *adj.* eight; *n., pron.*
  anything; *n.* possession;
  v. owe; own; ~**in** due;
  ~ **nor ocht** nothing at
  all; neither one thing
  nor another; ~**een** *adj.*
  eighteen. *cf.* **acht**
audiscence *n.* audience;
  hearing
aul(d) *adj.* old; ~**er** older;
  ~**est** oldest; ~**farrant** old-
  fashioned; **Auld Nick** *pr. n.*
  the Devil; **Auld Kirk, the**
  pr. n. established Church of
  Scotland; whisky. *See* **aal(d)**
aum *v.* thrash. *cf.* **aam**
aumrie *n.* cupboard (A);
  pantry; upper half of
  above (B1)

auncient *adj.* ancient
Australya *pr. n.* Australia
ava *adv.* at all
aven *adv.* even
Aw, aw *pron.* I. *See* **A**
awa *adv.* away; ~ **forrin** away
  abroad; **hine** ~ far away;
  keep her ~ change course to
  leeward (B). *cf.* **tee**
awaar *adj.* aware
awat *adv.* I wot, indeed, truly.
  cf. **awyte**
awcre *n.* acre
awe *v.* owe; **awin** owing
awee *adv.* a little while
aweel *adv.* well
aweers o *adv.* on the point of,
  just about to
awfu *adj.* awful. *cf.* **afa, aafa**
awmous *n.* alms. *cf.* **amous**
Awprile *n.* month of April.
  See **Prile eeran**
awpron *n.* apron; leather
  covering for use in open
  carriage
Aw'se *pron. with v.* I'll
awyte *pron. with v.* I wot,
  know; *adv.* assuredly
ay *adv.* yes
ay, ay *int.* hello
aye *adv.* always; still
ayoke *adv.* at work
ayon, ayont *adv., prep.* beyond
ayven *adv.* even

B

ba(a) *n.* ball

baabee *n.* halfpenny; *in pl.* money. *cf.* **bawbee**

Baabie *pr. n. deriv.* of Barbara

baal *n.* ball, dance

baathe *v.* bathe

babbity *n.* baby

babbity bowster *n.* (bab-at-the-bowster) an old country dance to end a ball etc

bacca bree *n.* the spittle of a tobacco-chewer

bachle *cf.* **bauchle**

bachlt *adj.* (of shoes) out of shape

back *n.* wooden vessel for carrying peat; outermost board of a sawn tree; **~ o** *prep.* just after (of time); **at the ~ o beyond** *phr.* far off the beaten track; **~-been** *n.* back-bone; **~bin** *n.* back band in harness; **~-birn** *n.* back burden; **~-cheyn** *n.* chain over saddle supporting cart shafts; **~-door** *n.* tail board of cart; **the ~e(y)n** *n.* autumn, winter; **~grun** *n.* background; **~gaen** *adj.* declining, not prospering; **~ie** *n.* back-green, back-garden; tether peg; **~in** *n.* address on a letter; **~lins** *adv.* backwards; **~set**

n. setback; *v.* disgust (BI); **~spier** *v.* question a speaker; **~s** *n.* refuse of sawmill

backart *adj.* backward

backet *n.* bucket; three-sided wooden box with hand-holes, used for carrying peats, sliced turnips or potatoes and predating sculls; wooden scuttle for carrying ashes; rubbish bin

bad *v. pt.* bade

badder *v.* bother. *cf.* **bather; ~ation** *n.* botheration; nuisance

bade *v. pt.* lived. *cf.* **bed**

baet *v.* beat; *ppl., adj.* beaten, defeated

baffies *n. pl.* slippers

baggerel *n.* worthless woman

bag-raip *n.* rope around eaves of stack

baignet *n.* bayonet

baikie *n.* short iron stake to hold tether for cattle and goats. *See* **backie**

bailie, baillie, bylie *n.* cattleman, alderman; water bailiff (M); **little ~** under-cattleman

baird *n.* beard

bairn *n.* baby, child; **~heid** *n.* childhood; **~ikie** *n.* little child; *v.* make pregnant

bait *n.* horse fodder

baith *adj., pron.* both
bajan(ella) *n.* first year student
at Aberdeen University
baket *n.* bucket. *cf.* **backet**
bale-fire *n.* bonfire. *cf.* **bondy**
Balfuff, at the baak o *phr.*
far away
ballant *n.* ballad
ballie *n.* ball (of)
ban *v.* to scold; curse, swear
bandie *n.* minnow, stickleback
bandster *n.* one who binds
sheaves. *cf.* **banster**
bane *n.* bone; **near the ~** tight-
fisted. *cf.* **been**
bang *v.* hasten (M)
bangstrie *n.* violence to person
or property
banie *adj.* boney
bannet *n.* bonnet
bannock *n.* round, flat cake
(usually of oatmeal) baked
on a girdle, oatcake (s)
banster *n.* one who binds
the sheaves. *cf.* **bandster**
banter *v. tr.* scold; tease
bantin *n.* a bantam
bap *n.* floury breakfast roll;
v. walk in a plodding; flat-
footed way
bapteese *v.* baptise; **~ment**
n. baptism
bar *n.* a joke, funny story;
bar of wood used to lock
door; *v.* lock door with

such a bar; **~ oot** *v.* lock
out; shut out
barbet *n.* arrow; **bow an ~**
bow and arrow
barbit-weer *n.* barbed wire
barfit *adj.* barefooted; **~ broth**
soup made without meat
bark *n.* the skin; preservative
for fishing nets; *v.* to skin;
~it *ppl., adj.* skinned;
encrusted with dirt, dirty
bark-an-bowff *n.* scolding
barleys-on *See* **parley**
barm *n.* yeast, ferment;
v. ferment; cause to ferment
barra *n.* barrow
barrie *n.* a baby's flannel
coat (BI)
barritchfu *adj.* harsh (G)
bash *n.* heavy blow
bass *n.* doormat
batchie *n.* bachelor
bather *v.* bother (s). *cf.* **badder**
Baubie *pr. n.* deriv. from
Barbara. *cf.* **Baabie**
bauch(-hertit) *adj.* shy, bashful;
timid
bauchl|e *n.* old shoe;
v. shamble; trouble (BI);
defeat (BI); **~ban** *n.* shoe-
lace (BI). **~t** (of shoes) out
of shape. *cf.* **bachle**
baud *n.* hare. *cf.* **bawd**
baudrins, bawdrons *pr. n., ref.*
to a cat; puss. *cf.* **bauldrins**

bauk *n.* uncultivated strip of land between fields; cross-beam between rafters

baukie *n.* bat (mammal)

baul *adj.* bold (A2); strong (B1)

bauld *adj.* bald; bold (J); ~ie-heidit *adj.* bald-headed. *cf.* **beld**

bauldrins *pr. n.*, ref. to a cat; puss. *cf.* **baudrins**

bawbee *n.* halfpenny; *in pl.* money

bawd *n.* hare (M). *cf.* **maukin**

baxter *n.* baker

beamfill, beamfull *v.* to fill up spaces in the walls of a house after beams are placed; to fill up completely; ~t *ppl., adj.* indulged, spoiled

bear *n.* four- or six-rowed barley

beardie *n.* the good-natured rubbing of a man's beard on a child's face

beas' *n. pl.* animals in general, cattle in particular (C)

beastle *n. pl.* farm animals. *cf.* **beas'**

beat *v.* lash a hook to a fishing line

beater *n.* heart

beck *v.* curtsey; do obeisance

bed *n.* bed; ~-claes *n. pl.* bed clothes; ~dal *n.* a bedridden person; ~die *n.* (small) bed; ~din *n.* old custom of putting bride and groom to bed; ~dit *ppl.* in bed, put to bed; ~-lids *n.* doors of box-bed; *v.* spread straw for animals for the night

bed(d) *v. pt.* lived. *cf.* **bade**

beddies *n.* hopscotch

bedeen *adv.* forthwith (often used to provide a rhyme)

bedraigle *v.* to bedraggle

beed *See* **beet**

beef *n.* beef; the term used on board fishing boats for all butcher meat (B)

beek *v.* warm before the fire

beel *v.* fester *eg,* **a ~t thoom**

beelin *n.* whitlow. *See* **futlie**

been *n.* bone. *cf.* **bane**

beerd *n.* board. *cf.* **buird**

beerial *n.* interment, funeral

bee-ruskie *n.* simple form of beehive, covered in ropes of twisted straw (T)

beery *v.* bury, *ppl.* beeriet; **~ Napoleon** bury contents of dry lavatory

beesom *n.* a broom; untidy woman (A1); disparaging term used of a woman. ~-ticht *adj.* swept-clean (B1); *cf.* **besom**

beet *n.* boot. *cf.* **buit**; *v.* bet; replace lost hooks on a fishing line; ~ikins *n. pl.* hobnailed boots. *cf.* **beat**

beet tae *v. pr.*, *pt.* must, had
to; (contraction of **be tae
be**); **that ~ ~ be gran** that
must have been grand.
cf. **beed**

beezer *n.* something of
huge size

befa *v.* befall

begarrie *v.* besmear; bespatter

begeck *n.* disappointment;
trick, shock, *v.* shock

begood *v. pt.* began

begouth *v. pt.* began (Abdn.,
rare)

begowk *v.* trick, fool

begrutten *adj.* tear-stained

begunk *n.* disappointment;
misfortune

behan, (aa) *adv.* (all) over,
past

behauden *adj.* beholden

behee|f *n.* behoof; **~ve**
v. behove

beheeld *v. pt.* beheld

beil, beilin *n.* boil, sore

bek (B1) *See* **beek**

belaabour *v.* belabour

belang *v.* belong; belong to a
place; **he ~s Aiberdeen**

beld *adj.* bald. *cf.* **bauld**

Beldie *pr. n.* deriv. of Isabella

belike *adv.* perhaps, likely

bellas, bellaws *n.* bellows

belly-ban *n.* harness,
belly-band

belly-flaucht *adv.* headlong;
flat on one's face

belly-rive *n.* indigestion

belly-thraw *n.* colic,
stomach-ache

belt *n.* narrow plantation

beltie *n.* water-hen (G1)

belyve *adv.* by-and-by, before
long

ben *adv., prep.* inside, through;
~ward *adv.* inward; forward;
~with *adv.* through the
house; inwards; **~maist,
~most** *adj.* innermost;
~-the-hoose, ~-i-hoose *adv.*
in the parlour of a
two-roomed cottage; **far
~ wi** intimate with; esp.
with God; *n.* hill,
mountain

bena *v. imp. neg.* don't be

bencape *adj.* first rate

ben-i-hoose *See* **ben-the-hoose**

Bennachie *pr. n.* well-known hill
near Insch, Aberdeenshire

bennin *n.* bend (T)

bensil *n.* heavy blow;
severe rebuke

bent *n.* coarse grass growing
near sea; hillock covered in
such grass; sand dune

ben-the-hoose *n.* inner room
of a but-an-ben cottage

benty *adj.* covered with
bent grass

bere *See* **bear**

besom *n.* broom; term of reproach for woman. *cf.* **beesom**

besom-shaft *n.* broom-handle

bess *n.* bass; *v.* sing bass

bestial *n.* cattle (A2)

bethral *n.* beadle

beuk *n.* book; *v.* register for proclamation of banns of marriage; **tae be ~it** to be so registered; **~in-nicht** night of registration. *cf.* **buik.**

bevie *n.* large fire (B1)

bewotifie *adj.* beautiful (B1)

bewutch *v.* bewitch; *ppl.*, *adj.* bewutcht

bey *n.* bay

bibblie-nibbit *adj.* snotty-nosed

bick *n.* bitch (in true sense)

bicker *n.* scrimmage; wooden brose basin; *v.* move quickly and noisily, scurry; ripple; laugh heartily; **in a ~** in a trice

bid *v.* ask, invite; tell; **~den** *ppl.* asked, invited, told, stayed; **~den gang** asked to go; **~din** *n.* invitation

bidden *See* **bid, bide**

bid|e *v.* live, stay; wait, remain; tolerate; *ppl.* **~den** (in passive) put up; **~e ye** *excl.* wait

bidie-in *n.* a live-in lover

biel, bield *n.* shelter; **~dy** *adj.* sheltered

bien *adj.* comfortable; well-to-do; **~less** *adj.* comfortless

big, bigg *v.* build; **~git** *pt.*, *ppl.* built; **~ger** *n.* builder; **~gin** *n.* building, house; **~git oot** *ppl.* having abundance of (B)

bigsie *adj.* conceited

bike *n.* nest of wild bees

bikk *See* **bick**

bil|e *v.* boil; **~t egg** boiled egg. *cf.* **bylt**

biler *n.* kettle

bilin *n.* a boiling (*eg*, of rhubarb)

billet *n.* lot; situation (A)

billie, billy *n.* fellow; comrade

billie *n.* notice posted in seaports with news of herring fleet catches (B)

bin *n.* humour, mood; *v.* to bind (rhymes with tin)

bin' *v.* to bind. *cf.* **bin**

binch *n.* bench

binder *n.* tall story; an outstanding thing of its kind (B)

bing *n.* crowd; heap; bin for corn, turnips etc

bink *n.* bench (M3); hob (B)

binna *v. neg. imp.* (of **be**) don't be

binner *n.* a quick movement; sounding blow, speed; *v.* move rapidly and noisily; buzz; whirr (K)

binnin *n.* binding for cattle

bird-alane *adj.* quite alone (B)
birdies' eenies *n. pl.* sago
   pudding (T)
birk *n.* birch tree; a youth
birken *n.* birch tree (C)
birkie *n.* lively, smart fellow
birl *n.* twirl; brisk dance,
   v. twirl
birn *n.* burden; large
   collection
birr *n.* force, energy, passion;
   whirr. *cf.* **virr**
birse *n.* bristle; bristle on
   cobbler's thread; beard;
   bruise; pressure, esp. of
   crowd
birse, birss *n.* fit of bad temper;
   get yir ~ up to get angry;
   set up yir ~ make you angry
birse *v.* press, squeeze, push;
   bruise, pressurise; **~ ben a**
   bit move along a bit; **~ tee**
   push to; **~ by** push past.
   cf. **birze**
birs|el, birstle *v.* toast, roast;
   ~let, ~lin *ppl.* scorched,
   scorching
birsin *ppl., adj.* out of breath
birst *n.* over-exertion causing
   injury; *v.* burst, split
birze *v.* squeeze, press;
   pressurise. *cf.* **birse**
bishop *v.* beat down earth or
   stones; *n.* device for doing
   this
bit *conj.* but; *n.* crisis;

at the ~ in a crisis;
oot o the ~ out of difficulty
bittock *n.* small bit
bizz *v.* buzz; hiss;
   cry ~ *phr.* make a fuss
bizzar *n.* jade (J) probably
   from **bizzard** buzzard
bizzin *n.* buzzing
blaa *v.* blow; boast; **~-aff**
   n. exchange of views
black *in phr.* **tae gae tae the**
   ~ gate to take the road to
   ruin; **~ yarn** *phr.* empty
   herring nets (B); **in ~ upo**
   fite in black and white;
blackguaird *v.* to blackguard,
   abuse
blackie *n.* blackbird.
   cf. **blaikie**
blad *v.* spoil. *cf.* **blaud**
bladderskite *n.* foolish,
   noisy talker
blade *n.* cabbage or kail leaf;
   piece of cooked flesh (M3)
blae *adj.* blue; bluish; black
   and blue (B1); **~berry**
   n. bilberry; **~wort** *n.* blue
   corn-flower
blaffert *n.* blast of wind (C).
   cf. **bluffert**
blaik(en) *v.* blacken
blaikie *n.* blackbird.
   cf. **blackie**
blain *n.* bare patch in field
   where grain has not sprung;

~y *adj.* covered with bare patches

blake *n.* black polish

blash *n.* splash, dash

blate *adj.* bashful

blatter *n.* sharp shower (C); *v.* dash noisily

blaud *v.* spoil. *cf.* **blad**

blauve *See* **blyaav**

blaw *v.* blow; brag; *n.* braggart

blawart *n.* harebell

bleart *ppl.* bleary-eyed

bleat *adj.* dull, stupid. *cf.* **blate**

bleb *v.* sip; tipple (A)

bleck *adj.* black; *n. joc.* blackguard, scoundrel (M2). (*cf.* **blake**); ~**en** *v.* blacken. (*cf.* **blaik**); *v.* puzzle; defeat; beat; prove too much for

bleckin *n.* blacking

bledder *n.* bladder; *v.* talk idly

bleed *n.* blood. *cf.* **bluid**; ~**y couter** nosebleed; ~**-jeelin** *adj.* blood-chilling; blood-curdling (G); ~**-reid** *adj.* blood-red

bleem *n.* bloom

bleery *adj.* bleary

bleeter *n.* blethering person, gasbag; an item of blether

bleeze *n., v.* blaze

bleezin *adj.* very drunk

blent *ppl.* blended

blether *n.* a talk, chat; *v.* chat; talk nonsense

blewart *n.* bluebell (B1)

blibber *v.* sip a small amount of liquid (T)

blicht *n.* blight

blickers *n. pl.* nonsense

blin *adj.* blind; ~**-bridle** *n.* bridle with blinkers; ~ **lump** *n.* boil; ~ **sieve** *adj., n.* sieve with solid base; ~ **tit** *adj., n.* blind teat

blink *n.* beam, ray; *v.* wink; flicker

blinter *v.* blink

bliss *v.* bless; ~**in** *n.* blessing

blithe(some) *adj.* cheerful, merry. *cf.* **blythe**

blivert *n.* bilberry. *cf.* **blaeberry**

blobbie-like *adj.* humid

blocher *v.* cough with phlegm in the throat

bloiter *n.* blast of wind. *cf.* **blouter**

blon *n.* blonde; girlfriend

blood *v.* bleed (S)

blouter *n.* blast of wind. *cf.* **bloiter**

blue *adj.* downcast (A1)

Bluemogganer *pr. n.* native of Peterhead

Blue Toon, the (nickname) Peterhead

bluffert *n.* blast of wind

bluichtie *adj.* bluish

blunk *n.* dull, lifeless person;
~**ie** *adj.* dull and lifeless

blyaav *v.* blow, pant; boast

blythe *adj.* glad, cheerful.
cf. **blithe**

boakie *See* **bokie**

bob *v.* curtsey

bobbie, bobby *n.* policeman

bobbinjohn *n.* tin cylinder
perforated at one end for
sowing turnip seed by hand
where it has failed in the
drills

bochert *adj.* stuck, held
up (M3)

bocht *v.* bought

bock *v.* vomit; **byre-bockit**
oozing from a byre (K)

bockie *n.* hobgoblin

Boddam Coo *pr. n.* fog horn
at Boddam Head (B)

boddom *n.* bottom

bode *n.* bid at a sale;
v. foretell

bodie *n.* person

bodin *adj.* full of foreboding

bodle *n.* small coin (K, J)

bodsie *n.* short, dapper person

body bulk *quasi-adv.*
physically

body-claes *n. pl.* clothes (M3)

bog *v.* stick in the mire or
bog; confuse, dumbfound;
~**git** bamboozled

boggle *n.* ghost (K)

bogie *n.* two-wheeled open
wagon

bogie-rowe *n.* bogie-roll
tobacco

bogjavelt (B1), **bogshaivelt**
adj. knocked out of shape,
distorted

bogle *n.* ghost (K); game of
'ghosties'

boiler *n.* kettle. *cf.* **biler**

boke *v.* belch; *ppl.* bokit (K)

bokie *n.* bogie, scarecrow;
fisher term for small
boy (B)

bole *n.* opening in wall for air
or light; **winnock ~** (K)

bondy *n.* bonfire (O)

bone *in phr.* **in richt ~** in fine
fettle (M2)

bone davie (davy) *n.* horse-
drawn manure distributor,
spreading fertiliser
including bone-meal (S, T)

bonnet *n.* a man's cap;
~~-**laird** *n.* yeoman farmer;
proprietor of the land he
farms

bonnie, bonny *adj.* lovely,
pretty; handsome;
attractive

bonspeil, bonspiel *n.* contest,
especially curling

boo *v.* bow; ~**t**, ~**'t** *ppl.*,
adj. bent; **boot twa faal**
bent over

boodie *n.* ghost (B1);
scarecrow (M1); *v.* haunt
(K). *cf.* **tattie-boodie**

booet, booit *n.* hand-lantern
(without glass)

bool, bowl *n.* a marble;
curved handle of a
kettle, pot

bools *n. pl.* marbles; bowls

boons *n. pl.* bounds; **oot
o kent ~** in unknown
territory; off the beaten
track

boorach(ie) *n.* group, crowd;
v. huddle. *cf.* **bour(r)ach**

boord *n.* board. *cf.* **brod**

boortree *See* **bourtree**

boo't *See* **boo**

bord *n.* ruffle, frill

bore *n.* crevice, chink, hole

borra *v.* borrow; **~t licht**
indirect light

bosie *n.* bosom; embrace

bosker *n.* something of
prodigious size

bosky *adj.* wild, unfrequented

boss *adj.* hollow

bossie *n.* large wooden bowl
used for oatmeal in
baking (B1)

bothy *n.* cottage where farm
servants were lodged and
cooked their own food

bottler *n.* bluebottle

bouch *v.* bark; cough

bouk *n.* size, build

boukit *adj.* large, bulky;
sma-~ of small build;
muckle-~ pregnant (B1);
nairra-~ of lean build

boun *n.* boundary

bourach(ie) *See* **boorach**

bourtree, boortree *n.*
elder tree

bout *n.* swathe cut by
scythesman, corn or hay cut
by a scythe and lying in rows

bow *n.* 1. boll, old Scottish
dry measure of not more
than six bushels; 2. the part
of the harness bent under the
neck of an ox to fasten the
yoke; the wooden yoke itself;
ower the ~s in a disorderly
way (A2); **gae throu the ~s**
misbehave (A2) and/or be
severely disciplined

bow-cheer *n.* armchair

bowden *v.* to fill; **~t** replete
(after eating); (of legs) bow

bowe *n.* fishing float

bowel-crappit *ppl.*, *adj.* (hair)
cut with a bowl

bowff *n.*, *v.* bark (of dog)

bow-hoched *adj.* bow-legged

bowie *n.* barrel; **~ cheer**
rocking-chair made from a
barrel

bowl *n.* pipe

bows *See* **bow**

bowsell *n.* iron cattle-binding
(F)

bowster *n.* bolster
bowsterous *adj.* boistrous
box *phr.* **i the same ~** in the same boat, or position
bracken *n.* fern. *cf.* **breckan**
braddie *n.* meat pie, savoury turnover. *cf.* **bridie**
brae *n.* hill, slope, steep road
braeset *adj.* situated on a slope
braggy *adj.* boastful
braid *adj.* broad
braig *v.* brag
brainge *v.* lunge. *cf.* **breenge**
braird *n.* first sprouting of young grain. *cf.* **breer**
braith *n.* breath (G). *cf.* **breith**
braivity *n.* show, splendour; finery
brak *v.* break; go bankrupt
brakfast *n.* breakfast
brak-fur *v.* plough shallow furrows (F)
bramble *n.* blackberry
brammle *See* **bramble**
brander *n.* gridiron; drain-cover
branert *adj.* baked on a brander
branks *n.* halter of wood or metal
brattle *v.* rattle; crash; thunder
braw *adj.* fine, handsome, excellent; *in pl.* fine clothes
brawlies *adv.* well, finely. *cf.* **brulies**
brawly *adv.* well, splendidly

braxy *n.* internal inflammation in sheep; sheep that has died a natural death (M)
break *n.* hollow in a hill
brecham *n.* collar for a draught horse
breckan *n.* fern. *cf.* **bracken**
bree *n.* liquid, juice; liquor; *See also* **sna-bree**; *v.* to drain boiled solids *eg*, **tae ~ the tatties; throwe the ~** (of potatoes) overboiled
breed *See* **breid**
breeder *n.* brother. *cf.* **bridder**
breek|s *n.* trousers; **~it** *adj.* wearing trousers. *cf.* **briks**
breem *n.* broom; a thatch of broom; **~-buss** *n.* broom bush
breenge *v.* rush forward impetuously; batter, bang
breer *n.* briar; first sprouting of a crop (A1). *cf.* **braird**; *v.* sprout. *See* **brier**
breest *n.* breast. *cf.* **breist**
breet *n.* brute (not always unsympathetic)
breeth *n.* breadth
breid *n.* bread; oatcakes (taken as dessert in bowl of milk) (F, T); **~-spaddie** oatcake lift; breadth
breist *n.* breast. *cf.* **breest**
breith *n.* breath (J)
brench *n.* branch. *cf.* **brinch**

brent *ppl.* burned (G1).
cf. **brunt**

bress *n.* brass

brevity *n.* fine show or display

brewster-wife *n.* woman who brewed or sold malt liquors

brich|t *adj.* bright; ~en
v. brighten

bridder *n.* brother. *See* **breeder, brither, broder**

bridegreem *n.* bridegroom

bridie *n.* beef or mutton pie (S)

brier *n.* eyelash; **by the ~s o the een** by the skin of his teeth (T)

brig *n.* bridge

briks *See* **breeks**

brinch *n.* branch. *cf.* **brench**

brinn *v.* burn

britchin *n.* breeching, the piece of harness that passes round the hind-part of a horse in shafts, to let it push back-wards; **intae the ~** into reverse

brither *n.* brother; ~heid *n.* brotherhood

brizz *v.* squeeze; crush

broadcast *n.* broadcast sowing machine (F)

brob *v.* to prick; ~bit *pt.*, *ppl.* pricked

broch *n.* burgh; halo round sun or moon (round moon, predicting storm); Pictish tower;

Broch, the *pr. n.* nickname for Fraserburgh; ~er *pr. n.* nickname for native of Fraserburgh

brochan *n.* oatmeal boiled thicker than gruel, with butter and honey

brocht *v. pt.* brought; ~upness *n.* (joc.) upbringing. cf. **upfessin**

brock *n.* grass and straw shaken out of corn after threshing (M3)

brod *n.* board; collecting box in church; *n., v.* prick; prod

broder *n.* brother (A2). cf. **breeder, bridder, brither**

brodmell *n.* brood (B1, A2)

broke *v. pt.* became bankrupt

broken *ppl., adj.* bankrupt

broncaidis *n.* bronchitis

broo *n.* brow; **~ o liking for**, inclination to

Broo *n.* Employment Office

broobin *n.* harness brow band

brook *n.* soot on pots; *v. pt.* broke. cf. **bruik**

brookie *n.* blacksmith (A); *adj.* sooty, grimy; **aal ~** "Old Maid" in the card game of that name "Ye're aal ~" (A1)

brookit *adj.* (of cattle, sheep) speckled

broom, sing the *phr.* cry
out in distress during
punishment (A1)

broon *adj.* brown

brose *n.* oatmeal or peasemeal
mixed with boiling water,
milk etc; a meal; **~-caup**
n. wooden bowl for
oatmeal dish

brosy *adj.* stout, well-fed

brow *adj.* handsome (M, R).
cf. **braw**

browdent upo *adj.* enamoured
of; fond of

browst *n.* a brew

bruckle *adj.* brittle, crumbly (C1)

brucklie *adj.* (of the weather)
changeable

bruik *v. pt.* broke. *cf.* **brook**

bruise-box *n.* corn-chest (F)

bruised corn *n.* pounded oats

bruk *v. pt.* broke (R). *cf.* **brak**,
bruik

brulies (B1) *See* **brawlies**

brulzie *n.* brawl

brunt *v. ppl.* burned. *cf.* **brent**

bubble *v.* blubber, snivel

bubbly *n.* paraffin torch used
at sea

bubbly-bairn *n.* cry-baby

bubbly(jock) *n.* turkey-cock

Buchan *pr. n.* Buchan's
Domestic Medicine

Buchaner *n.* native of
Buchanhaven, now part of
Peterhead

Buchanie, the *pr. n.* The
Buchan Observer

bucht *n.* a sheep-, cattle-fold

Bucker *pr. n.* native of Buckie

bucker *n.* annoyance;
nuisance (A); *v.* botch,
bungle (B1)

buckie *n.* refractory,
mischievous person;
periwinkle; spiral shell of
winkle; **as fou's a ~** drunk

buckle *v.* dress (for a
journey) (R)

buckle wi *v.* marry

bucklins *n. pl.* parphernalia of
marriage (A2)

buddick *n.* small useless fish
found in harbours (B)

buff *n.* nonsense; **~ an
nonsense** stuff and
nonsense

buffet steel *n.* square stool (B1)

buik *n.* bulk; book; *v.* book,
register; record names of
betrothed couple in church
register before marriage.
cf. **beuk, byeuck**

buikin-nicht *n.* the night on
which the names of persons
about to be married are
given to the church Session
Clerk to have the banns
proclaimed. *cf.* **beuk**

buird *n.* board; table.
cf. **boord, brod**

buirdin-squeel
n. boarding-school
buirdly *adj.* burly; fine-looking
buist *n.* box, chest
buit *n.* boot. *cf.* **beet**
bul(l) *n.* bull; bill; *v.* serve
a cow
bullaments *n. pl.* outer
garments usually ragged or
untidy (B1)
bullyrag *v.* scold, hector, treat
in a bullying manner
bum *v.* hum, drone
bumbaze *v.* confound; bewilder
bumbee *n.* bumble-bee
bumlock *n.* prominent stone;
sturdy fellow (M3)
bummer *n.* bumble-bee;
anything outstandingly large
bun, bunt *v. pt., ppl.* bound;
~-bed, ~-in bed, ~-breest
wooden bed shut in with
folding/sliding doors,
box-bed
buncher *n.* machine attached
to mill for making straw
bunches
bung *n.* ill-humour; huff (A);
rage; **in a** ~ in a temper; **on
the** ~ in the huff
bunkart, bunkert *n.* obstacle;
big heap of any material
bunnle *n.* bundle
bure *v. pt.* bore

burlaw *n.* district court of
neighbours; ~**man** member
of such a court
burn *n.* stream
burn the witchie *n.* burning
effigy on boat deck to
break bad luck (B)
buroo *n.* bureau
burr *n.* the uvular r; *v.*
pronounce the letter r in
the throat
burssen *ppl.* bursting
burssen-ile *n.* discarded
lubricating oil used to
soothe the skin of pigs (B)
and prevent rust on farm
machinery (T)
bushle, bussle *n.* bushel measure
busk *v.* dress; adorn
buss *n.* bush
but *prep.* across; *v.* must, had
to. *See* **beed, beet**
but-an-ben *n.* two-roomed
cottage; from end to end
but-bed *n.* the bed in the semi-
parlour end of the cottage
but-the-hoose *n.* kitchen
butt *n.* tail of a sheaf
butterflee *n.* butterfly (R).
cf. **buttery**
buttery *n.* butterfly (M1)
buttery (-rowie) *n.* flat
morning roll
buttock mail *n.* a spanking
buzness *n.* business

buzzle *n., v.* (of grain,
indicating ripeness) rustle

b'wye *interj.* by the way

by, by wi't *adv.* over, past;
~ the warst past the worst;
prep. besides, apart from

byaakin *n., ppl.* baking

bydand *old pr. ppl.* abiding,
steadfast. (Motto of the
Gordon family and the
Gordon Highlanders)

bye, byes *prep.* besides; except

byes *adv., conj., prep.*
compared with

byeuck *n.* book. *cf.* beuk, buik

bygaein, bygaun, bygyaun,
i the ~ *phr.* as you go by;
incidentally

bygane *adj.* (of time) past;
for a whilie ~ for some
time past; *n.* the past (also
byganes)

byke *v.* form a bees' byke

byl|e *n., v.* boil; ~t tae
spyooterie overboiled (M3).
cf. bile

bylie *See* bailie

bylin *n.* a boiling

byock *v.* vomit (B1).

byordnar *adj.* extraordinary

byous *adj.* extraordinary;
adv. exceedingly

byowt|y *n.* beauty; ~ifu *adj.*
beautiful

byre *n.* cowshed

bywye *n.* byway

C

ca, caa *v.* call; drive; knock;
~ awa persevere; ~ (him)
for aathing defame;
on the ~ on the move;
~ canny take care; ~ doon
demolish, knock down;
~ ower *v. tr.* knock over,
overturn; *v. intr.* fall over;
~ the kwintra go round the
countryside; ~ the crack
chat; ~ the door tee shut
the door; ~ad deen worn
out; ~-throw *n.* (of shops)
fleeting visit. *cf.* caw

caal *adj., n.* cold; ~ roch
shooers cold blustery
showers. *See* caul

caav *v.* give birth to a calf

cack *v.* defecate. *cf.* kich

cackie-stammackit *adj.*
having imperfect digestion;
squeamish (T)

caddis *n.* cotton-wool; flock;
padding; (cotton- or wool-)
fluff; any kind of fluff

cadge *n.* shake, jog; *v.* carry
loads; peddle wares; shake
roughly, knock about;
sponge

cadger *n.* carrier; itinerant
dealer, hawker; sponger;
~'s dizzen thirteen

cadgin *n.* a jolt

caff *n.* chaff; **~-bed, ~-seck** mattress filled with chaff. *cf.* **cauff**

caip *n.* cap

caird *n.* tinker. *cf.* **cyaard, kyaard**; *v.* card (wool); abuse, scold

cairga *n.* cargo (M3). *cf.* cargie

cairn *n.* loose heap of stones; *v.* form a cairn or heap

cairriet *adj.* light-headed (M3)

cairry *v.* carry; **~-on** *n.* carry-on

cairt *n.* cart; *v.* carry; **~er** *n.*carter; **~in** *ppl.* playing cards; **~s** *n. pl.* playing-cards

caithick *n.* monkfish

calfie's mooie *n.* small cowrie shell (B). *cf.* **Johnny Groatie, kysie**

callant *n.* stripling, lad

caller *adj.* fresh, cool, refreshing

cam *v. pt.* came; **~ in aboot** approached

camsteerie *adj.* perverse, quarrelsome

can *n.* ability, skill; drinking vessel

cankert *adj.* ill-humoured, fretful; (of weather) stormy, threatening; gusty

canle *n.* candle

Canlemas *n.* Candlemas

canna *v. neg.* cannot

cannas *n.* canvas, esp. that used in winnowing grain; **winnow o yir ain ~** fend for yourself

canny *adj.* prudent, cautious; gentle; frugal; safe; moderate in price; politic

cantle (up) *v. intr.* brighten (up), recover health or spirits; **~ doon** settle down

cantrip *n.* mischievous trick

canty *adj.* cheery, good-humoured

capawcity *n.* ability

capawshus *adj.* capacious

caper *v.* dance

capernicious *adj.* short-tempered, fretful

capernoity *adj.* peevish; whimsical

capital *adj.* excellent

cappernyam *adj.* very fussy, temperamental (B)

capshon, caption *n.* lucky acquisition, windfall, prize

captire, in *phr.* in suspense (B1)

car(r) *n.* calves. *cf.* **caur**; *v.* care

carant, carrant *n.* revel, escapade; uproar

carble *v.* cavil, carp (M3)

carcatch *See* **carkidge**

carefu *adj.* careful

carena *v. neg.* do not care; **~ doit** do not care in the least

cargie *n.* cargo. *cf.* **cairga**

cark *n.* care, anxiety; **nae ~ nor care** not a care in the world

carkidge *n.* carcase

carl *n.* churl; man; old man

carl-doddie *n.* stalk of rib-grass

carlers *n.* heavy seaweed. *cf.* **tangles**

carlie *n.* a little old man

carlin(e) *n.* old woman; witch

carn *n.* cairn (also in placenames)

carpets *n. pl.* slippers

carr *n. pl.* calves (M3)

carried *ppl., adj.* light-headed; delirious

carritch(es) *n.* catechism; *in pl.* the Shorter Catechism (M)

cartil *n.* cartload (B1)

carvel-biggit *adj.* (boat) built with planks edge to edge. *cf.* **clinker-biggit**

carvy, carvey, carvie *n.* caraway

case be *conj.* in case

cassen *ppl.* cast; (of snow) shovelled, cleared;

cassie *See* **causey**

cast *v.* cut with a spade (*eg*, peat); dig; to throw off (*eg*, coat); **~ up** *v.* turn up; **~-oot** *n.* a quarrel; fall-out

casen, cassen *ppl.* cast; (of colour) faded; **haes ~ up** *v. pt. perf.* has turned up

castell *n.* castle

castock *n.* stalk of kail or cabbage

catch|ed *v. pt.* caught; **~er** *n.* truant officer (S); townkeeper at weekends (F); **~ her** (*phr. used by fishermen*) fall asleep; **he's ~ed her**

catecheese *v.* catechise, instruct by question and answer by use of the Church Catechism

catechis *n.* catechism (A)

cat's dicht *n.* quick wipe or wash

cattie's tailie *n.* plaything made from scraps of knitting wool on makeshift loom, using a cotton reel and pins (B)

cattle-liftin *n.* raising of cattle to their feet in Spring after they'd become weakened by poor winter feeding

cattlie *n.* cattleman (S)

cauf(ie) *n.* calf

cauk *v.* to chalk; challenge for repayment of a debt; calk, fix guard on horse's hoof to prevent slipping

caul(d) *adj., n.* cold; **~ kail het** heated up broth; anything offered for a second

time; ~ **roch shooers** cold
blustery showers; ~ **steer**
sour milk or cold water
and meal stirred together.
cf. **caal**

cauldrife *adj.* cold, chilly

caulker *n.* iron rim fixed on
shoe to minimise wear

caum *n.* mould for ball,
spoon etc

caunle *n.* candle. *cf.* **canle**

caup *n.* wooden bowl;
~**er** *n.* maker of ~s,
wood-turner

caur *n.* calves. *cf.* **car(r)**

cause *conj.* because

causey *n.* causeway, paved
area; the granite sett or
cobblestone it is paved
with. *cf.* **cassie**

cautioner *n.* surety for
another

cavels, cavils *See* **kavils**

cavie *n.* lower half of an
aumrie or **meat-press** (K)

caw *v.* to drive. *cf.* **ca**

cawpable *adj.* capable

ceest *v. pt.* cast. *cf.* **coost,
keest**

ceety *n.* city

ceevil *adj.* civil

'cep, 'cepin: *prep., conj.* except

cert, certie *in phr.* **my ~,
my ~ie!** my word on it!

cess *n.* tax, rate

chaamer *See* **chaumer**

chack *n.* chalk; chequered
linen or calico; *v.* clack;
click

chackie *n.* farm worker's
bag (T)

chackie-mull *n.* death-watch
beetle

chackit *adj.* of a checked
pattern; chequered

chad *n.* compacted gravel;
~**dy** *adj.* gravelly

Chae *pr. n. deriv.* of Charles

chaep *adj.* cheap

chaetry *n.* cheating

chaff *v.* chafe

chafts *n.* chops; cheeks

chaip-john *adj., n.* cheapjack

chairge *n., v.* charge

chairity *n.* charity

Chairlie *pr. n. deriv.* of
Charles

chait *v.* cheat; *v. pt.* cheated;
~**-e-wuddie** *n.* one who
deserves to be hanged.
cf. **chate**

chalder *n.* dry measure, of
grain (16 bolls)

chancy *adj.* lucky, fortunate;
safe

chandler-chaftit *adj.* lantern-
jawed; gaunt, haggard

changefu *adj.* changeable

change-hoose *n.* alehouse, inn

changs *n. pl.* (of rheumatism)
twinges

channel-steens *n. pl.* curling stones

chanter *n.* the part of the bagpipes on which the tune is played

chantie, chanty *n.* chamber-pot

chap *n.* knock; *v.* hammer; knock; pound; mash; chop; (of clocks) strike; **the knock ~pit** the clock struck; **~pin** *n., ppl.* knocking; **~pit** knocked; **~pit neeps** mashed turnip; **~per** *n.* utensil for mashing potatoes, turnip etc

chape *adj.* cheap. *cf.* **chaep**

chaps me *excl.* (when a person chooses a particular thing) bags I, give me...

charge *n.* oath

chat *v.* tap in (a hobnail)

chate *n., v.* cheat; **or it ~s me** if I'm not mistaken. *cf.* **chait**

chatter *v.* shatter

chaumer *n.* chamber; best room; sleeping-place for farm workers in Banff and Buchan. In the Mearns, the bothy was more common. Unlike the bothy, no food was eaten in the chaumer (A, MI); *v.* to live in a chaumer; **~t up** *ppl.* shut up in a room

chaw *v.* chew

cheek *n.* doorpost; gatepost

cheekie-for-chowie *adv.* cheek by jowl; side by side

cheena *adj., n.* china

cheenge *n., v.* change. *cf.* **chynge**; **~less** *adj.* changeless

cheeper *n.* young or half-fledged bird

cheer *n.* chair; **~man** *n.* chairman

cheery-pyke *n.* tasty morsel, treat

cheest *n.* (human) chest

chessel, chesset *n.* cheese vat or press

chief (wi) *adj.* intimate, friendly

chiel(d) *n.* child; man, fellow; **wi ~** with child

chik *n.* cheek

chile *See* **chyle**

chill(ie) *n.* child. *cf.* **chiel**

chilp *n., v.* chirp

chilpit, chilpy *adj.* chilled

chim(b)ley, chimbly *n.* chimney. *cf.* **chimla**

chimla(y), chumla(y) *n.* chimney; grate, hearth, fireplace; mantelpiece; **~-cheeks** *n. pl.* the stone pillars at the side of the fire; the fireside; **~-heid** *n.* chimney top; mantelpiece; **~-neuk** chimney corner; **~-brace** *n.* mantelpiece

chine *n.* chain; **~-gaird** *n.* (on a bicycle) chain-guard

chingle *n.* shingle

chippit *adj.* tipsy

chirk *n.* squeak; creak

chirm *v.* complain; fret (A); sing, murmur (C1))

chirr-wirrin *n.* chatting back and fore, chin-wagging (S)

chirry *n.* cherry

chitter *v.* tremble, shiver; **~in-chow** bread eaten after open-air bathing; **chit-chow** good things to eat (B1)

chois *v.* choose. *cf.* **chyse**

chop *n.* shop

chore *v.* steal (Cant, Abdn.)

chouk *n.* cheek. *cf.* **chowks**

choup *n.* a cheep: **didna get a ~ oot o im**

chowdlers *n. pl.* teeth (F)

chowks *n.* cheeks; jaws

chowp aboot *v.* walk about (M3)

chowter *n.* term of endearment, mostly for children (B)

Chrissenmas *n.* Christmas (M3)

chucken, chucknie *n.* chicken; **~-hertit** *adj.* faint-hearted; **~wort** *n.* chickweed

chuckie-steen *n.* granite chipping; pebble

chuddy *n.* chewing-gum

chuff *adj.* chummy

chum *v.* be the friend of

chumla, chumlay *n.* mantel-shelf. *cf.* **chimbley**

chunner *v.* murmur plaintively

chuntie *n.* chamber-pot

chyle, chylie *n.* child. *cf.* **chiel, chile, chill**

chynge *v.* change. *cf.* **cheenge**

chyse *n.* cheese; *v.* choose. *cf.* **chois**

chyser *n.* team-picker in games

cla *n., v.* claw

clachan *n.* hamlet

clacht *n.* grip

claes *n.* clothes. *cf.* **clyes**

clag *v.* clog; cover with

claggieleerum (T) *See* **claggum**

claggum *n.* treacle toffee

claid *ppl.* clad. *cf.* **cled**

claik *n., v.* gossip, tittle-tattle. *cf.* **clash**

clair *adj.* clear; distinct; ready; correct, without fault. *cf.* **clear**

claith *n.* cloth; **aa ae ~** all the same

claithe *v.* clothe

claiver *n.* bit of tittle-tattle

clam(b) *v. pt.* climbed

clamjamfrey, clanjamfry *n.* noisy crowd, mob; company of people

clamp *v.* walk noisily, as with hobnailed shoes

clap *n.* pat; *v.* fondle, pat; **~ doon** settle down; **~ tae** *v.* adhere to

clappit *ppl,. adj.* shrunken in body

clapper *n.* butter-hand

clart *n.* bit of dirt or mud; *v.* daub; smear; ~**y** *adj.* dirty; muddy; sticky

clash *n., v.* gossip, tittle-tattle; tale bearing; ~**maclavers** *n.* idle discourse, silly talk

claught *v.* clutch, lay hold of

claw *n.* claw; *v.* scratch; ~**ed the caup** cleaned the dish (the last to rise in the morning had to clean the common bowl); *fig.* came to the end; ~**in post** scratching post for cattle, usually a stone (T); ~**haimmer coat** tailcoat

clay doddie *n.* clay marble (Abdn.)

clead *v.* clothe. *cf.* **claithe**

cleadin *n.* clothing

clean-lan *adj.* (field) cleared of turnips and ready for ploughing (T)

clear *adj.* undamaged, in good condition (S); **to be ~ wi** to get even with (A). *cf.* **clair**

cleathin *n.* mould-board (F)

cleck *v.* give birth to young (of rabbits); ~**in** *n.* brood, litter

cled *adj.* clad

cleek, cleik *n.* hook; device to set gird spinning (S); golfing iron; *v.* seize (with the claws); hook, catch up by or fasten (on hook); ~ **wi** hook arms with

cleekit shalt *n. with ppl.* pony suffering from string-halt

cleg *n.* gadfly, horsefly

clench *v.* clinch, settle; limp (A2)

cless *n.* class

cleuch *n.* narrow glen, ravine

clew *v. pt.* clawed; *n.* ball of straw-rope used in thatching. *cf.* **cloo**

clim *v.* climb. *cf.* **sclim**

climmer *n.* climber

clink *n.* cash, coin; resounding blow; *v.* mend by rivetting; hammer; weld

clinker-biggit *adj.* (boat) built with planks overlapping. *cf.* **carvel-biggit**

clinkum *n.* ringer of church bell

clip *n.* pert girl; *v.* cut

clipe *n.* tell-tale; *v.* to tell tales *cf.* **clype**

clish-ma-claver *n.* idle talk

clite *n.* lump, piece

clivver *adj.* clever; *n.* clover

clocher *v.* cough, wheeze; ~**ert up** (of the nose) blocked

clockin *ppl., adj.* (of hen) brooding, broody

clod *v.* pelt; ~**die** *n.* clod of earth; a peat

clog(gie) *n.* log; block of wood

clog-fit *n.* club-foot

cloo *n.* ball of rope, cord or wool, etc. *cf.* **clew**

clood *n.* cloud

clook *n.*, *v.* claw

cloon *n.* clown

cloot *n.* cloth; blow; *v.* mend; patch; ~**it** clothed; patched; **sair** ~**it** badly clothed; ~**ie-dumplin** *n.* sweet dumpling cooked in a cloth; ~**ie-rug** *n.* rug made from old cloths. *cf.* **clout**

Clootie, Cloots *pr. n.* the Devil

clootch *v.* clutch (A)

clorach *n.* phlegm; *v.* clear the throat, hawk

clort *n.* mud; anything soft and sticky; *v.* to besmear;

clortit *ppl.* smeared

clorty *adj.* dirty; messy

close, closs *n.* enclosure; farmyard; passage; alley; ~**-han't** *adj.* mean, tight-fisted; ~**n-in** *ppl.* closed in; ~ **tee** *adv.* close up

clossach *n.* bulk, body; carcase of a fowl; a mass; hoard of money

clour *n.* blow; *v.* strike, indent

clout, cloutie *n.* a cloth; ~**y-rug** (*cf.* **clootie-rug**); mend, patch; blow; *v.* mend, patch (incl. a kettle); beat, strike. *cf.* **cloot, clowt**

clowt *n.*, *v.* hit, strike. *cf.* **clout**

clud *n.* cloud (K)

clum *v. pt.* climbed. *cf.* **clim**

clunk *v.* make the sound of liquid from a bottle

clyack *n.* end of harvest; ~ **shafe** the last sheaf cut in harvest

clyock *n.* cloak

clyp|e *n.* a tell-tale; idle tales; *v.* to tell tales; (jibe for a tell tale) ~**ie**, ~**ie clash pye/pyot**; **ca'd aboot** ~ rumour. *cf.* **clipe**

clyse *n.* clothes. *cf.* **claes**

clyte *n.* a sudden or heavy fall; **cam** ~ fell suddenly; ~ **doon** *v.* fall heavily, thud

coach *n.* pram

coal-coom *n.* coal-dust

cobbly *adj.* rocky, unsteady (O)

coble *n.* pond for watering cattle; *v.* rock

Cock o the North nickname for the **Marquises of Huntly**

cock *v.* swagger, show off

cock-a-leekie *n.* chicken and leek soup

cockernon(n)y *n.* starched crown of a woman's cap; woman's hair gathered into a headband (K)

cockit on *ppl.*, *prep.* perched, mounted on

cockit up *ppl.*, *prep.* dressed up showily

cockle-ee *n.* an eye with a squint (B)

cof|f *v.* buy (G1); *ppl.* ~t

cog, coggie, cogue *n.* wooden pail for milking or herring guts

cog *v.* feed from the cog or pail

coggit *ppl.* fed from the caufie's cog (T)

colcannon *n.* dish of mashed potato and chopped-cabbage served with meat

cole, coll *n.* haycock; *v.* to make haycocks

colleague (wi) *v.* associate, consort with

colleeginer *n.* student at college (A1)

collieshangie *n.* uproar (C, M3)

collogue *n.* intimate chat; *v.* converse

come *in phr.* ~ **hairst** when harvest comes; ~ **at** *adj.* far gone, worn out; ~ **ower** *v.* befall; ~ **time** in course of time

comman *n.* command

commeenicant *n.* communicant

compl|een *v.* complain; ~**eent**, ~**int** *n.* complaint

concairn *n.* concern

concaited *adj.* conceited

condeeshun *n.* condition

conduck *n.* conduct

confeerin *adj.* corresponding; ~ **tae** *ppl.* corresponding to, accordant with

confoon, confoun *v.* confound

congregat *v. pt.* congregated

connach *v.* spoil; destroy; ~t *ppl.* destroyed; wasted; (of children) spoiled

conneck *v.* connect; *ppl.* ~it

constiteetion *n.* constitution

conteen|a *v.* continue (B1); *v. pt.* conteenit; ~**wal** *adj.* continual

conten *v.* contend

conter, contar *v.* contradict; *adj.* opposite; **i the ~ airt** in the opposite direction. *cf.* **cwanter**

contermashious *adj.* contrary

contermin't *adj.* contradictory; contrary, perverse

conterwecht *n.* counterweight

contrair *adj.* contrary; opposite

contreebit *v.* contribute

convainience *n.* convenience

convoy *v.* convey, escort

coo *n.* cow; ~'s **lick** hair over-hanging the brow at one side

cooard *n.* coward

cooch *n.* dog's kennel (A)

coof *n.* coward (M); fool (K)

coom-ceiled *ppl.* (used of an attic) having a sloping or arched ceiling. *cf.* **lie-in**

coomie *adj.* grimy; sooty.
cf. **brookie**

coonjer *v.* scold; intimidate.
cf. **counger**

coont *v.* count; ~**in** *n.* arithmetic

coontenance *n.* countenance

coonter *n.* (shop) counter;
~**-lowper** *n.* shop-assistant

coor *v.* cower

coord *n.* coward; ~**ie** *adj.*
cowardly; ~**y-lick** coward's
blow

coorie *See* **coory**

coorse *adj.* coarse; cruel (A);
evil, bad (MI); *n.* course; **an**
~, **of** ~ of course

coort *n.* cattle-court; *v.* court;

coory *v.* cower, crouch

coost *v. pt.* cast. cf. **ceest**

cooter *See* **couter**

corbie *n.* crow

core *n.* company, corps

corkit *adj.* constipated

corn *n.* oats; *v.* feed with
oats; ~**-kist** *n.* corn-chest;
~**-kister** *n.* farm-workers'
song; ~**-laft** *n.* grain-loft;
~**-yard** *n.* stack-yard

corp *n.* corpse

correck *v.* correct

corrie *n.* circular hollow on
mountainside; *v.* cower,
crouch. cf. **coorie**

corrieneuchin *ppl.* conversing
intimately

corter *n.* quarter; quarter of
oat-cake. cf. **korter**

cosh *adj.* cosy

cottar *n.* farm worker
occupying tied cottage; *v.*
to lead the life of a cottar;
~**-hoose** *n.* farm worker's
house

cotts *n. pl.* petticoats

counger *See* **coonjer**

coup *See* **cowp**

couper *n.* one who deals in
horses or cattle. cf. **cowper**

couple *n.* rafter (S). cf. **cupple**

coup-the-ladle *n.* the game
of see-saw

cout *n.* colt. cf. **cowt**

couter *n.* coulter, iron cutter at
front of plough; nose; **bleedy**
~ nosebleed. cf. **cooter**.

couthie, couthy *adj.* kindly;
pleasant

covin-tree *n.* trysting tree; tree
in front of an old mansion-
house, where the laird met
visitors

cow, cowe *v.* beat, outdo,
surpass; **yon ~s aa; that ~s
the gowan** that beats all,
that takes the cake

cowe *n.* twig of a shrub or
bush; *v.* prune

cower *v.* recover from, get
over, *eg*, **cower** an accident;
~**in** *adj.* curative, therepeutic

cowk *v.* retch; vomit (A)

cowman *adj.* common (M3);
  ~ality *n.* general public,
  commoners
cowp *v. tr.* upset; *intr.* fall over,
  overturn; bargain, deal
  (esp. in horses and cattle;
  ~ the creels upset a plan;
  ~it sheep overturned sheep;
  ~-the-cat children's game;
  ~in *n.* (of a boat) heaving.
  cf. **coup**
cowp *n., v. intr.* deal; **~er** *n.* a
  dealer (esp. in horses/cattle)
cowshus *adj.* cautious
cowt *n.* colt. *cf.* **cout**
coy *n.* heifer. *cf.* **quaik**
crabbit *adj.* bad-tempered,
  cross
crack *n.* talk, gossip; *v.* to
  chat; **~ie** *adj.* chatty,
  talkative
crackit *adj., ppl.* cracked
craft *n.* croft
crag *n.* throat. *cf.* **craig**
craggin *n.* jar, pitcher
craig *n.* throat. *cf.* **crag**
craighl|e *v.* cough huskily; **~y**
  adj. husky
craik *n., v.* croak
craiter, craitur *See* **cratur**
crame *n.* cream (S)
crank *adj.* (of a person)
  difficult, not easily
  understood
crannie *n.* the little finger

cran-the-net, a *n.* a good
  catch
crap *n.* crop; bird's crop;
  throat; highest part of
  anything; **craw in his ~**
  annoy, give cause for
  regret; **shook their ~s**
  expressed their feelings,
  grievances; **~ o the wa**
  highest part of an inside
  wall; *v.* crop land; *v. pt.*
  crept
crapper heid *phr.* head of cod
  scraped out, stuffed with
  oatmeal, onions and liver
crater, cratur *n.* creature;
  the ~ whisky
craver *n.* creditor; dun
craw *n.* crow; *v.* boast, exult;
  a ~ tae pluck a bone to pick
creeat *v.* create
creel *n.* basket for fish, used
  by fishwives
creenge *v.* cringe
creep doon *v.* shrink, bend
  with age
creepie *n.* low stool
creepin-eevie *n.* convolvulus;
  a very slow person (T)
creepit *v. pt.* crept
creesh *n.* fat, grease; *v.* thrash,
  beat; **~y** *adj.* greasy
creesis *n.* crisis
creesy *adj.* greasy. *cf.* **creeshy**
creetick *n.* critic

cries *n. pl.* banns (giving notice of impending marriage)

crinch *n.* small piece; *v.* crunch

crine *v.* shrink; shrivel

criticeese *v.* criticise

criv(e) *n.* enclosure (for poultry) *v.* enclose; ~ved up cooped up

crochl|e *n.* disease in the hind legs of cattle; *v.* limp; *adj.* crippled, also ~y

crockeneetion, crockaneeshin *n.* destruction; smithereens

crood *n., v.* crowd; ~it *adj.* crowded; ~le *v.* huddle together

crood|s *n. pl.* curds; ~s an fy curds and whey; ~-brakker *n.* curd-breaker (F)

crook *n.* iron hook from which pots and kettles were hung by chain over fire; twist. *See* links, swye

croon *n.* crown; the head; *v.* crown; wail, lament

croose *adj.* lively, bold, bright, confident. *cf.* crouse; ~ i the craw brisk and confident in conversation

croup *v.* croak. *cf.* crowp

crouse *adj.* lively, bold, bright. *cf.* croose

crowdy *n.* meal and water mixed cold (M). *cf.* caul steer

crowelty *n.* cruelty (M3)

crowp *v.* croak; complain. *cf.* croup

crowpie *adj.* querulous

cruisie *n.* old-fashioned oil lamp, with rush wick

crulg|e (doon) *v.* cower, crouch; ~t up curled up

crumlock *n.* crumb

crummie *n.* cow; cow's name

crummochie *adj.* crumbly

crunkle *v.* crease, crinkle

crusie *See* cruisie

cry *v.* call; publish bans; **fit-dae-ye-cry-him** what-do-you-call-him; ~ **in by** visit briefly; ~ **on** to call (on), visit; shout for; ~ **tee** call in by (B); **oot o** ~ out of hearing range

crydit *n.* credit

crynt *adj.* stunted. *cf.* crine

cubbirt *n.* cupboard

cud *v.* could; ~na *v. neg.* could not

cuddam wi *v.* get used to, get accustomed to (M3)

cuddy *n.* donkey

cuff *v.* winnow for the first time

cuffins *n. pl.* rough husks and hairs after first winnowing

cuif *See* coof

cuist *v. pt.* cast, threw. *cf.* ceest
cuitikins *n.* gaiters.
  cf. queetikins
Cullen skink *n.* fish soup
  made with smoked
  haddock, onion and
  mashed potato
cultivet *ppl.* cultivated
cupple *See* couple
curduddoch *adv.* close
  together (J)
curlie-wurlies *n.* hair in curl
  papers (B1)
curn, a *n.* a quantity;
  company; a gweed ~
  considerable number
currack *n.* coracle
curran *n.* currant; ~ daad fruit
  slice; ~-bap currant bun
currieboram *n.* confused,
  noisy crowd
curriehunkers *n. pl.* the hams;
  on yir ~ in a crouching
  position
cushie (doo) *n.* wood-pigeon
cut *v.* reap; castrate
cutchack *n.* small blazing coal
  or peat fire; the clearest part
  of the fire; the side of the fire
cutter *n.* small whisky bottle
cuttins *n. pl.* encouragement;
  ye'll get nae (short) ~ fae
  him
cuttit *v. pt.* cut

cutty *n.* short tobacco pipe;
  knife; short girl; worthless
  woman
cutty steel *n.* stool with
  short legs
c'wa *imp.* come away
cwanter *v.* contradict.
  cf. conter; ~-kine *adj.*
  contrary
cweel *adj., v.* cool
cweet *n.* ankle; thraw yir ~
  twist your ankle; ~ikins
  n. pl. gaiters. *cf.* queet
cwid *v. pt.* could; ~na could
  not
cwyte *See* kwyte
cyaard, cyaurd *n.* tinker
cyacks *n.* oatcakes
cyapper *v.* caper
cyarn *n.* cairn; number; a ~ o
  a number of (M3). *cf.* curn

D

daachter *n.* daughter (A2).
  cf. dother, dochter
daar *adj.* dear, expensive
Daavit *pr. n.* David
dab *v.* poke; *in phr.* let ~ give
  hint, give sign, let on; ~ han
  skilled exponent
dacent *adj.* decent. *cf.* daicent
dachle, dackle *v.* hesitate,

dawdle; (of the weather)
let up; cause to hesitate,
discourage (c)

dad *n.* lump; *v.* pelt; spatter.
cf. **daud**

dae *v.* do (*gen. pro.* dee; *pro.*
day by s, J); *ppl.* ~n;
~ **awa** do not so badly;
~ **doon** do down; ~ **wintin**
do without. *cf.* **dee, deen**

daff *v.* jest, sport (K); flirt (J)

daffie *n.* daffodil

daffin *n.* flirtation; romp

daft *adj.* foolish; frolicsome

dag *v.* confound; ~ **it** *excl.*
confound it; ~ **the bit** not a
whit (BI); ~ **the grain** not
at all (BI)

daicent *adj.* decent. *cf.* **dacent**

daidle *v.* dirty (s)

daily-day *adv.* every day

dainner *n.* dinner. *cf.* **denner**

dairk *adj.* dark (J)

daith *n.* death. *cf.* **deeth, deith**

daivert *adj.* fatigued; confused;
benumbed; stunned. *cf.* **daver**

dale *v.* deal

dall *n.* doll

dallies' cleysies *n. pl.* doll's
clothes; coloured seaweed (B)

dambrod *n.* draught board

dame *n.* mature woman;
mother; young woman.
cf. **deem**

dammer *v.* confuse;
astonish (R)

damn the bit, damn the fear
excl. not at all

dancers *See* **merry dancers**

dander *n.* temper; **tae get yir**
~ **up** to get angry

dandy *adj.* fine, light-hearted (J)

dane *ppl.* done. *cf.* **daen, deen**

dang *v. pt.* beat; dashed down.
cf. **ding**; *v.* used for *damn*

darg *n.* a day's work; *v.* work;
~**er** *n.* a day-labourer;
worker; ~**in** *n.* labouring

darksome *adj.* melancholy,
dismal

dask *n.* desk

dassint *adj.* decent.
cf. **daicent, dacent**

daub *n.* skilled exponent.
cf. **dab-han**

dauchle *v.* dangle; linger.
cf. **dachle**

daud *n.* stroke, blow; a large
piece; *v.* ~ **aboot** bang;
bump, bounce; jolt; pelt;
spatter

dauk *adj.* dark (K)

daumer *See* **dammer**

daunder, dauner *v.* stroll

daunert *See* **donnert**

daupet *See* **dawpit**

daur *v.* dare; ~**na** dare not;
~**sna** dares not

daut *n.* caress. *cf.* **dawt**

daver *v.* stun, stupify; benumb

daw *n., v.* dawn

dawpit *adj.* silly, stupid; benumbed

dawt *n.* caress; *v.* dote, fondle. *cf.* **dawt**

dawtie *n.* darling, pet

dazzle *n.* any fizzy drink

deal *n.* board, plank

deave *v.* deafen; pester with entreaties. *cf.* **deeve**

deddie *n.* daddy (M3)

dede *n.* death (K)

dee *v.* die; do. *cf.* **dae**; ~ **doon** do down; ~ **in** have a bad effect on the mind, head; ~ **wintin** do without

deece *n.* wooden seat or settle, which could be used as table or bed); turf seat out-of-doors; **haud doon the ~** rest, take it easy. *cf.* **deese**

deed *in phr.* **to be the ~ o't** to be responsible for (B); *adv.* indeed

deef *adj.* deaf. *cf.* **deif**

deegnity *n.* dignity

deelt (wi) *v. pt.* dealt (with)

deem(ie) *n.* a young girl; servant-girl

deen *ppl.* done; *adj.* exhausted; **caad himsel ~** wore himself out. *cf.* **daen**

deese *See* **deece**

deester *n.* (*often contemptuous*) doer; promoter; agent

deet *v. pt.* died

deeth *n.* death (A2). *cf.* **daith**, **deith**

deeve *v.* deafen; pester with entreaties. *cf.* **deave**

deevil *n.* devil; potato digger; **~itch** *adj.* devilish

deevilock *n. imp*, demon

defait *n., v.* defeat; *ppl.* defeated

defarred *v. pt., ppl.* deferred

defate *See* **defait**

defiet *v. pt.* defied

deft *adj.* bold; hard up

deg *See* **dag**

degraad *v.* degrade, *ppl.* **~it**; **~in** *ppl.* degrading

deid *adj.* dead; **~ly** *adj.* deadly; **~-thraw** *n.* death-throe; **i the ~-thraw** between one state and another, undecided

deif *adj.* deaf. *cf.* **deef**

deil, Deil *n.* devil; *adv.* no, not; **~ a muckle winner** not much wonder; **~ ane** not one **~-ma-care** *adv.* no matter; **~ the bit** not at all

deist *See* **dyst**

deith *n.* death (J). *cf.* **daith**

deleebrate(ly) *adj., (adv.)* deliberate(ly)

deleer *v.* intoxicate; render delirious; **~it** *ppl.* demented, gone mad

dell *n.* goal or base in children's games; **nae great**

~ no great shakes, of no great quality (T)

dell *v.* dig, delve;

dellt *ppl.* dug

delt *v.* fondle, cuddle (M2)

delve *v. in phr.* ~ **the bank** argue out the matter (B1)

dem *v.* dam

demoshel *n.* young, unmarried girl (M3)

den *n.* ravine

denner *n.* dinner; *v.* provide dinner. *cf.* **dainner**

denty *adj.* dainty (J)

denum *v.* confound

dern *adj.* dark; dismal

deroge *v.* decry, disparage

dert *n.* dart

descrive, descryve *v.* describe

designtly *adv.* deliberately

deteen *v.* detain

deuk *n.* duck

deval|l *n.* a pause, ceasing; *v.* to cease, stop; ~**vement** *n.* cessation, stop (M3)

deydie *n.* grandfather. *cf.* **gutcher**

deykon *n.* deacon. *cf.* **dykon**

dibber-dabber *n.* wrangle (B)

dicht *v.* clean; wipe up

diddle *v.* sing in a low tone without words; dandle a child (B)

didnin *v. neg. interrog.* didn't?

diffeekwalty *n.* difficulty (accent the second syllable) (A2)

dikesider *n.* bastard (M3)

dilet *adj.* stupid; crazed; confused; weary. *See* **dylt**

dilse *n.* dulse, edible seaweed

dince *n.* dance (S)

dindeerie *See* **dundeerie**

ding *v.* beat, over-come, excel; (of rain, snow) to fall heavily; ~ **in** inculcate, din

dinna *v. neg.* don't

din-rais|er *n.* trouble-maker ~**in** *adj.* quarrelsome, trouble-making

din-skinnt *adj.* weather-beaten, sunburned (T)

dinty *adj.* dainty. *cf.* **denty**

dip *v.* challenge; discuss; ~**pit him on't** challenged him over it

dipthairy *n.* diphtheria

dird *n.* a thud, thump, blow; heavy fall; *v.* beat, thump; ~**in** *n.* onslaught

dirdle *v. intr.* dangle; *tr.* bounce

dirdum(dree) *n.* loud noise, uproar

dirk *n.* long dagger

dirl *v.* tingle; vibrate

dirler *n.* chamber-pot

dirrum-dicht *n.* vigorous wipe (B)

dirry *n.* ash on top of a pipe (T). *See* **durrie**

dirten *ppl.* dirtied; mean, contemptible

diry *See* **dyrie**

dis *v.* does

disadvise *v.* warn against (A1)

disappint *v.* disappoint

disconvene *v.* inconvenience

discoont *n.* discount

discoorse *n.* discourse

dishabillay *n.* a state of undress

dish-cloot *n.* dish-cloth

dish o tay *phr.* cup of tea

disjaskit *adj.* downcast, dejected (J, M2)

disjeest *v.* digest

disjune *n.* breakfast (K)

disna *interrog.* doesn't

disnint *interrog.* doesn't it?

dispeace *n.* trouble, discord; **mak ~** cause trouble

displenish, displinis *v.* disfurnish; to sell off goods & stock on leaving farm; **~ing sale** *n.* auction sale of farm stock etc

dist *n.* dust; fine particles of meal and husk (F); **~er** *n.* duster; distillery draff for feeding animals

districk *n.* district

dit *v.* close, shut up; shut the mouth

dite *See* **doit**

div *v. pr.* do; *eg,* I div

divert *n.* entertainment, diversion; *v.* entertain

divnin *v. neg. interrog.* don't; **~ ye?** don't you

divot *n.* piece of turf

dixie *n.* severe scolding (A); **she gya him his ~** she gave him a dressing-down

dizzen *n.* dozen

doag *n.* dog (J). *cf.* **tyke**

dochter *n.* daughter (A1). *cf.* **daachter, dother**

dock *n.* buttocks; bottom. *cf.* **doke**

docken *n.* common dock plant

dockiment, *n.* document. *cf.* **dockyment**

dockit *ppl.* docked, cut short (*Eng. v.*)

docknail, docknell *n.* mainpin; nail used to fix handle on a scythe or plough; very experienced farmservant

dockyment *n.* document

dod *excl.* euphemism for God; **~ ay** yes indeed

Dod *pr. n.* nickname for George

dodd *v.* render hornless; **~it** *ppl., adj.* without horns

doddy mitten *n.* worsted glove with no separate division for the four fingers.

dog-birdie *n.* storm petrel (B)

dog-dirder *n.* whipper-in; kennel attendant

doilt *adj.* stupid, crazed. *cf.* **dylt**

doit *n.* old coin of little value; he caredna a ~

doit *v.* to grow feeble in mind; ~**it** *ppl.* in dotage; stupid

doke *cf.* **dock**

dome *n.* press-stud

dominie *n.* schoolmaster

donal(ie) *n.* glass of spirits (from Donald)

done *ppl.* outwitted

donnert *adj.* in dotage; dazed; stupid

Dons, the *pr. n.* nickname of Aberdeen football team

doo *n.* dove, pigeon

dooble *adj.*, double; two-faced (A1); ~**-jintit** *adj.* double-jointed; ~**-legs** *n. pl.* crutches

doocot *n.* dovecot

dook *n.*, *v.* bathe; ~**er** *n.* bather

dool *adj.* sorrowful; *n.* woe; grief; ~**some** *adj.* sad

dooms *adv.* extremely

doomsil *n.* domicile (B1)

doon *adv.*, *prep.* down; *adj.* depressed, fed up; ~ **i the moo** disconsolate, dejected; ~**-pressed (wi)** *ppl.* weighed down with ~**-by** *adv.* down yonder; ~**come** *n.* fall, decrease, drop; ~**fa**

n. downfall; ~**-i-toon** *adj.* rather common (Abdn.); ~**poor** *n.* downpour; ~**richt** *adj.* downright; ~**-sit** *n.* home (B1); ~**-sittin** *n.* settlement, usually at marriage

doorie *n.* (small) door; a game of marbles played against a door

door-cheek *n.* door-post; threshold

door-stane *n.* doorstep

doosht *n.* bump, heavy fall or throw

doot *n.*, *v.* doubt; ~**fu** *adj.* doubtful

dorb (of birds) *n.* a peck; *v.* grub, peck (R)

dorty *adj.* fastidious, hard to please, *eg,* ~ **wi their maet;** (of a person) spoiled (K)

dose *n.* large number of anything

doss *n.* bow; knot

dossie *n.* small quantity in the form of a cluster or heap; *v.* toss down (M3)

dother *n.* daughter (A, M). *cf.* **daachter, dochter**

dott|le *n.* the unconsumed tobacco left in a pipe; *v.* become stupid and fretful; ~**elt** mentally confused; in dotage; ~**ledom** *n.* dementia

douce *adj.* respectable,
  decent; quiet, gentle; kind;
  circumspect
douchty *adj.* doughty
doun *See* doon
doup *n.* buttocks. *cf.* dowp
Doup *pr. n.* nickname for
  village of Boddam
dour *adj.* grim, austere
dover (ower) *v.* doze (off)
dowf *adj.* melancholy,
  gloomy; hollow
dowie *adj.* sad; dismal;
  downcast
downa *v. neg.* don't
dowp *n.* buttocks;
  ~ doon *v.* sit down. *cf.* doup
doz|en *v.* to benumb, stupify,
  daze; ~ent, ~in *ppl.* in a
  benumbed state; stupid
dozen't *excl.* confound it!
draaght *See* dracht
draa *v.* draw; ~ bridle *phr.*
  rest (M3)
draars *n. pl.* long underpants
draavers *n. pl.* long drawers
  for men
drabble *v.* make wet or dirty,
  to besmear
drabbly *adj.* (of weather) wet,
  disagreeable
drablich *n.* muddy person (B1)
dracht *n.* a load; two or more
  cart-loads brought at one
  time; draught, drink

draff-hurlie *n.* iron trolley
  filled with distillery draff
  for feeding cattle
dra(i)ggelt *adj.* bedraggled
draigon *n.* child's paper
  kite (J)
drap *n., v.* drop; ~pie *adj.*
  rainy; *n.* drop; drink of
  alcohol; ~pin *adj.* dripping,
  rainy
drate *v. pr. & pt.* defecate;
  ppl. dritten
draucht *See* dracht
drauchtit *ppl., adj.* (of a
  horse) harnessed for work
drauchts *n. pl.* draughts
drave *v. pt.* drove
dree *v.* endure; ~ yir ain weird
  endure your fate
dreeble *v.* dribble
dreed *n., v.* dread. *cf.* dreid
dreel *n.* drill, small furrow
  for sowing seed; ridge
  with such furrow on top;
  practice; scolding; get yir
  ~s be punished
dreep *n.* drip; dripping
  condition; *v.* drip; empty to
  last drop
dreepin *n.* dripping; ~s
  n. pl. dregs
dreepin-pen *n.* fenced enclosure,
  where newly dipped sheep
  were held for dripping (T)
dreeve *v. pt.* drove

dregie *n.* refreshment given at a funeral

dreich *adj.* (of weather) dull; slow of motion; sombre; tardy; wearisome

dreid *n., v.* dread. *cf.* **dreed**

dreigh *See* **dreich**

drib *v.* draw the last milk from a cow

dribble, driblach *n.* drop, usually of alcohol

dribbly *adj.* drizzly

driffle *n.* scolding

drift *n.* driving or driven snow

drink, nae sma *phr.* of no small significance (M3)

drochle, drochlum *n.* dwarf; dumpy or puny person

droddum *n.* buttocks (M3)

drog *n.* drug; *v.* drug; dose

droggie, droggist *n.* druggist

drook *v.* drench;

drookit *adj.* drenched

droon *v.* drown, *pt. ppl* ~t drowned

drooth, drouth *n.* drought; thirst; drunkard, tippler. *cf.* **drucht**

droothy, drouthy *adj.* thirsty

drow *n.* fit of illness (A, A1)

drowse *v.* become drowsy; **the ~** drowsiness

drucht *n.* drought; dry weather; ~**it** *ppl.* in a state of drought; dehydrated (G). *cf.* **drooth**

drucht *n.* drying effect of air; **a gran ~** (B)

drucken *adj.* drunken

druckenness *n.* drunkenness

drumly *adj.* thick, muddy; gloomy (of water); sullen; troubled

drumster *n.* town drummer

drush *n.* peat dust (R); dross (K)

dry-darn *n.* constipation

dryster *n.* man who dried the grain before grinding

dubby, dubbit *adj.* muddy

dubs *n.* mud

ducksie *adj.* dull; lazy (A)

duddie *adj.* ragged

duds *n. pl.* rags; clothes

Duffer *pr. n.* native of Macduff

dule *See* **dool**

dumfoonert *adj.* dumbfounded

dummie *n.* a mute

dumpage, dumpitch *adj.* melancholy, depressed (A2)

dumpish *adj.* melancholy (K)

dumplin *n.* plum (or Christmas) pudding

dundeerie *n.* a great noise (M2)

dunderheid *n.* an outstanding fool

dune *ppl.* done. *cf.* **deen**

dung *v. pt.* (of ding) dashed down, smashed. *cf.* **dang**

dung-hack *n.* implement for clearing dung

dungers *n. pl.* dungarees

dunt *n., v.* thump; **the very ~** the very thing needed

durrie, hud on the *phr.* whip the horse (B)

dursna *See* **daursna**

durstna *v. pt. neg.* did not dare

dusht *ppl.* struck dumb, silenced

dutch *n.* ditch (G, M1)

dwaal, dwall *v.* dwell; **(~lin-) hoose** *n.* (dwelling-)house

dwaibly *adj.* feeble; shaky

dwam, dwaam, dwalm, dwaum *n.* a faint, fit of sickness; **tae tak a ~** to faint; **~ock** *n.* a faint

dwebble, dweeble, dweebly *adj.* feeble. *cf.* **dwaibly**

dweemly-dwamly *adj.* feeble (M1)

dwine *v.* languish, pine; waste away; diminish

dwobble *adj.* feeble. *cf.* **dwebble**

dyae, dyang *v.* go (M3). *cf.* **gae, gyang**

dyester *n.* dyer

dyke *n.* wall of stone or turf; **dry stane ~** wall made without mortar; **~r** *n.* builder of dykes

Dyker *pr. n.* native of Cellardyke

dykon *n.* deacon

dylt *ppl.* wearied, fatigued

dyod *excl.* euphemism for God

dyow *adj.* due; *n.* dew; **~ie** *adj.* dewy

dyowtie *n.* duty

dyrie *n.* dairy

dyst(e) *v.* fall, sit down or throw with a thud or bump; go up and down bumping

dytit *ppl.* in dotage; stupid. *cf.* **doitit**

dytlifiet *ppl., adj.* stultified

E

e, 'e *def. art.* the

each *n.* adze

ear, ear' *adj., adv.* early; **~er** *adj.* earlier

ear, 'ear *n.* year

ear *v.* plough; **~in** *n.* ploughing (A2)

Earl o Hell *pr. n.* the Devil; **blaik as the ~'s weskit**

earock *n.* a fowl of the first year

easedom *n.* ease; relief; comfort

easin *n.* eaves; point on rick where tapering began; **~-gang** row of sheaves projecting at at the eaves of a stack to keep the rain off. *cf.* **eezen**

easy *adv.* easily; **~-min't** *adj.* easy going; **~-osy** *adj.* easy-going

eattock *n.* dim. of **aet**, titbit, dainty

eave-raip *n.* rope around eaves of a stack

ebb land *n.* shallow soil

ebb-ploo *v.* to shallow plough (F)

echt *adj.* eight; **~een** *adj.* eighteen; **~y** *adj.* eighty; *cf.* **aicht, aucht**

echt *v.* owe; own. *cf.* **acht, yacht**

edder, edderan *conj.* either (can be used at end of sentence as in Eng.)

edder *v.* to rope thatch with an **~in** shuttle-shaped ball of rope (F)

eddica|shun *n.* education; **~t** *ppl., adj.* educated

edick *n.* edict

edifee *v.* edify; *ppl.* edifeein

ee *n.* eye; **hid a lang ~ at** was attracted to (G). *See* **een.**

eechie *n.* absolutely nothing (*in phr.* **eechie nor ochie**)

eediot *n.* idiot

eedle-oddle *adj.* easy-going, lacking character. *cf.* **eesie-osie**

eek *v.* add on or to; egg on; **eekin** *ppl.*

eeksy-peeksy, -picksy *adj.* exactly equal

eel *adj.* dry, empty (used of cows which have stopped giving milk). *cf.* **yeld**

Eel *pr. n.* Yule. *cf.* **Eile, Yeel**

eel, eelie *n.* oil; **~y** *adj.* oily

eemage *n.* image

eemaist *adj.* uppermost; **~ wynin** upper part of field

eemur *n.* humour

een *adj., pron.* one. *cf.* **ane**

een *n.* evening; *pl.* eyes. *See* **ee**

eence *adv.* once; **~ eeran** (A1) on a special errand; specially; **~ on a day** once upon a time, at one time. *cf.* **aince, ance**

eenin *n.* evening

eenoo *adv.* just now. *cf.* **eyvnoo**

eer *v.* err

eeran *n.* errand; **nae ~ tae** no right to. *See* **eence**

eesage *n.* usage; behaviour

ees|e *n.* (*pr.* eece) use; *v.* (*pr.* eeze) use; **tae ~e wuntin em** to do without them; **~t wi't** used to it; **~efu** *adj.* useful; **~eless** *adj.* useless

eeshan *n.* small child (M2); small puny person (B1)

eeshich *n.* small, untidy person (B1)

ee-sicht *n.* eyesight

eeswal(l) *adj.* usual; **~ly** *adv.* usually

eet *v. pt.* ate. *See* **aet**

eevie *n.* ivy; **creepin ~** convolvulus; a slow person

eezen(s) *n.* eaves. *cf.* **easin**

effeck *n.* effect

efter *prep., adv.* after; *adv.* afterwards; **~an-aa** after all. *cf.* **aifter**

efterhin *adv.* afterwards. *cf.* **efter**

efter|neen *n.* afternoon (A1); **~nin** *n.* afternoon (s)

eggs, clean aff his *phr.* in a state of excitement

egg shallies *n. pl.* egg shells; **aa ~** feeling fragile, fretful (B)

eichty *adj.* eighty. *cf.* **aichty, echty**

eident *adj.* diligent; industrious

eik, eke *n.* addition; *v.* add; **~ him up** egg him on (A2). *cf.* **eek**

eild *n.* old age; **~it** aged. *cf.* **eld**

Eile *pr. n.* Yule. *cf.* **Eel, Yeel**

eithly *adv.* easily

eke *adv.* also (*poet.*)

elbick, elbock, elbuck *n.* elbow; **~ jam** runny jam; **~-cheer** armchair (M3)

eld *n.* old age (C1). *cf.* **eild**

eldritch *adj.* unearthly, uncanny

eleeven, eleiven *adj.* eleven. *cf.* **aleyven**

elf-shoot *v.* shoot with elf arrow

ell *n.* Scottish measurement, the Scotch, equal to 37.0578 inches; **~-wan** *n.* yardstick

eller *n.* elder (of the church). *cf.* **elyer**

ellieson *n.* shoemaker's awl (B1). *cf.* **eshin**

elshin *n.* shoemaker's awl. *cf.* **ellieson**

elyer *n.* elder tree; church elder. *cf.* **eller**

emmenteen *n.* ant (M3). *cf.* **emmerteen**

emmers *n. pl.* embers

emmerteen *n.* ant (G)

en *n.* end

enew *adj.* enough. *cf.* **eneugh**

enfluence *n.* influence

engeen *n.* engine

enoo *adv.* just now

en-rig *n.* the land at the end of the furrow on which the plough is turned

enstinck *n.* instinct

enstrument *n.* instrument

enteetle *v.* entitle

enterdick *n., v.* interdict

enterfere *v.* interfere

enterin *adj.* favourable for beginning or entering on (s)

enterteenment *n.* entertainment

ere *prep.*, *conj.* before. *cf.* **or**
erf *adj.* loth, reluctant
errant *n.* errand (s)
erse *n.* arse, hind-quarters.
    cf. **doke**
erst *adv.* at first
esk *n.*, *v.* hiccup; **tak the ~**
    get hiccups
espeeshully *adv.* especially
ess *n.* ash, ashes. *cf.* **aiss**
essfu *adj.* useful. *cf.* **eesefu**
ether *n.* udder
etnach *n.* juniper (berry)
etsleel *n.* young child (B1)
ett *v.* eat; **~en** *ppl.* eaten; **~en**
    an spewed *phr.* in a poor
    state; **~ables** *n. pl.* eatables.
    cf. **aet, aeten**
ettercap *n.* spider.
    cf. **nettercap**
ettle *n.* aim, intent; *v.* aim at,
    aspire to, intend; be eager;
    begin
ettlin *ppl.*, *adj.* intending,
    eager
even *n.* evening. *cf.* **een**;
    at ~ in the evening
evendoon *adj.* sheer,
    downright
everlaistin *adj.* everlasting
excamb *n.* one piece of
    ground exchanged for
    another; *v.* exchange lands
exceesable *adj.* excusable
excep *prep.* except. *cf.* **'cep**

exerceese *n.*, *v.* exercise;
    ~-beuk exercise-book; **~d**
    wi/aboot pre-occupied with
exhibeetion *n.* exhibition
exkeesable *See* **exceesable**
expairience *n.* experience
expeck *v. e*xpect; **~it** expected
expoon(d) *v.* expound
exterordnar *adj.* extraordinary
eydent *See* **eident**
eyn *n.*, *v.* end, *ppl.* ended; **the**
    back~ the end of harvest;
    autumn; winter; **get ~s tae**
    rug thegidder make ends
    meet; **~less** *adj.* endless;
    ~rig *n.* end ridge. *cf.* **en, eynt**
eyntment *n.* ointment
eyven *adj.* even, straight; **set**
    yir tie ~ straighten your tie
eyvnoo, eynoo *adv.* just now.
    cf. **enew, eenoo**
eyzl|e *n.* a live coal, hot ember;
    ~y eet with eyes like
    burning coals

F

fa, faa *n.* fall; fate; *pron.* who;
    v. fall, befall; **~ clyte** fall
    heavily; **~ heir till** inherit;
    ~ tee fall to, begin
faamous *adj.* famous
faar *adv.* where
faavour *n.* favour; **for ony ~!**
    for goodness sake!

faavrit *adj.* favourite.
  cf. fauvrit
faceable *adj.* likely to be
  true; barely true (B1)
fack *n.* fact; *v.* make, shape,
  form (B1)
faddom *v.* fathom
fader, fadder *n.* father
  (A, M3). *cf.* faither
fae *n.* foe (A); *prep.* from.
  cf. frae
faem *n.* foam
faik *n.* plaid. *cf.* fayich, fyaak
fail-dyke *n.* turf wall.
  cf. feal-dyke
faimly *n.* family
fain *adj.* eager, anxious;
  inclined; *adv.* gladly
fair *adj.* fair; ~ hornie fair
  play; *adv.* very, quite,
  completely
fair-furth-the-gate *adj.* honest
  and straightforward (M3, R)
fairin *n.* treat, present bought
  at a fair
fairlie *See* ferlie
fairly *adv.*, *excl.* quite, surely
fairm *n.* farm; ~er *n.* farmer;
  ~hoose *n.* farmhouse;
  ~in *n.* farming; ~-servan
  n. farm-hand. *cf.* ferm
fairn *n.* fern
fairrier *n.* farrier
faist *adj.*, *adv.* fast. *cf.* fest
faisten *v.* fasten
faith *excl.* indeed; ~fu *adj.*
faithful
faither *n.* father (C1, F).
  cf. fader
Faithlie *pr. n.* Fraserburgh
fake *v.* make, shape. *cf.* fack
fald *v.* fold
fallow *n.* fellow
fan *adv.* when; *v. pt.* felt;
  found. *See* fin
fan, fanner *n.* winnowing
  machine
fancy *n.* fancy-cake
fang *n.* scamp; lout; large
  lump cut from something;
  ~ in tuck in (to food).
  cf. hing in
fank *n.* sheepfold
fant *n.* fainting fit; *adj.*, *v.* faint
fantoosh *adj.* very smart, grand
far *adv.* where; ~ever, ~ivver
  adv., *conj.* wherever;
  ~ idder *interrog. adv.* where
  else? *cf.* faur
far ben wi *phr.* intimate with,
  esp. in favour with God
fardel *n.* a large piece (B1)
farder *adv.* farther
fardin *n.* farthing; butter
  biscuit, originally four a
  penny (B)
Farfar *pr. n.* Forfar; ~ bridie.
  See bridie
farlan *n.* a long box into
  which herrings are emptied
  for gutting

farra *adj.* barren; **~coo** *n.* barren cow

farr|er *adj.* farther; **~est** farthest; **~est ootbye** farthest out

fas(t) *n.*, *v.* fast; **~ day** day in week preceding half-yearly Communion in Presbyterian Churches, treated as holiday, with service of preparation for the Sacrament; **Fasten's Een, Faster's Even** etc Shrove Tuesday. *cf.* **Festeren's Eve**

fash *n.*, *v.* trouble; **dinna ~ yir thoom** don't trouble yourself; **~ious** *adj.* fussy, hard to please; troublesome

fat *adj.* what; **~ever** *adj.*, *pron.* whatever; **~ for** *adv.* why; **~ gin** what if; **~ o** what a lot of; **~na** what sort of a; **~-ye-ca't** *n.* what-do-you-call-it

fat-hen *n.* weed growing among turnips

fattal *adj.* fatal

fattrels *n. pl.* ribbon-ends (B1)

fatty-bannocks *n.* fat person

faugh *n.* fallow land; **fairmers' ~ gars lairds lauch** (Prov.); *v.* rub; scratch, claw (B1); plough or harrow fallow land

fauchie *adj.* sickly-looking

faul(d) *n.* fold; sheep-fold; *v.* fold; fold sheep; **~ yir fit** sit down (R)

faur *v.* fare; **~-ye-weel** farewell. *cf.* **far**

faured, faurt *adj.* favoured. *See* **weel-faurt, ill-faurt**

fause *adj.* false

faut *n.* fault; **~-free** faultless

fauvrit *adj.* favourite. *cf.* **faavrit**

fawmous *adj.* famous

fawvour *n.*, *v.* favour; **~t** *ppl. adj.* favoured

fayich *See* **faik**

feal dyke *n.* wall built of sods

fear *n.* fright; *v.* frighten (Abdn. and coastal)

fear, for *conj.* in case, lest (*in neg. context*)

fearna *v. neg.* have no fear

feart *adj.* afraid; **~ things** *n. pl.* superstitious beliefs, the supernatural (A1)

feathers *n. See* **ploo**

feather-wisker *n.* feather-duster

fecht *n.*, *v.* fight

fechter *n.* fighter

feck *n.* abundance, quantity; **the ~ o** the majority, most; **~ly** *adv.* mostly

fecket *n.* waistcoat, under-jacket

feckless *adj.* weak, feeble; useless, incapable, incompetent

fedder *n.*, *v.* feather

fee *n.* a farm-hand's wage; *v.* engage a farm-hand; ~'t **man** hired hand; ~**in-fair**, **-mairket** *n.* hiring-fair, market for farm servants

feech *excl.* of pain or distress. *cf.* **feich**

feeder *n.* an ox fattened for market

feedle *n.* field (A, A2)

feel *n.* fool; *adj.* foolish; ~'s **eeran** fool's errand; ~**ish** *adj.* foolish; ~**ness** *n.* foolishness. *cf.* **fule**

feem *n.* state of sudden heat, a sweat; *v.* fume

feenal(ly) *adj., adv.* final(ly)

feenish *n., v.* finish

feer *v.* to set up the first furrow, when ploughing a field

feerd *n.* ford (M3). *cf.* **foord**

feerich *n.* bustle; state (of excitement); fit of enthusiasm; *v.* bustle; ~ **oot** fetch out

feerin *n.* furrow drawn out to mark the rigs before ploughing the whole field; ~ **pole** pole used as marker in setting up the first furrow (F)

feerious *adj.* furious; terrific; *adv. (used intensively)* exceedingly *eg,* a ~ **trait** a terrific treat

feeroch *See* **feerich**

feese *v. pt.* fetched

feesick *n.* medicine (T)

feet *ppl., adj.* employed

feesickle *adj.* physical

fegs *excl.* of surprise or emphasis: faith!

feich *excl.* of disgust. *cf.* **feech**

feignie *v.* feign

feint *See* **fient**

feish *v. pt.* fetched. *cf.* **feese**

fell *adj.* deadly; dangerous; *adv.* very, exceedingly; clever, shrewd (J); *n.* piece of turf, sod; *v.* kill; stun; knock down

fell-thocht *v. pt.* reconsidered, had second thoughts (B)

femisht *adj.* famished

fence-fed *adj.* (of animals) fed with titbits at the side of the fence; pampered

fen(d) *v.* defend; ~**less** *adj.* shiftless; weak, without energy or resource

fere *adj.* strong, sturdy; **hale an** ~ thoroughly healthy

ferich *See* **feerich**

ferlie, ferly *n.* oddity, wonder; a curiosity; *v.* wonder at

ferm *n.* farm. *cf.* **fairm**

fer-nothing *n.* dreadnought coat

fernyear *n.* last year; ~ **was a year** the year before last

ferny-tickle|d *adj.* freckled; **~s**
n. pl. freckles

ferr *n.* fear (s)

fersell *adj.* forceful, energetic

fesh, fess *v.* fetch, bring;
~ back bring to mind, recall;
~ up bring up (children);
~en in *ppl.* established

fest *adj., adv.* fast

Festeren's, Festren's Eve
See **Fasten's Een**

feth *n.* faith; *excl.* faith!

feuch *v.* smoke a pipe (R);
n. smoke (B1)

fey *adj.* disordered in
the mind; clairvoyant;
behaving in an excited way,
not oneself; doomed to
death or calamity

feyther *n.* father (J).
cf. **faither, fader**

fiars *n.* prices of grain legally
fixed for the year

ficher *n.* slow awkward work;
v. fiddle about

ficket *n.* woollen garment
with sleeves & buttoned
front, an undervest worn
under shirt

fidder *conj.* whether. *cf.* **fudder**

fiddley *n.* hatchway between
wheelhouse and funnel on
a drifter (B)

fidge *v.* fidget (B); be eager (B1);
~ fain to itch to; to champ
at the bit

fidgick *n.* tufted vetch;
~ piz small peas growing at
the roadside

fiedle *n.* field (A1). *cf.* **feedle**

fie na *excl.* not at all

fient *n.* fiend; the devil (used
in strong negations); **~ a**
not a; **~ een** not one; **~ a**
fears not likely; **~ haet**
not a bit, the devil a bit.
cf. **feint, fint**

fier *adj.* fit; healthy

Fiersday *n.* Thursday

fifety *adj.* fifty

fifteent *adj.* fifteenth

fikie *See* **fykie**

file *conj., n.* while; *v.* dirty,
soil. *cf.* **fool**

files *adv.* sometimes

filget, filjit *n.* untidy,
disreputable-looking person

filie *n.* a little while

filk *pron.* which

fillies *n. pl.* felloes of wheel

filock, filockie, (wee) *n.* a very
short time

fin *adv., conj.* when; *n.* touch;
tae the ~; to the touch;
v. find; feel; touch

fine *adj.* tasty; *adv.* very well,
perfectly

Finechty *pr. n.* local name for
the village of Findochty

fineerin *n.* fancy ornamentation

finger *n.* finger (*pro. as in*
singer); **~-eyns** *n.* fingertips;

~-pynts *n.* fingertips; **~steel** *n.* finger-stall

fingerin *n.* fine worsted from spun wool

fint *See* **fient**

fir, fir-candle *n.* pine-torch; **~-yowes** fir-cones; **~wood** bog wood, formerly used for candles

fire *v.* to discharge any missile; blister (the feet); **~-en** *n.* fireside (at the end of a room); **~-flaught** *n.* a flash of lightning. *cf.* **flacht o fire; ~hoose** *n.* dwelling house (M); farmhouse; **~wid** *n.* firewood

firlit *n.* a corn measure, the fourth part of a boll

firry *adj.* resinous

first-fit *n.* the first person to meet a marriage party or other procession (A2); the first visitor to cross the threshold on or after New Year's Day

fisher-loon *n.* fisher-boy

fisher-quine *n.* fisher-girl

Fishie *pr. n.* village of Fetterangus, near Mintlaw.

fist *v.* grasp with the hand (B1)

fit *adj., pron.* what; *rel. pron.* which (s); **~ like?** how are you? **~ wye** *adv.* how; why; **~ I leuch** how I laughed

fit *n.* foot; *v.* to foot it, *pt.* fittit; **first ~** first visitor of new year; **~-an-mou** foot-and-mouth disease; **gie (fowk) up their ~** rebuke; **o yir ~** on foot; **~ba** *n.* football; **~-roddie** footpath, track (M3); **~-socks** *n. pl.* short socks; the feet of stockings; **~step** *n.* footstep

fite *adj.* white; *v.* whittle; **~ the idle pin** pass the time away (M); **~-iron** *n.* tin ware; **~-oot** *n.* blinding snowstorm (s); **~-scoor** *n.* cattle ailment

fitininment *n.* a good footing (*fig.*); understanding

fit-socks *n. pl.* short socks; the feet of stockings

fitstep *n.* footstep

Fittie *pr. n.* Footdee. *cf.* **Futty**

fittie-fies *n. pl.* fault-finding; quibbles

fittock *n.* sock with the leg cut off, used over shoes on ice.

five-echter *n.* ordinary person or thing

fivver *n.* fever; **~t** *adj.* fevered

fizz *n.* bustle; fuss

flaa *v. pt.* flew

flacht *n.* flash, gleam; flash of lightning; **~ o fire** streak of lightning; **get the ~** suffer damage (B); flight. *cf.* **flaught**

flachter spad *n.* spade for cutting peat

flae *v.* flay, skin. *cf.* **flay**

flaesick *n.* spark from wood fire; wood-shaving. *cf.* **flezick**

flaff, flaffer *v.* flap, flutter

flag *n.* large snowflake: *v.* snow in big flakes

flagarie *n.* finery (*esp. in dress*); a gewgaw, piece of frivolity; dainty, delicacy

flaggit *ppl., adj.* (of floors) flagged

flake *n.* hurdle for penning sheep; hurdle used as a gate (M2)

flan *n.* a gust of wind; sudden down-draught in a chimney

flang *v.* flung

flannen *n.* flannel; ~ **broth** saps

flap *n.* a rest; *v.* flop

flate *v.* scolded. *cf.* **flite, flyte**

flaught *See* **flacht, flocht**

flaughtbred *adv.* at full length

flaughter-spaad *n.* two-handed spade for cutting turfs, peats

flech *n.* flea; ~y *adj.* flea-ridden

flee *n., v.* fly; ~ **aboot** dash about; ~**-b-nichter** *n.* fly-by-night; ~ **up** *imp.* get lost!; ~**-up** *n.* flighty person

fleech *See* **fleetch**

fleed *n.* head ridge on which the plough is turned

fleein *adj.* wildly intoxicated

fleem *n.* fleam, lancet

fleep *n.* lout. *cf.* **flype**

fleer *n.* floor; jeer (J)

fleerish *v.* flourish; **flint an** ~ flint and steel, used to strike a spark

fleetch *v.* flatter

fleg *n.* fright; *v.* frighten; *ppl.* ~**git**

flench *v.* flinch

fley *v.* frighten, scare; ~**ed**, ~**t** *ppl., adj.* frightened (A1). (*cf.* **fleggit**); **A'm** ~**t at** I'm afraid that; ~**t things** the supernatural

flezick *See* **flaesick**

flicher *v.* flicker

flicht *n.* flight

flichter *n.* a flap; *v.* flicker; flutter

flichty *adj.* flighty

flinrikin *n.* very thin cloth, a mere rag

flird *n.* anything thin or threadbare

flist *n.* lunge; **mak a** ~ **at** make a sudden lunge at (F)

flit *v.* leave a place, go elsewhere; move house

flite *v.* scold. *cf.* **flyte**

flittin *n.* house removal

flizzems (o fite shoories) *phr.* quick, sharp showers (F)

floan, tae hae a *phr.* (used of women) to hang over the fire (M3)

float *n.* lorry for carrying livestock

flocht *v.* excite, flurry; ~it *ppl.* in a state of excitement, worked up. *cf.* **fluchtit**

flooer, floor *n., v.* flower

floor *n.* (wheaten etc) flour

floorish *n.* blossom (G); *v.* flourish

flouk *n.* flounder; ~-mou'd *adj.* having a crooked mouth (K)

flow *n.* very small quantity of powdery substance, *eg* meal, dust

flozen *v.* become swollen

flucht *v.* agitate; ~it *ppl.* in a state of excitement

fluffer *v.* flutter. *cf.* **flaffer**

fluffert *n.* (of snow) a light shower (T)

flum(mer)gummery *n.* any useless thing or action; vain adornment, trimming (B1)

fly, fly-cup *n.* sly cup of tea (but taken ritually)

flype *n.* lout; *v.* turn inside out

flyte *v.* scold. *cf.* **flite**

foalie *n.* foal

fob *v.* pant with heat or exertion; ~bit yowe panting ewe

fochen *ppl.* fought; exhausted; ~ deen worn out with work

focht *v. pt.* fought

fodderin, foddrin *n.* fodder

fog *n.* long grass left standing in winter; moss, lichen; *v.* gather wealth; ~gin the waas stuffing wall cracks with moss; ~gage *n.* rank grass; grazing; second crop of grass after hay; ~gagy *adj.* (of grass) rank, tufted, matted (F); ~git *ppl., adj.* moss-covered; well off; ~gy *adj.* wizened, dry; mossy

foggie-bee *n.* yellow humble-bee

Foggieloan *pr. n.* nickname for Aberchirder

foifteen *adj.* fifteen (A2)

folk (G, M) *cf.* **fouk, fowk**

folla *n.* fellow; *v.* follow

folm *n.* a billow of mist; *v.* overturn

fommle *v.* turn over. *cf.* **whummle**

fond *adj.* foolish; *n.* fund

font *adj.* fond

foo *adj.* full; tipsy; *adv.* how; why

foodge *v.* (in marble-playing)
to take unfair advantage;
cheat

fooever *adv., conj.* however

fool *adj.* dirty; *v.* foul, soil;
cf. **file**; *n.* fowl (*dim.* **foolie**)

foon *ppl.* found (J)

foon(d) *n.* foundation.
cf. **founs**

fooner *v.* founder; *ppl.* ~t
exhausted, worn out

foont *n.* fount

foord *n., v.* ford

foorich *v.* work in a flurried
manner

foort *adj.* fourth; ~y *adj.* forty

foosh up *v. pt.* fetched up;
brought up

fooshtit *See* **foostie**

foosion *See* **fushen**

foostie, fooshtie, fooshtit
adj. fusty, musty; mouldy

footer *n.* bungler; silly, useless
person; troublesome,
fiddling job; *v.* fiddle with

footers *excl.* term of contempt

foraneen *n.* forenoon.
cf. **forenin**

forbeers *n. pl.* forebears

forbodin *adj.* ominous

forby(e) *adv.* besides; *prep.*
in addition to; compared
with

forbye|s *prep.* besides; far less;
not to mention; despite;
conj. whereas; ~'t *conj.*

apart from the fact that,
not to mention that

forcie *adj., adv.* active(ly),
forceful(ly); (of weather)
warm, dry, good for crops

fordal, fordel, fordle *n.*
progress, advancement; a
store; a spare; *v.* store up
for future use; **get ~t wi** get
ahead with (G)

forder *adj., adv.* further

forebeers *n. pl.* forebears.

forebreist *n.* front seat of a
gallery; front of a cart

for(e)nent *prep.* over
against, opposite, facing

forenicht *n.* interval between
twilight and bedtime

forenin *n.* forenoon (s).
cf. **foraneen**

foreshaida *v.* foreshadow

foreslings *n. pl.* for attaching
harness at front of cart shaft

foresta *n.* manger

forfairn *adj.* worn out;
forlorn (K)

forfecht (yirsel) *v.* overburden
(yourself), overdo

forfeffis *n.* heavy blow, wallop

forfochen, forfocht *adj.*
exhausted, worn out

forgaither *v.* forgather

forgat *v. pt.* forgot. *cf.* **foryat**

forgettle *adj.* forgetful

forgie *v.* forgive; ~ness *n.*
forgiveness

forgya *v.* forgave (A)

forhooie *v.* forsake; **~t** *ppl.*, *adj.* forsaken

forjeskit *adj.* fatigued, worn out

forkie(tail) *n.* earwig

forl *n.* whorl, small wheel on a spindle steadying its motion

forl(e)ith|y *n.* surfeit (B1); *v.* (upo) surfeit on; **~iet** *ppl., adj.* surfeited

fornent *prep.* over against, opposite, facing

forquant *v.* acquaint; intimate

forrit *adv.* forward(s)

forspeaker *n.* someone to speak for you; referee; spokesman

fort *adj.* fourth

forthink *v.* have second thoughts; *pt.* forthocht

fortiet *adj.* fortieth

fortig *n., v.* fatigue

fortin *n.* fortune

fortnat *adj.* fortunate

fortnicht *n.* fortnight

forty-faal *adj.* deceitful (B)

forty-fittit janet *n.* centipede

foryet *v.* forget, *pt.* foryat

fossy, fosy *adj.* (often used of rotten vegetables) soft, spongy. *cf.* **fozie**

fou *adj.* full, drunk; *n.* stone crop, saxifrage

fouk *See* **fowk**

foumart *n.* pole-cat; term of abuse

founs *n.* foundations

fousome *adj.* foul

fouth *n.* abundance; fill

fouty *adj.* mean; smutty

fower *adj.* four; **~teen** *adj.* fourteen

fowk *n.* people (A, A1, A2, C, J, R). *cf.* **fouk, folk**

foy *n.* farewell feast on leaving a place or finishing a job (B1)

fozie *adj.* soft, spongy

fraacht *See* **fraucht**

fracaa, fracaw *n.* hubbub, rumpus; fuss, palaver (M3)

frae *prep.* from (J). *cf.* **fae**

fraikie *adj.* coaxing, wheedling

fraise *n.* bit of flattery; *v.* speak flatteringly

fraisie *adj.* given to flattery

frap *n.* predicament (B)

fraucht *n.* freight or load; what can be carried or carted at one time: two pailfuls, cart-loads

fraughty *adj.* liberal, generous

Freday *n.* Friday

freely *adv.* particularly; completely, thoroughly; **~ fine** *phr.* remarkably fine

freen *n.* friend; **~ly** *adj.* friendly

freest *n., v.* frost

freet *See* **fret**

freevolous *adj.* frivolous

frem (K). *See* **fremt**

fremt, fremmit *adj.* foreign; strange, unknown; **the ~** *n.* strangers

fresh *adj.* (of weather) thawing; cold; open

fret *n.* superstition

freuch *adj.* brittle, dry

fricht *n.* fright

frich(t)en *v.* frighten; **~t** *ppl.* frightened

frien *See* **freen**

front shelvin *adj. with n.* movable board on front of box-cart

froon *n., v.* frown

frost *v.* to fit frost nails (F); **~-hole** *n.* frost nail hole (F)

frostit *adj.* inflamed by cold

frother *n.* hubbub, commotion (K)

frow *n.* big, fat woman

fry *n.* parcel of fish taken home by workers in the fishing industry

fu *adj.* full, tipsy; *adv.* very. *cf.* **fou**

fucher *See* **ficher**

fudder *v.* move hurriedly; run in excited or aimless fashion; *conj.* whether

fuff *n., v.* puff (of mist, smoke); *ppl.* **~in** puffing; **back in a ~** in a moment (M3)

fuffer *v.* (M1) *perh.* **fuffle** walk awkwardly, hobble, shuffle

fugie *n.* (*rhymes with* budgie) truant from school

fugle *v.* deceive (B1)

fuish *v. pt.* fetched, brought. *cf.* **feish, foosh**

ful(l) (*rhymes with* gull) *adj.* full; puffed up, conceited; *v.* fill, *pt.* fullt; *adj.* **~ (up)** replete after food; **at ~ teer** *phr.* at full speed; like the hammers; **a fully-up** *n.* refill

fulage *adj.* foolish (B1)

fule *n.* fool. *cf.* **feel**

fulk (whilk) *pron.* which

full *See* **ful**

fulp(ie) *n.* whelp; puppie

fummle *v.* fumble

fun, funn *n.* whin; **~ mull** *n.* whin mill for bruising whins for food for horses etc

fun *v. pt., ppl.* found; **~lin** *n.* foundling; **~ siller** unexpected or unearned money; windfall

fun *v.* to do something for fun; joke; **oot o aa ~** speaking seriously

fun(n) *n.* whin; **~ mull** *n.* whin mill for bruising whins for food for horses etc

fund *v. pt.* found (S)

fung *v.* throw

funk *n.* a breath (of wind) (B);
v. sulk (B1)

funtain *n.* fountain

funtainheid *n.* fountainhead

fup *n., v.* whip; ~-**han** whiphand; **in a ~** at once.
cf. **whup**

fur, furr *n., v.* furrow

fur-beast *n.* horse for walking
in furrow

furhooied *See* **forhooie**

furl *v.* whirl; ~**y** *adj.* whirly

furliefaa(s) *n.* elaborate
ornamentation

furligorum *n.* showy
ornament (G)

furliemageerum *n.* curiosity
(M3)

furm *n.* form, bench without
a back

furnitur *n.* furniture

furrer *n.* horse walking in
furrow

furth *adv.* forth, away

furth, the *adv.* outside; *n.* the
open air

furth-the-gait *adv.* honestly

fush *v. pt.* fetched. *cf.* **foosh**

fushach *n.* loose, untidy
bundle; **I carena a ~** *phr.* I
don't care a jot

fushen, fushon *n.* pith, vigour

fushenless *adj.* lacking vigour

fusion *See* **fushen**

fusker|s *n. pl.* whiskers; ~**t**
adj. whiskered

fusky *n.* whisky

fusome *adj.* disgusting.
cf. **fousome**

fussle *n., v.* whistle

fut *pron.* what; ~ **for nae** why
not. *cf.* **fat, fit**

futher *conj.* whether. *cf.* **fudder**

futlie (beelin) *n.* whitlow

futrat, futtrat *n.* weasel; small,
thin, hatchet-faced person

futtle *n.* short gutting knife;
v. whittle

Futty *pr.n.* Footdee. *cf.* **Fittie**

fy *n.* whey; **croods an ~** curds
and whey

fyaach *v.* fidget. *cf.* **fyke**

fyaachie *adj.* yellowish grey;
faded; (of liquids) pale,
colourless. *cf.* **f(y)auchy**

fyaak *n.* plaid. *cf.* **faik, fayich**

fye *excl.* of surprise

fyke *n.* fuss; difficulty;
v. fidget

fykie *adj.* troublesome,
tricky; restless

fyle *n., v.* while; ~**s** now
and then; *v.* to soil, make
dirty

fyou, fyow(e) *adj.* few; ~**er**
adj. fewer

G

gaad, gad *n.* goad, wand

gaager *n.* exciseman. *cf.* **gauger**

gaan *v.* go (coastal); *ppl.*
going. *cf.* **gaun**

gaan-aboot (hen) *ppl., adj.*
free-range (hen);
~ **folkies** travelling people;
travellers

gaar *n.* oozing vegetable
matter; **green** ~ growth
seen on piers and low on
the walls of houses

gab *n.* prattling talk; one who
talks incessantly; the mouth;
v. to chatter, prate; **~bin**
n. chattering

Gab o Mey *phr.* the last days
of April anticipating the
weather of May

gaberlunzie *n.* beggar

gad *n.* goad for driving horses
or cattle. *cf.* **gaud**

gadgie *n.* person (Cant)

Gadie *pr. n.* stream at the hill
of Bennachie, Aberdeenshire

gadsman *n.* person who
drives horses or cattle with
a gad; or uses gad to direct
corn to the scythe (B1) or
binder. *cf.* **gaudsman**

gae *v.* go (A, A1, A2, M, J, R).
(*cf.* **gyang, gang, ging**);
gae fae *phr.* stop

gae *v. pt.* gave (M, A2)

gaed *v. pt.* went; ~ **worth**
became as nothing

gae-lattin *ppl.* letting go;
n. the verge of bankruptcy

gaff *v.* laugh loudly, guffaw.
cf. **gauff**

gager *n.* exciseman. *cf.* **gaager**

Gaimrie *pr. n.* local name for
the village of Gardenstown;
~ **knottie** biscuit

Ga'in *pr. n.* Gavin

gaird *n., v.* guard

gairden *n.* garden

gairdy *n.* the arm (A)

Gairtly *pr. n.* Aberdeenshire
village of Gartly

gaist *See* **ghaist**

gait *See* **gate**

gaither *v.* gather. *cf.* **gedder,
gether, gidder; ~er** *n.* one
who gathers grain to make
sheaves. *cf.* **lifter**

gaivel *n.* gable (G). *cf.* **gale,
gavel**

gale *n.* gable (M)

galleeperus *See* **gillieperous**

galliart *adj.* bright, gaudy (B1)

gallus *adj.* wild, high-spirited

galluses *n. pl.* trouser braces

galore *adv.* in abundance

galshachs, galshochs *n. chf.
in pl.* sweets, titbits; treats,
goodies; junk foods

gamey, gamie *n.* gamekeeper

gan *v. pt.* went (K). *cf.* **gaed;**
(poet.) began

gane *v. pt.* gone

gang *v.* go (A2, M, M1, R);
~ **yir gait** go your way.
cf. **gyang, ging, gae**

gange *n.* projecting lower jaw; tedious prating; *v.* prate

gangrel *n.* vagrant, tramp; toddler

ganjie *See* **gansey**

ganner *n.* gander

gansey *n.* guernsey, a seaman's jersey. *cf.* **ganjie**

gant *v.* yawn

gapus *adj.* stupid; *n.* fool

gar *v.* compel, cause to

gardie *n.* arm. *cf.* **gairdie**

garron *n.* small horse

gartens *n.* garters; **green ~** given by girl to her elder sister, if marrying before her

gash *adj.* ghastly, gruesome; affable; witty (K); *v.* talk, prattle

gast *n.* fright; shock; gust

gat *v. pt.* got

gate *n.* way; route; **aa ~** everywhere; **the richt ~** properly; **dee the richt ~** do the right thing; **some ~s** in some places; **fat gate?** in what manner?; **~-ganger** *n.* wanderer, tinker

gatefarrin *adj.* presentable; comely

gaud *See* **gad**

gaudsman *See* **gadsman**

gaun *v.* go (coastal) *ppl.* going. *cf.* **gaan**

gaup *v.* gape; eat voraciously (A1)

gavel *n.* gable. *cf.* **gaivel**

gavel *n.* tail of sheaf (F)

gaw *n.* trick; **widder~** trick of the weather; cut or abrasion (*eg*, **girssgaw**)

gawk, gawkie *n.* silly, clumsy person; **~it** *adj.* stupid, clumsy; **~itness** *n.* stupidity; uncouth silliness

geal *See* **jeel**

gean *n.* wild cherry tree

gear *n.* property, wealth

geck *n.* disdainful toss of head; *v.* turn the head in a foolish or coquettish way; toss the head in scorn; mock, scorn; **~ neck** *phr.* twisted neck; **~-neck(it)** (having) a twisted neck

gedder *v.* gather; **~t** *v. pt., ppl.* gathered; *adj.* well-to-do. *cf.* **gaither, gether, gidder**; **~er** *n.* (usually female) gatherer in the harvest field; **~in** *n.* gathering

gee *n.* sullenness; stubbornness; whim, foolish notion; **tak the ~ wi** take offence at someone; *v.* stir, move; **~ up** *imp.* forward! (command for a plough-horse in Buchan)

geed *adj.* good (F); *v. pt.* went.
cf. **gaed, gid**

geems *n. pl.* gums

Geery *pr. n.* Garioch (a
district in Aberdeenshire).
cf. **Gerry**

geet *n.* child

gell *v.* bawl; quarrel noisily

genteel *adj.* courteous; well
bred; ~ity *n.* gentility

geordie *n.* (yellow) guinea;
country yokel

Geordie *pr. n.*, deriv. of
George

Gerry *pr. n.* Garioch (a
district in Aberdeenshire).
cf. **Geery**

gether *v.* gather (R). cf. **gaither,
gedder, gidder**

get on tae *v.* scold, *eg,* **dinna
~ them**

gey *adj.* great, considerable;
~, ~an *adv.* very, somewhat,
rather; ~lies *adv.* rather;
nearly; pretty well

Geylic *pr. n.* Gaelic

ghaist(ie) *n.* ghost

gheelie *n.* man or boy
attending sportsman; ghillie

gibbles *n. pl.* wares;
dirty dishes (M3)

gid *See* **gaed, gied**

gidder *v.* gather. cf. **gaither,
gedder, gether; ~in**
n. gathering. cf. **gedderin**

gie *v.* give; ~ **intae trouble**
scold; ~d, gid *v. pt.* gave

gif *conj.* if (B1). cf. **gin**

giglet *n.* girl (O)

gilgal *n.* (hard *g*) hubbub;
uproar (B1)

gillieperous, gileepris *n.*
(hard *g*) fool; rough,
ungainly person (B1,T)

gilp *See* **jilp**

gimmer *n.* ewe from one to
two years old; or not yet
having borne young

gin *conj.* if, whether; if only
(M2); than, by the time
that; *prep.* (used of time) by

ginch, ginge *n.* ginger

ginch-breid *n.* gingerbread

ging *v.* go (A, S). cf. **gyang**

ginkmen (B1) *See* **ginkum**

ginkum *n.* trick, dodge; fancy

gintles *n. pl.* gentry

gird *n.* child's hoop; *v.* drive
farm animals; strike

girdin *n.* rope or girthing used
to secure saddle or lash
load to a cart

girdle *n.* circular iron plate
with bow handle for
baking oatcakes, etc

girge *See* **jirg**

girn *n.* snare; whimper;
fretful fault-finding;
v. complain peevishly,
grumble; snarl. cf. **grin**

girnal, girnel *n.* meal chest or barrel

girn-bleater *n.* snipe (Abdnsh.)

girnie, girnin *adj.* peevish

girs|e, girss *n.* grass; **~-hyeuk** *n.* metal strut on scythe; **~in** *adj.* (of farm animals) grazing; put out to grass; **~sy** *adj.* grassy

girsle *n.* gristle

gizzen *n.* throat (M3); *v.* dry up; shrivel; **~t** *adj.* parched; shrivelled; warped

glaar *See* **glaur**

glack *n.* fork of a tree; ravine; point where two things branch off

glaff *n.* glance (K)

glagger *v.* gasp; *also in phr.* **the daith ~** the death rattle (terminal respiratory secretions)

glaid *adj.* glad. *cf.* **gled**

glaik *n.* gleam; glance

glaiket, glaikit *adj.* senseless; stupid

Glaisga *pr. n.* Glasgow

glammach, glammoch *n.* morsel; *v.* grasp, grab; *phr.* **lat ~ at**

glamour, glamourie *n.* magic

glamp (aboot) *v.* grope (about)

glaur *n.* mud; ooze; phlegm (M3)

gleck *n.* glance

gled, gledsome *adj.* glad

gled, gleed *n.* kite (bird of prey)

gleebrie *n.* large piece of (waste) ground

gleg *adj.* keen, sharp; eager; *n.* gadfly

glegsome *See* **gleg** *adj.*

glen *n.* narrow valley

glent *n.* glance

gless *adj.* glass; *n.* mirror **~es** *n.* spectacles

gley *n., v.* squint; **~ed ee** eye with a squint

gliberal *n.* large piece of waste ground (B1). *cf.* **gleebrie**

gliff *n.* shock, scare (B1)

glim *n.* gleam. *cf.* **glisk**

glimp *n.* glimpse

glimsh *n.* glimpse

glint *n.* glimpse (M)

glisk *n.* gleam. *cf.* **glim**

glive *n.* glove (A2)

gloam, gloamin, gloomin *n.* twilight. *cf.* **glowmin**

glorious *adj.* highly stimulated by alcohol (M2)

glowe *n., v.* glow

glower *n., v.* gaze; scowl; stare

glowm *v.* darken at dusk; **~min** *n.* twilight (M3). *cf.* **gloamin**

gluff *n.* shock; inhalation of air; whiff; *v.* eat greedily (B)

glumf *v.* to look sulky

glunch *n.* frown; scowl

gnap *n.* bite, mouthful

gnappin *in phr.* **in ~ earnest** in dead earnest (B1)

gnauve *v.* gnaw

gneck *v.* notch

gnidge, gnige *n.* squeeze

gnipper *n. in phr.* **~ for/and gnapper** the very smallest particle (deriv. from sound of mill when grinding); every bit

go-ashores *n. pl.* fishermen's dress for going ashore; casual wear (B)

Goavermint *n.* Government

gobbinfae *See* **gowpenfu**

gock *n.* cuckoo; fool. *cf.* **gowk**; **~it** *adj.* foolish

gog *n.* nestling (S). *cf.* **gorbel**

gollach, goloch *n.* beetle; **hornie-~** earwig

gollar *n.* shout(ing); *v.* shout incoherently

gomeril *n.* fool, blockhead

good al meggins! *excl.* probable euphemism for God Almighty

goodman *n.* husband (A2). *cf.* **guidman**

goodwife *n.* wife (A2). *cf.* **guidwife**

goon *n.* gown

goor *n.* mud; slime from fish

goranichy *adj.* complaining feebly (B1)

gorbel, gorblin *n.* unfledged bird. *cf.* **gog**

gorbellt *adj.* state of egg with young bird partially formed

goshie *excl.* gosh!

gosky *adj.* coarse; luxuriant

gou *n.* taste; smell

goup *v.* gawp, stare. *cf.* **gowp**

gousty *See* **gowsty**

govie-dick(s) *excl.* of surprise (M1)

gow *n.* seagull (Buckie); *v.* induce, persuade; gull (A2). *cf.* **goy**

gowan *n.* daisy

gowd *n.* gold; **~en** *adj.* golden

gowdie *n. in phr.* **heels ower ~** head over heels

gowf(f) *n.* golf; ruin, destruction; **gae tae the ~** to be ruined; **~er** *n.* golfer

gowk *n.* cuckoo; fool. *cf.* **gock** **~it** *adj.* foolish. *cf.* **gockit**

gowp *v.* gawp, stare. *cf.* **goup**, **gype**

gowpenfu (-fae) *n.* as much as two cupped hands can hold

gowsty *adj.* pale, sickly; ghostly

gowt *v. pt., ppl.* got

goy (ower) *v.* allure, entice; convince (B1). *cf.* **gow**

graavit *n.* scarf; cravat. *cf.* **grauvit**

graen, grain *n.*, *v.* groan
graidiwal *adj.*, *(adv.)* gradual(ly)
graip *n.* large fork used in farming; *v.* fork
graith *n.* accoutrements, harness; substance, riches; clothes
graivel *n.* gravel
gralloch *v.* disembowel the carcass of a deer
gran *adj.*, *adv.* grand
granda *n.* grandfather
grane *v.* groan. *cf.* **graen, grain**
gran'eur *n.* grandeur
granfadder *n.* grandfather
Granny's John *n.* coddled boy
grape *v.* grope (J)
grat *v. pt.* wept; **roared an ~** wept noisily. *cf.* **greet**
grauvit *n.* cravat; scarf
grease *n.* disease affecting horses' legs
great-hertit *adj.* overcome by emotion; having a full heart
gree *n.* palm, prize; **tae bear the ~** carry off first prize (K); *v.* agree
green *n.* lawn; grassland; *v.* **~ (efter)** long, yearn (for) (BI); **~-brees** *n.* cesspool; pool by dunghill; **~-hoose** *n.* greenhouse; **~ichtie** *adj.* greenish

greep *n.* open drain in cowshed; middle part of byre
greeshach *n.* flameless fire of red-hot embers (AI)
greet *v.* weep; **~in fou** in an advanced stage of intoxication
greff *n.* grave (A)
grein *See* **green**
greybeard *n.* earthenware bottle
grieve *n.* farm overseer
grimmy *n.* Grimsby boat or fisherman (B)
grin *n.* snare. *cf.* **girn**
grindie (-tocher) *n.* small greenish crab (B)
grinsteen *n.* grindstone
grippit *ppl.*, *adj.* seized with pain; hard up, pressed for cash (R)
grippy *adj.* stingy, tight-fisted
grizzelt *ppl.* turning gray (G)
grofe *adj.* coarse, rough
groanach *v.* groan, complain
groncie *n.* anything large or fine of its kind
groo *v. See* **grue**
groogle *v.* disorder; pucker up *eg*, **~ yir broos**
grow|e *v.* grow; **~en folk** *n. pl.* adults; **~in shoorie** light rain good for plants and crops (T); **~the** *n.* growth;

vegetation; ~-the-midden
n. compost heap; ~thy *adj.*
(of weather) conducive to
growth; (of a season) of
good growth

grozart *n.* gooseberry

grubb|er *Eng. n.* agric.
implement clearing ground
of roots etc; ~it *ppl.* (of land)
cleared with a grubber

grue *v.* shudder

gruggl|e *v.* to render sub-
standard by much
handling; ~t creased

grum|mle *v.* grumble; ~lie *adj.*
grumbling, fault-finding

grumph *n., v.* grunt; ~ie *n.* pig

grun|(d) *n.* ground; ~ offisher
n. manager of an estate (A2);
~sel *n.* groundsel; *v.* ground,
pt. ~nt;

grunny *n.* grandmother

grunter *n.* fisher word for the
pig, where the word *pig* is
taboo. *cf.* **Sandy Campbell**

gruntle *v.* grunt

grup *v.* grip

grutten *ppl.* wept; *adj.*
tear-stained

gryte *adj.* great; ~ lins
heavy fishing lines (B); nae
~ shot no great shakes;
~-hertedness *n.* tender-
heartedness; compassion;
~-hertit *adj.* emotional;
moved

guaird *n., v.* guard. *cf.* **gaird**

guddle *v.* catch fish with the
hands by groping below
the banks of a stream

Gude, gude (K) *See* **Gweed,
gweed;** ~man *n.* master of
the house

gudge *n.* small, thickset fellow

guff *n.* smell

guffa *n.* guffaw

guid *adj.* good. *(cf.* **gweed);**
~-brither etc *See* **gweed-;**
~man *n.* master, head of
household; husband (J);
~wife *n.* female head of
house, the mistress; wife (J);
~willie *adj.* generous (R).
cf. **gweed-wully**

guise *v.* to go mumming,
masquerade. *cf.* **gyse;**
~er *n.* mummer; child in
disguise who goes round
doors at Halloween
offering entertainment in
return for gifts or money

guiss *v.* guess (M3)

guizard *n.* mummer (J)

gull *n.* haze, mist

guller *n.* gurgling sound in
throat

gullie *n.* large knife

gumbile *n.* gumboil

gumfleers, gumfloors *n. pl.*
artificial flowers for ladies'
bonnets (B1)

gummeraagus *n.* idiot (M3)

gumption *n.* common-sense
gundy *n.* candy; toffee
gunge aboot *v.* run around
  aimlessly, awkwardly
gunpouther *n.* gunpowder
Gurdon *pr. n.* Gourdon
gurk *n.* a short fat person;
  strong man
gurl *n., v.* growl; ~ie, ~y
  adj. gnarled; (of weather,
  sea) stormy, threatening
gurr *n.* growl; drive, spirit;
  v. to growl
gurron *n.* an ample specimen
gushet *n.* gusset; triangular
  piece of land; corner of a
  building
gustfu *adj.* with relish
gutcher *n.* grandfather (M).
  cf. **deydie**
gutsy *adj.* greedy
gutter(s) *n.* mud, mire (S)
gutter *v.* work untidily, dirtily
g'wa *imp.* go away
gwana *n.* guano fertiliser
Gweed *pr. n.* God;
  ~-**forsyaaken** *adj.* God-
  forsaken; *excl.* ~ **kens**
  goodness knows; ~ **keep's**
  aa God keep us all;
  ~ **preserve's** God preserve us;
  ~ **send** God grant
gweed *adj.* good; ~ **fegs** *excl.*
  good faith; *n.* good; **tak the**
  ~ **o** take advantage of;
  ~-**brither, -breeder**

n. brother-in-law; ~-**dother**
n. daughter-in-law;
~-**father** *n.* father-in-law;
~-**lie** *adv.* godly; ~-**mither**
n. mother-in-law; ~-**naturt**
adj. good-natured; ~**ness**
n. goodness; ~-**nicht** *int.*
goodnight; ~-**sin** *n.* son-in-
law; ~**wife** *n.* wife; ~-**words**
n. pl. prayers; ~-**wull** *n.*
goodwill; ~-**wully** *adj.*
good-hearted; generous (B1).
cf. **guid-willie**
gweel *n.* corn marigold
gwestie, gweeshtie,
  gweeshtens *excl.* goodness!
gwite *n.* a narrow rocky inlet
gya *v. pt.* gave (A)
gyad(-sakes) *excl.* of
  revulsion, usually over food
gyana *v. pt. neg.* did not give
gyang *v.* go (A, A1); *n.* a
  gang; row; ~ **forrit** attend
  Communion; ~ **tae**
  Padanaram wi ye (M3) *excl.*
  away with you!
g(y)angrel *n.* vagrant, tramp;
  child beginning to walk.
  cf. **gangrel**
gyaaps *n.* poultry disease
gyaun, gyaan *ppl.* going;
  a-~ going about; ~-**ower**
  n. examination
gye *v.* guide, *eg,* ~ **a bike**; ~**s**
  n. handlebars (of a bike)

gyke-neckit *adj*. descriptive of
some one whose neck is
held slightly to one side (B).
cf. **geck-neckit**

gyp|e *n*. a fool; *v*. stare
foolishly, gawp. *cf*. **gowp**;
~ery *n*. foolishness, silly talk;
~it *adj*. foolish

gyse *See* **guise**

gyte *adj*. mad, crazy

H

ha *n*. hall

haach *n*. phlegm; *v*. hawk,
clear the throat. *cf*. **hachle**

haad, haud *v*. hold; **~ aff** (o)
defend

haak *v*. hawk; cough; **~er**
n. hawker

haar *n*. (sea) mist

haaver *n*. half share; *v*. divide
in two. *cf*. **halver**

habber *v*. stutter, stammer

hachle *v*. clear the throat.
cf. **haach**

hack *n*. chap, the effect
of severe cold; notch;
~-a-thraw *n*. nickname for
a joiner; **~(ie)** *n*. a certain
amount; a bit; *eg*, **a ~ie
langer**; **~-stock** *n*. stump
used for chopping wood

had *cf*. **haad, haud, hud**

haddie *n*. haddock

hae *v*. have, *pt*. **~d**; *ppl*. **~n**;
neg. **~na** have not. *cf*. **hinna**

haet *See* **hait**

haethen *n*. heathen

haflin *See* **halflin**

haffets *n*. temples; sides of the
head

hag *n*. brushwood

hagger *n*. wound (A); *v*. hack

haibit *n*. habit

haik *n*. rack for fodder; trek;
v. tramp, trudge; **livin at ~ an
manger** living extravagantly;
on the ~ for on the look-out
for. *cf*. **hake**

hail(|) *adj*., *n*. whole. *cf*. **hale**;
~-heidit *adj*. (of time)
without a break; **~-stanes**
n. *pl*. hailstones; **~ teer** *phr*.
with great vigour

Hail(|) Eel *n*. the old
Christmas season
extending from 25 Dec
to Twelfth Night; **tae had
~ ~** to make merry,
celebrate with abandon

haill *v*. heal

haimal(t), haimil(t) *adj*. homely,
plain; without ceremony

haimle *See* **haimal(t)**

haimmer *n*., *v*. hammer.
cf. **hemmer**

haims *n*. curved pieces of iron
attached to horse's collar;
pit the ~ on: (*fig*.) bring

someone into line; curtail; restrict

hain *v.* save, husband; hoard; ~ **o** *v.* deprive of; **a great ~in** a great saving; *v.* spare

hair *in phr.* **nae a ~ o't** not a bit of it

hairbour *n.* harbour. *cf.* **herbour**

hairm *n.*, *v.* harm; **~less** *adj.* harmless

hairrial *n.* something that impoverishes, costly expenditure. *cf.* **herrial**

Hairry *pr. n.* Harry

hairry *v.* harry

hairse *adj.* hoarse

hairst *n.*, *v.* harvest; **~-hyook** scythe (*cf.* robsorbie); **~-park** harvest field

hairt *n.* heart. *cf.* **hert**

hairth *n.* hearth (J). *cf.* **ingle**

hairy-tatties *n.* hash made with potatoes and dried, salted fish (B)

hait *n.* atom, particle; **fient ~** not a bit; nothing at all

haith *n.*, *excl.* (of surprise) faith

haive *v.* heave, throw

haiveless *adj* careless; unmannerly (A2)

haiver *v.* talk nonsense. *cf.* **haver**; **~s** *n.* nonsense. *cf.* **havers**

haivins *n. pl.* (good) behaviour; manners (M3)

hake *n.* wooden frame for drying fish. *cf.* **haik**; *v.* wander

hale *adj.* whole; **~ an fere** whole and entire. *cf.* **hail**; **~some** *adj.* wholesome; **~-wheel** *adj.* wholesale

half-hung-tee *adj.* irresponsible (T)

halfie *n.* half-holiday

halflin *adj.* half-grown; *n.* half-grown boy, youth; farm- or stable-boy

half roads *adv.* half-way

halla *adj.* hollow (C). (*cf.* **boss**); *n.* hollow (F)

hallach *adj.* high-spirited; crazy

hallan *n.* partition between a cottage door and fireplace

halver *v.* divide in two. *cf.* **haaver**

hallyrackit *adj.* boistrous, romping

halycut *adj.* wild, giddy

hame *n.* home; **fae ~** away from home; **~-drauchtit** *adj.* selfish, keen to further ones own interests; **~-fairm** *n.* home farm; **~l** *adj.* belonging to home; homely; (*cf.* **haimal**); **~owre, -ower** *adj.* homely,

humble; ~**sick** *adj.*
homesick; ~**spun** *adj.*,
n. homespun; ~**ward**
adv. homewards; ~**with,**
-**wuth** *adv.* homewards;
~**worth** *adv.* homeward (K)

hammer *v.* work or walk in
clumsy, noisy way

hamsh *v.* eat noisily,
voraciously

han *n.* hand; **at aa ~s** at
every opportunity; **tak**
throw ~ deal with, discuss;
~-**breed** *n.* hand-breadth; in
a ~**clap** *phr.* in an instant;
~**fu** *n.* handful; ~**key** *n.*
handkerchief; ~**le** *n.*,
v. handle; ~-**leem** *n.* hand-
loom; ~**lin** *n.* hand fishing
line (B); ~**sel** *n.* handsel;
first money received (B1);
v. tr. handsel; ~**shak** *n.*
handshake

hane *ppl.* had. *cf.* **haen**

hang|ie *n.* hangman; a soft
cheese (F); ~**man cheese**
curds in cloth, salted and
hung to dry (T)

hank *v.* fasten, secure; tie
tightly, constrict

hanlin *n.* going-over, critical
assault (A1)

hantle *n.* large quantity or
number, a lot; ~**s** *pl.* lots

hap *n.* cover; ~-**warm** *n.* a
warm wrap or covering;

v. happen; hop; cover;
~ **in/up** cover over; ~**pit**
ppl. covered

hape *n.* heap (S)

happer *n.* basket or container,
esp. of seed for sowing

harassment *n.* fatigue (A2)

hard *adj., adv.* hard; ~ **tee/tae**
hard against; ~-**vrocht** *adj.*
hard-worked; *n.* hardship;
v. pt. heard

harden *(adj.), n.* (of) very
coarse cloth made of **hards**

hards *n. pl.* the coarse refuse
of flax or hemp separated
by heckling

hare-shard *n.* hare-lip (B1)

harigals *n. pl.* animal entrails

harken *v.* listen

harl|e *v.* rough-cast a wall with
mix of mortar and small
gravel; ~**in** *n.* rough casting

harn *n.* coarse cloth, sackcloth

harn|s *n.* brains; ~ **pan** the
skull

harp *n.* (a mason's) wire
screen for cleaning sand
or gravel

harra *n.* harrow

harrach *v.* clear the throat

harry *v.* plunder bird's nest,
bee's bike. *cf.* **herry**

hash *n.* bustle *v.* slice, cut
up; work at high pressure,
hustle, hurry; ~**t** *ppl.*
pressed, harrassed

hasp *n.* clasp; latch

haste-ye-back *phr.* come back soon!

hat *v. pt.* hit

haud *n., v.* hold; ~ **aff o** keep clear of, away from; ~ **awa fae** except for; **~in hame** going home; ~ **in wi** keep in with; ~ **oot** maintain; ~ **oot-ower** keep away; ~ **redd o** keep clear of (R); ~ **the cat an play wi the kitlin** sit on the fence; ~ **yir tongue/yir wheesht** be silent; **nae tae ~ nor bin'/ bin** not to be held down, out of control

haud *v.* continue, to go on; ~ **awa** go on; ~ **gyaan** keep going; ~ **stracht on** go straight ahead; ~ **up** (a road) go up

hauden *pt. ppl.* held; ~-**doon** *adj.* inhibited, constrained; (of husbands) hen-pecked; ~ **in aboot** *ppl.* constrained

haudin *n.* (small)holding (A, M)

hauf *adj.* half; ~**lins** *adv.* halfway

haugh *n.* low-lying ground beside a river; clearing of throat

hauld *n.* stronghold

hault *See* **hult**

haumer *v.* stamp about noisily

hause *n.* throat (K). *cf.* **hawse**

haved *v. pt.* heaved

haveral *n.* half-witted person; fool; garrulous person

haw *adj.* bluish-gray or pale green

hawse *n.* throat. *cf.* **hause**

haythen *adj., n.* heathen

heal *n.* health

heapie-on, a *n.* boy's game

hearken *v.* listen

heart(e)nin *See* **hertnin**

hearthsteen *n.* hearthstone, hearth

heater *n.* glazed, sugared bun; warming drink of liquor

hech *v.* pant (J)

heck an manger, to live at to live extravagantly. *cf.* **haik**

heckle *n.* hackle, steel flax-comb

hed *v. pt.* had (A2)

hedder *n.* heather

hedger *n.* hedgehog

heedie craw *See* **hoodie craw**

heediepeers *n. pl.* people of the same height

heelabalow *n. var. of* hullabaloo

heeld *v.* held; (of time) spent (A1)

heelster-gowdie *adv.* head over heels

heelster-heid *adv.* head first

heelie *v.* hail

heely, heely *excl. of correction*: slowly! or wait!

heemlin *ppl.*, *adj.* humbling

heepochondreech *adj.* listless, gloomy (B1)

heepocrat *n.* hypocrite

heepocreet *n.* hypocrite

heerican *n.* hurricane (G)

heerin *n.* herring

heese, heeze *v.* heave; lift; exalt; intensify

heesh *int.* make hissing sound to drive animals away. *cf.* **hish**

heeven *pr. n.* heaven (C)

heeze *n.* crowd, swarm; *v.* swarm (with); teem. *cf.* **heese**

heft *n.* haft, knife handle; *v.* lift up; carry aloft; ~it coo unmilked cow with full udder

heich *adj.* high; *adv.* aloud; ~er, ~est *adj.* higher, highest; ~-heidit *adj.* haughty; ~t *n.* height. (*cf.* **hicht**); ~en *v.* heighten

heid *n.* head; headmaster; ower the ~s o because of; ~-bummer *n.* leader; ~ dooster leader; ~-hurry *n.* busiest time; ~maister *n.* headmaster; ~piece *n.* (*joc.*) head; brain; ~-rig *n.* head ridge; ~-stall *n.* head-stall, part of **halter**; ~-shafe, ~in-shafe *n.* last sheaf on top of a stack

heidie, heidy *adj.* clever; head-strong; opinionative; ~peers *n. pl.* (young) people of exactly the same height

heir *v.* inherit; fa ~ till inherit; ~skip *n.* heirship, inheritance

heist *v.* lift with effort

hell *v.* heal (M3)

helm *n.* a crowd

helpender, helpener *n.* helper (minister's) assistant

helter *n.* halter

hemmer *n.* hammer

hems *See* **haims**

hen *n.* hen; ~-hertit *adj.* chicken-hearted; ~shine *n.* party for females; ~wife *n.* woman in charge of poultry

hench *v.* to launch missiles by striking the hand against the thigh

hennie *n.* familiar name for a henwife; ~-hertit *adj.* timid, faint-hearted

herbour *n.*, *v.* harbour. *cf.* **hairbour**

herd *n.* herdsman, -boy, one who tends cattle or sheep; *v.* tend cattle, sheep

hereaboot *adj.*, *(adv.)* local(ly)

heretick *n.* heretic

herp *n.* harp

herrial *n.* means of harrying; cause of ruin. *cf.* **harrial**

herrin *n.* herring; ~ **fivver** herring fever, condition caused by poor fishing (B)

herry *n.* plunder; *v.* plunder, rob birds' nests. *cf.* **harry**

hersel *pron.* herself; *pred. adj., adv.* by herself, alone

hert *n.* heart; (*cf.* **hairt**); ~ **oot** *v.* build up heart of a stack or cart-load of grain; ~**nin** *n.* encouragement; strengthening; ~**sca(u)d** *n.* heartburn; a disappointment (B1)

hesp *n.* hasp

het *adj.* hot; *v. pt.* heated (A1) ~ **fit** hot foot; ~ **an reekin** newly baked

heth *excl.* faith!

heugh *n.* a crag; rugged steep

heuk, heuck *n.* hook; reaping-hook, scythe. *cf.* **hyeuk**

hey *n.* hay; ~-**hoose** *n.* hayshed (S); ~-**makker** *n.* haymaker; ~-**ruck** *n.* haystack; ~-**soo** *n.* rectangular haystack

hey-ma-nannie *n.* (play) havoc; (get) a scolding; punishment

hi! *imp.* turn left! (instruction for a plough-horse in Buchan) (T)

hich *adj.* high; ~**t** *n.* height; ~**en** *v.* raise. *cf.* **heich, heicht**

hid *n. v.* hold (S). *cf.* **haad, haud**

hid *v. pt.* had; ~**na** had not. *cf.* **haed, haedna**

hide|-bind *n.* disease of horses and cattle in which skin sticks closely to the bones; ~**bun** *adj.* suffering from this disease

hidholie *n.* hidiehole

hie *adj.* high (S); ~**r** higher. *cf.* **heich**

hielan|(t) *adj.* highland; ~**der** *n.* Highlander

hilpinder *See* **helpender**

himpen *adj.* hempen

himsel *pron.* himself; *pred. adj., adv.* by himself, alone

hin *adj.* of the back or rear; ~**maist** *adj., n.* last; ~-**shelvin** *n.* movable board on back door of box cart (A2); ~**sicht** *n.* hindsight; ~-**slings** *n. pl.* part of **britchin,** for attachment to rear of cart shaft (F); ~**t** *n.* end; **the ~t o hairst** the end of harvest

hinch *n.* haunch

hinder-, hinner-en *n.* latter or final part, the extremity; the end; death; the remains of anything; **at the ~-en** in the end

hindmost *adj.* last. *cf.* **hinmaist**

hine *adv.* far; ~ **awa** far off, far away. *cf.* **hyne**

hing *v. tr. & intr.* hang; ~ **in** *v.* get on with something, persevere; eat up; *pt.* **hang in**; ~**in** *n.* a hanging; ~**in-luggit** *adj.* having drooping ears; disappointed

hinna *v. neg.* have not. *cf.* **haena**

hinner *n., v.* hinder; ~**ation** *n.* hindrance; ~**eyn** *n.* bottom, buttocks

hinny *n.* honey

hint *See under* **hin**

hippen, hippin *n.* baby's nappy; ~~-**towie** *n.* rope for hanging nappies

hipper *n.* hip flask

hippick, the *n.* hiccups; **tak ~** get hiccups. *cf.* **esk**

hippit, hip-grippit *adj.* having stiff hip-joints and lower back

hir|e *v.* 1. hire; engage as an employee; ~**hoose** *n.* farm labour or service; the place or house where servant is engaged; ~'**t** *ppl.* hired 2. season food; ~**in** *n.* seasoning; ~'**t** *ppl* seasoned

hirple *n.* limp; *v.* limp; hobble

hirsel *n.* flock of sheep

hirstle *v.* to move with grazing or friction (M); rustle. *cf.* **hurschle**

his *v.* has; ~**na** has not. *cf.* **haes, haesna**

hish *v.* drive animals, esp. poultry. *cf.* **heesh**

hishty-wishty *adj.* hush-hush

hissel *pron.* himself. *cf.* **himsel**

hist *n.* a great number; *v.* haste; ~ **ye back** come back soon

hit *pron.* it

hiv *n.* hoof; *v.* have

hive *v.* swell, cause to swell

hivven *n.* heaven

hiz *pron.* us

hize *See* **hyze**

hizzie *n.* housewife; hussy, used jocularly or disparagingly of young frivolous woman or servant girl

hoast *n., v.* cough; **a kirkyaird ~** severe cough

hoaver a blink *phr.* wait a moment

hobbl|e *n.* predicament; swarm of any kind; ~**in wi** *phr.* teeming with; ~**et** *adj.* perplexed

hoch *n.* lower part of human thigh; leg (M3) *eg,* **rax oot yir ~s** stretch out your legs; hind-leg joint of animal

hod *v.* hide, *pt.* hid, ~**den** *ppl.* hidden

hodden *n.* homespun cloth of wool of the natural colour; **~-grey** *n.* grey homespun

hodge *v.* move or walk awkwardly or jerkily

hoffin *n.* clumsy, awkward person

hog, hogg *n.* young sheep before first shearing

Hogmanay *pr. n.* New Year's Eve

hole *n.* puddle; shallow pool

holipie|d *adj.* having holes worked in sewing or knitting and stitched around; **~ thingies** work of this kind

hollach (aboot) *v.* lark (about)

hoo *adv.* how; why. *cf.* **foo**

hooch *n.* dance (s); loud cry esp. when dancing; *v.* shout when dancing

hoodie(-craw) *n.* hooded or carrion crow

hooer *n.* whore. *cf.* **hure**

hooever *adv., conj.* however. *cf.* **hoosomever**

hooick *n.* small rick of corn or hay (T). *cf.* **scroo**

hooie *v.* barter, exchange (incl. knives between boys)

hoolet *n.* owl. *cf.* **howlet**

hoomble *adj.* humble

hoose *n.* house; **~fu** houseful; **~brakker** *n.* burglar; **~-room** *n.* house-room; **~wifeskip** *n.* housewifery

Hoose, the *n.* the laird's house

hoosomever; hoosomediver (M3) *adv.* however

hoot|(s) *excl.* of doubt, contempt, irritation; **~ awa wi** down with; **~ ty** oh, yes

hooze, the *n.* disease in sheep and cattle

horn-en, -eyn *n.* best room in two-roomed cottage

hornie *in phr.* **fair ~** fair play

hornie *pr. n.* the Devil

horny-golach *n.* beetle; earwig

horrifie *v.* horrify

horseman's wird *n.* code word revealed on joining horsemen's secret society

horse-troch *n.* horse-trough

hose *n.* stocking(s); **~ an sheen** *lit.* shoes and stockings; *fig.* exaggeration (B)

hotch *See* **hodge**

hotchin *adj.* infested, seething, overrun

hotter *v.* move unsteadily; simmer, sputter; *n.* a seething mass; the noise or motion of the crowd; jolting movement; the sound this produces; **gie a vrang ~** make a wrong move

hottle *n.* hotel

houff'd *See* **howff, howffed**

hough *n.* thigh

houk *v.* dig. *cf.* **howk**

houp(ie) *n.* mouthful of food or drink. *See* **howp**

hoven *ppl., adj.* swollen, blown out

howder *n.* sudden gust of wind; push; a thrashing (M3); *v.* bluster

howdie *n.* midwife; **~-wifie** *n.* midwife (S); **at ~ haste** at high speed

howe *adj.* hollow; *n.* hollow, valley; **~-backit** *adj.* hollow-backed

Howe o the Mearns *pr. n.* valley of the Mearns

howff *n.* a place of resort, or evil repute; tavern; a haunt; *v.* lodge, reside, shelter; **~t** *v. pt., ppl.*

howfin *n.* clumsy, senseless fellow

howk *v.* dig. *cf.* **houk**

howlet *n.* owl (G1). *cf.* **hoolet**

howm *n.* holm (J)

howp *v.* hope; **~fu** *adj.* hopeful; *n., v.* gulp

hubber *v.* stammer. *cf.* **habber**

hucky-duck *n.* team game for boys (S)

hud *v.* hold; **~ in wi** keep in with; **~den** *ppl.* held; **~den-doon** *adj.* inhibited. *cf.* **ha(a)d, haud**

hudd(e)ry *adj.* unkempt, dishevelled

huick *See* **hooick**

hull *n.* hill

hullick, hullock *n.* hillock, heap; **~s o** lots of

hull-run *adj.* uncouth

hult *v.* halt

hum an hae *phr.* hum and haw

hummel, hummle *adj.* without horns; **~-doddie** *adj.* hornless **~-doddies** *n. pl.* woollen mittens without fingers

hummel-thrummy mittens *n.* unknown, perhaps synonym for above

humoursome *adj.* affably disposed

humph *n.* hump, curvature of the back or spine; *v.* carry, lug, lift something heavy; **~ie-backit** *adj.* hunchbacked; round-shouldered

humsh *v.* eat noisily and greedily, munch

hun *n., v.* hound

hunger *n.* (*ng* pronounced as in singer) hunger; a mean or avaricious person

hungert *adj.* hungry

hungry *adj.* mean; avaricious; **~ Angus** mean person

hunker *v.* squat down on the haunches; *n. pl.* the haunches resting on the heels; **doon on yir ~s** squatting; **~t up** *ppl.* curled up; **~-slidin** *n.* evasive behaviour

hunkit *See* **hank**

hunky *n.* handkerchief

hunner *adj., n.* hundred; **~wecht** *n.* hundredweight

hup *adv.* up

hurb *n.* clumsy, awkward fellow; displeasing person; good-for-nothing

hurdies *n. pl.* the buttocks

hure *n.* whore. *cf.* **hooer**

hurkle *v.* cripple. *cf.* **hirple**

hurl||(ie) *n.* 1. lift on a vehicle; **~barra** *n.* handcart; **~ie** *n.* barrow; handcart; **~ie-bed** *n.* low bed on castors, stored under box-bed. 2. the sound of laboured breathing due to phlegm in the throat; **~ in the throat** (when *r* is pronounced gutturally)

hurry-burry *n.* noisy confusion

hurschle *v.* move along a seat without rising (A). *cf.* **hirstle, hushle**

hushie *n.* stash, hoard

hushl||e *v.* move (M3); **~t up** curled up *cf.* **hirstle, hurschle**

huz *See* **hiz**

hyaave *adj.* sallow; grey

hyeuk *See* **heuk**

hyne *See* **hine**

hyow(e) *n., v.* hoe

hyowman *adj.* human

hypal *adj.* crippled (B1)

hypothec, hale *phr.* whole concern, lot, or collection

hyse *See* **hyze**

hyste *n., v.* hoist, lift. *cf.* **heist**

hystergowdie *adv.* head over heels (T). *cf.* **heelster-gowdie**

hyter *v.* walk unsteadily; stumble

hyze *n.* banter; frolic, sport; a practical joke; **tae hae a ~ wi** to have a joke with, play a trick on; *v.* joke

I

I *pron. (when unstressed, pro.* A) I. *cf.* **A, AW**

i *prep.* in; **~ mauger o** *conj.* in spite of

ice-tangle *n.* icicle

idder *adj., n., pron.* other

idelty *n.* idleness; *in pl.* idle frolics

identifee *v.* identify

idleset, idleseat *n.* idleness

ile *n.* oil; **~-cake** *n.* oil cake (for cattle); **~-skin** *adj., n.* oilskin

ilk, ilka, ilky *adj.* each, every

ill *adj.* ill; bad, *eg,* **~ widder**; wicked; unkind, cruel;

hard, difficult; *adv.* badly.
(*cf.* **ull**); **~-aff** *adj.* badly off;
~ baabee *phr.* bad penny;
~-deen *adj.* unkindly done;
~-deer *n.* evil-doer,
malefactor; **~-eesage** *n.*
ill treatment; **~-eese,**
~-ess *v.* ill use, abuse;
~-farrant *adj.* unpleasant in
behaviour; bad-mannered;
~-fashence (*See* **~-fashions**);
~-fashioned, -t *adj.* bad-
mannered, esp. inquisitive
~-fashions *n.* bad manners,
esp. inquisitiveness;
~-faured, -faurt *adj.* ugly;
unbecoming; **~-gatit,**
~-gettit *adj.* badly behaved,
perverse; **~-gruntit** *adj.*
ill-natured; **~-guide**
v. maltreat; **~-hung** *adj.*
(of the tongue) impudent,
sharp; **~-jaw** *n.* abusive
talk; **~-naturt** *adj.* ill-
natured; **~-pairt, the** *pr.*
n. hell; **~-pairtit** *ppl.* badly
shared out; **~-peyt (for)** *adj.*
sorry (for); **~-shakken-up,**
-shooken up *ppl.* (of dress)
disordered, untidy; **~-teen**
n. bad mood; **~-thochtit**
adj. having suspicious
thoughts; ill-disposed;
~-tongue *v.* abuse;
~-trickit *adj.* mischievous;
~-tricks *n.* mischief;

-willer *n.* adversary; one
wishing you harm; **~-willie**
adj. ungenerous; **~-win**
n. abusive language (A2);
scandal, slander
ily-lamp *n.* oil lamp. *cf.* **crusie**
imaagin|e, imaigin (A1)
v. imagine; **~ashun**
n. imagination
immas, immis *adj.* variable
(B1); (of weather) dark, wet
and gloomy (A2)
immed(i)antly *adv.* immediately
impident *adj.* impudent
impreevement *n.* improvement
impruv *v.* improve
in aboot, come *phr.* approach
in-by(e) *adv.* inside; (with
verb of motion) from
outside to inside
inch, insch *n.* island; stretch
of higher ground in the
middle of a plain
inchie *n.* small amount
income *n.* internal ailment of
unknown cause
indraacht *n.* suction of air, breath
induck *v.* induct
inflooensie *n.* influenza
ingan, ingin *n.* onion
ingine *n.* engine
ingle *n.* fire; hearth, fireside;
chimney-corner;
~-cheek *n.* fireside;
~-lowe *n.* blazing fire;
~-neuk *n.* chimney corner

in-haudin *adj.* currying
favour with one, fawning
inklin *n.* slight desire (B)
in'o *prep.* into
inower *prep.* in and over
inquar *v.* inquire; ~y *n.*
inquiry
In'rurie *pr. n.* Inverurie
insnorl *v.* entangle, entrap
instanter *adv.* straightaway
interaistin *adj.* interesting
intil, intill *prep.* into;
~'t into it
intimat *adj.* intimate
intimmers *n. pl.* intestines;
inner workings of anything
intoon *n.* land nearest the
farm-house
invaad *v.* invade
inveet *n.* invitation (A); *v.* (AI)
inveetor *n.* inventory; value
of goods inventoried
I'se *pron. with v.* I shall;
~ warn I'll warrant you,
I guarantee
isna *v. neg.* is not
isnint *v. interrog.* is it not?
ither *adj.* other; ~weese
adv. otherwise
itmost *adj.* utmost
iv(v)er *adv.* ever
iverleevin *in phr.* at the ~
gallop at high speed (T)
ivnoo *adv.* just now. *cf.* eyvnoo

J

jaa *n.* jaw; talk, chatter; dash
of water; ~-hole *n.* plughole
(M3). *cf.* jaw
jabb *v.* fatigue, exhaust; ~it
adj., ppl. exhausted
jabby *See* jobby
jaicket *n.* jacket
Jaicobeet *pr. n.* Jacobite
jainus *n.* genius
jallop *n.* dose of (medicinal)
fluid
jalouse *v.* guess; suspect;
imagine
jamaica *in phr.* he jist
aboot hid a ~ he almost
lost control
jamb *n.* anything large and
clumsy
Jamie *pr. n.* deriv. of James
jamph *v.* mock, sneer, jeer
jamphin *n.* mockery
jandies, the *n.* jaundice
jannie *n.* school janitor
jant *n., v.* jaunt
Janwar, Janiwar *n.* January
jassamine *n.* jasmine
jaud *n.* a jade
jaup *v.* fatigue, weary; ~it
ppl. weary
jaw *n.* chatter; (abusive)
talk; (at sea) wave; *v.* talk;
chatter. *cf.* jaa
jaw-hole *n.* sink; hole in the
wall for dirty water

jee *n.* side motion, swerve;
v. to move, stir. *cf.* **gee**

jeedge *v.* judge; ~**ment**
n. judgment (B1)

jeel a*dj.* cold as ice;
n. extreme cold; *v.* freeze;
congeal

jeely *n.* jam; ~ **pigs** jam jars

Jeems *pr. n.* deriv. of James

Jeen *n.* month of June

jeest, jest *n.* joist

jeesty *adj.* normally used in
the *neg.* **nae ~** no joking
matter

jeho(y) *v.* cease, give over

jelly *adj.* jolly

jest *See* **jeest**

jibble *n.* small quantity of
liquid (contemptuous term);
~ **ower** *v.* brim or spill over

jile *n., v.* jail

jilp *v. tr.* spill, cause to splash;
intr. splash about; *n.* a
splash of liquid

jimp *adj.* small of stature;
neat; slender; *adv.* scarcely

jine *n., v.* join. *cf.* **jyne**

jine-on *n.* playground game

jiner *n.* joiner, carpenter.
cf. **jyner**

jing-bang *in the phr.* **the hale**
~ the whole party or affair

jings *excl.* gosh

jink *n.* sudden turn; *v.* elude;
dodge; cheat

jinkie *adj.* jaunty (R)

jinnip(e)rous, jinipperous
adj. trim, spruce; ingenious;
natty; finicky, over-particular

Jinse *pr. n.* Janet

jint *n.* joint

jip *n.* pain (sometimes
retributive)

jipperty *n.* jeopardy

jirg *v.* creak, grate

jist *adv.* just. *See also* **jyst**

jivvle *n.* a gaol; house as
uncomfortable as a gaol

jo *n.* boyfriend, sweetheart
(J, K)

job *v.* prick;

jobby *adj.* prickly;
~ **nickles** stinging nettles

Jock *pr. n.* John

Jocktober *n.* October (T)

joco *n.* jovial (G)

jog *v.* keep a steady pace

Johnny Groatie *n.* small
cowrie shell (B). *cf.* **kysie**

joodge *n.* judge

joog *n.* jug

joogle *v.* joggle, jerk repeatedly

joost *adv.* just (A2); ~**ice** *n.*
justice (A2). *cf.* **jist**

jorum *n.* whisky jug

jot *n.* job; piece of work;
a ~ wark a job of work

jougs *n. pl.* instrument
of public punishment,
sometimes in church,
consisting of iron collar

attached to wall and placed around offender's neck

jouk *v.* dodge, duck, swerve; ~ **an lat the jaw gae by** yield to circumstances

joukerie pawkery *n.* trickery, roguery

joundie *v.* jog with the elbow

jow *n.* sound of bell; judder; *v.* move (with a rocking motion); ring

jowdy *v.* shake (K)

jummle *n.*, *v.* jumble

junny *n.* wrench; severe jolt

jurr *v.* (of water) gush (K)

jyne *v.* join; ~**r** *n.* joiner, carpenter. *cf.* **jiner**

jynt *n.* joint

jyst *n.* joist

K

(*k* is usually pronounced before *n*)

kail *n.* colewort; ~ **runt** kail stalk; also term of abuse; **caul ~ het** (*fig.*) a stale story; ~ **throu the reek** severe criticism or scolding

kaim, kame *n.*, *v.* comb

kavils *n. pl.* lots; **ceest ~ drew** lots. *cf.* **cavels, cavils**

kebar *n.* rafter (K). *cf.* **couple**

kebbuck *n.* round of cheese

keckle *v.* cackle, chuckle

keeble *See* **kibble**

keech *See* **kich**

keeger *v.* mess, puddle (*eg,* through mud)

keek *n.*, *v.* peep

keek-a-bo *n.* game of peep-bo

keel *n.* any marking substance (*eg,* for sheep) (M2)

keelupper *n.* fall, tumble (from upturned keel)

keeng *n.* king; ~**dom** *n.* kingdom

keeperin *n.* the work of a gamekeeper

keepit, keept (A) *v. pt.* kept

keep tee *v.* keep up

keer *n.*, *v.* cure

keerio|us *adj.* curious, strange; keen, desirous; ~**sity** *n.* curiosity

keest *v. pt.* cast. *cf.* **ceest**

kell *n.* caul; the puckered part of a woman's **mutch** which rises over the back part of the head

kelpie *n.* water sprite

ken *n.* knowledge; *v.* know; ~**na** don't know

ken|le, kennle *v.* kindle; light; ~**nelt** ablaze with colour; ~**nlin** *n.* kindling

kenspeckle *adj.* easily recognised

kent *v. pt., ppl.* knew, known ~**na** *v. pt. neg.* did not know

kep *n.* cap; **~steen** *n.* capstone; *v.* catch; keep; meet; intercept; **~ the win** keep the wind out

kerridge *n.* carriage

Kersey *Eng. pr. n.* coarse woollen cloth used to make trousers

keuk *v.* cook. *cf.* **kyeuk**

kibble *adj.* strong, sturdy; well-built; active; agile

kich *n.* excrement; *v.* defecate

kickup *n.* uproar

kil *n.* kiln

kil(l) *n.* wooden tripod round which hay- or cornstack is built

kilt *v.* tuck up (skirts, sleeves etc)

kiltimmer *n.* term of abuse for a woman of doubtful character; a rough woman; virago

kiltit *adj.* kilted

kimmer *n.* a gossip; married woman; wife

kin' *adj.* kind; *n.* kind, nature, sort; *adv.* rather; **caal ~** rather cold; **~-kine** *n.* kind, sort; **aa-kine o** all kinds of

kinallie *n.* (Fr. canaille) mob

kindlin *adj.* blushing, ruddy (J)

kine *v.* cattle (A)

kinkhoast *n.* whooping cough

kinkind, -kine *n.* kind, sort, variety

kinkin-pin *n.* pin or lever for twisting ropes tight

kinlin *n.* kindling. *cf.* **kennlin**

kinsh *v.* twist; wind (a rope) (T)

kintra *n.* country. *cf.* **kwintra**

kipple *n.* couple; *v.* partner

kire *n.* choir. *cf.* **kyre**

kirk *n.* church; **to be ~it** *v.* to be at church; **~ton, -toon** *n.* village or hamlet with parish church; **~-yaird** *n.* churchyard

kirn *n.* butter churn; mess, state of confusion; *v.* churn butter; stir, mix up; mess about

kirsen *v.* christen; **~in** *n.* christening

kis(s) *conj.* because

kist *n.* chest; coffin; *v.* to put into a coffin

kitchie *n.* kitchen; seasoning, an addition to plain fare, *eg,* **tak a piece an mak ~ o yir egg; ~-deem** *n.* kitchen-maid

kite *n.* stomach. *cf.* **kyte**

kithe *See* **kythe**

kitlin *See* **kittlin**

kittl|e *v.* anger; annoy; caress; excite; please; tickle; upset; *adj.* skilful; (of a person) touchy; (of a task) tricky, difficult, not easily

managed; (of an issue)
controversial, sensitive;
~**esome** *adj. See* **kittle** *adj.;*
~**et** (**up**) *ppl., adj.* excited;
~**ie,** ~**y** *adj.* tickly; ticklish
kittlin *n.* kitten. *cf.* **kitlin**
kittyneddie *n.* sandpiper
klyack *See* **clyack**
knablich *n.* small hillock (A2)
knablick *adj.* nobbly
knack *v.* to knock; crack, snap
knag *n.* knob or pin
knap *n.* knoll; *v.* knock; snap
with the teeth; starve (B1);
~~**at-the-win** a mere bite
(*ref.* to stray dog) (M2)
knapdarloch *n.* matted dung
on the hind-quarters of
cattle or sheep (T)
kneef *adj.* healthy and active
kneevlick *n.* a big lump (of
cheese, beef etc). *cf.* **knyte**
kneggum *n.* sharp or nasty
smell or flavour
kneip *v.* knock, strike smartly;
~ **on** *v.* press on
knibloch *n.* clod of earth;
lump (used as mild insult)
knicht *n.* knight; ~**it** *adj.*
delighted; flattered; proud
(M3)
knief *adj.* active, alert; healthy.
cf. **kneef**
knock *n.* clock
knoit *n.* blow. *cf.* **knyte**

knottit *adj.* lumpy (as of
porridge)
knotty-tams *n.* dish of boiled
milk with meal
knowe *n.* knoll; steep field;
head; ~~**heid** *n.* top of a
hillock
knowpert *n.* crowberry
knurlin *n.* dwarf
knyte *n.* large piece, lump
korter *n.* quarter; quarter of
oatcake. *cf.* **corter**
kowe *See* **cowe**
kowk *v.* retch; vomit
kwile *n.* coal
kwintra, kwintry *n.* country
kwite, kwyte *n.* coat; oilskin
skirt with bib worn by
women in the herring
curing yards (B); petticoat
kyaak|s *n. pl.* cakes (usually
oatcakes); ~ **o breid** round
of oatcakes
kyaard *n.* tinker; *v.* abuse;
~~**tonguet** given to loose or
unwholesome talk
Kyack *pr. n.* nickname for the
village of Pitsligo
kyarn *n.* large heap, cairn.
cf. **carn**
kye *n.* cows
kyeuk *n., v.* cook. *cf.* **keuk**
kyne(-hertit) *adj.* kind(-hearted)

kyp(i)e *n.* scooped out hollow in ground for use in game of marbles

kyre *n.* choir. *cf.* **kire**

kysie *n.* small cowrie shell (B). *cf.* **Johnny Groatie, calfie's mooie**

kyte *n.* stomach. *cf.* **kite**

kythe *v.* show, display, reveal (B1)

L

laad *See* **lad**

laag *v.* talk volubly, chatter. *cf.* **laig, lyaag**

laan *n.* land; lawn

laain *See* **lawin**

lab *v.* lap

lab(b)ach *n.* long story about nothing (R); small quantity to drink (B1)

labster *n.* fisher term for lobster. *cf.* **partan**

lacer *n.* shoe-lace. *cf.* **pint**

lach *n., v.* laugh. *cf.* **lauch**

lachter *n.* laughter; a sitting of eggs. *cf.* **lauchter**

lad *n.* lad; boy-friend; sweetheart; **a bit o a ~** rascal; lady's man; **~ o pairts** clever lad from small country school; **~die** *n.* small boy

lade *n.* canal carrying water to a mill; load; lead (metal) (s)

ladle *n.* small wooden box with long handle, formerly in use in collecting offerings in church

laft *n.* loft; upper storey; church gallery

lagamachie *See* **lamgamachie**

laich, laigh *adj.* low; **~-in** *adv.* in a low voice or confidential tone; **~-braid** *n.* short, stocky person or animal (T); **~en** *v.* lower; **~en yir wird** lower your voice. *cf.* **laigh**

laid *n.* load; *ppl.* (of a crop) flattened

laidle *See* **ladle**

laig *v.* talk idly. *cf.* **lyaag**

laigh *n.* stretch of low-lying ground

laimiter *n.* a cripple

lair *n.* mud, mire; burial place reserved in graveyard; *v.* sink in bog or mud; **~-stane** *n.* gravestone; **~y** *adj.* muddy

laird *n.* squire; landowner; **~skip** *n.* lordship; right as proprietor; **~lifu** *adj.* generous

lairge *adj.* unrestrained in talk

lairn *v.* learn; teach. *cf.* **leern;** ~**in** *n.* learning (J). *cf.* **lear**

laist *adj., v.* last. *cf.* **lest**

laiteran *See* **lettrin**

lallan *adj.* lowland

lame *n.* crockery, earthenware; shard of earthenware. *cf.* **leems**

lamgamachie *n.* anything long and loose in movement; rigmarole

lamikie *n.* little lamb

Lammas *n.* beginning of August, a Scottish term

lammie *n.* lamb

lamp *n., v.* stride

lan *n.* land; ~**d** *n.* tenement (K); ~**side** *n.* side of the plough next the unploughed land; ~**ner** *n.* land-side horse; ~**warth** landward; *v.* land; ~**nit** *v. pt.* landed. *cf.* **laan**

lane *pred. adj., adv.* alone. *cf.* **lccn**

lang *adj. v.* long; ~ **acre** *phr.* grass verge at roadside (T); ~**-gane** *adj.* long-gone; ~**-heidit** *adj.* intelligent; shrewd; ~**-leggit** *adj.* long-legged; ~**-nebbit,** **-nibbit** *adj.* prying; critical; acute in understanding; (of words) difficult to pronounce or understand; ~ **sandy** *n.* heron; ~**some** *adj.* wearisome; ~**someness** *n.* tedium; ~**syne** *adv.* long ago; *v.* long

langer *n.* languor, tedium; **haud oot o** ~ keep from boredom, amuse

langidge *n.* language; words

lanstell *n.* parapet of a bridge

lant *v.* jeer

lanter (wi) *v.* leave in the lurch (with) (B)

lantren *n.* lantern; ~~**-chaftit** *adj.* lantern-jawed

lap *v. pt.* leaped

lapper *v.* clot, congeal; (of water) lap

lapsteen *n.* stone on which shoemaker hammered leather

larrie, larry *n.* long, flat low wagon, horse-drawn or motorised; lorry

lass|(ie), lassock *n.* girl; ~**ikie,** ~**ockie** *n.* young girl

lat *v. pr. and pt.* let; ~~**-aff** *n.* lay-off, ramble. *cf.* **leet, loot**

latch *v.* be slow; idle, loiter; ~**ie** *adj.* slow; tardy; lazy (M2)

latten *pt. ppl.* let; ~ **be** let alone

latter-oot *n.* the letter-out, the one who feeds in the straw in rope-twisting (F)

lauch *v.* laugh; **~en at** *ppl.*
laughed at

lauchter *See* **lachter**

lave *n.* the rest; the remainder;
v. leave (s). *cf.* **lea, ley;**
v. ladle out (B1)

laverock, lavrock *n.* skylark.
cf. **livrock**

lawbor, lawbour *n.* labour

lawfu *adj.* lawful

lawin *n.* tavern-bill; reckoning

lawlands *n. pl.* lowlands

lawvyer *n.* lawyer

lay *v.* to put more iron on a
sock or coulter

lay-aff *n.* harangue;
rigmarole; *v.* talk volubly,
spout

lay on *v.* work hard; beat
severely

lea *v.* to leave (A1). *cf.* **ley, lave**

lead *v.* cart in the corn from
the field (A1); **~in** *n.* carting
hay, straw (s)

leal *adj., n.* loyal; **~-loved**
well-loved (T)

leam *n.* gleam

lean *in phr.* **~ yirsel doon** take
a seat

lean-tee *n.* lean-to, shed

lear *n.* learning

leasure *n.* leisure. *cf.* **leesure**

leavie-oh *n.* catching game

ledd *v.* lead (K)

ledder *n.* leather; a ladder;
v. thrash, belabour

leddy *n.* lady

lee *n., v.* lie

leear *n.* liar

Leebie *pr. n.* deriv. of
Elizabeth

leeberary *n.* library

leeberty *n.* liberty

leebral *adj., n.* liberal

leed *n.* lead. *cf.* **lade, leid**

leeft *v. pt., ppl.* left

leefulane *adj.* all alone

leein *ppl., n.* lying

lee-lang *adj.* (of the day)
livelong

leems *n. pl.* implements;
apparatus; earthenware;
in ~ in bits, smithereens.
cf. **lames, lems**

leen *adj.* alone; **ma~** by
myself; **him~; them~** etc

leenity *n.* lenity, mercy

leepie *n.* measure of oats;
wooden box for measuring
corn for horse's feed (T)

leerie(-man) *n.* lamp-lighter

leern *v.* learn; teach. *cf.* **lairn;**
~in *n.* learning. *cf.* **lear;**
~t *adj.* learned

leery-bows *in phr.* **tae gang by
the ~** (B1) meaning unclear,
perhaps to do mischief

leese-me-on *phr.* expression of
pleasure in, or affection for
person/thing, eg **~ the Enzie
fowk** (C)

leeshens, leeshins *n.* licence

leesome *adj.* pleasant

leesure *n.* leisure. *cf.* **leasure**

leet *n.* list; *v.* let (M3), *pt.* let (A1); ~ **at him** assailed him; ~ **off** reeled off (M3). *cf.* **lat, loot**

leeterary *adj.* literary

leethe *n.* a shelter; *in phr.* **in the ~ o** ye through your influence (B). *cf.* (B1) **lythe**

leetiny *n.* litany

leevin *n.* living being; person

lefts-an-richts *n.* soup made from turnip and potato

leg *v.* walk quickly; *pt.* ~**git**; **draa ma ~** pull my leg

leid *n.* language; dialect; lead; ~**en** *adj.* leaden

lems *n. pl.* shards of earthenware (M3). *cf.* **leems**

len *n.* loan; *v.* lend; ~**nit** *ppl.* lent; **tak a ~ o** take advantage of

lench *v.* launch

lenth *n.* length; **damn the ~** not at all; ~ **o lang** at long length

lerb *n.* lick, mouthful of fluid (A1); *v.* lap with tongue

lest *adj.*, *n.*, *v.* last. *cf.* **laist**

let off *v.* break wind anally

leuch *v. pt.* laughed; **fit I ~** how I laughed

leuk *v.* look

ley *n.* lea, unploughed land; grass land; ~**-corn** oats grown on ploughed-up grassland; *v.* leave (s). *cf.* **lea, lave**

lib *v.* castrate

licht *adj.*, *n.* light; *v.* light, alight ~ **on** *v.* land on; **let ~ that** let it be known that; **think ~fu o**, *phr.* despise; ~**hoose** *n.* lighthouse; ~**lifie** *v.* to make light of; belittle; ~**nin** *n.* lightning ~**some** *adj.* pleasant; cheerful; lively

lichts *n. pl.* lungs (human/animal)

lick *n.* smack, blow; **at a gweed ~** at high speed; *v.* thrash

lickened (wi) *ppl.* likened (to)

lickin *n.* thrashing

lickly *adj.*, *adv.* likely

licky *adj.* lucky

liefer *adv.* rather

lie-in *n.* the part of an attic room lying under slope of roof

lie-money *n.* money retained by employer for lie-time

lie-time *n.* the time before pay day for making up accounts, in which work has been done but payment remains or lies over till next pay day

lift *n.* sky

lifter *n.* one who gathers grain to make sheaves. *cf.* **gaitherer**

liftit *ppl., adj.* elevated; overjoyed

lig *v. (lit.)* lie, recline, rest

like *adj., prep.* like; ~**r** *adj.* more like; ~**st** *adj.* most likely; ~, ~**in** *adv.* (used at the end of sentences to modify or intensify) that's to say; do you mean?; ~**in** *ppl.* as; *adv.* like as; for example; ~**n tae** *adj.* apt to; *v.* like, ~**t**, **likit** *v. pt.* liked

limerin *n.* thrashing

limmer *n.* woman of loose morals; playful or derog. term applied to a female; rascal

linder, linner *n.* woollen or flannel undershirt (B)

ling *n.* long thin grass (J)

linga *n.* lingo

linglairy *n.* long story, rigmarole (B)

link *v.* walk hand-in-hand, arm-in-arm; ~ **at** work vigorously

links *n. pl.* chain by which a pot hung over a fire from the **crook**; iron chains formerly used on farm to remove surface weeds from seed bed

linn *n.* precipice over which water falls; the cascade of water

lint *n.* flax

linth *n.* length. *cf.* **lenth**

lintie *n.* linnet

lip *v.* to be full to the brim; brim over; ~**pin fou** brimming full

lippen (tae, till) *v.* trust; depend on; ~**able** *adj.* trustworthy; ~**ance** *n.* trust

lippie *n.* fourth of a peck; container for such a measure

lirk *n.* crease, fold. *cf.* **lurk**

list *v.* enlist

lit *v.* let. *cf.* **lat**

litchie *adj.* light-headed

lith *n.* joint; segment; *v.* disjoint, dislocate *(eg, the necks of hens)*; ~**it** *ppl.*

lithe *adj.* gentle; soft

little ane, littlean, littlin *n.* small child

liveliheid *n.* livelihood

liv(v) *n.* palm of the hand (M3)

liver *v.* unload a catch of fish (B)

livrock *n.* skylark (G). *cf.* **laverock**

loaf *n.* bread

loamin *n.* leg (K)

loan *n.* a small common; uncultivated land about

a homestead; ~ing(s)
n. village common green

loch *n.* lake

lochan *n.* small loch

locker *n.* small compartment
in the end of a chest

lod *excl.* Lord!

lodesteen *n.* magnet

lodomy *n.* laudanum

loe *v.* love

londer *v.* tramp wearily,
trudge

lood *adj.* loud

loon *n.* lad; boy; ~ikie *n.* little
boy

loos|e *n.* louse; ~ie *adj.* lousy

loot *v.* bend, bow, make
obeisance; let; *v. pt.*
permitted, let; ~ ye doon sit
down

loo-warm *adj.* lukewarm

lordlifu *adj.* sumptuous;
extravagantly liberal

losen *See* **lozen**

losh *excl.* euphemism for
Lord; ~ins *excl.* of surprise
(A); ~tie (be here) *excl.* of
surprise; ~tie-goshtie guide's
excl. good Lord guide us!

loss *v.* lose. *cf.* **tine**

lounder *See* **lownder**

loup *v.* leap. *cf.* **lowp**

Lourenkirk *pr. n.*
Laurencekirk (s)

lout *v.* stoop

lowder *v.* plod

low door *adj., n.* entrance at
ground floor level

lowe *n., v.* glow, flame, blaze;
sweer blue ~s swear
vehemently; ~ **for** *v.* hunger
for, crave (M3)

lower *v.* frown, look
threatening; (of weather)
be overcast; ~in *ppl.*
frowning, overcast

lown *adj.* sheltered,
unfrequented; (of weather)
calm, still

lowp *n.* leap; loop, stitch;
v. leap. *cf.* **loup**

lowp-the-cat *n.* (of a person)
term of contempt

lowrie *n.* long, heavy, steel
hook used on the market
floor

lowerin *See* **lower**

Lowrin *pr. n.* Lawrence

lows|e *v.* unyoke, leave off
work; loose, loosen; *adj.*
loose; suffering from
diarrhoea; ~er *n.* one
who cuts bands on
sheaves during threshing;
~in-shooer *n.* heavy shower
of rain putting a stop to
outdoor work on farm (T);
~in-time *n.* the end of the
day's work; the time for
unyoking horses;

lowss *See* **lowse**

lowssen *v. tr.* loosen
lozen *n.* window-pane
lucken-gowan *n.* globe flower
Luckie, Lucky *pr. n.* form of address for old woman
luckpenny *n.* sum of money given for luck, *eg,* returned by the seller to the buyer as discount
lucky daddy *n.* grandfather (A2)
lucky minnie *n.* grandmother (B1)
ludgement *n.* a place to rest
luft *v.* lift
lug *n.* ear; handle; ~**git bonnet** one with ear pieces; ~**babs** *n.* earrings; knot of ribbons over the ears
luggie *n.* small wooden vessel with two handles, for table use
lum *n.* chimney; ~**hat** *n.* black tile hat
lumbaga *n.* lumbago
lunder, lunner *v.* beat
lundies, landies *n.* double ropes for skipping
Lunnon *pr. n.* London
lunt *n.* column of fire and smoke; puff of smoke from a pipe; blaze; ~**er** *n.* pipe; *v. intr.* smoke; catch fire; burn; blaze; *v. tr.* smoke a pipe; set fire to; ~**in** *ppl.,* *adj.* smoking
luppen *ppl.* leaping (M3)

lurk *n.* fold, crease. *cf.* **lirk**
lut *v.* let; ~**ten** *ppl.* let. *cf.* **lat**
luve *n.* love
lyaach *adj.* low. *cf.* **laich, laigh**
lyaag *v.* to talk idly and at length. *cf.* **laig**
lyart *adj.* streaked with grey
lyen *ppl.* lain
lyin *ppl.* lying; ~**-holes** *n.* patches of corn or barley flattened by heavy rain, unsuitable for the binder (T); ~**-shafts** *n. pl.* main beams under box cart (F)
lyooch *See* **leuch**
lyook *v.* look. *cf.* **leuk**
lyter *v.* loiter
lythe *n.* shelter; *adj.* sheltered; **in the ~ o** on the strength of

M

ma *pron.* me; my
maa *n.* seagull. *cf.* **maw, myaave**
maamie *See* **maumie**
maasie *n.* jersey (G)
mackerels' backs an meers' tails *phr.* high cirrus clouds (B)
mad *adj.* angry
madden-dreem *n.* madness; folly; mad pranks (B1)
madder, maddie *n.* lunatic
mae *adj.* more

maet *n.* food; **aff o's ~** off his
food; *v.* feed, **~it** *ppl.* fed;
~-haill *adj.* able to take
one's food; **~ oot** *v.* feed
animals. *cf.* **meat**
mager *See* **mauger**
Maggie Rennie *in phr.*
a different ~ a different
kettle of fish (B)
maggot *n.* whim, caprice,
fancy; **~ive** *adj.* full of
whims, moody
maiden *n.* designation once
given to farmer's eldest
daughter
maijesty *n.* majesty
maik *n.* halfpenny; **~st** *n.* a
halfpennyworth
mailin *n.* purse
maillyer *n.* the quantity of
oatmeal received from the
mill at one time
main *n., v.* moan
mainners *n.* manners.
cf. **menners**
Mains o Backchines *pr. n.*
fictitious farm representing
an inferior fee (T)
mair *adj.* more
mairch *n.* boundary; *n., v.*
bound; march; **~(in)-dyke**
n. boundary wall
Mairch *n.* month of March
mairdle *See* **merdle**
mairket *n.* market. *cf.* **mercat**

mairrage *n.* marriage;
wedding. *cf.* **mairritch**
mairritch *n.* marriage;
wedding. *cf.* **mairrage**
mairry, mairry on (to)
v. marry; *ppl.* **mairret,
mairrit**
mairt *n.* ox killed at
Martinmas for winter use
(A); beef (M3). *cf.* **mart**
maist *adj.* most; *adv.* **~ly**
mostly
maister *n.* master; stale
urine used as detergent;
~-pig jar containing such
urine; *v.* master
mait *See* **maet**
maitter *n.* matter
maive *n.* maggot
mak *v.* make; reach; **~ nae
odds** make no difference;
~sna, disna ~ does not
matter; **~ yir feet yir
freen** it's best to go; **~ on**
n. pretence; *v.* pretend; **~ins**
(O) *n.* makings (of)
maker, makker *n.* poet
malagruze *v.* bruise
mallie *n.* fulmar (B)
mamen(t) *n.* moment
mammy *n.* mother
man *n.* husband; man; **~heed**
n. manhood; **~nie** *n.* man;
pl. **mannies**. *cf.* **mennies**;
~nikie *n.* little man; term of
endearment for small boy

maneeplate *v.* manipulate (M3)

mang *v.* long for eagerly; **~in tae** dying to

manniwal *adj.* manual

man|swear *v.* commit perjury; **~sworn** *ppl.* perjured

mant *n., v.* stammer

mappie *n.* rabbit (used on board ship to avoid taboo word, *rabbit*)

mardle *n.* crowd

Marget *pr. n.* Margaret

mark *n.* darkness (A); **~ness** *n.* darkness (A2)

marless *adj.* not matching

maroonjus *adj.* wild, obstreporous; surly; harsh; outrageous (A)

marra, marrow *n.* match, equal; **~less** *adj.* unmarried

marra-been *n.* marrowbone

mart *n.* ox killed at Martinmas; market; building used for agricultural auctions; such a sale. *cf.* **mairt**

Martimas *n.* Martinmas

masel(lie) *pron.* myself; *pred. adj., adv.* by myself, alone

mashlach, mashlich *n.* mixed grain. *cf.* **mashlie**

mashlie *n.* mixed grain, peas & oats

mask *v.* infuse (tea)

mason's mear *n.* trestle

match(-paper) *n.* brown papers soaked in saltpetre solution, used with flint and steel for lighting pipes etc

mauger, maugre *prep.* in spite of (M); **i (the) ~ o** in spite of (A); *v.* act in spite; master (B1). *cf.* **mager**

maumie *adj.* mellow

maun *v.* must; **~(n)a** must not

maut *n.* malt; **the ~ was abeen the meal** (leading to intoxication)

mavis *n.* thrush (M)

maw *n.* mouth; seagull (M1); *v.* mow, cut with a scythe

mawkin *n.* hare (A, M). *cf.* **myaakin**

mawmie *See* **maumie**

maxie *n.* a maximus, the gravest error in Latin prose composition

maze *n.* state of amazement

meal *n.* oatmeal; **~-an-ale** mixture of oatmeal, ale, sugar and whisky, traditional fare at harvest-home celebrations; the celebration itself; **~-bowie** *n.* barrel for oatmeal; **~-bunk** (s) *See* **meal-kist; ~er** (s) *See* **meal-kist; ~ie puddin** *n.* oatmeal pudding; **~-kist** *n.* meal-chest in which farm servant stored meal and other eatables; ~ock *n.* crumb of oatcakes etc; ~y-mou't *adj.* mealy-mouthed

mean *n.* moan; cry of sorrow; sound of pity; (expression of) sympathy; **I mak nae ~ for** I've no sympathy with; *v.* pity; ~fu *adj.* full of regret

meangie *adj.* tight with money, mingy

mear *n.* mare. *cf.* meer

meat *n.* food (C. J). *cf.* maet

meathes *n. pl.* bearings; **tint ma ~** lost my bearings

mebbe *adv.* perhaps

meellyin *n.* million; ~aire *n.* millionaire

meen *n.* moon; ~licht *n.* moonlight. *cf.* mune

meen *See* mean

meeninit *n.* mignonette

meenister *n.* minister. *cf.* minaister

meenit *n.* minute

meent *ppl.* meant

meer *n.* moor. *cf.* muir; *n.* mare. *cf.* mear

mees (in) *v.* blend (in); smooth

meesic *n.* music; ~-fan *n.* musical instrument

meesrable *adj.* miserable

meet *in phr.* ~ the cat have a spell of bad luck (B)

meev|e *n., v.* move; ~ie nor mavie not a movement, sound or whisper; ~ement *n.* movement

meggie-monyfeet *n.* centipede (B)

meggins alive *excl.* of surprise (MI)

megreem, megrim *n.* migraine

megstie me *excl.* of surprise (MI)

meikle *adj.* big, large, great. *cf.* muckle

mell *n.* mallet, heavy hammer; *v.* hammer; mix; meddle

melt *n.* the spleen

meng(y)ie *n.* crowd, huddled mass (A)

menner *n.* manner; *pl.* ~s manners; **weel ~t** well-mannered

mennies *n. pl.* men (AI). *cf.* mannies

mense *n.* common sense

mensefu *adj.* courteous, respectful; well-bred

menseless *adj.* rough, unmannerly; incalculable *eg,* **a ~ amoont o siller**

menteen *v.* maintain

mercat *n.* market. *cf.* mairket

merch *v.* march. *cf.* mairch

merchan *n.* shopkeeper, retailer

merciment *n.* mercy; tolerance

merdle *n.* confused crowd of people or animals. *cf.* **mardle**

merry dancers *pr. n.* aurora borealis. *cf.* **northern lights**

mertyreese *v.* torture as a martyr

mervel *n.* marvel

messages *n. pl., in phr.* **go the ~** do the shopping

mett *v.* feed (M3). *cf.* **maet**

mettlesome *adj.* spirited

Mey *n.* month of May

micht *n.* might, strength; **~y** *adj.* mighty, powerful; **~y me** *excl.* of surprise

midden *n.* dunghill; dirty, slovenly woman (K); **~-bree** *n.* moisture from dunghill; **~-plunk** *n.* wooden plank up which barrowload of dung could be wheeled up midden; **~-tap** *n.* top of the dunghill

midder *n.* mother. *cf.* **mither**

middle *v.* meddle

middlin *adj., adv.* moderate(ly); semi-

midgeck *n.* midge (T, M3)

midgie *n.* midge

midrig *n.* mid ridge

mids(e) *n.* middle, midst; the open furrow between two ridges; a halfway point; *adv.* halfway; **there's a ~ i the sea** everything in moderation

mildyow *n.* mildew

milk *n.* milk; **~-brose** *n.* dish of milk and raw oatmeal; **~-broth** *n.* dish made with milk and barley; **~er** *n.* milk cow; **~ness** *n.* the business of preparing milk (A2)

mill *See* **mull**

millert *See* **mullart**

milt *n.* spleen of an ox

mim, mim-like *adj.* prim; as **~'s a Mey poddock** *phr.* (M3); **~-mou'd** *adj.* prim

min *n.* man (used as form of address) **hey, ~!**

minaister *n.* minister (A2)

mind, min' *n.* mind; a memory; *v.* remember; remind

mink *n.* noose

minker *n.* ne'er-do-well; vagrant

minna *v. neg.* might not. *cf.* **mithna**

min(n)eer, mineerum *n.* great noise; fuss

minnie *n.* mother; pet name for a mother

minnon *n.* minnow; any small fresh-water fish

minse *See* **mense**

mint *n.* aim, intention; *v.* attempt, endeavour; **~ at** hint, insinuate; **~it** *pt. ppl.*

mirk *n.* darkness. *cf.* mark
mirky *adj.* smiling; merry
mirl *v.* crumble
mirly *adj.* speckled, spotted
mirra-hine, merry hyne
  int. off you go and good
  riddance
mirrles, the *n. pl.* measles (B)
misca *v.* speak ill of; abuse;
  slander
mischancy *adj.* dangerous
mischeef, mischief *n.* mischief;
  severe hurt
mischieve *v.* injure, hurt
miscomfit *v.* displease, offend;
  disappoint (B1)
misdoot *v.* doubt, disbelieve;
  ~ yirsel *phr.* mistake
  yourself
misfortnat *adj.* unfortunate
mishachlt *ppl., adj.* deformed;
  misshapen (B)
mishanter *n.* accident
misken *v.* not to recognise
mislippen *v.* neglect (A);
  mismanage; deceive (M);
  distrust (A2, M3); ~ment
  n. misfortune
missaucre *v.* destroy, hurt
  severely
misser *n.* measure. *cf.* missour
missie *n.* female teacher
missionar *n.* missionary
missour *n., v.* measure.
  cf. mizzor
mistaen *ppl.* mistaken

mistak *n.* mistake
misteuk *n.* mistake (K)
misthrive *v.* fare badly, *ppl.*
  misthriven
mith *v.* might; ~na, ~nin
  might not. *cf.* minna
mither *n.* mother (A); ~ wit
  native wit. *cf.* midder
Mither Tap *pr. n.* topmost
  peak of the hill, Bennachie
mitten *v.* grab hold of, seize (B)
mixter *n.* mixture; ~-maxter
  adv. in a state of confusion;
  n. mixture
mizzer, mizzor *n., v.* measure;
  ~ment *n.* measurement
moch *n.* moth; ~-aeten
  adj. moth-eaten; ~-baas
  n. pl. moth balls; ~ie
  adj. muggy, misty, damp;
  moth-eaten
moderat|e *v.* to preside at a
  Presbyterian Church court
  or at the election, calling
  or ordination of a minister;
  ~or *n.* one who presides at
  a Presbyterian Church court
modren *adj.* modern
moggan, moggin *n.* stocking,
  (sometimes used as purse);
  footless stocking
moleskins *n.* trousers of thick
  cotton
molie *n.* molecatcher
'mon *prep.* among
Monanday *n.* Monday (A)

moniment *n.* monument;
spectacle

mony *adj.* many; ~ **een** many
a one

monyfaulds *n. pl.* entrails
(consisting of many folds),
intestines

moo *n.* large rick of hay
or corn; mouth; **~-bag**
n. feeding-bag for horses;
~fae mouthful; ~ **o hairst**
opening of harvest; **~-ban**
v. utter, articulate; mention
(B1). *cf.* **mou**

moocher *n.* scrounger

moold *n., v.* mould

mools *n. pl.* moulds; earth of
a grave

moose *n.* mouse

moosewob *n.* cobweb

moothie, mouthie *n.* mouth
organ

morn, the *adv.* tomorrow; **~'s
nicht** tomorrow night

mornin *n.* morning dram

mortal *adj.* dead drunk

mortifiet *ppl., adj.* humiliated

moss *n.* moor where peats
are dug; **~-hags** broken
ground of a peat-bog; **~in**
n. peat-cutting

mott *n.* mote; particle of
dust; **a ~ in yir ee** *phr.* a
nuisance; **~y** *adj.* full of
motes or specks

mou *n.* mouth; **~fu** mouthful

moulter, mouter *n.* multure,
miller's fee for grinding corn

mowdie(warp), mowdiewart
n. mole

mowse *adj.* appropriate; safe,
harmless; *used in neg.* **nae ~,
nae a ~ concairn** no joking
matter; not safe; **nae ~ job**
no easy job

mowser *n.* moustache

moyen *n.* influence, means;
v. accomplish by means;
entice

muck *n.* dung; dirt; refuse;
v. to clean a **byre** or stable;
~ **the line** clear putrid bait
from fishing line; **~-barra**
n. manure barrow; **~it** *adj.*
dirty. *cf.* **fool**

muckle *adj.* large; *n., adv.*
much; **~-boukit** *adj.*
pregnant (B1); burly; bulky

muddim *n.* madam

mudgeon *n.* facial expression;
he gied nae ~s he heard (M2)
no indication that he heard

mudge *v.* budge

muggl|e *v.* drizzle; **~y** *adj.*
drizzly and foggy (B)

muir *n.* moor; **~-cock** *n.* moor-
cock; **~lan** *n.* moorland.
cf. **meer**

muldoan, muldoon *n.* the
basking shark (B)

mulfa *n.* tinful (deriv. from **mill** a tin) (R)

mull *n.* meal- or threshing-mill; snuff-box; tin box with a lid; ~ **coorse** circular path trodden by horses driving a threshing mill (A1); ~ **sheels** mill sails; **snuff** ~ snuff box; ~**art**, ~**er(t)** *n.* miller; ~**art's wird** *n.* supposed secret password among millers

multiteed *n.* multitude

mum, mummle *v.* mumble

mump *v.* grumble

muncey *n.* mess; **mak a** ~ **o't** (M3)

mune *n.* moon; ~**licht** *n.* moonlight. *cf.* **meen**

munsie *n.* the knave in cards; someone in a fix (B1); contemptible figure (A2)

munt *v.* mount

muntin *n.* mountain

murgeon, murjin *n.* grimace; gesture. *cf.* **mudgeon**

murl|e *v.* crumble; ~**y** *adj.* crumbly; ~**y tuck** oatcakes crumbled into milk

murlin *n.* basket fitting into top of the fish-wife's creel

murn *v.* mourn; ~**er** *n.* mourner; ~**ins** *n. pl.* mourning clothes

musaeum *n.* museum

mutch *n.* woman's cap

mutchkin *n.* liquid measure equal to English pint

muther *n., v.* murder

muv *v.* move (B1). *cf.* **meeve**

myaakin *n.* hare (G). *cf.* **mawkin**

myaave *n.* seagull (Fraserburgh) (B)

myn *n., v.* mind; **weel** ~**t** *phr.* well-intentioned

myn *v.* remember

myowte *n.* sound; whisper; murmur

N

na *adj., adv.* no. *Also used to turn verb neg. eg,* **cudna, camna**

naarhan *adv.* nearly. *cf.* **nearhan**

nab *v.* seize; steal; take into custody

nabal *See* **nabble**

nabble *n.* churlish person; *adj.* ill-natured, churlish; grasping

nace *adj.* destitute

nackety *adj.* neat; *n.* a neat person

nacky *adj.* dexterous, adroit, skilful; ingenious

nae *adj.* no, not; ~**body**, ~**een** *pron.* no one; ~ **weel** not well, ill; ~**gait** *adv.* nowhere; ~**handy** *pred. adj., adv.* a lot

of; of great size; **there wis
cyaaks ~handy, a queue
~handy; ~thing** *n.* nothing;
~wye *adv.* nowhere; on no
account (s)
naet *adj.* neat
naether *conj., pron., adj.*
neither. *cf.* **nether, naither**
naftie, naphtie *n.* liquor (from
Eng. naphtha)
naider *conj., pron., adj.*
neither (M3). *cf.* **naither**
naig *n.* nag. *cf.* **nyag**
nain *adj.* own; **haud yir ~**
hold your own; **yir ~sel**
one's own self
nairra *adj.* narrow; **~-myn(d)it**
adj. narrow-minded
naisty *adj.* nasty
naith *prep.* below, beneath.
cf. **ablo, aneth; ~most** *adj.*
lowest; **~most wynin** lowest
part of field (F)
naither *conj., pron., adj.*
neither. *cf.* **nether, naether**
naitional *adj.* national
nait|ur *n.* nature; **~ur-girss** *n.*
natural herbage; **~ral** *adj.*
natural. *cf.* **natur**
nakit *adj.* naked. *cf.* **nyaukit**
nammle *adj.* enamel (B)
nane *adv., pron.* none
napkin, naipkin *n.* pocket
handkerchief
napper *n.* head
napron *n.* apron (B1)

nar *adj., adv.* near(ly);
mean (B1)
na-say *n.* denial; refusal;
v. deny, refuse
natheless *adv.* nevertheless
natur, Natur *n.* Nature.
cf. **naitur**
navus-bore *n.* knot-hole in
wood
near *adj.* mean, stingy;
~-beg(y)aun *adj.* miserly;
~-beg(y)aunness *n.*
niggardliness
nearhan *adv.* nearly; close by.
cf. **naarhan**
neb *n.* beak; nose
necessar *adj.* necessary
nedder, nedderin *pron., conj.*
neither; *adj.* lower
neebour *See* **neiper**
Neebra *pr. n.* village of
Newburgh near Ellon
need-a *v.* need to
needcessity *n.* necessity, need
needsna *v. neg.* does not need
neen *pron.* none; *adv.* at all
eg, **nae ~ pleased**
neep *n.* turnip; *v.* to feed
turnips **~-click** *n.* tool
for pulling turnips (F);
~-hasher *n.* implement for
slicing turnips for fodder;
~-heid *n.* fool; **~(ie)-lantrin**
n. turnip-lantern; **~-pluck**
n. tool for pulling turnips
(F); **~-reet** *n.* land cleared

of turnips for grain crop
to follow (F); **~-rinner**
n. old fashioned implement
for hoeing turnips;
~-rinnin *n.* turnip-hoeing;
~ watch *n.* turnip watch

neeper *See* **neiper**

ne'er *adv.* never

neer-dee-weel *n.* ne'er-do-well

neest, neesht *adj.* next.
cf. **neist**

neeze *v.* sneeze

neffy *n.* nephew

negleat *v.* neglect (B1)

negleck *v.* neglect. *cf.* **negleat**

neibour *See* **neiper**

neibourheid *n.* neighbour-
liness

neiper, neipor *n.*, *v.*
neighbour. *cf.* **neebour,
neibour, neeper**

neiper-like *adj.* neighbourly

neist *adj.* next. *cf.* **neest**

neive *n.* fist; **~fu** fistful;
steekit ~s clenched fists.
cf. **nieve, niv**

nemkin *n.* handkerchief;
napkin (M3)

nep *adj.* hairy (B)

nepkin *n.* napkin

nerra *adj. See* **nairra**

nervish *adj.* nervous

nether *conj.*, *pron.*, *adj.* neither;
adj. lower. *cf.* **naither**

nettercap *n.* spider. *cf.* **ettercap**

neuk *n.* corner

neukit *adj.* having corners,
crooked

new *adv.* newly

new-fungelt *adj.* newfangled

newlans, -lins *adv.* newly,
recently

news(e). *n*, *v.* chat

news-gizzent *adj.* news-starved

newsy *adj.* chatty; full of news

nib *n.* nose, beak. *cf.* **neb,
niz, nob**

nibawa *adj.* snappy, crusty

nicher *n.* (of horses) neigh,
whinny

nicht *n.* night; **~-boun** *adj.*
overtaken by night;
~-mutch nightcap

nick *n.* notch; *v.* make
pregnant (B). *cf.* **bairn**

Nick, Aul *pr. n.* the Devil

nicket *adj.* disappointed

nickum *n.* mischievous boy

Nicky Cloots *pr. n.* the Devil

nicky-tams *n. pl.* buckled
leather straps worn below
the knee by farmworkers.
cf. **waal-tams**

niddert *ppl.* subject to cold,
hunger

niddry *adj.* shimmering

niev(e) *n.* fist. *cf.* **neive**

niffer *n.* deal; *v.* to barter,
bargain; exchange

nimp *n.* a very small part

nineteen *n.* 19-year period of land lease

nip *n.* advantage in bargaining; **get a ~ o some een** steal a march on; speed; *v.* snatch; **deil a ~** not a bit (M2)

nippit *adj.* tight-fitting; curt in manner, testy; **~-like** *adv.* testily

nippock(ie) *n.* very small piece

nirl *v.* cause to shrink or shrivel; **~t** *ppl.* shrivelled (G)

niv *See* **neive**

niver, nivver *adv.* never; **~ een!** *excl.* not likely! (B)

niz *n.* nose (A). *cf.* **nib, nob**

nizzer *n.* serious situation; blow; facer

nizzin *n.* drubbing; sharp reception; exposure to the weather

no *adv.* not (C1, G1, K, S). *cf.* **nae**; (*used as interrogative after positive statement*) isn't he, hasn't it etc (A2)

nob *n.* nose (A). *cf.* **nib, niz**

nocht *n.* nought, nothing

nochtie *n.* puny in size. *cf.* **noughtie**

noddle *n.* head

nominat *ppl.* nominated

non *n.* name given in mid 18th C. to non-intrusion section of the Church of Scotland

noo *adv.* now; **~ an than** now and then; also **~ an aan, ~s an aans** (T); **~adays** *adv.* nowadays

nor *conj., quasi-prep.* than

norlan *adj.* northern

Noroway *pr. n.* Norway

noshun *n.* notion, idea; **~ o** romantic fancy for; liking for

nosy-wax *n.* simpleton (B1)

not, nott *v. pt., ppls.* needing, needed; had to; **~na** did not need

noth *n.* nothing. *cf.* **naething**

notice *v.* take care of (A1)

notion *n.* high opinion; **~ate** *adj.* opinionative

noughtie *adj.* puny, trifling. *cf.* **nochtie**

nown *adj.* own

nowt *n.* (collective) neat, cattle; (*sing.*) an ox, steer (A1)

nummer *n.* number

nyag *n.* nag (horse). *cf.* **naig**

nyaakit *adj.* naked. *cf.* **nyaukit**

nyatter *v.* speak fretfully, angrily; grumble (A, M1)

nyattery *adj.* peevish, grumbling, ill-tempered

nyaukit *adj.* naked. *cf.* **nyaakit**

nyod *excl.* euphemism for God

nyow(e) *adj.* new

O

o, o' *prep.* of; on; ~ **the sly**
on the sly; ~ **the tae han,**
~ **the tither** on the one
hand, on the other

obaidient *adj.* obedient

objeck *n.* object; creature
diseased or deformed;
v. object

obleege *v.* oblige

occupee *v.* occupy

och *excl.* oh

ocht *n.* aught, anything;
v. ought; ~**na** ought not

od *excl.* God

odder *adj., n., pron.* other.
cf. **ither**

odds *n.* difference

oe *n.* grandchild (M). *cf.* **oy**

o'er *prep.* over; *adv.* across;
too much. *cf.* **ower**

o'ercome *n.* burden of a
discourse

o'erleuk *v.* overlook

o'ertak *v.* overtake

offeecial, offeeshal *adj.* official

offeeshyat *v.* officiate

offen *v.* offend

offisher *n.* officer; policeman

oilie *n.* fisherman's oilskin
frock, made from oiled
canvas now replaced by
plastic (B); oil lamp.

'oman *n.* woman. *cf.* **umman**

on- *neg. particle used with*
pr. and pt. ppl. without
eg ~-**been** without having
been; ~-**deen** without
doing; ~-**hed** without
having; ~-**leet** without a lie;
~-**taal somebody** without
telling anybody

on- *prefix* un- (C); ~**speshifiet**
adj. unspecified; ~**streekit**
ppl. adj. not stretched out
(after death). See **oon-**

on *prep.* ~ **aboot** talking about;
~ **for** keen on; in the mood
for; **far** ~, **weel** ~ tipsy; ~ **o**
on to

on-cairry(ins) *n. (pl.)* carry-
on, carryings-on

ondeemas *adj.* extraordinary

onding *n.* a heavy fall of rain
or snow

ong(y)aun) *n.* activity; *in pl.*
proceedings, goings-on

ontill *conj.* till; *prep.* on to

onwal *adj.* annual

ony *adv., pron.* any;
adv. at all; ~**body**
n., pron. anybody; ~**een**
n., pron. anyone; ~**gait,**
~**road** *adv.* anyway; ~**thing**
n., pron. anything; ~**wye**
adv. anyway; anywhere;
anyhow; **gin it's** ~ **weet** if
it's wet at all

oo *n.* wool; ~ ruskie basket
for wool
oof *n.* Moray Firth name for
the monkfish. *cf.* **caithick**
ooie *adj.* woolly
ook, ouk *n.* week
ool *v.* treat harshly; ~t *pt. ppl.*
oolet *n.* owl (A). *cf.* **hoolet**
oonbapteest *adj.* unbaptised
ooncanny *adj.* uncanny;
dangerous
ooncarin *adj.* uncaring
oonchancie *adj.* uncanny;
risky, not safe to meddle
with
ooncommon *adj.* uncommon
oonder *prep.* under. *cf.* **ooner**
oondergrun *adj., adv.*
underground
oondevallin *adj.* unceasing
oondisjeestit *adj.* undigested
oondootitly *adv.* undoubtedly
oonendin *adj.* unending
ooner *prep.* under. *cf.* **oonder**
oonerstan *v.* understand
oonertakin *n.* undertaking
oonexpeckit *adj.* unexpected
oonfashed *adj.* untroubled
oonfeelin *adj.* unfeeling
oonfersell *adj.* lacking energy
oongrutten *adj.* not wept over
oonhandy *adj.* unhandy
oonhappy *adj.* unhappy
oonheedin *adj.* unheeding
oonhonesty *n.* dishonesty

oonjustice *n.* injustice
oonkent *adj.* unknown
oonlawfu *adj.* unlawful
oonless *conj.* unless
oonmynit o *adj.* unmindful of
oonnaitral *adj.* unnatural;
supernatural
oonpossible *adj.* impossible
oonprenciplt *adj.* unprincipled
oonrichteous *adj.* unrighteous
oonrizzonable *adj.* unreasonable
oonslockened *adj.* unquenched
oonstable *adj.* unstable
oontill *conj.* till
oontirin *adj.* untiring
oonwashen *ppl., adj.* unwashed
oonweel *adj.* unwell
oonwullin *adj.* unwilling
oonwuttin *adj.* unaware,
unwitting
oopie stiff(ie) *excl.* (on lifting
a heavy weight)
oor *n.* hour; *adj.* our
oorie *adj.* eerie; dismal
oorlich *adj.* (of people)
miserable-looking from
cold, hunger etc; (of
weather) dull and cold;
melancholy; *n.* starved-
looking, stunted person
oorly *adv.* hourly
oors *pron.* ours
oorsels *pron.* ourselves; *pred.*
adj., adv. by ourselves, alone

oot *adv., prep.* out; ~ **amint**
adv. out of things;
~ **amon** *prep.* out of; **~-by**
adv. outside; out in the
fields; out and a little way
off; **~bye fae** *prep.* away
from; ~ **the door** facing
ruin; ~ **o han** beyond
control; **~ower, ~owre** *prep.*
out and over; out of; *eg,*
~ower the cairt; ~ **wi** out
of favour with; **~-win** wind
off the sea; ~ **o yir box**
painting the town (B)
ootbrak *n.* outbreak
oot-by *adj.* out of the way;
distant
oot-cry *v.* protest
ootdang *v. pt.* outdid
ootding *v.* outdo
ootfeedle *n.* outfield
ootgang *n.* outgoing,
departure *eg,* from a
tenancy at end of season
oothoose *n.* outhouse
ootin *n.* outing
ootlat *n.* outlet; expression
ootlay, ootlie *n.* outlay
ootlin *n.* stranger; outcast
ootmaist *adj.* outmost
oots-an-ins *n. pl.* hairpins
oot wi *v.* take out *eg,* **he**
oots wi

ootwith, -wuth *adj., adv.*
outward; *adv.* outwardly,
fully
opeenion *n.* opinion
opingan *n.* opinion
or *conj., prep.,* before; until
ordeen *v.* ordain
ordinar *adj.* ordinary
orpi(e)t *adj.* peevish,
querulous (A2)
orra *adj.* odd; idle,
worthless; shabby; coarse;
~-beaster *n.* the man who
worked the odd horse on
a farm (T); ~ **loon** boy
who did odd jobs on farm;
~ls *n.* anything left over,
refuse; ~ **man** man who did
odd jobs on farm; wire-
tightning lever (F); ~ **wark**
odd jobs
ou *excl.* oh
ouk *n.* week; **this day** ~ a
week today. *cf.* **ook**
ousel *n.* blackbird (M)
outdang *v. pt.* outdid (K)
outding *v. pr.* outdo (K)
outer *n.* one who goes out
socialising
overly *adj.* incidental
ow awa *excl.* of sympathy
owdience *n.* audience
ower, owre *adv., prep.* over;
across; *adv.* too much;
~ **the heids o** because of;

~ **e watter,** ~ **e road** in jail
(Craiginches, Abdn.)

owercassen *adj.* (of weather)
overcast

owercome *n.* a frequently
repeated phrase or chorus,
burden or message

owercowp *v.* spill out

owergaan *n.* severe reproof;
close examination (B)

owergae *n.* dressing-down;
v. go over; pass (through or
over); exceed *eg*, (of horse
in foal) **she canna ~ an
ouk or twa** (A2)

owergeen *adv.* (of time) past

owerhead *adv.* for the most
part

owerheid *adj., adv.* overhead

owerlay *v.* overlay, cover over

owernicht *adv.* overnight

owersman *n.* person with
authority over others

owerturn *n.* turnover

own *v.* admit; ~ **baet** admit
defeat (A1)

owse *n.* ox; *pl.* **owsen**

owsen-bow *See* **bow** 2.

owthereese *v.* authorise

oxter *n.* armpit; bosom;
v. embrace; **~fu, ~lift** *n.*
armful; **~-pooch** *n.* inside
pocket; **~-staff, -stav**
n. crutch

oy *n.* grandchild (K). *cf.* **oe.**

P

paal *n.* mooring post or
bollard; *v.* puzzle. *cf.* **paul**

paamer (aboot) *v.* wander
(about)

paans *n. pl.* afterbirth of premature child

paap *n.* breast, pap

Paapist *n.* Papist

paavie *n.* frenzy, panic (M3)

Pace *See* **Pase**

pack *adj.* intimate

pack-merchants *n. pl.* small
scudding clouds

paewae *adj.* sickly, unwell (T)

pailace *n.* palace

pair, pairie *n.* pair of horse

pairis *n.* parish

pairl *n.* pearl

pairt *n.* part; *v.* part; divide;
~ oot *v.* share-out (S); **~in**
n. share-out; parting; *ppl.*
parting; **~-tak** *v.* side with;
defend; **~-teen, to be** *v.* to
have your part taken

pairtner *n.* partner

pairtrick *n.* partridge (M, C).
cf. **paitrick**

pairty *n.* party

paitrick *n.* partridge (S, M1).
cf. **pairtrick**

palaiver *n.* (of a person)
show-off; palaver (K)

palin *n.* paling, stake fence

pammer *v.* walk about aimlessly, saunter; stamp around noisily. *cf.* **paumer**

pandy *n.* smack, cane stroke on palm

pang *v.* cram; stuff full

pan loaf *adj.* loaf with hard crust; *fig.* affected way of speaking

pap *n.* teat; sea anemone

Pape *n.* the Pope

papen *v.* pamper

park *n.* field (A). *cf.* **fiedle**

parley *n.* period of truce in games, after the cry ~s-on

paroch *n.* parish

parochin(e) *n.* parish (K)

parritch *n.* porridge (J)

partan *n.* the common crab

parteeclar(ly) *adj., adv.* particular(ly)

Pase *n.* Easter; ~-ree wreath of snow at Easter (M3). *cf.* **Pess, Pesch**

pass *n.* passage

passin *prep.* after; more than

pastur *n.* pasture

pat *n.* pot; small ball of butter; *v. pt.* put; ~ tee put by, put aside

patcher *n.* turnip-seed sowing device (F)

Patie *pr. n. deriv. from* Peter

pattren *n.* pattern

paul *v.* baffle, puzzle

paut *v.* stamp (feet)

pawky *adj.* shrewd; sly

pawmie *n.* a stroke on the palm with a **tawse** or cane (J)

pawrent *n.* parent

pawtron *n.* patron; ~age *n.* patronage; ~ise *v.* patronise

peanny *n.* piano

peat *n.* peat; ~-backet *n.* peat-bucket; ~delf *n.* hole peat has been dug from; ~-fog *n.* peat-moss; ~-hagg *n.* hole peat has been dug from

pech *v.* pant

peek *v.* cheep; complain; ~in-eevie discontented girl

peel *n.* pill; pool; *v.* skin; ~-an-aet tatties *n. pl.* potatoes boiled in their skins and peeled just before eating; *adj.* even, at level pegging *eg*, **aat's us peel**

peelie-wally *adj.* sickly

peelin *n.* skin; thrashing

peen *n.* pane of glass

peenge *v.* complain, whine

peenie *n.* pinafore

peeny *n.* peony (rose)

peer *adj.* poor. *cf.* **puir;** ~(s)hoose *n.* workhouse

peerie *n.* spinning top

peerman *n.* holder for fir candle

peer-man *n.* wire-tightening lever in fencing (F)

peer wi *v.* match, equal

peesie(weep) *n.* lapwing (s).
cf. **pee-weet**

peetrol *n.* petrol

peet|y *n., v.* pity; ~ifu *adj.*
pitiful

pee-weet *n.* lapwing (M, R).
cf. **peesie**

pelt *n.* trash, rubbish

peltin-pyock *n.* worthless rag

pend, pen(n) *n.* arch; arched
passageway or entry, esp.
one leading from the street
into a back court

penner *n.* penholder

pensy *adj.* (would be) stately

pent *n., v.* paint (rhymes with
hint)

peppen *v.* rear delicately

pepper *n.* paper; newspaper

perfit *adj.* perfect

perjink *adj.* precise; neat in
appearance; prim; fussy

perlyaag *n.* rubbish; mixture
of odds and ends, esp.
rubbishy food; goodies (B1)

pernickety *adj.* very
particular; over-fastidious

perswaad *v.* persuade

perteen *v.* pertain

pervoot *ppl., adj.* abandoned,
deserted. cf. **forhooiet**

Pesch (A1) *See* **Pase, Pess**

peshifie *v.* pacify (B1)

Pess *n.* Easter (M1). cf. **Pase**

pet, the *n.* pique; the huff

peter *in phr.* pit the ~ on bring
to a sudden stop, bring up
short

peuchert *adj.* adversely
affected by the heat

pey *n., v.* pay

peyed-thankless *adj.* ungrateful (B)

peymen *n.* payment

pheesic *n.* medicine. cf. **feesick**

philander *v.* caper

phizog *n.* face

physeeshun *n.* physician,
doctor

picher *n.* state of nervous
excitement (B1); *v.* fiddle,
mess

picht *n.* Pict; small person

pick *n.* small quantity; pitch;
as mark's ~ as dark as
pitch; ~-mirk *adj., n.* pitch-
dark; *v.* peck

picker *n.* lever for removing
staples

pickie *n.* a little bit

pickiesae *n.* hat similar to
deerstalker

pickthank *adj.* ungrateful.
cf. **pykethank**

picter, pictur *n.* picture

piece *n.* portable snack;
e ~ *phr.* apiece, each

pig(gie) *n.* pitcher; earthenware
jar; stone hot-water bottle

pike *n.* frost-nail. *See* **pyke**

pilget *n.* fight, struggle, plight: in a ~ wi pain (B1)

pilk *v.* pilfer

pilla *n.* pillow

pilpert *n.* cold, badly fed child (B1)

pin *n.* clothes peg

pin, pit in a *phr.* call a halt

pine *n.* pain. *cf.* **pyne**

piner *n.* animal that does not thrive

pink *v.* trickle

pint *n., v.* (near rhyme with *hint*) paint; *v.* (rhyming with Eng. *pint*) point; *n.* (rhyming with Eng. *pint*) shoe-lace. *cf.* **pynt**

pint stoup *n.* drinking vessel with a handle containing a Scots pint

pirk *v.* prick

pirl *v.* poke, stir; trifle; *intr.* ripple

pirn *n.* reel on which yarn or thread is wound; spinning top made from reel, with spindle through centre

pirn-taed *adj.* pigeon-toed

pirr *n.* sudden burst of activity; **on the ~** active

pirr o win *phr.* breeze; **~-winnie** *n.* breeze

pish *v.* urinate

pit *v.* put; *ppl.* ~**ten**; ~ **aff** *v.* postpone; ~ **past** *phr.* put away; ~**-on** *n.* affectation; ~, ~**ten oot** *phr.* put out, discomfited, worried (A1); ~ **aboot** *v.* to inconvenience

pitawtie *n.* potato (B1)

pit-black *adj.* dark as pitch

piz *n. pl.* peas; ~**-meal, ~zers** *n.* pease-meal

place *n.* laird's residence

placie *n.* place; small farm, croft

plack *n.* small coin (J)

plaid *n.* long piece of woollen cloth with chequered or tartan pattern, outer article of Highland dress, worn over the shoulder; also used as a blanket

plaik *n.* plaything (M1)

plaise *v.* please (S)

plaised *adj.* pleased (S, C1, G1) *cf.* **pleast**

plaister *n.* plaster

planesteens *n. pl.* pavement

plank *v.* place, lay

plantin *n.* plantation

plashie, plash fluke *n.* plaice

playackin *n.* acting

playgreen *n.* playground

playgrun *n.* playground

pleast *adj.* pleased. *cf.* **plaised**

pleece *n.* police

pleege *v.* plague (B1)

plees|ur(e) *n.* pleasure; **~int** *adj.* pleasant

pleiter *See* **plowter**

plenish *v.* furnish a house; stock a farm; ~ing *n. pl.* furnishings; deadstock

plett *n.* plate

pleuch *n.* plough (A, M1). *cf.* ploo

pleura *n.* pleuro-pneumonia

plicht *n.* plight

plisky *n.* mischievous trick; plight (B1)

plivver *n.* plover (A1)

plizzant *adj.* pleasant

ploiter *n., v. See* plowter; ~ o dubs *phr.* mess of mud

ploitery *adj.* wet; muddy

ploo *n.* plough; ~man *n.* ploughman; ~-feather *n.* projecting wing on the sock of a plough, which cuts out the furrow; ~-sock ploughshare; ~-stilts *n. pl.* plough handles

plook *n.* pimple; ~y *adj.* pimply

plot *v.* plunge into boiling water; scald; burn, scorch; ~tin *adj.* (of weather/ people) very hot

plowt *n.* blow, punch

plowter *v.* splash in mud or water, squelch; work messily; potter; *n.* the act of working or walking in mud or water. *cf.* pleiter, ploiter

ploy *n.* frolic, escapade

pluff *v.* shoot (peas) through a tube

pluffy *adj.* chubby; puffed up

plump-churn *n.* plunge churn (F)

plunsh *v.* plunge

plunk *n.* plank of wood

plunkie *n.* homemade sweetmeat made with treacle or syrup and flour (A2)

plyaak *n.* toy (A1, A2)

plyoo|ch *n.* plough (M3); ~man *n.* ploughman. *cf.* plooman

plype *n.* the sound of a splash; *v.* fall *plop* into water

plyper *v.* walk in mud or water

pob *n.* the refuse of flax

pock, poke *n.* bag. *cf.* powk, pyock; pocket (J). *cf.* pooch

poddick *n.* frog (G); P~-etter *pr. n.* Frenchman (M3). *cf.* puddock

points *n. pl.* shoe-laces. *cf.* pints

poleetics *n.* politics

politeeshun *n.* politician

pollis *n.* police (J)

pom-pom *n.* the Field Marshall diesel tractor, the nickname deriv. from sound of engine

pooch *n., v.* pocket

poochle *See* puchal

pooder *n.* powder; **lattin oot the ~** divulging the secret

pooer *n.* power; **~ o pot an gallows** the old feudal power to hang or drown (A2); **~fae** *adj.* powerful

pookie *n.* little bag

poond *n.* pound sterling (J). *cf.* **pund**

poopit *n.* pulpit

poor *v.* pour; **~in haill waater** *phr.* pouring rain

poortith *n.* poverty

pooshan, pooshin *n.*, *v.* poison; **~ous** *adj.* poisonous. *cf.* **pushion**

pooter *v.* walk backwards and forwards

poother *See* **pouther**

porritch *n. pl.* porridge (*takes pl. v.*) *cf.* **pottich**

port *n.* lively tune on the bagpipes

poseetion *n.* position

postie *n.* postman

pot *n.* pit; pool

potestatur *n.* prime

pot fit *n.* foot of a cauldron; **stick oot like a ~** stick out like a sore thumb

potterlow *n.* ruined condition; unsightly mess; **geen tae ~** gone to pot, spoiled

potti(t)ch *n. pl.* porridge (A1). **He made his ~ an suppit them.** *cf.* **porritch**

pottiestattur etc, *See* **potestatur**

pottit-heid *n.* dish made from head of ox or pig, boiled to a jelly

potty *n.* putty

pouch *n.* pocket. *cf.* **pooch**

poun *n.* pound sterling

pouther *n.* powder; **~-deevil** *n.* primitive home-made firework; **~y** *adj.* powdery

pow *n.* head, poll

powk *n.* bag; *cf.* **pock, poke**; *v.* poke

powser *n.* cat (O)

powsowdie *n.* sheep's head broth

powster *n.* posture; position, situation

practeese *v.* practise

praisent *n.* present

pran *v.* crush; hurt severely or fatally

preceese(ly) *adj.*, *adv.* precisely

precent *v.* lead the psalmody in a Presbyterian church

precunnance *n.* condition; footing; **on ony ~s** in any circumstances

pree *v.* taste; experience

preef *n.* proof. *cf.* **pruif**

preen *n.*, *v.* pin; **~-heidit** *adj.* pin-headed; unintelligent

preevacy *n.* privacy

preevilege *n.* privilege

prefairrance *n.* preference

prefar *v.* prefer

prejudeece *n.* prejudice

prence *n.* prince

prenciple *n.* principle

prent *n.*, *v.* print

press *n.* wall-cupboard

prick *v. intr.* (of cattle) to stampede to escape insect bites

pridefu *adj.* proud (J). *cf.* **prood**

prig *v.* plead

'Prile *n.* April; **~ eeran** April (fool's) errand

prile *n.* three cards of equal value, *eg*, **a ~ o queens**

primpit *adj.* prim (R)

prink *v.* make pretty; deck out; **~it oot/up** decked out

prizintor *n.* precentor, praise leader

prob *v.* to pierce, prod; release gas from stomach of cattle by piercing

prodeegious *adj.* prodigious

projeck *n.* project

pron *n.* residue of oat husks and oatmeal left over after the milling process, bran

prood *adj.* proud

prop *n.* ploughing marker (F); land mark or memorial

prophesiet *v. pt.* prophesied

proteck *v.* protect

prot(t)ick *n.* rash or idle adventure; bit of mischief; scheme; trick

protty *adj.* pretty; **a ~ penny**

proveesions *n. pl.* provisions

providin *n.* bride's trousseau

pruif *n.* proof. *cf.* **preef**

pruv, pruve *v.* prove

pu *v.* to pull

puchal, puchil *adj.* reserved, proud; self-important (A2). *cf.* **poochle**

puckle *n.* a small quantity, some

puddick *See* **puddock**

puddins *n. pl.* innards, intestines

puddle *v.* play with hands or feet in water

puddock *n.* 1. frog; **~'s eggs** *phr.* nickname for sago or tapioca pudding; **~-steel** *n.* toadstool; **~ crood**; frogspawn; 2. flat, wooden platform for transporting heavy loads on farms *cf.* **puddick, poddick**

puggled *ppl.* worn out

puir *adj.*, *n.* poor. *cf.* **peer**

puke *v.* vomit (B1)

pule *n.* seagull (Gardenstown) (B)

pul-throwe *n.* cord with which cleaning rag is pulled through rifle

pultice *n.* poultice

pump *v.* break wind anally

pumphel *n.* pen for cattle; square church pew

pun, pund *n.* pound (in weight)

punctwal *adj.* punctual

purchase *n.* a hold or grip

purpie *adj.* purple

purvoy *v.* abandon, drop (an aquaintance)

pushion *See* **pooshan**

putt *v.* push, shove; **ae ~ an row** a hard struggle

putten *ppl.* put; sent

pye *n.* magpie; a counting-out rhyme in children's games and the serving of food *eg*, **say a ~**

pye-wae *adj.* sickly

pyk|e *n.* 1. spike (of a railing); **~it** *ppl.* spiked; **~it weer** *phr.* barbed wire (F). *cf.* **barbit-weer.** 2. pique; **tak a ~ at** be piqued at; *v.* pick; steal; **~ their pooch** cost them a lot. *cf.* **pike**

pykethank *See* **pickthank** *adj.* meagre-looking

pykit *adj.* meagre-looking

pyne *n.* pain. *cf.* **pine**

pyner *n.* animal suffering pain (M2)

pyocher *n.* troublesome cough; *v.* to clear the throat

pyock *See* **poke** etc

pyooch *v.* cough

pyot *n.* magpie. *cf.* **pye**

pyowter *n.* pewter

pyshon *See* **pooshan**

Q

quaet *adj.* quiet. *cf.* **quait**

quaetly *adv.* quietly

quaetness *n.* quietness, peace

quaich *n.* drinking cup with two handles

quaikin-aish *n.* aspen

quairt *See* **quait**

quait *adj.* quiet. *cf.* **quaet**

quake, quaik *n.* heifer

quarterer *n.* tramp with quarters on farm in exchange for work (F)

quat *v.* quit; stop what one is doing

queed *n.* cud; **chaw the ~** chew the cud

queeger *n.* mess, muddle; mixture

queel *adj., v.* cool

Queenie arabs *n. pl.* inhabitants of the Queenie (Keith Inch) in Peterhead (B)

queet *n.* ankle

queetikins *n.* gaiters. *cf.* **cuitikins**

quern *n.* stone hand-mill

queyn *See* **quine**

queyston *n.* question (M3).
cf. **quisson**

quig *n.* mix up

quigger *n.* mess, muddle;
mixture

quile *n.* coal; burning coal.
cf. **kwile**

quin|e *n.* girl; ~**ockie** *n.* little
girl

quinkins *n. pl.* dregs;
something of no value

quirky *adj.* tricky

quisson *n.* question

quite *See* **quyte**

quivvy, o the *phr.* all of a
quiver

quo *v.* quoth

quyte *n.* coat; petticoat.
cf. **kwite**

R

raa *adj.* raw; *n.* row

raan *n.* fish roe

rack *n.* mist (K)

rackle *n.* chain of tin pipe-lid

rackon *v.* reckon

rade *v. pt.* rode. *See also* **redd**

radge *n.* term of abuse for a
man (Abdn., *poss. corr.* of
vratch)

rael *adj., adv.* real; really

raelly *adv.* really

raeper *n.* reaper; **tiltin-~**
reaping-machine, requiring
a man to knock off the
sheaves with a rake

raff *n.* riff-raff

raffy *adj.* plentiful (M); *n.* a
rank growth (A1)

raggit, raggity *adj.* ragged;
~ **robin** *n.* (flower) lychnis
floscuculi

ragi|e *adj.* raging; scolding;
n. rage; ~**n** *n.* scolding

raiffle *See* **reffle**

raik *v.* to rake; roam about;
reck, care; **fat ~s?** what
does it signify? (A2).
cf. **rake**

raikins *See* **rakins**

raip *n.* rope. *cf.* **rape**

rair *v.* roar

raise *v. tr.* excite, infuriate,
madden; ~ **din** make
trouble; ~ **him wull** drive
him crazy;

raist *adj.* excited, angry

raise *v. pt. intr.* (of rise) got
up;

raise-o-the-win *n.* a stroke of
good luck (T)

raith *n.* quarter of a year;
term at school

raither *adv.* rather. *cf.* **redder**

raivel *v.* entangle; wander
in speech; ~**t** *adj.* tangled;

mentally confused; ~t roast
confused situation (M3)

raiverie *n.* rumour (M2)

rake *n.* great energy; cam mair
~ worked faster, with more
energy; *v.* range, roam,
wander; stray; search.
cf. raik

rakins *n.* gathering of loose hay
or strands of corn which
escape the reaping-machine

rally (on) *v.* scold; speak
angrily to

rammack *n.* rough piece of
wood; worthless article

rammy *n.* uproar

rampauge *n.* fury, rage; *v.* to
rage

ramsh *adj.* hasty, rash;
foul, rank; sour to taste

ramshackle *adj.* disorderly;
unmethodical; thoughtless;
headstrong

ranagant *n.* wild, loose-living
person (B1); good-for-
nothing

ran-dan *n.* carouse; rumpus
(A); oot on the ~

randy *n.* virago; loose-
tongued woman; loose
woman/person

ranegill *adj.* renegade; rough
character; criminal

rank *v.* get ready, esp. dress to
go out; ~ oot *v.* bring out,
look out in preparation

rant *n.* lively tune

ranter *v.* mend, stitch; put
together

rantletree *n.* the beam across
the chimney from which
the crook is suspended

rantree *n.* mountain ash.
cf. rowan

rap, gang *v.* knock on or at

rape *n.* rope, esp. of straw.
cf. raip

rare *adj.* excellent

rase *v. pt.* rose. *cf.* raise

rash *n.* rush; as stracht's a ~ as
straight as a ramrod

rassor *n.* razor

rattle *n.* sound made by pro-
nouncing the letter r in the
throat

rauchle *adj.* noisy, clamorous

rave *v. pt.* tore. *cf.* rive

raw *adj.* raw; *n.* row

rawn-tree *n.* mountain ash.
cf. rowan, rodden, rantree

rax *v.* stretch; hand;
~ ower hand over

readin-sweetie *n. pl.*
conversation lozenge

ream *n.* cream; *v.* foam; buzz
(of thoughts); overflow;
~ ower overflow; ~in fu
brimming

rebat *v.* retort; speak again;

speak back

reca *v.* recall

recaipt *n.* recipe

reck *v.* to take heed of

recreet *v.* recuperate

redd *adj.*, *adv.* read(il)y, willing(ly): **as ~ wirk as nae;** *v.* clear out, to rid; **~ up** *v.* tidy up; (a person) criticise; **~ yir thrapple** clear your throat; **~ yir crap** get something off your chest; *ppl.*, *adj.* rid; **win ~ o** get rid of; **like tae ~ fire** in haste; **~ance** *n.* riddance

redd *v. pt.* rode (M3). *cf.* **rade**

redder *adv.* rather. *cf.* **raither**

rede *v.* advise (J)

red-lan *n.* ploughed land

red-wud *adj.* raging mad (K)

ree *n.* enclosure; hen run

reed *adj.* red; **~~-het** *adj.* red-hot *cf.* **reid**; *n.* rood by measurement

reef; *n.* roof; **~ a ditch** roof a ditch, vacate your home with no other to go to (T)

reek *n.*, *v.* smoke. *cf.* **rik** **~-bouk** *n.* belch of smoke (R); **~-hen** *n.* a hen exacted for every smoking chimney or inhabited house

reel, oot o *phr.* out of sorts; in disorder

reem *n.* cream. *cf.* **ream**

reemis(h) *n.* resounding crash, din; *v.* move with such a sound; rummage; **~in** *vb.* *n.* uproar; clatter

reenge *v.* range, roam

reerie *n.* row; **kick up a ~** create a rumpus

reesle, reeshsle *v.* rustle; hustle noisily

reest *n.* roost; *v.* distrain for debt; *v. intr.* roost; sit; refuse to move; *v. tr.* arrest; bring to a halt; **~ the fire** bank up the fire. *cf.* **reist**

reet *n.* root; **the ~ an the rise o't** beginning and end of it, the whole story, affair; **~ an crap** through and through, completely

reetch *v.* retch. *cf.* **kowk**

reeve *v. pt.* tore. *cf.* **rive**

reevin *adj.* (of wind) high, strong; (of fire) burning brightly

reeze *v.* praise; *n.* high praise

refar *v.* refer

refeese *v.* refuse

reffle *v.* ransack

regaird *n.*, *v.* regard

reglar *adj.* regular

reid *adj.* red; **a ~ een** a new net (B); **~ fish** the salmon (this being a taboo word at sea); **~-biddy** *n.* mixture of cheap red wine and methylated spirit or other alcohol; ~-**cheekit** *adj.* red-cheeked; ~-**heidit** *adj.* red-headed; ~-**het** *adj.* red hot; ~-**kaimed** *adj.* red-combed; ~-**wud** *adj.* mad; harum-scarum. *cf.* **reed**

reist *v.* roost; sit; bank up a fire. *cf.* **reest**

reistin *adj.* restive

reive *v.* to plunder; ~**r** *n.* plunderer; thief. *cf.* **riever**

releegio|n *n.* religion; ~**us** *adj.* religious

remeid *n.* remedy

remis *See* **reemis**

remorse *v.* express regret about; repent (A2)

remuv *v.* remove

repoort *n., v.* report

repree *v.* reprove

requar, requair *v.* require

residenter *n.* resident

respeck *n., v.* respect

retour *n.* a renewal, replacement

reuch *adj.* rough (J). *cf.* **roch**

revarse *n.* *r*everse

reverie (B1) *See* **raiverie**

reyn *n.* rain. *cf.* **ryne**

rheumatics, the *n.* rheumatism

ribbet *n.* rabbit (S). *cf.* **rubbit**

richt *adj., n., v.* right; ~**it** righted

richteous *adj.* righteous

rickle *n.* loose heap or stack (*eg*, of peats set up to dry)

rickmatick *n.* concern, affair; collection

riddel *n.* sieve

rideeclous *adj.* ridiculous

riever *n.* thief

rift *n., v.* belch

rig *n.* ridge; space between furrows; section of a field; practical joke; frolic; **play a ~** play a trick; *v.* dress; ~-**oot** *n.* outfit; ~ **oot** *v.* prepare (a ship for the fishing season) (B); ~**git-oot** *ppl., adj.* all set; equipped (S)

riggin *n.* ridge, roof; head, skull; ~ **crap** *n.* rooftop; ~ **o the nicht** middle of the night

rig-lamb *n.* male lamb with only one descended testicle (T)

riglin *n. as above*

rik *n.* smoke. *cf.* **reek**

rime *n.* hoar-frost

rim-rax *n.* a good feed (B1)

rin *v.* run; (of a cow) be in heat (F); ~-**awa** *adj.* runny; ~-**oot** *n.* urination; ~-**the-wuddie** *n.* fugitive from the gallows; ~-**watter** *n.* natural flow of water, esp. one which will drive a mill-wheel without a dam; *fig.* just enough money to pay one's way

rine *n.* rein. *cf.* **ryne**
ring *v.* surround
ring in *v.* give up, yield
ringel-een *n.* wall-eyes
ringle *n.* wallop
ringum-tringum *adv.*
  higgledy-piggledy
rink *v.* clamber; range about
  noisily; ransack, rummage.
  cf. **rank**
rinnins *n.* main outlines
rint *n.* rent
ripp *n.* a handful of
  unthreshed corn or hay
ripper *n.* hand-line for
  catching cod; **~-yole** *n.* yawl
  used for ripper-fishing
rippit *n.* uproar (M, B1)
rise *n.* joke at someone's
  expense; **hae a ~ oot o, tak
  the ~ o** play a trick on
risp *v.* rasp
rist *n., v.* rest; *v.* make up fire
  for the night; **~less** *adj.*
  restless
riv *n.* enclosure; chicken-
  run. *cf.* **ree, criv(e)**
riv|e *n.* tear; bite, large
  mouthful; gap, breach,
  hole; **faan i the ~** (A2);
  v. pull forcibly; burst
  asunder; tear; **hae a ~ aff**
  score off (someone);
  ~ven *ppl.* pulled apart; torn
rivin *adj.* grasping; *n.* romp (K)

rizzar *n.* redcurrant
rizzon *n., v.* reason; **~able**
  adj. reasonable
road *n.* way; **i the ~** in the
  way; **oot o the ~** out of the
  way; *v.* take the road; **~it**
  adv. on the road, on one's
  way; **get ~it** set off. *cf.* **rodd**
roasen, roassen *ppl.* roasted;
  adj. roasting hot
Robbie *pr. n., dim. of* Robert
robsorby *n.* a make of scythe,
  synonymous with the
  implement (T)
roch *adj.* rough; **~ an richt**
  phr. rough in manners;
  ~ian *n.* ruffian
rock *n.* distaff
rockin *n.* evening gathering
  of neighbours with rock
  and spindles; a spinning-
  bee (M)
rocky-on *n.* sea-shore game
  involving stone cairn (B)
rodd *n.* road, way; **fat ~** how;
  why
rodden *n.* mountain-ash (berry)
rodden-, roddin-tree *n.*
  mountain ash or rowan
rogie *n.* little rogue, term of
  endearment for a child
rone *n.* a slide
Room *pr. n.* Rome (A2)
room, the *n.* the best room in
  a small house

roon *adv., prep.* round; **~-shoodert**
  adj. round-shouldered
roos|e *n.* praise (O).
  cf. **reeze**; *v.* rouse (to
  anger); salt (*eg,* herring);
  ~in-tub *n.* tub in which
  herring were salted
rooser *n.* watering-can
Roos(h)ian *n.* rabbit (Russian)
roost *n., v.* rust; **~ty** *adj.* rusty.
  cf. **rousty**
rosit *n.* resin; **~ie** *adj.*
  resinous; **~ie eyn** resined
  thread used for sewing
  leather
rottack *n.* useless, discarded
  object; *pl.* lumber, junk
rottan *n.* rat
rounder *n.* an ungutted fish
roup *n., v.* auction; **~ oot**
  v. sell up by auction
roupit, roupy *adj.* hoarse
roust *v.* 1. roar, bellow (also
  of animals); 2. rust; **~in**
  adj. rusting; **~y** *adj.* rusty.
  cf. **roost, roosty**
rout *v.* roar, bellow. *cf.* **roust**
routh (o) *n.* plenty (of); *adj.*
  abundant. *cf.* **rowth**
rowe *v.* roll; wheel (a barrow)
rowie *n.* a morning roll
rowle *n., v.* rule; **~r** *n.* ruler
rowt *v.* (of cattle) bellow, roar
  (G1). *cf.* **rout, roust**
rowth (o) *n.* plenty (of).
  cf. **routh**

royd, roy(i)t *adj.* (of children)
  wild, unruly, capering
rozet *n.* resin; cobbler's wax.
  cf. **rosit**
rubbit *n.* rabbit
ruck *n.* rick, stack; **het ~**
  steaming stack built
  before crop has dried out;
  thackit ~ stack thatched
  for winter; **wattert ~** badly
  built and porous (T); **~-foon**
  n. stack foundation;
  ~-ledder *n.* stack ladder;
  ~-post *n.* wooden support
  for off-centre stack
rug *n.* high profit, bargain
  perhaps to the seller's dis-
  advantage (A1); tug; *v.* pull
  sharply, tug
rumigumshun (A1). *See below*
rum(mil)(mle)-gumption *n.*
  common sense (M1, M3)
rummle *v.* rumble; *ppl.*
  rummlin
rumple *n.* rump; rump-bone
runch *n.* wild radish (F)
rung *n.* heavy staff or stick
runk *n.* old, outworn animal;
  contemptuous term for a
  woman of ill repute
runklt *ppl., adj.* wrinkled.
  cf. **wrunklt**
runt *n.* cabbage or kail stalk;
  withered hag, *m.* or *f.*
runtit (o) *ppl., adj.* having
  lost all (as in the game

of marbles); completely
deprived of

ruskie *n.* straw basket;
beehive; strong person

ryne *n.* rein. *cf.* **rine**

rype *v.* ransack, rifle; steal

S

's *pron.* his; **aff o's maet** off
his food

sa, saa *v. pt.* saw, *neg.* ~**na**,
~**wna**

saabre *n.* sabre

saach *n.* willow. *cf.* **sauch**

saadist *n.* sawdust

saan *n.* sand. *cf.* **san**

saar *n.* savour; ~**less**
adj. taste-less, insipid.
cf. **saurless**

saatit an set by *phr.* (of a
single woman) on the shelf

sab *v.* sob

Sacrament the *n.* holy
communion

sad *v.* grow solid

sae *adv., conj.* so

sae-be *conj.* provided that, so
long as

saeven *adj.* seven; ~**ty** *adj.*
seventy. *cf.* **seyven**

saff *adj.* safe

saft *adj.* soft; weak; simple;
~**ie** *n.* weak(-minded)
person; slipper (G); ~**ness**
n. softness

saft(-like) *adj.* (of the
weather) damp, drizzly

saick *n.* sack; **a ~fu o sair
beens** *phr.* a hiding

saicret *n.* secret

saiddle *n.* saddle; ~**r** *n.* saddler.
cf. **seddle**

said-say *n.* hearsay

sailary *n.* salary

sain *v.* bless; make sign of
the Cross

saip *n.* soap

sair *adj.* sore; *n.* sore; ailment;
adv. 1. sorely, badly; ~ **aff**
badly off, hard up; ~ **awa
wi't** worn out; in a bad
state; ~ **come at** far gone,
worn out; ~ **dung** hard-
pressed; **a ~ fecht** hard
struggle; ~ **heid** headache;
~**-heidie** *n.* sponge-cake in
paper cup; ~ **hert** heavy
heart; ~ **made** hard pressed,
at a loss, desperate; ~ **on**
hard on (clothes etc);
~ **suited at** not pleased
with. 2. very much, greatly;
~ **maetit** well-fed (A1); ~**ly**
adv. badly

sair *v.* serve; satisfy (esp.
with food/drink) (M1);
satiate, sate (G); **weel-~t**
well satisfied with food or
drink; **ill-~t** not having had

enough; **sick ~t** satiated; **~t
her richt** served her right;
~in *n.* serving, helping;
deserts; fill; **she got her ~
o't.** *cf.* **ser**

sairgint *n.* sergeant

sairious *adj.* serious.
cf. **sarious**

Saiterday, Setturday
n. Saturday

saitisfie *v.* satisfy; *ppl.* **saitisfiet**

saiven *adj.* seven

sakeless *adj.* innocent

sal *See* **saul**

sall *v.* shall. *cf.* **saul**

salvenda (B1). *See* **solvendo**

same *n.* (pig)fat, lard.
cf. **semm**

samen *adj.* same

san *n.* sand; **san-gless** *n.*
hour-glass. *cf.* **saan**

sang *excl.* blood!

sang *n.* song

sanna *v. neg.* shall not

sanshach *adj.* saucy;
disdainful; irritable

sant *n.* saint; **~ifie** *v.* sanctify
~ly *adj.* saintly

sappy *adj.* moist, full of juice;
heavy in the water, laden
with fish (B); **~ sodjers** ball
game

saps *n.* bread with milk and
sugar

sarious *adj.* serious. *cf.* **sairious**

sark *n.* shirt; chemise; **~et, ~it**
n. undershirt; shirt or jersey

sate *n.* seat

satteral *adj.* stiff; tart

sattle *v.* settle

sauch *n.* willow tree. *cf.* **saugh**

sauchen *adj.* unsociable

saugh *n.* willow; **~-wans**
willow wands; **~y** *adj.*
abounding in willows.
cf. **saach**

saul *n.* soul; also used as *excl.*;
~less *adj.* soulless; wicked;
pt. ppl. sold

Sauners *pr. n.* Alexander

saurless *adj.* tasteless; spiritless

saut *n.* salt; **wirth ~ till his
kail** worth his salt;
~-backet *n.* salt-box; **~er**
n. salter; one who can
do difficult things; **~ie**
adj. tasting of salt;
~ie-bannocks *n.* oatmeal
pan cakes; **~-lick** *n.* salt
brick for cattle (T)

saw *n.* salve, ointment

saw *v.* sow (S); **~er** *n.* sower

Sawboth *n.* Sabbath

sawna *v. pt. neg.* did not see

Sawney *pr. n. deriv. of*
Alexander

Sawtan *pr. n.* Satan

sax *adj.* six; **~-pair toon**
farm with 6 pairs of horses;
~pence *n.* sixpence; **~teen**
adj. sixteen; **~ty** *adj.* sixty

say-awa *n.* discourse, narrative, monologue; *imp.* have your say

say wi *v.* agree with

scaa *n.* barnacle. *cf.* **scaw**

scaad *v.* scald

scaam *See* **scam**

scabbie *adj.* scabbed

scabbit *adj.* scabby; shabby

scadden *n.* person of spare figure; contemptuous term for person or thing

scaffy *n.* street-sweeper

scaith *n.* injury; damage

scaivy *v.* rush, scramble

scalder *n.* stinging jellyfish

scam *n., v.* singe, scorch; scald slightly. *cf.* **scaum**

scance *n.* a look; *v.* scan

scarecraw *n.* scarecrow

scart *n., v.* scratch (A). *cf.* **scrat**

scashle *n., v.* quarrel

scaul *n.* scolding; *v.* scold;

scaum *v.* singe, scorch, scald slightly. *cf.* **scam**

scaup *n.* land of thin, poor soil; bank of mud or soil exposed at low tide

scaur *adj.* timid; *n.* bare place on side of hill; cliff

scavie *n.* mishap (B1)

scaw *v.* fade; ~t *ppl.* faded. *cf.* **scaa**

scawm *See* **scaum**

schaim *n.* scheme

scholar *n.* school pupil

schule *n.* school (J)

scienteefic *adj.* scientific

sclaff *n., v.* stroke

sclaffert *n.* blow; a stroke with the palm of the hand; slap

sclairt (on) *v.* smear

sclait *n.* slate. *cf.* **sklate**

sclaive *See* **sclave**

sclap *v.* walk in flat-footed or shuffling way. *cf.* **sclaup**

sclarry *v.* daub, smear (J)

sclaup *See* **sclap**

sclave *n.* gossip, scandal-monger; *v.* spread a story by gossip

sclaver (M2). *See* **sclave** *v.*

sclim *v.* climb. *cf.* **clim**

sclinner *adj.* slender, slim

sclyter *v.* fall heavily, tumble

scob *v.* put in splints

scog *v.* hide; shelter

scomfice (K). *See* **scomfish**

scomfish *v.* suffocate (A1)

scone *n.* girdle baked cake of flour; *v.* beat with open hand; ~ **yir doke** *phr.* smack your bottom

scoof *n.* quick swig; *v.* swallow food or drink quickly. *cf.* **scowf**

scool *v.* scowl

scoon(e)ral *n.* scoundrel

scoor *n.* smack; wallop (*eg,* ower e heid); *v.* scour;

scamper; ~in-buird *n.*
scrubbing-board
scoosh *n., v.* squirt
scooshle *v.* shuffle
scoot *n.* term of contempt
applied to man or woman;
v. hurry off. *cf.* **scout**
scooth *n.* scope. *cf.* **scowth**
score, over the *phr.* beyond
what is reasonable
scorie-hornt *adj.* calloused (G)
scouf *See* **scoof**
scoug *n.* shelter; pretence, ruse
scouk *n.* evil look; scowl;
v. scowl, skulk. *cf.* **skook**
scoukin *adj.* furtive; sullen
scout *v.* hurry off. *See* **scoot**
scouth *n.* freedom of movement,
elbow-room, scope
scouth-an-routh *phr.* freedom
to range and plenty of food
scowff *v.* scoff at, mock (R)
scowth *n.* freedom to move;
scope. *cf.* **scouth, scooth**
scraich *n., v.* shreik
scran *n.* food, victuals;
v. scavenge for; ~ner *n.* one
who scavenges
scrat *n.* shallow furrow;
scratch; *v.* scratch (M).
cf. **scart**
scrath *n.* cormorant
scrauch *n., v.* screech
screed *n.* long piece of writing
screef, screeth *n.* surface of
water

screeve *n.* a large scratch;
v. scratch, scrape
screeve, screive, scrive *v.* write
screid *See* **screed**
scrie *v.* cry; proclaim; ~s-buird
n. church announcement
board
scriff(an) *n.* membrane,
film, thin cover, surface.
cf. **striffin**
scrimp o *phr.* short of
scrimpit *ppl.* straitened;
pinched
scrog *n.* stunted bush; term of
abuse
scronach *n.* shrill cry; fuss,
outcry (A2); ~in *n.* fuss
scroo *n.* small rick of corn
or hay. *cf.* **hooick**
scrow *n.* rain shower
scruff *n.* riff-raff
scrunt *adj.* stunted; *n.* anything
stunted in growth
scry *v.* cry; proclaim, advertise
scryach *v.* screech
scryaap *v.* scrape
scud *n.* skin; **scud, the** *n.* slap
with a **tawse** on the open
hand
scuddl|e *v.* mess about at
domestic work; ~in claes
second-best clothes
scuddy *adj.* niggardly
scudge *n.* kitchen drudge;
v. do rough, menial work.
cf. **skudge**

scudlert *n.* maid of all work. *cf.* **scudge**

scuff *v.* touch lightly in passing

scuff o rain *n.* sudden, passing shower

scull, skull *n.* shallow wicker basket. *cf.* **skull**

scum *v.* skim; **scummin(s)** anything skimmed

scumfish *v.* suffocate. *cf.* **scomfish**

scunfice *v.* smother. *cf.* **scomfice**

scunge *v.* scour (M3)

scunner *n., v.* disgust; **~t o** or **wi** *ppl., adj.* disgusted; bored, fed up, sick of; **tae tak a ~ till** to go off something; **~ashun** *excl.*, *n.* offensive sight/thing; **~fu** *adj.* disgusting, loathsome

scur(l) *n.* scab

scurry *n.* seagull (Peterhead) (B); **~-waster** *n.* seagull (M1)

scushle *v.* shuffle

scutter *n.* messy or difficult work; nuisance; *v.* potter, work messily, awkwardly; **~ aboot** mess about; **~ification** *n.* palaver; **~ie jobbie** messy or trifling job

scypal *n.* rascal, rogue. *cf.* **skypal**

scythe-brod *n.* sharpening board for scythe

seagoo *n.* seagull (A1, R)

seama(w) *n.* seagull (M1)

sea-myow *n.* seagull (M3)

search *n.* milk strainer (F)

seck *n.* sack. *cf.* **saick**; **~-apron** *n.* sackcloth apron. *cf.* **harn-apron**

seck-lifter *n.* hand-barrow (F)

secrifeece *n., v.* sacrifice

sedarin *n.* scolding, dressing-down

seddle *See* **saiddle**

see(d)g(e) at *v.* scold

seek *adj.* sick (S); **~ener** *n.* sickener, something upsetting *v.* look for; ask for; invite; desire; **fit are ye ~in?** what do you want, what are you looking for?

seel *adj.* blessed, happy; *n.* happiness; **~y** *adj.* (*now poetic*) lucky, happy, blessed; **~y court** fairy court; **~yhoo** *n.* the caul rarely found on the head of a new-born child and thought a good omen

seelfu *adj.* blessed; happy; **~ness** *n.* happiness

seelen|ce *n., v.* silence; **~t** *adj.* silent

seemit *n.* under-shirt, vest. *cf.* **semmit**

seen *prep.* since; *adv.* soon; ago

seenit *n.* Synod

seer *adj.* sure (A, B1, M3);
  ~ly *adv.* surely

seerup *n.* syrup

seet *n.* site; building-ground

seetivation *n.* situation

seg *v.* sag; **~git** *ppl., adj.*
  sagged, sunk down

seg(g)s *n.* sedge; the yellow iris

seil *See* **seel**

seiven *adj.* seven; **~teen** *adj.*
  seventeen; **~ty** *adj.* seventy

sel *n.* self; **~lfitness** *n.* selfishness

seleck *v.* select

sell *n.* chain to bind cattle (F)

selt *v. pt., ppl.* sold

semm *n.* (pig)fat, lard.
  cf. **same**

semmit *n.* undershirt

sen *n.* messenger sent ahead of
  a bridegroom to summon
  the bride; *v.* send

ser *v.* serve. *cf.* **sair**

ser'in *See* **sairin**

servan *n.* servant

serve's *excl.* preserve us!

set *n.* kind; manner; *v.* lease,
  let; place a hen on eggs for
  hatching; plant (seedlings
  or tubers); suit; **~tin** *n.* a
  clutch of eggs a hen sits on
  to hatch

set tee *v.* begin

settril *adj.* slightly stunted in
  growth

severals *n. pl.* several people

sey *n.* sieve; *v.* strain through
  a sieve, strain milk; try.
  cf. **sye**

seyven *adj.* seven (A1).
  cf. **saeven, saiven**

shaave *v.* sow. (A1) *cf.* **shauv**

shachle *v.* shuffle. *cf.* **shochle**

shacklebane, -been *n.* wrist-bone

shadda, shaeda *n.* shadow

shaef, shafe *n.* sheaf. *cf.* **shaif**;
  the croonin ~ the last straw,
  the tin lid

shafter, shaftit weskit *n.*
  sleeved waistcoat (F)

shaggie *n.* sheepdog

shaif *n.* sheaf. *cf.* **shaef,
  shafe, shave**

shair *adj.* sure (S). *cf.* **seer**

shak *n., v.* shake; **the Big Shak**
  the near-ruinous shaking of
  barley by high winds one
  night in the 1960s; **~ker**
  n. part of a threshing mill
  which shakes out the straw;
  ~ky *adj.* shaky; **~ky-doon** *n.*
  make-shift bed on the floor

shak a fa *n.* wrestling bout
  (M); *v.* wrestle

Shakkin Briggie *pr. n.* bridge
  across the River Dee at
  Cults near Aberdeen

shakkin-spoot *n.* wooden chute
  conveying corn to the elevator
  lifting it to the corn loft

shall *n.* shell; **~y** *adj.* abounding in shells; **~ san** shell sand, used as grit for hens (T)

shalla *adj.* shallow

shallie o tay *phr.* old term for a cup of tea (B)

shalt(ie) *n.* pony; **~-loon** *n.* farm-boy looking after the ~ (F); groom

shammelt *adj.* uneven, irregular

shan-dre-dan *n.* any old rickety vehicle; jalopy

shangie *n.* fight; scrimmage

shank *n.* leg; stocking being knitted; *v.* to knit; **to ~ it** to walk; **~s' meer** shanks' pony; **~ redd o** send off without ceremony; **~less** *adj.* having no leg(s)

shanna *v. fut. neg.* shall not; *cf.* **sanna**

shapit *ppl.* shaped

sharg|art *ppl.* stunted; **~er** *n.* stunted person/animal; lean, scraggy person

sharn *n.* cow-dung; **~-bree** liquid cow-dung; **~-hole** *n.* bored in outhouse for dispatch of dirty straw dung; **~y** *adj.* dung-covered; dirty

sharp *n.* frost-nail; *v.* sharpen

sharrie *n.* quarrel; fight

shauchle *v.* shuffle in walking

shauv *v.* sow (S); **~en** *ppl.* sown. *cf.* **saw**

shave *n.* sheaf. *cf.* **shaif**

shaven *ppl.* shaved

shaw *n.* green leaf; small wood (J); *v.* sow; show

sheaf *n.* slice (of bread)

shear *v.* reap

sheath *n.* holder for needles during knitting

sheave *n.* slice (of bread)

shed *v.* part the hair or sheep's wool

shee *n.* shoe; *pl.* **~n**; *v.* to shoe. *cf.* **shoon, shune**

sheel *n.* shovel; *v.* 1. shovel; **~t** *ppl.* (of a road) snow-cleared by shovel; 2. to shell

sheelock *n.* corn husk; unfilled ear of corn

sheelter *n.* shelled mussel (B)

sheemachan, sheemich *n.* person or thing of no value

sheen *n., v.* shine; *pl. of* **shee**

sheers *n. pl.* scissors

sheet *n.* shoot; *v.* shoot; fall (used of rain between intervals of sunshine)

sheet-iron *n.* corrugated iron

sheilin *n.* temporary dwelling for shepherds

shellin steen *n.* (in meal mill) stone to remove corn husks

shelt(ie) *n.* pony. *cf.* **shalt, shult**

shelvin *n.* movable board on box cart, to increase capacity

sheugh *n.* ditch; furrow; hollow, trench

shew *v.* sew; ~**in-machine** *n.* sewing-machine. *cf.* **shoo**

shiel *n.* shovel; scoop for fish

shiffle *n.* shovel. *cf.* **sheel**

shillans *n.* grain freed from husks

shilpit *adj.* feeble; puny

shim *n.* horse-hoe, small plough for weeding

shine *n.* party. *cf.* **henshine**

shippie *n.* steam drifter (B)

shirra *n.* sheriff

shirrameer, shirramineer (B1) *n.* tumult, uproar

shirry *n.* sherry

shiv, shive *v.* shove, push

shochle *n.* icicle; *v.* waddle; shuffle

shog, ~gle *n.*, *v.* shake; jolt; ~**gly** *adj.* shaky; ~**gly-wullie** *n.* a table jelly. *cf.* **shoogle, shoogly**

shoo *v.* sew; ~**in** *n.* sewing; *v. pt.* sowed. *cf.* **shew, shaw**

shood|er *n.*, *v.* shoulder; ~**rin** *ppl.* shouldering; -**erheid** *n.* shoulder joint; ~**er-e-win** *n.* a hunched back. *cf.* **shouder**

shooer *n.* shower

shoogl|e *v.* to shake; ~**y** *adj.* unsteady (of a table etc). *cf.* **shoggle**

shool *n.* shovel (K). *cf.* **sheel**

shoon *n.* shoes. *cf.* **sheen, shune**

shoorie *n.* light shower

shoot *n.* suit (including cards); *v.* suit

shoother *n.* shoulder. *cf.* **shooder**

shoppie *n.* small shop

shore *v.* cut; scold; *v. pt.* sheared (a sheep)

short *adj.*, *in the phr.* ~ **i the trot** quick-tempered; irritable; ~**comes** *n.* shortcomings; ~**some** *adj.* amusing, making the time seem short

shot *n.* the *shooting* of a fishing net; the catch

shottie *n.* turn

shoud, showd *n.*, *v. tr. & intr.* rock; swing; ~**en-boats** *n.* swing-boats at carnival

shouder, shouther *n.*, *v.* shoulder. ~**-the-win**, *n.* (having) one shoulder higher than the other. *cf.* **shooder**

shrood *n.* shroud

shud *v.* should

shue *v.* sew. *cf.* **shoo**

shuit *v.* suit. *cf.* **shoot**

shullin *n.* shilling

shult *See* **shelt**

shune *n. pl.* shoes. *cf.* **sheen, shoon**

shuner *adv.* sooner (s)

shunner *n.* cinder; **harn bags an ~s** sackcloth and ashes

shyve *n., v.* throw (of rope or fishing line only) (B)

sib *adj.* closely related, akin; **~best** *adj.* most nearly related; **~ness** *n.* relationship

sic, siccan *adj.* such; **~-an-~** such-and-such; **~like** *adj.* such-like; **~likes** *n.* things like that; *prep.* just like

siccar *adj.* secure, certain; dependable, reliable

sich *n.* sigh

sicht *n.* sight; **a ~ for sair een** a welcome sight

sick lamb *n.* pet lamb brought up on the bottle, drawn by the call *sick*

sid *n.* seed; *v.* should; **~na** shouldn't. *cf.* **sud**

sideboord *n.* sideboard

sidelins *adv.* sideways

siderig *n.* side ridge

side-shelvin *n.* movable board on side of box-cart

sidiewyes *adv.* sideways

sids *n. pl.* oat husks, used for **sowans**

siftin-riddle *n.* riddle for small seed

signaatur *n.* signature

sik *v.* seek; desire; **nae ~ken't** don't want it. *cf.* **seek**

sile *n.* sand-eel (B). *cf.* **sunnel**

siller *n.* silver; money

silly-made-up *adj.* (of a child) mischievous

simmer *n.* summer; **~-hoose** *n.* summer-house

sin *n.* son; sun; **~-brunt** *adj.* sun-burned; **~doon** *n.* sundown, sunset

sin *prep.* since; **~seen, ~syne** since then

sinacle *n.* vestige, trace (BI)

sinder *v.* separate, sunder. *cf.* **sinner**

sindry *adv.* asunder

sine *n., v.* rinse

sing *v.* singe

single *v.* hoe turnips

sing-sang *n.* singsong speech

sinker *n.* weight for fastening horse in stall (F)

sin|ner *v.* part company, separate, sunder. *cf.* **sinder** **~rin** *n.* separation

sinny *n.* senna

sinry *adj.* sundry

sipper *n.* supper

siree *n.* soirée

sitiwat *ppl.* situated

sit saft *v., adv.* enjoy an easy life

sitt *n.* soot

siven *adj.* seven; **~teen** seventeen; **~ty** seventy

sivven *n.* raspberry

size *n.* chives

sizzon *n.*, *v.* season

skaalie *n.* slate pencil. *cf.* **skeily**

skaas, for ony *phr.* for any sake (M3)

ska(i)ken *v.* feel disgust at, be nauseated by (food); *ppl.* ~t wi't. *cf.* **skechan**

skaikit *ppl.* bedaubed; besmeared

skail *v. tr.* spill; *intr.* disperse (school pupils etc); *v. tr.* dismiss. *cf.* **skale**

skaillie *n.* slate-pencil. *cf.* **skaalie**

skaillies *n. pl.* something spilt or scattered

skaim *v.* scheme. *cf.* **skem**

skair *n.* share, portion

skaith *n.* harm

skale *n.* school (S). *cf.* **skweel**; *v. tr.* dismiss; spill; *intr.* scatter. *cf.* **skail, skel**

skalie, skallie *n.* slate pencil. *cf.* **skaalie, skeily**

skance *n.* glance; view

skate *n.* jade (term of contempt)

skech *v.* go about in a silly, vain way

skechan *See* **skaiken**

skeegin *n.* walloping

skeek *v.* strike with open palm

skeel *n.* skill; *v.* prove, test; ~y *adj.* skilful

skeigh *adj.* timid; coy

skeily *n.* slate pencil. *cf.* **skaalie**

skel *v.* spill. *cf.* **skale**

skelb *n.* splinter

skelf *n.* shelf; thin flat fragment or slice; splinter esp. lodged in skin

skellach *n.* 1. wild mustard, charlock; 2 *n.*, *v.* shriek, scream

skelp *n.* smack, whack; chunk, slab, sizable area; *v.* dash, run

skelve *n.* shelf (B1); *v.* laminate (B1). *cf.* **skelf**

skem *v.* scheme. *cf.* **skaim**

skep *n.* beehive; *v.* handle beehives

skew *adv.* askew; ~-fittit *adj.* splay-footed. *cf.* **skyow-fittit**

skice *v.* to run off quickly. *cf.* **skyce**

skichent *adj.* showing contempt. *cf.* **skaiken, skech**

skicy *adj.* mean, unfair

skiff *v.* rain, snow, hail lightly

skiffin *n.* light fall (of rain, snow)

skiffie *n.* scivvy (S)

skiken *See* **skaiken**

skink *n.* shin or knuckle of beef from which soup may be made (*joc.*) leg

skinnymalink *n.* a thin person

skip *v.* slide on ice

skire *See* **skyre**

skirl *n., v.* scream

skirl(ie) *n.* squall of wind with rain or snow

skirlie *n.* oatmeal cooked with onions, dripping and seasoning; a very small quantity (A1)

skirlie-wheeter *n.* oyster-catcher (F)

skirp *n., v.* splash; *n.* fragment

skirt *v.* hurry off, run away (A)

skiry *adj.* gaudy. *cf.* **skyrie**

Skite *pr. n.* nickname of Drumlithie

skit|e *v.* slip or slide suddenly; run off quickly; rebound, ricochet; squirt, splash; *n.* slip or skid; squirt of liquid; small amount of liquor, a dram; ~ie *adj.* slippery

skitter(s) *n.* diarrhoea

sklaik *n., v.* lick, smear with the tongue. *cf.* **slaik**

sklate *n.* slate; **a ~ aff** *phr.* mentally abnormal; ~r *n.* slater

sklent, sklint *v.* slant, slope (off); glance

sklett *See* **sklate**

sklush *n.* slush

skyalloch *v.* screech

sklype *n.* derog. term for someone of dirty habits

sklyte, sklyter *v.* slip awkwardly, fall heavily; *n.* a heavy fall; expanse (G)

skook *v.* skulk. *cf.* **scouk**

skowf *v.* quaff; drink off. *cf.* **scoof**

skraich *v.* screech

skreefer *n.* skimmer for surface soil and weeds (F)

skreek o day *phr.* dawn

skrie *v.* shriek, cry; proclaim

skudge *v.* do rough menial work. *cf.* **scudge**

skug *v. tr.* shelter. *cf.* **scog**

skull *n.* shallow wicker basket. *cf.* **scull**

skum *v.* skim

skurken *v.* dry out; shrink, shrivel

skwaal *v.* squall, scream

skweel *n.* school. *cf.* **squeel**

skweenge *v.* scrounge (of dogs and people)

skwyle *v.* squeal. *cf.* **squile**

skyce *v.* scurry. *cf.* **skice**

skycie *adj.* unsporting, ungenerous

skylie *n.* slate pencil. *cf.* **skaalie**

skyow *v.* to go askew; ~-fittit splay-footed. *cf.* **skew-fittit**

skypal *n.* (*var. of* **skybald**) rascal, rogue. *cf.* **scypal**

skyr|e *v.* shine or glitter gaudily; **~ie** *adj.* gaudy, showy; **~rin** (of colours) clashing. *cf.* **skire**

skyte *See* **skite**

slabber *n.* mud; slush; slop

slack *v.* slake or quench thirst

slaik *v.* lick, smear with the tongue. *cf.* **sklaik**

slaiver *n., v.* slaver

slammach *n.* gossamer, webs of small spiders

slap *n.* opening, gap in wall or fence

slater *n.* wood-louse

slauchter *n., v.* slaughter; **~-hoose** *n.* slaughter-house

slaw *adj., adv.* slow

sled *v. pt.* slid

slee *adj.* sly; **~ly** *adv.* slyly

sleed *v. pt.* slid (s)

sleek *n.* alluvial deposit of mud left in tidal rivers. *cf.* **slich**

sleekit *adj.* smooth, glossy; sly, sneaky

sleepit *v. pt.* slept; **~ in** overslept

sleicht *n.* sleight

sleumin *n.* hint; surmise

slewie *v.* walk with heavy, swinging gait (B1)

slich *See* **sleek**

slicht *adj., n.* slight

slidder *n.* ice (M3); **~y** *adj.* slippery

slider *n.* retaining rod for cattle-binding; harness fitment on cart shaft; ice-cream between two wafers

slip *n.* loose frock or pinafore; *v.* let slip; forget; **~ the timmers** *phr.* die (M)

slipe *See* **slype**

sliv(v)er *n., v.* slaver; **~-doctor** *n.* harmless jellyfish (B)

Sloch, the *pr. n.* village of Portessie

slocher *v.* (of a pig) wallow in mud

slock, sl(y)ocken *v.* slake (thirst)

slooch *v.* slouch

sloosh *n., v.* drench(ing); rinse; sluice

slorach *n.* wet or dirty, disgusting mess (B1)

slubber *v.* sip noisily

slung *n.* a low fellow

slype *n.* worthless fellow

sma *adj.* small. **sing ~** say little (as matter of discretion); **~ drink** of no consequence; **~ lins** small fishing lines; **~ watter** calm waters (B); **~ weet** a soft drizzle

smachrie *n.* hotch-potch of foods, esp. sweets

smack *n.* kiss (K)

smad *n.* blemish, smudge

smarrach *n.* confused crowd. *cf.* swarrach

smatchet *n.* pert, impudent person

smatterie *n.* heap of small objects

smeddum *n.* intelligence; shrewdness; mettle; spirit

smeeky *adj.* smoky (G1)

smeerich *n.* a kiss. *cf.* smoorich

smeerless *adj.* lacking spirit, energy, sluggish; handless (B1)

smeeth *adj.* smooth

smeirless *See* smeerless

smert *adj.* smart

smiddy *n.* blacksmith's shop

smiler *n.* small farm rake pulled by a rope from the shoulder

smird *n.* smut, smudge. *cf.* smad

smirr *n.* drizzle, fine rain

smit *v.* infect; ~tin *adj.* infectious; gie some-een the ~ *phr.* to infect

smith *n.* blacksmith

smoocherin *n.* fine rain

smook *n.* smoke (K)

smoor *v.* smother (J). *cf.* smore

smoorich *n.* kiss. *cf.* smeerich

smor|e *v.* smother; ~n i the caal having a heavy cold; smore drift dense drift (M3);

~ichin *ppl.* smothering. *cf.* smoor

smout *n.* term of endearment for a young animal or child

smucht *v.* choke; ~y *adj.* smoky; stifling;

smuchter *v.* smoulder

smyteral *n.* collection of small objects

sna, snaave *n., v.* snow; ~vie *adj.* snowy (S, M3). *cf.* snaw, snyaave

snap-an-rattle *n.* dish of oatcakes crumbled into milk (F). *cf.* murly-tuck

snapper *n., v.* (of a horse) stumble

snappus *adj.* testy, snappy (A2)

snaw *n., v.* snow; ~-bree *n.* melted snow; slush; ~-fite *adj.* snow-white. *cf.* sna

sneck *n.* latch; *v.* sneak; ~-drawin *adj.* crafty, sly (A2)

sneck-harl *v.* rough-cast a wall with mortar

sned *n.* scythe handle; *v.* cut; prune; chop; fit a shaft to a scythe

sneesh *v.* take snuff; ~in *n.* snuff; pinch of snuff

sneevil, sneevle *v.* snivel

snell *adj.* (of the wind) cold, sharp

snicher *v.* snigger, laugh up one's sleeve

snifter *v.* sniff, draw air through the nose

snipe *n.* smack. *cf.* **snype**

snippet *adj.* having a white streak down the face

snisty *adj.* impudent, saucy

snocher *v.* sniff; breathe noisily; snore

snochters *n. pl.* nasal mucus

snod *adj.* tidy; neat; *v.* tidy up (C); **~-in-aboot** *n.* hair-cut (T)

snoot *n.* snout, nose; peak of a cap; **~it** *adj.* (of a cap) peaked

snoove *v.* move smoothly, glide, slip

snorl *n.* tangle, difficulty

snot *n.* dolt; *contemptuous term for* a person

snotter *n.* nasal mucus; *v.* let mucus run from nose; snuffle; blubber; doze; **~ aff** doze off

snout *See* **snoot**

snowk *v.* (of an animal) smell about

snuff *v.* sniff

snyaave *n.* snow. *cf.* **sna, snaav**

snyp|e *n.* rebuff; reverse of fortune; setback, let-down, loss by cheating; *v.* cheat, defraud; **~it o** cheated by

snyte *v.* blowing the nose with finger and thumb

sober *adj.* weakly; of spare figure

socht *ppl.* sought. *cf.* **seek**

sock *n.* ploughshare

sodger *n.* soldier

softie, soft biscuit *n.* a kind of plain floury bun

sole *n.* window-sill

solvendo *adj.* fixed, firm, to be depended on

some *adv.* rather, to some extent; **~ caul** rather cold; **~ like** rather as if

some-ane, -een *n., pron.* someone

son-afore-the-father *n.* flowering currant (the blossom appearing before the leaves

sonsy *adj.* plump and pleasant

soo *n.* sow; rectangular stack of hay or straw; **~-moo't** having projecting upper jaw; chinless

sooch *See* **souch**

sooder *n., v.* solder

sooie *n.* dough trimmed off edges of oatcake before baking, given to children

sook *v.* suck; **~er** *n.* tree sucker; cow suckling calves; **~in caafie** *ppl.* & *n.* suckling calf

soom *n.* sum; *v.* swim (C, K). *cf.* **sweem**

soon(d) *n.*, *v.* sound. *cf.* soun

soop *n.*, *v.* sweep

sooperaniwat *ppl.* superannuated

soople *adj.* supple. *cf.* souple
soor *adj.* sour; ~ness
n. sullenness; surliness

soord *n.* sword

soorocks *n.* sorrel

soosh *v.* beat severely, flog;
sue at law

sooter *n.* cobbler. *cf.* souter

sooth *adj.*, *n.* south;
~-kwintra *adj.* southern;
English. *cf.* suddron

sorn *v.* sponge upon; beg; loaf

sorra *adj.* sorry; *n.* 1. sorrow;
she hisna her ~s tae seek
she has plenty trouble on
her hands; 2. the Devil,
used impatiently *eg*, **fat ~
idder?** what other?; **faar ~?**
where the devil? ~fu *adj.*
sorrowful

sort *v.* mend; see to, attend
to, deal with (sometimes
harshly); ~in *n.* scolding

soss *n.* mess

sotter *n.* disgusting mess

souch *n.* sigh; sough;
whistling or rushing sound;
moaning; *v.* sigh, make
rushing sound. *cf.* sough

soud *n.* as in ~ o siller sum of
money. *cf.* sowd

souder *n.* solder

souff, sowf(f) *v.* whistle in a
low tone; *n.* fool, simpleton

sough *See* souch

soun *adj.*, *n.* sound; *adv.* soundly

souple *adj.* supple

souter *n.* shoemaker; ~'s
deevil shoemaker's last.
cf. sooter

southron *adj.* southern

sowans, sowens *n.* dish made
by steeping and fermenting
the husks or siftings of oats
in water, then boiling

soward *n.* sword

sowd *n.* a large sum; a quantity.
cf. soud

sowff *See* souff

sowl *n.* soul

spaad, spad *n.* spade. *cf.* spaud

spaal *See* spaul

space *n.* pace

spae *v.* to tell fortunes; ~-wife
n. female fortune-teller

spaingie, spainyie *n.* W. Indian
cane, sometimes smoked
by boys; osiers for basket-
making among
fishermen (B)

spairge *v.* bespatter; scatter

spak *v. pt.* spoke

span *n.* span of life

spang *n.*, *v.* spring, stride;
span, outstretched width
of hand

spar *v.* spare; ~**t** spared

spark *v.* splash, mark with drops of water. *cf.* **sperk, spirk**

sparry *n.* sparrow (J)

sparty tow *n.* coir yarn

spat *n.* spot

spate *n.* river-flood

spaud *See* **spaad**

spaul *n.* leg, limb; shoulder; shoulder or forequarter of an animal

spaver *n.* trouser fly

spavie *n.* the spavin in horses, affecting walking

spawcious *adj.* spacious

spean *v.* wean

speecial *adj.* special

speel *v.* climb

speen *n., v.* spoon; ~ **aboot** spoon about as farmworkers shared the same broth bowl

speer, speir, spier *v.* ask

speerit *n.* spirit

speeshal(ly) *adj., adv.* special(ly)

speet, speeth *n.* spate, river-flood (B1). *cf.* **spate**

speldin *n.* fresh haddock, split open, salted and dried in the sun

spell *n.* wood shaving

spell-beuk *n.* spelling-book

spen *v.* spend; wean (F); spawn (B). *cf.* **spean**

spengie *adj.* Spanish; *n.* West Indian cane. *cf.* **spaingie**

spence *n.* spare room

sperk *v.* splash

spew *v.* vomit. *cf.* **spue, spoot**

spiel *v.* climb. *cf.* **speel**

spik *n.* speech; conversation; subject of talk or gossip; *v.* speak

spile *v.* spoil

spinner, at a *phr.* at a smart rate of speed, at a dash

spinnle *n., v.* spindle; ~-**shanks** spindly legs

spiritool *adj.* spiritual

spirk *n.* spark; drop of rain; splash or spot; *v.* splash; rain slightly. *cf.* **sperk, spark**

spit *v.* to rain slightly

splairge *n.* splodge

splatch *n.* splash

splay *v.* to mend a tear in cloth by sewing edges together without patching

spleeter|s *n. pl.* spillings, splashings; ~ **o weet** *n.* heavy shower of rain

spleet-new *adj.* quite new

spleuchan *n.* tobacco-pouch. *cf.* **splochan**

splew *v.* spit out, spue; ~**in** *n.* vomit; term of abuse, *eg,* **ye lazy splewin**

split *n.* quarrel; *v.* separate

split-the-win *adj., n.* Y-junction

splochan, splyoochan
(M3) *n.* tobacco pouch.
cf. **spleuchan**

sploiter *v.* splash, spill

splore *n.* frolic; party; revel

splouter *v.* splutter

spluen (B1) *See* **splewin**

splutrich *n.* a scattered
mess (B1)

splyaader *n.* mess (M3)

splyter *See* **sploiter**

spoot *n.* spout; rone pipe;
v. vomit. *cf.* **spew, spue**

spot *n.* dram

sprachle *v.* sprawl. *cf.* **sprauchle**

sprag *n.* piece of wood or iron
used to block a wheel;
medium-size cod

spraikle *v.* speckle

spraing *n.* streak, usually
glittering

sprauchle *See* **sprachle**

spree *adj.* spruce

spreeth *n.* a large number (B1)

sprent *ppl.* strewn; *n.* spring or
elastic force of anything (B1)

spring *n.* lively tune

spring-cairt *n.* cart mounted
on springs

sprod *n.* an implement for
dislodging limpets from a
rock

sproot *n.* Brussels sprout;
v. grow, sprout

sprot *n.* reed, rush; a coarse
grass

sprung *adj.* tipsy

spue *v.* vomit. *cf.* **spew, spoot**

spull *v.* spill; **~ins** spillings.
cf. **skale**

spulyie *v.* plunder, despoil

spunk *n.* a match; mettle,
energy; courage

spunkie *n.* will-o-the-wisp;
the devil

spur-bauk *n.* cross-beam in
the roof of a building (B1)

spurdie *n.* house-sparrow

spurgie *n.* house-sparrow (O)
~-hoched *adj.* thin-legged

spurk (J) *See* **spirk** etc

spurkle, spurtle *n.* wooden
rod for stirring porridge etc;
~-shanks *n. pl.* thin legs;
cf. **theevil**

spyauck *n.* example, guide;
a gryte ~ a good example

squaar, squarr *adj., n., v.*
square

squallach *v.* squeal; **~ty** *adj.*
loud, shrill

squatter *v.* scatter

squeams *n. pl.* squeamishness

squeeb *n.* firework

squeel *n.* school. *cf.* **skweel**

squeerie *v.* (often of animals)
roam, gad about

squile *v.* squeal. *cf.* **skwyle**

sta(a) *n.* stall; place

staamer *v.* stagger

stacher *v.* stagger

stack *n.* a pile of peats; *pt. ppl.* stuck; ~**it** *ppl.* (*eg, of* hay) built into a stack; ~**yaird** *n.* rick-yard

staffy *n.* a staff; ~**-nevel** *adj.* staff-in-hand; ~**-nevel job** a fight with cudgels

stag-moss *n.* alpine club moss

staig *n.* stallion

stail *v.* steal (S). *cf.* **stale**

stainch *adj.* staunch. *cf.* **stanch**

stairch *n., v.* starch

stairt *n., v.* start, begin

stairv|e *v.* starve; *cf.* **sterve**; ~**ation** *n.* starvation

staito *n.* statue (A2)

staiver *v.* saunter, wander

staivy *v.* saunter; stagger

stale *v.* steal. *cf.* **stail**

stamach, stam(m)ack *n.* stomach; *v.* stomach; endure

stame *n.* steam; ~**-mull** *n.* steam-driven threshing-machine; ~**-mull breid** thick, poorly-made oatcakes (F). *cf.* **stem-mull**

stammack *See* **stamach**

stammergast *v.* flabbergast

stammygaster *n.* shock; *v.* flabbergast

stan *v.* stand; ~**nin** *ppl.* standing

stance *n.* site; station

stanch *adj., v.* staunch. *cf.* **stainch**

stand *v.* hold out; last

stane *n.* stone; ~**-cast** *n.* stone's throw. *cf.* **steen**

stang *n.* sting; pole; steering-rod; tongue of a Jew's harp; ~ **o the trump** the best of all, best of a family

stank *n.* pond; ditch; marshy ground; (*fig.*) **help a chiel ower a ~; a muckle ~ luppen** *phr.* a big step forward (M3)

stap *n.* step; *v.* stop; block up; stick, stuff; ~**pit fu** stuffed full

stapple *n.* a pipe stem

stark *adj.* naked

starkly *adv.* strongly, bravely

starn, starnie *n.* star; small quantity, pinch

sta(r)shie *n.* row, uproar. *cf.* **stushie**

staucher *v.* to stagger

staw *v. pt.* stole

steadin *n.* steading, farmstead

stech *v.* cram; satiate, gorge; create a stifling atmosphere; ~**t** *ppl., adj.* overheated (G)

steed *v. pt.* stood. *See* **stan**

steek *n.* stitch; *v.* shut; clench; stitch

steel *n.* stool; fellow (B1)

steelbow *n.* system under which farm stock, implements etc could be held by the tenant under contract to the landlord

steen *n., v.* stone; **~-chackert** *n.* stonechat (M). *cf.* **stane**

Steenhive *pr. n.* nickname for Stonehaven

steeny *adj.* stony

steepin *n.* a wetting, drenching; stipend, minister's salary

steepit loaf *ppl. & n.* bread poultice (B)

steepy *adj.* steep

steer *n., v.* stir, bustle

steeroch *n.* (of a pot) stir

steigh *v.* fill with bad air or fumes

steil *See* **steel**

steilert *n.* steelyard, weighing machine (F)

stem *v.* (nautical) keep a certain course

stem-mull *n.* steam-driven threshing-machine. *cf.* **stame-mull**

stench *v.* staunch

sten(d) *v.* stride (A2)

sten(n) *n., v.* spring

stent *n.* extent of task, stint; *v.* stint

stepple *n.* staple

sterv|e *v.* starve. *cf.* **stairve**; **~ o/wi the caul** feel chilled; **~ation** bitter cold

stey *adj.* steep; *n.* stay, support; *in pl.* corsets; *v.* stay

stibble *n.* stubble; **~ ruckie** mini-cornstack built by cottar loons from stubble roots (T)

stick *v.* stick; come to a premature halt in a job etc; **~ in** *v.* to persevere; **~it** *ppl., adj.* gored; **~it minister** student of the ministry who has failed to be licensed as a preacher;

stickly *adj.* (of peat) fibrous, woody

stiffen *n.* stiffening, starch

still an on *adv.* nevertheless

stilp *v.* to stalk

stilpert *n.* stilt; long-legged, lanky person or animal

stilt *n.* handle of plough (F)

stime, styme *n.* a tiny amount

stinch *adj.* staunch; strict. *cf.* **stanch**

stirk *n.* young bullock; a stupid fellow

stirkie's sta *n.* the place in the cowshed reserved for the stirk; the place of a child, (*eg*, father's lap) when the mother has a younger baby

stirlin, stirrie *n.* starling

stite *n.* nonsense; stumble. *cf.* **stoit, styte**

stiter *v.* stumble; **~y** *adj.* unsteady. *cf.* **stoiter**

stob *n.* thorn; stake; **~bit, ~-thackit** thatched by means of a stake; *v.* stub (the toe etc)

stock *n.* chap, fellow

stockit *adj.* (of a person) hard; obstinate

stodge *v.* walk slowly, stomp

stoit, stoiter *v.* stagger, totter. *cf.* **stite, styter, stotter**

stoker *n.* odd job-lot of fish, sold by a ship's crew for cash (B)

stoo *v.* cut (off) (animal's tail, shoots of tree, a fishing net)

stook *n.* a shock of eight or more standing sheaves; *v.* to put into shocks; **~in** *n.* the arrangement of corn in shocks, usually 12 sheaves per shock

stookie *n.* stucco, plaster of Paris

stoon(d) *n., v.* ache; throb. *cf.* **stound**

stoor *n.* flying dust; store (M3); *v.* pour (can be used of rain); gush; **~ie** *adj.* dusty. *cf.* **stour.**

stoorum *n.* gruel

stoot *adj.* stout; strong, fit (A, A2),

stop *v.* live or stay at an address

store the kin *phr.* to keep the human race in existence by living on; *fig.* to survive, to keep going, last out in general (A2, M)

stot *n.* castrated bullock older than a stirk; *n., v.* bounce; walk with a spring; stagger; **the aal ~** *phr.* the old routine; **~s-and-bangs** *adj., adv.* intermittent(ly); *n.* occasional work

stotter *v.* stumble. *cf.* **stoiter**

stound *See* **stoond**

stoup *n.* deep, narrow vessel for holding liquids: flagon; jug; *in pl.* props, supports; the two pieces of a cart projecting beyond the body; **~ie** *n.* small liquid measure; cream pot (B1)

stour *n.* dust; a downpour; **~ie** *adj.* dusty. *cf.* **stoor**

stovies *n.* stoved potatoes cooked in stew-pan with onion, fat and meat scraps

stow *v.* steal; *ppl.* **~en** stolen; **~n-wyes** *adv.* by stealth, secretly

stowff *n.* slow, measured gait; *v.* stump; plod

stra *v.* straw *in phr.* **~ his beets** put straw (as soles) into his boots (formerly a custom of farm servants) (R). *cf.* **strae**

straaberry *n.* strawberry

strab *n.* stalk of loose straw lying on the field after harvesting or sticking out from a sheaf or stack; anything adhering loosely to clothes

strach|t *adj., adv.* straight; ~-edge strip of iron used to align the **couter** and **sock** with the body of the horse plough (T); ~-oot-the-gate *adj.* straight-forward. *cf.* **straucht**; ~en *v.* straighten. *cf.* **straichen, strauchen**

strack *v. pt.* struck

strade *v.* strode

strae *n.* straw; *v.* to give straw to animals; ~ **his beets** put straw into his boots for warmth (T). ~-soo *n.* long stack of straw. *cf.* **stra**

straichen *See* **strachen**

straik *n.* sharpening board or stone for scythe; wooden cylinder for levelling a bushel measure (F)

straik *n., v.* stroke *n.* streak. *See* **strake**

strainer, strainin post *n.* post taking the strain of the wire in fencing (F)

strait *adj.* rigid

strake *v.* stroke; *v. pt.* **strak**. *cf.* **straik**

stramash *n.* uproar, commotion

strang *adj.* strong; *n.* urine; ~-hole *n.* drain for liquid discharge; cesspit, (-pool)

strapper *n.* young farm servant looking after the shalt (F). *cf.* **shalt-loon**

strappin *adj.* tall, handsome and agile

strathspey *n.* Highland dance

strauch|t *adj.* straight. *cf.* **stracht**; ~twye *adv.* straightaway; ~en *v.* straighten (A1). *cf.* **strachen, straichen**

stravaig *v.* wander

streck *adj.* strict. *cf.* **strick**

streek *v.* stretch; *ppl.* ~it stretched out; dead. *cf.* **streetch, rax**

streen, the *n., adv.* yester-day evening; last night; yesterday. *cf.* **yestreen**

streetch *v.* stretch (A2). *cf.* **streek, rax**

streeve *v. pt.* strove; struggled; fell out, quarrelled

strenth *n.* strength

strick *adj.* strict; *v.* strike

stridelins *prep.* astride

striffin *n.* thin, membranous film

strik *See* **strick**

strin *n.* jet of milk from a cow's teat

stripe *n.* small open drain.
  cf. **strype**
strive *v.* quarrel; **~n** *ppl.*
  having quarrelled, fallen
  out
stroop(ie) *n.* spout (of teapot
  etc); water tap; outlet at
  spring
stroud *n.* silly song
strucken *ppl.* struck
strunge *adj.* surly, gruff,
  morose
strush, strushie *n.* quarrel;
  disturbance
strushel *adj.* untidy, slovenly
strushlach *n.* untidy woman
struve *v. pt.* strove
strype *n.* small stream;
  v. draw the last milk from
  a cow
stucken *ppl.* stuck
studdy *n.* anvil
stue *n.* dust. *cf.* **styoo, stoor**
stumpart, stumper *v.* walk
  clumsily in a stumping way
stur *n., v.* stir. *cf.* **steer**
sturken *adj.* sulky, sour
sturt *n.* strife (C)
stushie *n.* uproar
styoo *n.* dust. *cf.* **stoor**;
  ~ie *adj.* dusty. *cf.* **stoorie**
styoomer *n.* foolish person
styter *v.* stumble, totter;
  ~in fou incapably drunk.
  cf. **stoiter**
sub *n., v.* advance wages

subjeck *n.* subject
succar *n.* sugar
sucken *n.* the district thirled
  to a mill; generally, the
  district in which anyone
  carries on business (A2)
suddent *adj.* sudden (C);
  hasty (A); *adv.* suddenly;
  ~ty *n.* suddenness; **in/on a**
  ~y suddenly
sudderinwid *n.* southernwood
suddron *adj.* southern;
  English
sug *n.* easy-going individual
sugh *See* **sough**
suit *v.* please; **wasna ower sair**
  ~ed aboot was displeased;
  ~in *adj.* suitable
sumph *n.* fool, simpleton
sune *See* **seen**
sung *ppl., adj.* singed
sunnel *n.* sand-eel (B)
sunsheen *n.* sunshine
sup *n.* sip, small quantity;
  v. take food or liquid, esp.
  with a spoon; **~pie** *n.* sip,
  small quantity
superannuat *ppl.*
  superannuated
suppersteetion *n.* superstition
supplicant *n.* a beggar
surtoo, surtout *n.* old-
  fashioned coat
suspeck *v.* suspect
swack, swak *adj.* supple, nimble
  ~en *v.* make supple, pliant

swad *n.* swede, Swedish turnip; **~dish neep** *n.* swede

swadge *v.* (*from* assuage) relax (*eg,* after a meal)

swaleheidit (s). *See* **swall-heidit**

swall *v.* swell; **~-heidit** *adj.* swollen-headed

swalla *n.* swallow (bird)

swally *v.* swallow

swankie *n.* smart young man or girl

swap *v.* to rope thatch with a **cloo**

swarf *n., v.* faint, swoon

swarrach *n.* crowd, swarm. *cf.* **smarrach**

swashy *adj.* grand, dashing

swat *n., v.* sweat, *pt.* sweated; **~tit** *v. pt.* sweated (M). *cf.* **swate, swyte**

swatch *n.* sample

swate *v.* sweat (A2). *cf.* **swat, swyte**

sweel *v.* swill, rinse; swirl

sweem *v.* swim; **~er** *n.* swimmer; **twenty-minute ~er** doughball (B)

sweeng *n., v.* swing

sweengletree *See* **swingle-tree**

sweer *v.* swear; **~(-wird)** *n.* swear(-word)

sweer(t) *adj.* lazy; unwilling

sweer-tree, puin the a game in which two people sit on the ground, holding a stick between them and try to pull each other up

sweesh *v.* swish, brush

sweetie *n.* sweet; **~-boolie** *n.* round sweet; **readin ~s** *n. pl.* conversation lozenges; **~-wife** *n.* female sweet-seller; emasculate man

sweevle *v.* swivel

sweir *See* **sweer**

sweirty *n.* laziness

swey *v.* sway, swing

swick *n.* cheat, fraud; *v.* swindle; **~it** *ppl.* cheated

swidder *See* **swither**

swig *v.* sway, move from side to side (J)

swine's hoose *n.* pigsty

swingletree *n.* (as in Eng.), bar in a plough-draught to which the **theats** are attached

swipe *v.* sweep. *cf.* **swype**

swippert *adj.* nimble. *cf.* **swyppirt**

swite *n., v.* sweat. *cf.* **swyte**

swith *adv.* swiftly

swithe *v.* hasten, get away

swither *n.* quandary; *v.* to be undecided; hesitate. *cf.* **swidder**

swourd *n.* sword

swult *v.* sob deeply (B)

swuppert, swyppirt *adj.* nimble, agile; swift

swye *n.* pivoted rod in chimney for hanging pots

over the fireplace; sway,
influence; *v.* sway

swype *v.* sweep. *cf.* **swipe**

swyte *n.*, *v.* sweat. *cf.* **swat,
swate**

swyth *adv.* swiftly. *cf.* **swith**

sye *v.* strain liquid; pour
milk through a sieve

syer *n.* milk strainer. *cf.* **syre**

sympathees|e *v.* sympathise;
~**in** *adj.* sympathetic

syne *adv.* since, ago; then

syp|e *v.* seep, drip; ~**it** *ppl.*
soaked

syre *n.* drain in street gutter,
incl. the covering grating.
cf. **syer**

T

taal *ppl.* told

taapie *n.* foolish fellow

tabbie *n.* cigarette end (Abdn.)

tablin *n.* top stones on a gable

tack *n.* lease of a farm; leased
farm; ~ **o life** lease of life

tacket *n.* stud, hobnail;
~**y beets** hobnailed boots

tackie, takie *n.* the game
of tag

tae *adv.* (*pro. when stressed*
tee) too; *prep.* to; for; by;
n. (*pro.* tay) toe. *cf.* **tay**

tae, the *num. adj.* the one,
contrasted with the other.
cf. **the tane**

tae-ee *n.* a pet

taen *ppl.* taken (s). *cf.* **tane, teen**

tag *n.* leather strap, tawse;
i the ~ hard at work

taik *n.* stroll; **tak** ~ take stock (T)

taikle *n.* harness; tackle

tailer *n.* tool for taking roots
off turnips (F)

tail *in phr.* **i the** ~ **o** at the end of;
~**-eyn** *n.* the tail end

tailyer *n.* tailor. *cf.* **tyler, tylie**

taings *n. pl.* tongs, hinged
wire-tightener in fencing

tait *n.* lock of hair, wool etc;
small portion

tak *v.* take; ~ **aboot** *v.* take
care of, look after, see to;
(of a crop) take in;
~ **aff** *v.* copy down;
~ **in** cultivate; ~ **in han**
v. undertake; ~ **throwe-han**
v. discuss; ~**-on** *n.* undertaking; ~ **sheet** *v.* take flight
(*orig. naut.*) (B, T); ~ **tent**
pay attention

takkie *n.* the game of tag, tick
and tack. *cf.* **tackie**

Tam *pr. n.*, *deriv.* of Thomas

Tamintoul *pr. n.* Tomintoul
village

tamteen *n.* a tontine

tane *adj.* the one. *cf.* **taen**

tangles *n. pl.* kind of seaweed

tangs *n. pl.* tongs. *cf.* **tyangs**

tansy *n.* ragwort; tansy

tantaleeze *v.* tantalise

tap *n., v.* top

tapdress *n.* manure on the surface

tapner *n.* tool for removing turnip-tops (F)

tappit *adj.* crested; ~-hen *n.* crested hen; Scottish quart measure of ale or claret, with a knob on its lid

tapsalteerie *adv.* topsy-turvy

tapster *n.* the person at the top

tare *n., v.* tear

tares *n. pl.* beans and peas grown among oats for cattle feed (T)

tarick *n.* Arctic tern (B)

tarlach *n.* mean fellow (M3)

tarlich *n.* a puny, worthless creature

tarraneese *n., v.* (*lit.* tyrannise) tease, torment

tarry-fingert *adj.* light-fingered

tase oot *v.* tease out (S)

tashed, tasht *adj.* fatigued; well worn

tasment, tastement, tesment *n.* will, testament

tass(ie) *n.* drinking cup; glass; goblet

tatterwallop *n.* ragged person; ~s *n. pl.* rags and tatters; ~y *adj.* ragged

tattie, tatie *n.* potato; ~-boodie *n.* scarecrow (A, T); ~-bootie *n.* scarecrow (C); ~-chapper *n.* potato masher; ~-clamp *n.* earth pit for storing potatoes; ~-doodle *n.* scarecrow (S); ~-dulie *n.* scarecrow (J); ~-howker *n.* potato-digger; ~-howkin *n.* potato harvest; ~-liftin *n.* potato harvest (J); ~-shaws *n.* potato foliage

taucht *ppl.* taught

tauk *n., v.* talk

taul *v. pt.* told. *cf.* **telt**

tawpie *n.* stupid fellow, blockhead

tawse *n.* leather strap for punishment

tay *n.* tea; ~speen *n.* teaspoon; ~spenfae teaspoonful

tchach *excl.* of disgust, contempt, impatience etc

tchoot *int.* tush!

ted *n.* toad, applied to men as term of contempt, to children, young women or animals as term of endearment; youngster

tedder *v.* tether (M3)

tee *adv.* too; also. *cf.* **tae**

tee, keep her *naut. phr.* alter
course to windward (B)

teel *n.* tool

teem *adj., v.* empty; ~ yir crap
get it off your chest; spill
the beans. *cf.* redd yir crap

teemsteen *n.* tombstone

teen *n.* tune; humour, temper;
ill ~ bad mood; *ppl.*
taken; ~ in cultivated;
~ wi charmed by, pleased
with; ~ on wi fascinated
by; *adj.* the ~ the one, (in
contrast with the tither the
other. *cf.* tak, taen

teep *n.* type

teer *n.* tare; tear; *v.* tear

teet *v.* peep

teeth *in phr.* a ~ in the sky a
broken rainbow (T); ~ache
n. toothache; ~fu *n.* swig;
~less *adj.* toothless; ~ on
nail *phr.* vigorously

teetle *n.* title

teind *n., v.* tithe. *cf.* tiend

telt *v. pt., ppl.* told

temp *v.* tempt

ten *v.* tend; ~nit *ppl.* attended;
looked after

tenner *adj.* tender

tent *n.* care, heed; tak ~
give heed to; *v.* attend, pay
heed to; ~ily *adv.* carefully,
attentively; ~less *adj.*
neglectful; ~y *adj.* careful,
attentive

term-time *n.* end of working
contract: Whitsunday;
Martinmas

terrible *adv.* exceedingly

terrifee *v.* terrify; ~t *ppl.*
terrified

testament *n.* will

teuch *adj.* tough. *cf.* tyeuch

teuchat, teuchit *n.* lapwing;
~'s storm wintry weather in
March, when the lapwings
arrive

teuchter *n.* (*sometimes
disparaging*) *ref. to*
anyone from the North,
to a Highlander or
Gaelic-speaker

teuk *v. pt.* took

thack *n., v.* thatch; ~it *ppl.*
thatched

thae *adj.* those (S, J, C)

thaese *See* thase

thairm *n.* cat-gut; fiddle
string (K)

than *adv.* then; ~-an-awa long
ago

thase *adj.* these

that *adv.* so, *eg,* it wis ~ caul

theat *n.* trace by which horses
draw plough etc, kick owre
the ~s kick over the traces,
become reckless; lat the
~s slack take it easy; oot o
~ unreasonable

theek *v.* thatch (J). *cf* thack

theet *See* theat

theevil *n.* wooden rod for stirring porridge. *cf.* **spurtle**

thegidder, thegither *adv.* together

theirsels *pron.* themselves; *pred. adj., adv.* by themselves, alone; ~s **twa** just the two of them

thenk *v.* thank (s)

thereoot *adv.* outside; in the open air

thestreen *adv., n.* yesterday

thewless *adj.* feeble

thick *adj.* intimate

thiefie *adj.* thief-like, sneaky

thig *v.* beg, borrow, be a genteel beggar; generally applied to the practice of begging seed oats to sow first crop on entering a farm; ~**ger** *n.* genteel beggar

thingumboob, thingumenderry *n.* thingummybob

thin-skint *adj.* sensitive, easily upset

thir *adj., pron.* these; those

thirl *v.* to thrill; tingle; to bring under legal obligation; ~**t** *ppl.* bound, enthralled; ~**age** *n.* bondage

thoara *adj.* thorough (M3)

thocht *n., v. pt., ppl.* thought; ~**-been** *n.* wish-bone; ~**ie** *adv., n.* a little bit

thole *v.* bear; endure; tolerate

thon *pron.* that; *adj.* that, yonder; those. *cf.* **yon**

thoom, thoomb *n., v.* thumb; ~**-piece** oatcakes buttered with thumb; ~**-raip** thumb rope; **keep yir** ~ **on't** keep mum

thoosan(d) *n.* thousand

thorther, thorter *v.* cross harrow (F)

thow *n.* thaw

thowless *adj.* lacking energy or mettle

thraan *adj.* stubborn. *cf.* **thrawn**

thrammle *n.* chain on cattle-binding, for attaching **sell** to a stake

thrang *n.* throng; *adj.* crowded; busy; intimate. *See* **throng**

thrapple *v.* throttle; *n.* throat

thrash *n.* threshed grain; ~**in-mull** *n.* threshing-mill

thraten *v.* threaten

thrave *n.* two **stooks** or 24 **shaifs**; *v. pt.* thrived

thraw *n.* twist; *v.* throw; twist; ~**s o fate** twists of fate

thrawart *adj.* twisting; crooked (K)

thrawcruik, thrawheuk *n.* implement for twisting straw ropes

thrawn *adj.* stubborn; twisted

thraws, in the *phr.* in the grip of (*fig.*)

threep *n.* a vehemently held opinion; *v.* argue, quarrel; insist

threeple *adj.* triple, threefold; *v.* treble

threeplets *n. pl.* triplets

threesh *v. pt.* thrashed; threshed

threet *n.* threat; **-en** *v.* threaten; **~nin** *ppl., adj.* threatening

three-threids-an-a-thrum *phr.* cat's purr (G)

threeve *v.* throve

threip *See* **threep**

thretty *adj.* thirty (K)

thrimble *v.* fumble out

thrissle, thristle *n.* thistle

thrist *n.* thirst; **~y** *adj.* thirsty

throng *adj.* intimate, pally. *cf.* **thrang**

thro(u) *prep.* through. *cf.* **throw**

throw(e) *adj.* finished (M3); *prep.* through; **~ the bows** (of behaviour) over the top; *adj.* finished. *cf.* **throu**; **~-beerin** *n.* livelihood, means of sustenance (A1); **~-come** *n.* ordeal; **~der** *adj.* untidy; muddled; in a confused state; **~-gang** *n.* passage; **~-han** *adv.* under consideration;

tak ~-han discuss; **tak some-een ~-han** run someone down; **~-idder, -ither** *adj., adv.* confused(ly). *cf.* **throwder ~-the-muir** *n.* quarrel;

thrum *n.* end of yarn; *in pl.* purring of a cat; **span her ~s** purred

thrummy *n.* name for a weaver

thruve *v. pt.* thrived. *cf.* **thrave**

thummle *n.* thimble

thunner *n.* thunder; **~-stane** *n.* thunder clap

tials *n. pl.* strings to tie up

tice (wi) *v.* coax

tich|en *v.* tighten; **~t** *adj.* tight

tick an tack *n.* the game of tag. *cf.* **tackie**

ticket *n.* someone of untidy appearance

tickie *n.* piece of, bit of; some

tidder *adj., n.* the other. *cf.* **tither**

tiend *n., v.* tithe. *cf.* **teind**

Tiesday *n.* Tuesday. *cf.* **Tyesday**

tift *n.* state, condition; mood (K)

tig *n.* fit of ill-humour; sudden whim; **tae tak a ~** (R) to take a notion; *v.* touch lightly, tap; **~ wi** dally; have to do with; **~-tire** a practical joke; state of suspense; **tae haud in ~-tire** *phr.* to keep in suspense

tike *n.* dog; unpleasant man;
~ **aal** *adj.* very old

till *prep.* to; compared to

tillie-pan *n.* metal pan used as
a scoop (F)

tillygraph *n.*, *v.* telegraph

tillyphone *n.*, *v.* telephone

tilter *n.* used for tilting loose
sheaves off an old-fashioned
mower or reaper

timeous *adj.* keeping time,
in time

time-sairin *adj.* time-serving

timmer *n.* timber; **wun-~**
seasoned timber (T);
~ **mairket** ancient fair held
in Aberdeen in August; *adj.*
wooden

timmer on, up *v.* work
vigorously

timoursome *adj.* timorous

timpin *adj.* tempting

tin *n.* money (A)

tin-can *n.* corrugated iron

tin|e *n.* prong, spike; *v.* lose;
~**t** *pt.*, *ppl.* lost

tink *n.* (term of contempt)
foul-mouthed, quarrelsome,
vulgar person; ~**ie** *n.* tinker,
one of the travelling people;
~**ie's maskin** tea made in
the cup

tinkler *n.* tinker; ~**'s curse**
something of no value

tint *ppl.*, *adj.* lost; *n.* tent

tippen *n.* hair that binds a
hook to a fishing line

tipperteen *n.* bit of card with
pin passed through it
resembling a teetotum, a top

tire *n.* tiredness; ~**teese** *adj.*
(A2) *(baby talk for a child)*
tired

tirl *n.* vibration; short bout of
anything; *v.* vibrate; rattle;
~ **the sneck** twirl the handle
of the latch

tirment *n.* (*lit.* torment) an
annoyance; *v.* annoy

tirr *v.* strip off; uncover,
undress; unroof, tear off
slates/thatch; ~**t nyaakit**
stripped naked

tirran *n.* tyrant; awkward or
exasperating person; ~**eese**
v. tyrannise

tirravee *n.* commotion

tirr-wirr *n.* quarrel, wrangle

tit *n.* teat; *v.* jerk, twitch, pull

tither, the *adj.* the other.
cf. **tidder**

tittersome *adj.* (of weather)
unsettled; (of a horse)
restless

titty *n.* (child's word) sister

tobacca *n.* tobacco

tocher *n.* dowry. *cf.* **doonsittin**

tod *n.* fox

toddle *n.* toddling walk

toggery *n.* clothes

toit *v.* trot; totter from age

tolerat *v.* tolerate

tongue *v.* scold, abuse

tongue-betroosht *adj.* outspoken

tongue-tackit *ppl., adj.* tongue-tied

too-fa *n.* lean-to shed

tool *n.* towel

toom *adj.* empty (GI, M, J); *v.* empty (K). *cf.* **teem**

toon *n.* a town; farmstead. *cf.* **toun**

toondie, toondy *See* **toonkeeper**

toonkeeper *n.* the person left in charge of a farmstead on Sunday. *cf.* **catcher, toondie**

toonser *n.* town-dweller

toopachin, toopican *n.* pinnacle, summit; steeple, turret

toor *n., v.* tower; ~in *ppl.* towering. *cf.* **tour**

toorie *n.* topknot (on bonnet)

toosht *v.* handle carelessly

tooshtie *n.* small quantity

toosle, toozle *v.* dishevel; tussle

toosy *adj.* tousled. *cf.* **tousy**

toot fie *excl.*

tooter *v.* work ineffectually

tooteroo *n.* wind instrument

tootie *n.* dram

toot-moot *n.* low muttered conversation; whispering (B1)

topper *n.* first class person or thing

toppers *n. pl.* rubber knee boots worn by fish workers (B)

tory *n.* grub of cranefly, which consumes germinating grain

tossel, toshil *n.* tassle

tossle *v.* tousle. *cf.* **toosle, touzle**

tottum, totum *n.* a teetotum, four-sided top spun in games of chance; the game itself

touchtie *n.* a little

toun *n.* farm. *cf.* **toon**

tour *n.* tower; ~in *ppl.* towering. *cf.* **toor**

tousy *adj.* tousled, dishevelled. *cf.* **toosy**

touzle *v.* ruffle, dishevel. *cf.* **toosle, tossle**

tow *n.* rope; strong twine; **claes** ~ washing line

tow-heidit *adj.* fair-haired (G)

towmond, towmon *n.* twelve-months, year

trachel, trachle *n.* burden, hindrance, struggle; *v.* draggle; trudge; overwork. *cf.* **trauchle**

trachelt *adj.* overburdened, draggled. *cf.* **trauchlet**

track *n.* an oddity (used of untidy person); *v.* to train an animal to go in traces or harness

trackie *n.* earthenware teapot

traecle *n.* treacle

traet *v.* treat. *cf.* **trate**

trag *n.* trash

traik *n.* long, tiring walk, trudge; *v.* trudge

traikle *n.* treacle. *cf.* **traekle, trykle**

trail *n.* dirty, untidy woman; part, portion; *v. intr.* tramp, trudge; *v. tr.* drag

trail the rape old Hallowe'en spell consisting in dragging a straw rope round the house (M); witchcraft device to put a cow off yielding milk

traivel *n.* journey; walk; *v. tr., intr.* travel; walk

traleel *n.* something long and trailing; a tall person (B1)

tram *n.* shaft of barrow or cart

trammle *n.* chain on cattle-binding. *cf.* **thrammle**

tramp-cole *n.* large haycock, made up of smaller ones (F)

trampit *v. pt.* tramped

trams *n.* shafts as of a cart

trance *n.* passage in a house; entrance-hall

transack *n.* transaction; deal; dealings; *v.* transact; **~ins** *n. pl.* dealings

trate *n.* treat. *cf.* **traet**

trauchelt *See* **trachelt**

trauchle *See* **trachle**

travail *n.* work; exertion

travise, trevis *n.* division between stalls in cowshed

trebble *n.* trouble (B1). *cf.* **tribble**

treesh *v.* curry favour; treat in a friendly, flattering way; call to cattle

treetle *v.* trickle; trot (G, M3)

treid *v.* tread (J)

trett *n.* treat

tribble *n., v.* trouble; problem; **~r** *n.* a troublesome thing (A). *cf.* **trebble**

trickit *adj.* tricky; wicked; delighted (S) *eg,* **fair ~ wi masel; ~ (up)** *ppl.* dressed (up). *cf.* **triggit**

triffle, trifflie *n.* trifle; small sum

trig *adj.* tidy; *v.* to tidy up, dress smartly; *ppl., adj.* **~git (oot)**

trincher *See* **truncher**

trink, trinkie *n.* narrow channel; rut

trinkle *n., v.* trickle

trippin *in phr.* **his face wis ~ im** he looked glum, displeased

troch *n.* watering trough for cattle and horses

trock *See* **troke**

trockins *n. pl.* dealings

trogs *excl.* troth! (as an oath)

troke *n.* goods of no value; trash; truck, dealings; *v.* exchange, barter; **~s** odds and ends. *cf.* **trock**

troo *v.* trust; believe

trool *n.* trowel

troonk *n.* lobster pot (term used in St Combs)

troosers *n. pl.* trousers

troot *n.* trout; ~ i the waal *phr.* child in the offing (M3)

trot, the backdoor *phr.* diarrhoea

troth *int.* truly; *n.* truth

trowth *n., int.* truth; **~fu** *adj.* truthful

true *v.* play truant; also ~ **the squeel**

truff *n.* a turf

trummle *v.* tremble. *cf.* **chitter**

trump(e) *n.* Jew's harp; **stang o the ~** best of the lot

trumph *n.* trump; **fat's ~?** what's doing?

truncher *n.* trencher, wooden platter

trykle *n.* treacle

trypal *n.* tall, lanky, ill-shaped person

tryst *v.* appoint a meeting; entice; *n.* an appointed meeting

trytle *v.* lag (A1)

tsil *n.* child. *cf.* **chill**

tull *prep.* to; till. *cf.* **till**

tulzie *n.* quarrel

tummle *n., v.* tumble; **~-doon** *adj.* tumbledown; ~ **the cat** *phr.* do a somersault (O); **~-tam** *n.* hay-gatherer (F)

tummler *n.* glass tumbler

turk *adj.* angry, annoyed (A1)

turkis *n.* a pair of pincers

turned-gyang *n.* row of sheaves on a stack, with the shear underneath (F)

turnkwite *n.* turncoat; backslider

turn-oot *n.* attendance

turn ower *v.* fare moderately well

Turra *pr. n.* nickname for Turriff

Turra Coo *pr. n.* dairy cow confiscated from a Turriff farmer who refused to stamp the insurance cards of his workers, when the Health Insurance Act was introduced in 1913. A riot ensued when the cow was put up for sale

turse *v.* dress; adjust one's clothes

twa *adj.* two; **~-faul** double; **~-han** two-handed; **~-three, (a)** *adj.*, (*n.*) two or three, a few, several

twae *adj.* two. *cf.* **twa**

twal *adj.* twelve; **~mont(h)** *n.* a twelve-month period; year

twa're, a *See* **twa-three**

tweeshtichen *n.* small quantity

tweetle *v.* tootle on a wind instrument

tweezlock, tweezlick *See* thawcruick

twig *n.* glance; *v.* glance; catch sight of; see through a dodge

twine *n.* string; *v.* turn, twist; ~r *n.* rope-twister

twinty *adj.* twenty

twise *adv.* twice (A1)

tyach *excl.* of impatience

tyaave, tyauve *v.* work strenuously, struggle; *n.* struggle

tyangs *n. pl.* tongs

tyce *v.* entice

tye *excl.* giving assent. *cf.* ay

tye wye or e tidder *phr.* one way or another (M3)

Tyesday *n.* Tuesday (A). *cf.* Tiesday

tyeuch *See* teuch

tyeuk *v. pt.* took

tyeuve *v. pt.* struggled. *cf.* tyauve

tyke *n.* dog; ticking for beds. *cf.* tike

tyler *n.* tailor

tylie *n.* tailor

tyne *See* tine

typ|e *v.* labour hard; a ~in job physically exhausting job (A1); ~it *ppl., adj.* worn out by hard work

U

ug *v.* to feel disgust; ~git disgusted; ~some *adj.* disgusting, ghastly, horrible; tak an ~ at *phr.* take a dislike to

ulkie *adj.* each, every. *cf.* ilka

ull *adj.* ill, bad; ~ baabee *phr.* bad penny; ~-less-guid-less *adj.* harmless; ~-mynit *adj.* evil-minded; the ~ place *phr.* hell (*cf.* the ill pairt); ~-wull *n.* ill will; tak an ~-wull at take a dislike to. *See* ill, ill-

ulzie *n.* oil (K)

umberella *n.* umbrella

umman *n.* woman. *cf.* 'oman

umquhile *adj.* former

umrage *n.* umbrage

unbehauden *adj.* not obliged

unca *adj.* odd, strange, peculiar; unknown, unfamiliar; extraordinary; ~ man stranger; *adv.* extremely; very. *cf.* unco

uncanny *adj.* dangerous, threatening (supernaturally); unearthly, ghostly; weird

unce *n.* ounce

unceevil *adj.* uncivil

unco *adj.* strange, unknown ~-gweed *adj., (n.)* self-

righteous (person). *See* **unca**
uncolies *adv.* strangely; very
   much, extremely
unctioneer *n.* auctioneer.
   cf. **ungshineer**
undevaulin *adj.* unceasing
unedicat *adj.* uneducated
ungshin *n.* auction; ~**eer**
   n. auctioneer
unlade *v.* unload
unnersteed *v. pt.* understood
uphaader *n.* supporter (M3)
unsocht *ppl., adj.* unsought
unthocht-lang *adj.* without
   getting bored
unvrocht *adj.* unworked
   (land)
unweirdy *adj.* ill-fated;
   unfortunate
up-castin *n.* rising of clouds
   above horizon threatening
   rain
upcome *n.* quick-witted
   remark
upfessin, upfeshin *n.*
   upbringing
uphaud *v.* uphold
upmakker *n.* one who invents
   a story (M3)
upo *prep.* upon
uppish *adj.* ambitious,
   aspiring; upwardly mobile
upple *v.* (of weather) clear
upsettin *adj.* pretentious;
   forward

upsides wi *adv.* equal with,
   on a par with
up-tail *v.* depart in a hurry;
   run off
uptak *n.* apprehension
up-through *n.* upper part of
   the country
upthrow *adj.* upland
upwith, -wuth *adv.* upwards,
   rising (as of a market)
ur *See* **or**

V

vaig *n.* idler
vaigabon *n.* vagabond
vailyable *adj.* valuable
vailye *n., v.* value
vainish *v.* vanish
valinteen *n.* valentine
vauntie *adj.* vain; exultant;
   ostentatious
vawcant *adj.* vacant
vawpour *n.* vapour
veelent *adj.* violent
veeper *n.* viper
veeperate *adj.* venomous,
   vicious; bitterly abusive
veeshus *adj.* vicious
veesion *n.* vision
veesit *n.* visit
veesitor *n.* visitor
vengefu *adj., adv.* vengeful(ly);
   vindictive(ly)
vennel *n.* alley, narrow lane

ventur *n.*, *v.* venture; **vintrin** *ppl.* venturing

vera, verra *adj.*, *adv.* very

verlies *adv.* actually

verty *adj.* eager; wide-awake; early up

veshel *n.* vessel

vex *v.* distress, upset; ~ed *ppl.* distressed; sorry; worried

viackle *n.* vehicle

vice *n.* voice. *cf.* **vyce**

vintrin *ppl, adj.* venturing

virr *n.* force, vigour, "go"

vive *adj.* clear, vivid

vizzie *See* **vizzy**

vizzy *n.* look; view; ~ **backart** backward look

vogie *adj.* proud

vokie *adj.* jocular (A2). *cf.* **vyokie**

voo *v.* vow

vooch *v.* vouch

vrack *n.* wreck, ruin

vran *n.* wren

vrang *adj.*, *n.* wrong

vrap *v.* wrap. *cf.* **wap**

vrapper *n.* working smock, overall; woman's loose jacket, blouse

vrastle *v.* wrestle (B1). *cf.* **warsle**

vrat *v. pt.* wrote

vratch *n.* wretch

vreath *n.* a wreath of snow

vreet *v.* write; *n.* handwriting; (something in) writing; ~ter *n.* writer; ~in *n.* handwriting; ~in-dask *n.* desk; ~in-paper *n.* writing paper

vricht *n.* wright, joiner, carpenter

vring *v.* wring

vrocht *v. pt.* wrought, worked

vrote *v. pt.* wrote

vrung *ppl.* wrung

vrutten *ppl.* written. *See* **vreet**

vyaig *n.* loose woman

vyce *n.* voice. *cf.* **vice**

vyokie *adj.* jocular. *cf.* **vokie**

vyow *n.* view

W

wa *adv.* away; *n.* wall; way; **come yir ~s ben** come away in or through. *cf.* **awa**

waages *n. pl.* wages

waal *n.* well

waakrife *adj. See* **waukrife**

waal-tams *n. pl.* Buchan name for **nicky-tams**

waan *n.* wand; fishing-rod

waar *adj.* worse; ~ **o the weer** the worse for wear; *v.* spend. *cf.* **waur, wair, ware**

waares *n.* wares

waav *n.* wave

wab *n.* web, woven fabric; ~ster *n.* weaver

wabbit *adj.* exhausted

wabble *n.* insipid drink (M3)

wa-cast *adj., n.* (anything) worthless

wacht *n.* draught (of ale etc); weight. *cf.* **weicht**

wachy *adj.* stale (B)

wad *v.* 1. wed, marry; ~**din** *n.* wedding; ~**dit** *v. pt.* wedded, married; 2. *v.* would, ~**na** *v. pt. or cond., neg.* would not. *cf.* **wid**

wadge *v.* brandish threateningly

wadset *v.* mortgage

wae *n.* woe; *adj.* sad, sorrowful; sorry; ~ **for** sorry for; ~**'s me** woe is me!; ~**fu** *adj.* woeful; ~**some** *adj.* sorrowful, sad

waff *n.* puff of wind; whiff, odour

waffle *adj.* limp from weakness; shaky

wag *v.* wave, shake; carry on, proceed; fare; ~**-at-the-wa** *n.* wall clock with pendulum

wa-gawn *adj.* departing; *n.* departure

waif *adv.* astray (K)

waik *adj.* weak; ~**ness** *n.* weakness. *cf.* **wyke**, **wykeness**

wainished-like *adj.* (vanished), pinched, thin

wair *v.* spend. *cf.* **ware**

waister *n.* something, someone of no further use, due to infirmity, disease etc

waistry *n.* waste. *cf.* **wastrie**

waldies *n. pl.* wellington boots

wale *n.* choice, selection; *v.* choose; *int.* well (S). *cf.* **weel**

walgin *n.* bundle; pouch; something large and roomy

wall *n.* well. *cf.* **waal**

wallant *adj.* (of flowers) withered

wallet *n.* bag for carrying personal items on a journey

walloch *n.* Highland dance; *v.* cry, shriek, wail

wallop *v.* dance (K); ~**in** *n.* dancing (K)

wally-draggle, -draigle *n.* sloven; good-for-nothing; insignificant, untidy person. *cf.* **warridrag**

walthy *adj.* wealthy

waly *excl.* of woe

wame *n.* belly; stomach. *cf.* **wime**

wamfle *adj.* flexible

wammle *v.* overturn; turn over; roll; undulate; writhe

wan *adv.* way: Kintore ~ in the direction of Kintore; *n.* wand; fishing-rod; *v. pt.* won; ~ **aff** got off

wandocht *n.* silly creature

wan'er, wanner *v.* wander

wanworth, wanwurth *n.* a
mere nothing, something of
little value (A1)

wap *n.* sharp stroke;
v. strike sharply; flap; wrap.
cf. wip, wup

war *v. pt.* were; ~na were not

wardl|e *n.* world; ~y *adj.*
worldly. *cf.* warl

ware *n.* cash (S); wire (S).
cf. weer; *v.* spend. *cf.* wair

wark *n.* work; ~hoose *n.*
workhouse; ~leem, ~loom
n. tool, implement;
a ~ a job; fuss; sic a ~ what
a fuss; *v.* (rarely) to work.
cf. wirk

warl, warld *n.* world. *cf.* wardle

warly-wise *adj.* worldly-wise

warn *v.* warrant. *cf.* warran

warna *v. pt. neg.* were not

warple *v.* entangle; twist

warrandice *n.* warranty

warri(e)drag, warriedraggle
n. good-for-nothing;
under-sized person or
animal; slowcoach; ~s,
**towrags an swypins o the
pier** riff-raff (B)

warsh *adj.* insipid. *cf.* wersh

warsle, warstle *v.* wrestle,
struggle

warst *adj., n.* worst

was *in phr.* ~-a-year a year ago

washen *ppl.* washed

waskit *n.* waistcoat. *cf.* weskit

wast *adj.* west; ~er western;
~ward *adv.* westward

wastrie *n.* waste. *cf.* waistry

wastrifeness *n.* waste

wat *adj.* wet; *v. pt.* wet;
v. pt. waited (M3); *v.* know;
~na *v. pt. neg.* wot not, did
not know

watrence *n.* an entry cut
through hedge or bank
to give stock access to
drinking water

watter *n.* water; ~-brash
n. heartburn (with
watery acid eructations);
~fa *n.* waterfall; ~-gless
n. water-glass, solution
used for preserving eggs;
~-kelpie *n.* water sprite;
~y *n.* lavatory

wattery *adj.* watery; -nibbit
adj. having a nasal drip

wauble *adj.* of a weak watery
flavour; wobbly; *v.* wobble

wauch *n.* swig

wauchle *v.* struggle;
waddle; wade

waucht *n.* large draught;
weight; ~y *adj.* weighty,
heavy. *cf.* wecht

wauger *n., v.* wager

wauges *n.* wages. *cf.* waages

wauk *n., v.* walk; ~er *n.*
walker; **by ~er's bus** on

Shanks' pony, on foot; ~ie
n. walk; walkway, path

wauk|en *v.* waken; ~ent
ppl., adj. awake; ~rife *adj.*
sleepless

waur *adj.* worse; ~st worst;
v. spend (money); ~ i the
weer *phr.* the worse for
wear

wean *n.* child (A, K, M) (*pro.*
ween)

wear awa *v.* to take one's
leave; to fade away; die

weariet *adj.* wearied

weasen, weason, weazen,
weazon *n.* gullet; windpipe

wecht *n.* weight; sieve with
solid base. *cf.* **wacht, waucht**

wedder *n.* wether, castrated ram

wee *adj.* small; *n.* a little bit;
a little while; **bide-a-~** stay
a while

weeda *n.* widow

weel *adj., adv., excl.* well;
~-a-wat *excl.* assuredly;
~-a-wins (wuns) *excl.* of
soothing and endearment;
~-a-wite *excl.* assuredly;
~-faured, -faurt *adj.* well-
favoured, handsome;
~-geddert *adj.* well off;
~-kent *adj.* well-known;
~-prenciplt *adj.* having
strong principles

weelins *vbl. n.* full use of one's
limbs or faculties, *eg,* **tae**
hae the ~ o yir airms (B1)

Weelum *pr. n.* William

weemen, weemin *n.* women

weemple an wample *phr.* turn
and twist

weeng *n.* wing

weepies *n.* ragweed (J)

weer *n.* wear; wire; knitting-
needle; *v.* wear; ~in geylies
throu nearly finished; ~ in
get underway, go ahead;
~ on (of time) approach;
~ tee come to, recover

weers o, on the *phr.* just
about (to), on the point
of; in the way of (M3).
cf. **aweers**

weesh(t) *v. pt.* washed

weesht *imp.* hush

weet *adj., v.* wet; ~ichtie
adj. wettish; ~y *adj.* rainy

weezhin *n.* baby

weffle *adj.* pliable

weich|t *n.* weight; ~en (doon)
ppl. weighed down.
cf. **wacht**

weird *n.* fate, destiny; ~less
adj. ill-fated; improvident;
worthless

weit *See* **weet**

welkin *n.* sky (K, M1)

went *n.* glance; glimpse; blink

wersh *adj.* tasteless. *cf.* **warsh**

we's *pr. with v.* we'll; we're

weskit *n.* waistcoat. *cf.* **waskit**
weyk *adj.* weak. *cf.* **wyke**
wha *pron.* who (GI). *cf.* **fa**
whaal *n.* whale
whack *n.* slice; large portion of food and drink
wham *pron.* whom
whang *n.* blow; lash; chunk
whapper *n.* lie
whaup *n.* curlew; empty peapod (T)
whaur *adv.* where (GI). *cf.* **far**; ~ **awa** *adv.* whither
whause *pron.* whose
whazzle *v.* wheeze. *cf.* **wheezle**
wheeber *n.* whistling sound
wheeble *See* **wheeple**
wheech, wheek *v.* move through the air with a whizzing sound; whisk away; flick
wheel *n.* spinning wheel
wheelie-birr *n.* child's imaginary toy car (T)
wheen *n.* number; quantity
wheep *n.* whip; ~**han** *n.* whiphand, upperhand; ~**er-in** *n.* school attendance officer. *cf.* **whup, fup**
wheeple *n.* shrill, intermittent note with little variation of tone; *v.* whistle; call (of birds)
wheeriorums *n. pl.* intricate pieces of machinery
wheetie *adj.* mean, shabby

wheetie-like *adj.* having the appearance of meanness
wheezle *v.* wheeze. *cf.* **whazzle**
whigmaleerie *n.* a fantastic, useless ornament; foolish fancy; contraption
whilie *n.* a little while
whilk *rel. pron.* which
whip-the-cat *n.* tailor with no fixed place of business, who goes from house to house (M)
whirligig *n.* any rapidly revolving object
whitet-, whitie-broons *n. pl.* unbleached thread
whittle *n.* long knife
whom(m)le *v.* upset (K); (of liquid) churn (K). *cf.* **whummle**
whotten *a excl.* what a. *cf.* **fit a, fut a**
whummle *v. tr., intr.* overturn (J)
whundyke *n.* fence consisting of furze bushes.
whup *v.* whip; *cf.* **wheep, fup. in a** ~ in a trice; ~~**-the-cat.** *See* **whip-the-cat**
whurl *v.* whirl
whusky *n.* whisky
whust *n.* whist
whylock *n.* little while
wi *prep.* with

wice *adj.* wise; **~-like** *adj.*
  seemly, respectable;
  sensible. *cf.* **wyce**
wicht *n.* wight; person
wick *n.* corner; corner of the
  eye or mouth
wicket *adj.* wicked
wid *adj.* mad (A1); *n.* wood;
  v. would. *cf.* **wud**
widda *n.* widow. *cf.* **widdie**
widden *adj.* wooden
widder *n.* weather. *cf.* **wither**;
  ~-gaw trick (**gaw**) of the
  weather; *v.* wither
widdie *n.* small wood; gallows;
  widow (J) (*cf.* **weeda**);
  haddock dried without
  being split; **as dry as a ~**;
  ~fu *n.* rogue; scamp;
  ~-waan *n.* willow wand
wide *n.* weed; *v.* wade. *cf.* **wyde**
widna *v. pt., neg.* would not
wif|e, wifie, *n.* woman,
  married or not; **~ockie**
  n. little woman, wife
wik *n.* week; **~-en** *n.* weekend
wil *adj., adv.* wild, wildly.
  cf. **wull**
wile *v.* choose, select; **~ warst**
  the worst of the selection.
  cf. **wale, wyle**
wilipen *v.* (vilipend), vilify,
  defame
willieway *v.* (wellaway! alas!)
  bewail, lament
wime *n.* belly; stomach

wimple *v.* (of a stream) wind;
  meander
win *n.* wind; **~-casten** *adj.* cast
  aside by the wind; *v.* dry
  (stooks); earn; harvest; go,
  reach a place; get; reside
  ~ aff asleep fall asleep;
  ~ awa go away; **~ by** pass;
  ~ hame get home; **~ oot**
  get out, escape; **~ redd o**
  get rid of; **~ tee wi** get even
  with; catch up with; **~ up**
  wi catch up with
winceys *n.* petticoats made of
  wincey
windae *n.* window; **~-sneck** *n.*
  window catch. *cf.* **winnock**
windlestrae *n.* tall, thin,
  withered stalk of grass
  of various kinds; crested
  dogstail grass
windlin *See* **winlin**
windy *n.* window (J)
wingle *v.* dangle loosely
wink *v.* brim
winker *n.* eyelash. *cf.* **brier**
winlin *n.* bundle (of straw)
winna *v. fut. neg.* will not
winner *n., v.* wonder; **~fu** *adj.*
  wonderful
winnerstan *v.* understand (M3)
winnister *n.* fan for
  winnowing corn
winnock *n.* window (A1, K)

winny *adj.* windy; boastful;
  v. winnow (S)
winraa *n.* gathered row of
  hay (F)
winrin *ppl.* wondering
wint *n.*, *v.* want, lack; desire
winter, to get *phr.* to clear the
  fields of harvested grain
wi'oot *prep.* without.
  cf. **withoot, athoot**
wip *v.* wrap, bind tightly.
  cf. **wup**
wir *pron.* our
wird *n.* word
wire intae *v.* set to work on
wires *n. pl.* knitting needles.
  cf. **weers**
wirk *v.* work; **~er** *n.* worker
wirm *n.* worm
wirry *v.* worry; **~-coo** *n.*
  bugbear (K)
wirsels *pron.* ourselves.
  cf. **oorsels**
wirsit *adj.*, *n.* worsted
wirth *n.* worth
wis *v. pt.* was
wise *v. tr.* advise (someone in
  a matter); instruct
wish! *imper.* turn right!
  (command to Buchan
  plough-horse) (T)
wisht! *int.* hush!
wiskar *n.* woven container
  worn round knitter's waist
  to hold needles (M3)

wisna *v. pt. neg.* was not
wiss *n.*, *v.* wish. *cf.* **wuss**
wissen *v.* wither, shrivel
wistna *v. pt. neg.* did
  not know
wite *n.*, *v.* blame. *cf.* **wyte**
wither *n.* weather. *cf.* **widder**
withershins *adv.*
  anti-clockwise
withoot *prep.* without.
  cf. **athoot**
withouten *prep.* without (K)
witriffe *adj.* wild to madness,
  raging
witril, wittrel, witterel *n.*
  peevish, waspish person
witter *n.* barb of a dart or
  hook; *in pl.* the throat;
  v. struggle
wivven *ppl.* woven
wizzen *n.* gullet; *v.* wither,
  shrivel
wob *n.* web; **~by** *adj.* covered
  with cobwebs
womle *v.* be squeamish;
  (of the stomach) rumble
  queasily
womble-bree *n.* soup made
  with offal
won *v. pt. of* **win** resided
wonner *n.* wonder
woo *n.* wool. *cf.* **oo**
woorlich (B1). *See* **oorlich**
woorthy *n.* worthy
wordle *n.* world. *cf.* **wardle**
wordy *adj.* worthy, deserving

wormit *n.* wormwood
worn awa *ppl.* deceased
worry *v.* choke; strangle
worsit *n.* worsted; woollen
  yarn, knitting wool; **~t-bag**
  n. wool-bag
worth *in phr.* **gaed ~** went to
  pot
wot *v.* to know; *pt.* knew
wowff *n.* wolf; *v.* swallow,
  swig
wow's me *excl.* woe is me
wrack *n.* wreck; destruction
wraith *n.* (of snow) drift;
  wrath; spectral apparition
  of a living person (K)
wrang *adj.*, *n.* wrong; **~ spy**
  mistaken identity
wranglesome *adj.* argumentative
wrapper *n.* working apron,
  overall. *cf.* **vrapper**
wratch *n.* wretch. *cf.* **vratch**
wreathe *v.* writhe
wreith *n.* wraith, ghost
wreth (B1). *See* **raith**
wricht *n.* carpenter. *cf.* **vricht**
wrocht *v. pt.* worked. *cf.* **vrocht**;
  ~-up *adj.* overwrought
wrunkelt *adj.* wrinkled
wud *adj.* mad; **clean reed ~**
  stark staring mad; *n.* wood;
  v. would; **~na** would not.
  cf. **wid**
wudden *adj.* wild; mad;
  ~-dream *n.* sudden frantic
  motion or effort

wuddie, wuddy *n.* gallows.
  ~fu *n.* ne'er-do-well;
  scamp. *cf.* **widdie**
wulk *n.* whelk; periwinkle
wull *adj.* wild; bewildered;
  adv. astray; **~cat** wildcat;
  ~-like *adj.* as if lost; *n.*, *v.*
  will; **~in** *adj.* willing; **o ~** of
  one's own accord; **A hinna
  ~** I've no desire
Wull, Wullie *pr. n.* William
wully-goo *n.* grotesque person
wumman *n.* woman
wummle *v.* turn over and
  over. *cf.* **whummle**
wumple *n.* tangle of objects;
  v. (of a river) twist, turn
wun *v. pt.* wound; harvested.
  See **win**
wund|a, ~ockie *n.* window
  (M3)
wunna *v. fut. neg.* will not
wunt *v.* want; **~in't** without it
wup *v.* bind, bandage, wrap.
  cf. **wip**
wur *v. pt.* were. *cf.* **war**
wurr *n.*, *v.* growl
wu(r)th, gaed *phr.* went to
  pot, to ruin. *cf.* **worth**
wusp *n.* wisp
wuss *n.*, *v.* wish. *cf.* **wiss**
wut *n.* wit; *in pl.* wits
wutness *n.* witness
Wutsunday *n.* Whitsunday
wutten *ppl.* wet
wutter *n.* barb on a fish hook

wutteroch *n.* weasel; also used as term of endearment (M3)

wyce *adj.* wise. *cf.* **wice**

wyde *n.* weed; *v.* wade. *cf.* **wide**

wye *n.* way; **there's nae twa ~s aboot it** there's only one possibility; *v.* weigh; **~d, ~t** *ppl.* weighed

wyke *adj.* weak; **~ness** *n.* weakness

wyl|e *v.* choose; **~in** *n.* selection. *cf.* **wile**

wyme *n.* belly; womb

wynd *n.* narrow lane or street

wynin *n.* division of a field (F)

wyte *n.* blame; fault; *v.* wait

wyve *v.* weave; knit

wyver *n.* spider

wyvin *n.* weaving; knitting **~ weer** *n.* knitting needle (M3)

Y

yaamer (M3) *See* **yammer**

yaaws *See* **yauws**

(yab-)yabber *v.* talk excitedly

yab-yabble *n.* gabble

yacht *v. pr. & pt.* own, owned; owe

yafa *adj.* awful (M). *cf.* **aafa**

yaird *n.* yard (unit of measurement); farm garden. *cf.* **yard**

Yakkie *pr. n.* Peterhead name for the Eskimo, deriv. from Yaqui (B)

yaldie *n.* yellow-hammer (C)

yall *n., v.* yell

yalla *adj.* yellow; *n.* yellow turnip; **~ geordie** guinea; **~ yite** *n.* yellowhammer (M3)

yammer *v.* chatter; clamour; cry aloud; jabber

yamph *adj.* hungry, ravenous (AI)

yap *adj.* hungry; **~py** hungry-looking

yard *n.* farm garden. *cf.* **yaird**

yark *v.* jerk; push; tug; work hard; **~ in** drive in

yarlins *n.* device for winding yarn into skeins

yarp *v.* carp, complain

yarr *n.* corn spurrey

yaucht *See* **yacht**

yaum *n.* foolish talk (R)

yaummer *v.* cry out. *cf.* **yammer**

yauws *n. pl.* arms *eg,* of a windmill

yavil *n.* second year crop; **~-broth** *n.* second day's broth

yavin *n.* awn, the beard of oats or barley

yawfu *adj.* awful. *cf.* **yafa**

ye *pron.* you

yea *adv.* yes; (before a *v.* used for the 2nd time) again and again *eg,* **threepit an yeathreepit**

yearock *n.* hen not exceeding a year old, pullet. *cf.* **earock**

Yeel *n.* Christmas. *cf.* **Yule, Eel**

yeld *adj.* (of an animal) barren; not yielding milk. *cf.* **eel**

yeldrin *n.* yellow-hammer

yelloch *v.* scream; bawl

yer *pron.* your. *cf.* **yir**

yerd *n.* yard (unit of measurement)

yerl *n.* earl

yersel *pron.* yourself; *pred. adj., adv., phr.* by yourself, alone;

youkie *adj.* itchy. *cf.* **yockie**

ye's *pron. with v.* you'll

yestreen *adv., n.* yesterday evening. *cf.* **the streen**

yett *n.* gate

yill *n.* ale

yim *n.* thin film or coating on a surface

yir *pron.* your. *cf.* **yer**

yird *n.* earth, soil; the earth (ᴋ); *v.* bury; ~**it** *ppl.* buried; covered in earth, dirty

yirl *n.* earl

yirlin *n.* yellow-hammer (ᴍ). *cf.* **yalla yite**

yirn *v. tr., intr.* curdle; ~**t milk** curds and whey; ~**in** *n.* rennet; the stomach of a calf; the human stomach (ᴀ2)

yirsel *pron.* yourself; ~**s twa** the two of you. *cf.* **yersel**

yist *v.* hiccup

yitt *See* **yett**

yivvery *adj.* eager, hungry for

yoam *n.* steam; vapour; *v.* to blow with warm air; steam, belch

yock *n., v.* itch; ~**ie** *adj.* itchy

yok|e *n.* yoke, wooden spar for pulling a plough; *v.* to attach horse to plough, harness, etc; to start work; begin; **get** ~**it** start work; ~**e intae** begin; ~ **tae** begin; **weel** ~**it** well-matched; ~**in** *n.* working period during which horses are in harness; ~**in-time** *n.* the time to begin or resume farm work

yole *n.* yawl, small two-masted sailing-boat

yon *adj.* that, those

yonner *adv.* yonder

yont *adj.* distant; yonder; that; those; *adv.* yonder, farther away

you eens *pron. pl.* you

youkie *adj.* itchy. *cf.* **yockie**

youthheid *n.* (in abstract) youth

yowden-drift *n.* wind-driven snow

yowder *n.* bad smell of fumes from burning

yowe, yowie *n.* ewe; fir cone
yowff (doon) *v.* gobble (M3)
yowm *n.* vapour. *cf.* **yoam**
Yule *pr. n.* Christmas;
   Christmas Day; the
Christmas season till after
New Year, *now mainly lit.*
cf. **Yeel, Eel.**
yunkers *n. pl.* children

Part Two

English – Doric

A

abandon *v.* (forsake) forhooie;
   (an acquaintance) purvoy;
   ~ed *ppl., adj.* forhooiet;
   pervoot (M3)
Aberchirder *pr. n.* (nicknamed)
   Foggieloan
Aberdeen *pr. n.* Aiberdeen
Aberdeen football team the
   Dons
Aberdour *pr. n.* Aiberdour
ability *n.* can; capawcity
ablaze *adv.* alow(e); alunt
about *prep.* aboot
above *adv., prep.* abeen;
   aboon (K); atheen.
Aboyne *pr. n.* Abyne
abreast *adv.* abreist
abundance *n.* feck; fouth;
   rowth; (to have) to be biggit
   oot; **in ~** galore
abundant *adj.* rowth, routh
abus|e *v.* ill-eese; (verbally)
   caird; ill-tongue; kyaard;
   misca; tongue; ~ive *adj.*
   (bitterly) veeperate; ~ive
   language ill-win
accept *v.* accep, *ppl.* acceppit
accident *n.* amshach; mishanter
accommodate *v.* accommodat
accompany *v.* convoy
accomplish *v.* (by means) moyen
accord, of one's own *phr.* o wull
account *n., v.* accoont; **on**
   no ~ naewye (S)

accountable *adj.* accoontable
accoutrements *n. pl.* graith
accumulate wealth *v.* fog
accustomed to, get *v.* cuddam
   wi (M3)
ache *n., v.* stoond, stound
acquaint *v.* (intimate) forquant
acquaintance *n.* acquantance
acquainted *ppl.* acquant (G);
   acquaint (B); acquint (S)
acre *n.* aacre; awcre
across *prep.* athort; but
act *v.* ack; ~ing *n.* playackin
action *n.* ack
active *adj.* forcie; kibble; on
   the pirr
actor *n.* ackir
actually *adv.* verlies
acute *adj.* (in understanding)
   lang-nebbit, -nibbit
adapt *v.* adap; ~ed adappit
add (on or to) *v.* eek, eik, eke
addition *n.* eek, eik
addition to, in *prep. phr.* forbye
adept *n.* da(u)b; a dab haan
adhere to *v.* clap tae
admit *v.* own; ~ **defeat** own baet
adorn *v.* busk
adornment *n.* (vain or
   fanciful) flumgummery
adroit *adj.* nacky
adults *n. pl.* growen folk
advance *n., v.* (wages) sub
advancement *n.* fordal, fordle
advantage *n.* (in bargaining)
   nip; **take ~ of** tak the gweed

o; tak a len o; **steal a march on** get a nip o some-een

advertise *v.* scry

advise *v.* rede (J); wise

adze *n.* each

aerated drink *n.* ale

affable *adj.* humoursome; gash

affair *n.* rickmatick; **the whole ~** the hail rickmatick

affectation *n.* pit-on

afflicted *adj.* afflickit

afford *v.* affoord

afraid *adj.* feart; fleyt; **don't be ~** dinna be feart; fearna; **I'm ~ that** A'm fleyt that

after *prep., conj.* aifter, efter; passin; **~ an hour** passin an oor; **~ all** efter-an-aa

afternoon *n.* aifterneen (A); aifternin (S)

afterwards *adv.* aifter, efter; efterhin, aifterhin

against *prep.* agane (K); agin

aged *adj.* eildit

agent *n.* aagent; deester

agile *adj.* keeble; kibble; swuppert

agitate *v.* flucht; **~d** fluchtit

ago *adv.* syne; seen; **a year ~** a year syne; was-a-year

agree *v.* gree

ahead *adv., prep.* aheid; **get ~ with** get fordalt wi

ailment *n.* (*in pl.*) sairs; (of unknown cause) income

aim *n.* mint; *v.* ettle; mint

ajar *adv.* ajee, agee

akin *adj.* sib

alarm *n.* alairm

alas *excl.* alis(s)

alder *n.* arn-tree (J)

ale *n.* ale; yill. *cf.* **aerated drink**

alehouse *n.* chynge-hoose

alert *adj.* knief

Alexander *pr. n.* Ake; Akie; Ackie; Saaners, Sauners; Saaney, Sawney; Sandy

alight *v.* licht

alive *adj.* alist

all *adj.* aa; **~ over** *adv.* athort; **not at ~** deil the bit

alley *n.* vennel

allow *v.* alloo; *v. pt.* alloot

allure *v.* goy

Almighty *adj.* Almichty

almost *adv.* amaist; gey near; near; nearhan

alms *n.* a(w)mous

alone *pred. adj., adv.* aleen, alane; masel etc (maleen, yirleen, oorleen, himleen, herleen; their, themleen); **all ~** aa maleen etc; **let well ~** lat weel abee; **quite ~** bird-aleen; leefulleen, -lane

along *prep.* alang

aloof *adj.* abeech, abeich

aloud *adv.* heich

already *adv.* aready

also *adv.* an aa; as weel; tee;
tae (s)
always *adv.* aye
am not *v.* neg. amnin; **am
I not?** amnin aw?
amazement *n.* (state of) maze
ambitious *adj.* uppish
amends *n. pl.* amens
ammunition *n.* ammuneetion
among *prep.* amang; amo;
amon; amin (s); 'mon
amount *n.* amunt; (small)
inchie
amusement *n.* ameesement
amusing *adj.* shortsome
ancestor *n.* forbeer
ancient *adj.* aancient, auncient
and *conj.* an
Andrew *pr. n.* Andra; Andro
Andrewmas *pr. n.* Anersmas
anger *v.* kittle
angry *adj.* mad; raist; turk; **get
~** get yir birse/dander up
animal *n.* (old, outworn) runk;
farm ~s *n.* beastle (M3)
ankle *n.* cweet, queet;
twist your ~ thraw yir
cweet
announce *v.* lat licht that;
~ment board *n.* (at church)
scries-boord
annoy *v.* kittle; **~ed** *adj.* turk;
~ing *adj.* angersome; **~ance**
n. bucker; tirment
annual *adj.* annwal; onwal

anoint *v.* anynt; *ppl.* anyntit
another *adj., pron.* anidder;
anither; anodder (A2)
ant *n.* emmenteen (M3);
emmerteen
anticlockwise *adv.* withershins
anvil *n.* studdy
anxious *adj.* airch (A2); arch
(*ch* gutteral)
any *adj., adv., pron.* ony;
~body *n., pron.* onybody;
~how *adv.* onywye; **~one**
n., pron. ony een; **~thing**
n. aacht, ocht; onything;
~thing at all ocht nor flee;
~way *adv.* onygait, onygate;
onyroad; onywye; **~where**
adv. onywye
apart *adv.* apairt
apiece *adv.* e piece
apology *n.* affcome
apparatus *n.* leems
apparently *adv.* appearandly
appeal *n., v.* appale
apple *n.* aipple
appoint *v.* appynt; (a meeting)
tryst; **~ed meeting** *n.* tryst
apprehension *n.* uptak
approach *v.* come in aboot;
(of time) weer on
appropriate *adj.* mowse;
not ~ nae mowse
approve *v.* appruv
April *n.* Awprile; Prile

apron *n.* aapron; naapron;
(working) wrapper; (of
sackcloth) seck-aapron

apt to *adj.* liken tae

arch *n.* airch; (arched
passageway) pend, pen(n)

Archie *pr. n.* Airchie

Arctic tern *n.* tarick

argu|e *v.* argie; argie-bargie;
argle-bargle; threep, threip;
~e the matter delve the
bank (B1); ~ment *n.* argie-
bargie; argle-bargle;
argiement; ~mentative *adj.*
wranglesome

arithmetic *n.* coontin

arm *n.* airm; gardy (A2);
gairdy (A); *n. pl.* (*eg*, of a
windmill) yaaws, yauws;
hook ~s cleek (wi); ~chair
n. airm-cheer; bow-cheer;
elbock-cheer (M3); ~ful
n. oxterfu; oxterlift; ~pit
n. oxter

army *n.* airmy

around *adv.* aroon; roond an
aboot; *prep.* aroon

arrange *v.* arreenge

arrest *v.* nab; reest

arrow *n.* barbet

arse *n.* erse; doke

art *n.* airt

articulate *v.* moo-ban

as well *adv.* an aa; as weel; tee

ash, ashes *n.* aiss; ess; (on top
of a pipe) dirry; ~-cann *n.*
aissbacket; ~-heap *n.*
aiss-midden

ask *v.* (request) bid; (for) sik,
seek; (a question) speer, speir

askance *adv.* asklent

askew *adv.* skew

asp *n.* aisp

aspen *n.* quaikin-aish

aspire *v.* ettle

aspiring *adj.* uppish

assail *v.* lat at

assistant *n.* (minister's)
helpender

associate *v.* (with) colleague
(wi)

assure *v.* asseer; asser

assuredly *adv.* awyte; *excl.*
weela-wat; weel-a-wite

astir *adv.* asteer

astonish *v.* dammer (R)

astray *adv.* wull; waif (K)

astride *adv.* stridelins

asunder *adv.* sindry

at all *adv.* ava; neen (nae neen
pleast); ony (gin it's ony
weet)

ate *v. pt.* eet (rare)

atom *n.* (particle) hait; styme

attach *v.* (horse to plough) yoke

attempt *v.* mint

attend *v.* atten; ~ to *v.* sort

attendance *n.* turn-oot;
~ **officer** *n.* (school)
wheeper-in

attent|ion *n.* tent; **pay** ~ tak
tent; **pay** ~ **to** tent; ~**ive** *adj.*
tenty; ~**ively** *adv.* tentily

attract|ed to, to be *v.* tae hae a
lang ee at; ~**ive** *adj.* bonnie,
bonny

auction *n.* rowp, roup; ungshin
sell up by ~ rowp oot; ~**eer**
n. ungshineer

audience *n.* owdience

aught *n.* ocht

August *n.* Aagist

aurora borealis *pr. n.* the
merry dancers

austere *adj.* door, dour

Australia *pr. n.* Australya

author (of invented story)
n. upmakker

authorise *v.* owthereese

autumn (winter) *n.* backeyn

aware *adj.* awaar

away *adv.* awa; wa; furth;
~ **abroad** awa foreign; **far** ~
hine awa; ~ **you go!** gyang
tae Padanaaram!

awful *adj.* aafa, affa, aafu;
yafa

awl *n.* (shoemaker's) ellieson;
elshin

awry *adj.* agee; ajee

axe *n.* aix

axle *n.* aixle

B

babbler *n.* gab

baby *n.* bairn; bairnikie;
babbity; weezhin (M3); ~**'s
flannel coat** barrie

back *n.* back; ~ **band** *n.* (of
harness) backbin; ~**-bone**
n. back-been; ~**-garden** *n.*
backie; ~**ground** *n.* back-
grun; ~**side** *n.* doke; doup;
~**slider** *n.* turnkwite;
~**ward** *adj.* backart; ~ **look**
vizzie backart; ~**wards**
adv. backlins

backart *adj.* backward

bad *adj.* coorse; ill; ull;
adv. ill; ull; **in a** ~ **state** sair
awa wi't; ~**-mannered** *adj.*
haiveless (A); ill-farrant;
ill-fashiont; ~ **manners**
n. pl. ill-fashions, -fashence;
~**-tempered** *adj.* crabbit;
cankert; ~**ly** *adv.* ill; sairly;
~**ly off** *adj.* ull-aff; sair-aff;
~**ly behaved** *phr.* ill-gatit,
ill-gettit

bade *v.* bad

baffle *v.* paal, paul

bag *n.* pock, poke; powk;
pyock; walgin;
(farmworker's) chackie;
(for personal necessities
on journey) wallet; (small)
pookie; ~**s I!** chaps me!

baggage *n.* (loose woman) limmer

baker *n.* baxter

baking *n.* byaakin

bald *adj.* beld; baaldie-heidit

ball *n.* (bouncing) ba; ballie; (of rope, cord, wool) clew, cloo; (of butter) pat; (dance) baal

ballad *n.* ballant

bamboozled *ppl., adj.* boggit; bumbazed

bandage *v.* wup

bang *v.* daud

bang about *v.* breenge

bankrupt, go *v.* brak; *pt.* broke

bank up *v.* (a fire) reest, reist

banns *n. pl.* (giving notice of impending marriage) cries

bantam *n.* bantin

banter *n.* hyze

baptise *v.* bapteese

baptism *n.* bapteesement

barb *n.* (of a hook) witter; wutter

Barbara *pr. n.* Baabie, Baubie

barbed-wire *n.* barbit-weer; pykit-weer

bare *n.* nakit; nyakit; ~ **patch in field** *n.* blain

barefooted *adj.* barfit

bargain *v.* cowp; niffer

bark *v.* (of a dog) bowff; bouch

barley *n.* (when 4 or 6-rowed) bear, bere

barnacle *n.* scaa, scaw

barrel *n.* bowie; (for oatmeal) meal-bowie

barren *n.* (of an animal) eel; farra; yeld; ~ **cow** farracoo

barrow *n.* barra; hurlie; secklifter

barter *v.* hooie; niffer

base *n.* (in children's games) dell

bashful *adj.* blate; bauch

basin *n.* (wooden for brose) bicker

basket *n.* ruskie (for wool) oo ruskie (M3); (for fish) creel; (fitted into top of fish-wife's creel) murlin; (shallow, wicker) scull, skull; (esp. for sowing seed) happer

bass *n.* bess; **to sing** ~ bess

bastard *n.* dykesider (M3)

bat *n.* baakie; baukie

bathe *v.* baathe; dook

bather *n.* dooker

bayonet *n.* baignet

be *v.* be; ~ **not** *v. neg.* (don't be) binna; ~ **without** *v.* wint

beadle *n.* bethral (K)

beak *n.* neb, nib

beam *n.* (of sun) blink; (across chimney from which the crook is suspended) rantle-tree

bear *v.* thole

beard *n.* baird; birse; (of oats
or barley) aan, awn
bearings *n. pl.* meathes;
lose your ~ tine yir meathes
beat *v.* (surpass) baet; bleck;
cow; ding; (strike) clowt;
dird; lownder; swinge;
(severely) soosh; **~en** *ppl.*
baet; **that ~s everything**
yon cows aa; **~en track, off
the** *prep. phr.* at the back o
beyond; oot o kent boons
beaut|y *n.* byowty; **~iful** *adj.*
byowtifu; bewotifie
because *conj.* cause; (of) ower
the heids o
beckon *v.* gie (us) a wag
bed *n.* (small) beddie; (wooden,
shut in with doors) bun-
bed; (bed doors) bed-lids;
(bed in semi-parlour end
of but-an-ben) but-bed;
(low, on castors) hurlie-
bed; (makeshift) shakky-
doon; **in ~, put to ~** beddit;
~-clothes *n. pl.* bed-claes;
bedaub *v.* skaik
bedraggle *v.* bedraigle; **~d** *ppl.*
adj. bedraiglt; dragglet;
draigelt
bedridden person *n.* beddal
bee *n.* **bumble-~** bumbee;
(in Buchan) (Auchmacoy-)
bummer; **yellow humble-~**
foggie-bee; **~hive** *n.* skep;
(of straw) (bee-)ruskie

beef *n.* mairt (M3)
beetle *n.* gollach, goloch;
hornygollach
befall *v.* befa; come ower; fa
before *adv., prep.,* afore; ere,
or; *conj.* ere, or; **~ long**
belyve; **~hand** *adv.* aforehan
beg *v.* sorn; thig
began *v. pt.* begood; (*poet.*)
gan
beggar *n.* gaberlunzie;
supplicant; (threatening)
sorner; (genteel) thigger
begin *v.* fa tee; set tee; stairt,
stert; yoke tee; **~ning**
n. aff-go
behaved, badly *adj.* ill-gatit,
-gettit
behaviour *n.* (esp. good)
haivins
beheld *v. pt.* beheeld
behind *adv., prep.* ahin(t)
beholden *adj.* behauden
behoof *n.* beheef
behove *v.* beheeve
belabour *v.* belaabour
belch *n., v.* rift; (of vapour
etc) yoam; (*fig.*) boke
believe *v.* troo
belittle *v.* lichtlify
bell *n.* (sound of) jow
bellman *n.* clinkum
bellow *v.* bullie (of cattle)
rowst; rowt (G1)
bellows *n. pl.* bellas

belly *n.* wame; wime, wyme;
~-**band** *n.* (of harness)
bellyban
belong *v.* belang; **he ~s to**
Buckie he belangs Buckie
below *prep.* aneth; ablo(w),
alow (s); in alow
bench *n.* binch; bink
bend *n.* bennin
bend *v.* boo; loot; (with age)
creep doon; *ppl.* boo't; **bent**
double boo't twa-faal
beneath *See* below
benighted *ppl., adj.* nicht-boon,
-boun
benumb *v.* daver; dozen
beside *prep.* aside
besides *adv.* forby(e); forbyes;
prep. by; (apart from) byes
besmear *v.* begarrie (K);
drabble
bespatter *v.* spairge; begarrie
best *n.* ~ **of the lot** stang o the
trump; ~ **room** the room;
~ **room in two-roomed**
cottage horn-en, -eyn
bet *v.* beet; **I'll ~** I'se warran
between *prep.* atween;
atweesh; ~ **times** atween
hans
bewail *v.* willieway
bewilder *v.* bumbaze; ~**ed** *adj.*
bumbazed; dozent; wull
bewitched *ppl., adj.* bewutcht
beyond *adv.* ayon; ayont
bid *n.* (at sale) bode

big *adj.* muckle; meikle
bilberry *n.* blaeberry; blivert
bill *n.* bull; laain, lawin
billy-o, like *intensive phr.*
ful teer
bin *n.* (for corn, turnips) bing
bind *v.* bin'; bin (rhyme with
tin); (tightly) wip; wup;
~**ing** *n.* (for cattle) binnin
birch *n.* birk; birken (C)
bird *n.* (unfledged) gorbel;
gorblin; gog (s); (state
of egg with young bird
partially formed) gorbellt
birth, give *v.* (of rabbits) cleck
biscuit *in phr.* **that takes the ~**
that cowes the gowan.
bit *n.* (small) bittock; pickie;
thochtie; tickie; wee; **not a**
~ **of it** nae a hair o't; fient
hait; deil a nip
bitch *n.* bick
bite *n.* gnap; rive; (a mere)
knap-at-the-win
black *adj.* bleck; blaik; ~ **and**
blue blae (B1); ~**berry**
n. bramble; brammle;
~**bird** *n.* blackie; blaikie;
ouzel (M); ~**smith** *n.* smith;
brookie; ~**smith's shop**
n. smiddy; ~**en** *v.* blaik;
blaiken, blecken; ~**ing** *n.*
bleck; bleckin; **in ~ and**
white *phr.* in black upo fite
(M3)

blackguard *v.* blackguaird;
  (*joc.*) bleck
bladder *n.* bledder
blame *n.* wyte
blanket *n.* (fisher term) plaid
blast *n.* (of wind) blaffert;
  bluffert; bloiter; blouter
blaze *n.* bleeze; lowe
bleak *adj.* (of weather) oorlich
bleary-eyed *adj.* bleart; bleery
bleed *v.* blood (s)
blend *v.* blen, *ppl.* blent; mees
bless *v.* bliss; sain; ~ed *adj.*
  seely; ~ing *n.* blissin
blight *n.* blicht
blind *adj.* blin
blink *n.* went; *v.* (weakly)
  blinter
blockhead *n.* gomeril; tawpie
block up *v.* stap
blocked *ppl.* (of the nose)
  clochert
blonde *n.* blon
blood *n.* bleed; ~-curdling
  adj. bleed-jeelin; ~-red *adj.*
  bleedreid
bloom *n.* bleem
blossom *n.* floorish
blow *n.* clour; cloot, clowt;
  daad; knoit; lick; plowt;
  sclaffert; whang; (heavy)
  bash; bensil; forfeffis;
  (of a sounding kind)
  binner; (resounding) clink;
  (disappointment) nizzer;
  v. blaa; blaave; blyaav;

(the nose with finger and
  thumb) snyte; (with warm
  air) yoam
blown out *ppl.* (of cattle,
  having overeaten) hoven
blubber *v.* bubble; snotter
blue *adj.* blae; **black and ~**
  blae; ~**bell** *n.* blewart;
  ~**bottle** *n.* bottler
bluish *adj.* blae; bluichtie
blunt *adj.* (of speech) aff-han
blushing *ppl.*, *adj.* kindlin (J)
bluster *v.* howder
board *n.* brod; boord; (plank)
  deal; (moveable on front
  of boxcart) front shelvin;
  (at rear) hin shelvin;
  (for sharpening scythe)
  scythebrod; straik
boarding-school *n.* buirdin-
  squeel
boast *v.* blaw; braig; blyaav;
  craa, craw; ~**ful** *adj.*
  braggy; winny
boat *n.* (built with planks
  edge to edge) carvel-biggit;
  (built with planks overlapping) clinker-biggit; **in the
  same ~** i the same box (AI)
bob *v.* cobble
Boddam *pr. n.* (nickname)
  Dowp
bogie-roll *n.* (tobacco)
  bogierowe

boil *n.* beil; beilin; blin lump;
  v. bile, byle; ~**ing** *n.* (*eg,* of
  rhubarb) bilin, bylin
boistrous *adj.* bowsterous;
  hallyrackit
bold *adj.* baul; bauld; croose;
  deft
boll *n.* (old Sc. measure) bow
bollard *n.* paal
bolster *n.* bowster
bolt *v.* tak sheet
bondage *n.* thirlage
bone *adj. n.* been; **a ~ to pick**
  a craa to pluck
boney *adj.* beeny
bonfire *n.* bale-fire; bondy (O)
book *n.* beuk, byeuk
boot *n.* beet; buit (S); (rubber
  knee boot worn by
  fishworkers) topper
bore *v. pt.* bure
bored (with) *ppl., adj.*
  scunnert (O, wi)
borrow *v.* borra; thig
bosom *n.* bosie; oxter.
  cf. **armpit**
botch *v.* bucker
both *adj., pron.* baith
bother *n., v.* badder,
  bather; fash
bottle *n.* (earthenware) pig;
  (hot water) pig; (with
  handle(s) for holding
  liquor)) grey-beard

bottom *n.* boddom;
  (buttocks) doke, dowp;
  hinnereyn
bought *v. pt.* bocht; coft (G1)
boulder *n.* bumlock (M3)
bounce *v.* stot; daad, daud
  (aboot); (up and down) dyst
bound *v. pt., ppl.* bun; bunt;
  thirlt
boundary *n.* boon, boun;
  mairch; ~ **wall** mairch-dyke
bow *adj.* (of legs) bowdent;
  n. (tied) doss; *v.* boo;
  loot; ~ **and arrow** bow
  an barbet; ~-**legged** *adj.*
  bow-hoched
bowl *n.* (for bowling) bool;
  (large wooden for baking)
  bossie; (wooden dish for
  oatmeal) brose caup
box *n.* buist
box-bed *n.* bun(-in) bed;
  bunbreist (M3)
boy *n.* loon; loun; laddie;
  (small) laddikie; (fisher
  term) bokie; (coddled)
  Grunnie's John; (term of
  endearment) mannikie;
  ~**friend** *n.* jo; laad
braces *n. pl.* (for trousers)
  galluses
bracken *n.* breckan
brag *v.* blaa, blaw; blyaav;
  braig
brain(s) *n.* harns
brainless *adj.* glaikit

bran *n.* pron
branch *n.* brench, brinch
brandish *v.* (threateningly)
   wadge
brass *n.* bress
bravely *adv.* starkly
brawl *n.* brulzie
bread *n.* loaf; breed, breid
breadth *n.* breeth; breid
break *v.* brak; ~ **down**
   v. (from drink, exhaustion,
   illness) fooner; ~ **wind** *v.*
   pump, let off; **without a ~**
   phr. hail-heidit (M3)
breakfast *n.* brakfast;
   disjune (K)
breast *n.* breest, breist; paap
breath *n.* braith (G); breith (J);
   indraacht; (of wind) funk;
   out of ~ birsin
breeching *n.* (part of harness
   round hind-part of shaft
   horse to allow backward
   movement) britchin
breeze *n.* pirr o win; pirr-
   winnie
brew *n.* browst
bridegroom *n.* bridegreem
bridge *n.* brig
bridle *n.* (with blinkers) blin
   bridle
bright *adj.* bricht; (brisk, bold)
   crouse; (gaudy) galliart (B1)
brighten *v.* brichen; (of person)
   intr. cantle up

brim *v.* (be full to the brim,
   brim over) lip; ream; wink;
   ~**ming** *ppl., adj.* lippen f(o)u;
   reamin fu
bring *v.* fesh; fess; ~ **out** rank
   oot; ~ **to a halt** pit the peter
   on; ~ **to mind** fess back;
   ~ **up** fess up
bristle *n.* birse
brittle *adj.* bruckle; freuch
broad *adj.* braid
broke *v. pt.* brook, bruik;
   brak; bruk
bronchitis *n.* broncaidis
brood *n.* cleckin; brodmell;
   ~**ing**, ~**y** *adj.* (of hen)
   clockin
broom *n.* (brush) beesom,
   besom; ~**-handle** *n.* besom-
   shaft; (shrub) breem;
   ~**-bush** *n.* breem-buss
brother *n.* brither; breeder;
   bridder; broder (A2);
   ~**hood** *n.* britherheed;
   ~**-in-law** *n.* gweedbrither,
   -breeder, -bridder
brought *v. pt.* brocht; foosh.
   cf. **fesh**
brow *n.* broo; ~**-band** *n.* (in
   harness) broobin
brown *adj.* broon
bruise *n.* birse; malagruze
brush *n.* beesom; besom;
   v. sweesh
brushwood *n.* hag
brute *n.* breet

Buchanhaven native *pr. n.*
Buchaner
Buchan Observer, the *pr. n.*
the Buchanie
bucket *n.* backet
Buckie native *pr. n.* Bucker
budge *v.* mudge
bugbear *n.* wirrycoo
build *n.* book, bouk; **of small**
~ sma-bookit, -boukit;
of lean ~ nairra-bookit;
v. big(g); *pt. ppl.* biggit; ~**er**
n. bigger; ~**ing** *n.* biggin;
~**ing-site** *n.* seet
bulk *n.* book, bouk; ~**y** *adj.*
(muckle-)bookit, boukit
bull *n.* bul
bullock *n.* (young) stirk;
(older, castrated) stot
bully *v.* bullyrag
bumble-bee *n.* bumbee; in
Buchan, (Auchmacoy)
bummer
bump *n.* doosht; *v.* (up and
down) dyst
bumpkin *n.* gillieperous;
gileepris (hard *g*)
bun *n.* (floury) bap; (glazed,
with sugar on top) heater;
(plain) soft biscuit, softie
bundle *n.* bunnle; walgin (M3)
(loose, untidy) fushach
bungle *v.* bucker
bungler *n.* footer
buoy *n.* bowe

burden *n.* birn; (of a discourse)
owercome
bureau *n.* buroo
burgh *n.* broch
burglar *n.* hoosebrakker
burial *n.* beerial; ~ **place** *n.*
(reserved in graveyard) lair
buried *pt. ppl.* beeriet; yirdit
burly *adj.* buirdly;
mucklebookit, -boukit
burn *v.* brinn (K); *pt., ppl.*
brunt; brent (GI); plot;
~**ing brightly** (of fire)
reevin
burst *v.* birst; (asunder)
rive; ~**ing** *ppl.* burssen
bury *v.* beery; yird (doon)
bush *n.* buss; (stunted) scrog
bushel *n.* bushle; bussle
business *n.* buzness
bustle *n., v.* steer; feerich;
hash
busy *adj.* thrang
but *conj.* bit
butter churn *n.* kirn
butterfly *n.* butterflee (R);
buttery (MI)
butterhand *n.* clapper
buttocks *n. pl.* dowp, doup;
droddum (M3); hurdies;
(*vulg.*) dock, doke
buy *v.* buy; coff (GI)
buzz *v.* bizz; (of thoughts) ream
buzzing *n.* bizzin
by *prep.* by, b'; (used of time)
gin; ~ **7 o'clock** gin seyven

o'clock; ~ **the time that**
gin; ~ **the way** *inter.* b'wye;
~-and-~ *adv.* belyve;
~way *n.* bywye

C

cackle *v.* keckle
cairn *n.* carn; cyarn
calf *n.* caaf, caafie; **calves**
n. pl. car
calk *v.* (fix guard on horse's
hoof) caak, cauk
call *v.* ca, caa; ~ **on** *v.* cry on;
cry in by; cry tee
callous *adj.* scorie-hornt
calm *adj.* (of the weather) lown
calve *v.* caav; **~s** *n. pl.* calfies;
carr (M3)
came *v. pt.* cam
candle *n.* cannle, cunnle
Candlemas *pr. n.* Cannlemas
candy *n.* gundy
cane *n.* (West Indian)
spaingie; spainyie
cannot *v. neg.* canna
cantankerous *adj.*
contermashious
canvas *n.* cannas
cap *n.* (man's) bonnet;
caip, kep; (woman's) mutch
capable *adj.* cawpable
capacious *adj.* capawshus

caper *n.* cyaaper; *v.* philander;
~ing *adj.* (of children) royd,
royt
caprice *n.* maggot
capstone *n.* kepsteen
carcase *n.* carkidge; (of a fowl)
clossach
card *n.* (playing) cairt; **to play**
~s cairt; *v.* (wool) caird
care *v.* car; raik; **don't ~ at all**
carna doit; **take ~** ca canny,
tak tent; **take ~ of** *v.* notice;
tak aboot; *n.* tent; (anxiety)
cark; **not a ~ in the world**
nae cark nor care; **~ful** *adj.*
carefu; tenty; **~fully** *adj.*
tentily; **~less** *adj.* haiveless
caress *v.* daat, dawt
cargo *n.* cargie
carouse *n.* ran-dan; **on the ~**
oot on the ran-dan
carp *v.* carble (M3); yarp
carpenter *n.* jyner; vricht,
wricht
carriage *n.* kerridge
carrier *n.* cadger
carrion crow *n.* hoodie(-craw)
carry *v.* cairry; cairt; (loads)
cadge; (something heavy)
humph; ~ **on** *v.* ca awa; wag
on/awa; **~-on** *n.* cairry-on;
on-cairry
cart *n.* cairt; (mounted on
springs) spring-cairt;
v. (corn in from field) lead;

~er *n.* cairter; ~ing *n.* (corn, hay) leadin; ~load *n.* cartil

case, in *conj.* case be; (*in neg. context*) for fear

cash *n.* clink

cast *v.* cast; *pt.* ceest, keest

castle *n.* castell

cast-off *n.* aff-cast

castrate *v.* cut; lib

casual dress *adj., n.* go-ashores

catch *n.* (of fish) shot; **a good ~** a cran-the-net; *v.* cleek; (with the hand) kep; (fish with the hands) guddle; **~ sight of** twig; **~ up with** win tee wi

catechise *v.* catecheese

catechism *n.* carritch(es); catechis

cattle *n. pl.* beas' (C); bestial (A2); kine (A); kye; nowt; **~ disease** *n.* fite scoor; (disease in the hindlegs) crochle; (to call to cattle) treesh; **~ fold** *n.* bucht; **~man** *n.* bail(l)ie; bylie; cattlie (s)

cattle binding *n.* (iron) bowsell; (retaining rod for binding) slider; (rope or chain on binding to attach **sell** to a stake) thrammle

caught *v. pt.* catcht

caul *n.* kell; seelyhoo

cause to *v.* gar

causeway *n.* causey; cassie

caution *n.* haud-again

cautious *adj.* canny; cowshus

cavil *v.* carble

cease *v.* devall; jeho(y)

ceiling *n.* (below sloping roof) lie in; **having a sloping ~** coom-ceiled

celebrate *v.* haud haill Eel

centipede *n.* meggie-monyfeet; forty-fittit janet

certain *adj.* siccar

cessation *n.* devall; devalvement

cesspool *n.* green-brees; stranghole

chafe *v.* chaff

chaff *n.* caff; **~ mattress** caffbed; caff-seck

chain *n.* chine; (by which pot hung over fire from crook) links; (to bind cattle) sell

chair *n.* cheer

chairman *n.* cheerman

chalk *n.* chack; *v.* caak, cauk

challenge *v.* dip; (for repayment of a debt) caak, cauk

chamber *n.* chaamer, chaumer (esp. for sleeping place for farm servants in Banff and Buchan; **to live in a ~** tae chaamer, chaumer

chamber-pot *n.* chantie, chanty, chuntie; dirler

change *n., v.* cheenge; chynge; **~able** *adj.* changefu; (of

weather) brucklie; ~less
adj. cheengeless
channel n. (narrow) trink(ie)
chap n. billie; chiel; stock;
(effect of cold) hack
characterless adj. eedle-oddle
charge n., v. chairge
charity n. chairity
Charles pr. n. Chae; Chairlie
charlock n. skellach
charmed with phr. teen wi
chat n., v. blether; crack;
newse; phr. ca the crack;
~ty adj. crackie; newsy
chatter n. jaa, jaw; v. bledder;
blether; chirr-wirr (s); gab;
jaa, jaw; yammer; ~-box
n. gab; ~ing n. chirr-wirrin
(s); gabbing
cheap adj. chaip, chape; ~jack
n. chaip-john
cheat v. chait, chate; jink;
snype, swick; (in marble-
playing) foodge; ppl. snypit;
swickit; ~ing n. chaitry
checked adj. (of a pattern)
chackit
cheek n. chik; chowk (F);
chaft; ~-by-jowl cheekie-for-
chowlie; (impudence) chik
cheep n. chowp; peek; not a ~
nae a chowp
cheerful adj. blithe(some),
blyth; crouse; ~ness n.
crouseness
cheery adj. canty

cheese n. chyse; (a round)
kebbuck; (soft) hangie;
~ press n. chessel; chesset
chemise n. sark
chequered linen n. chack
cherry n. chirry; ~ tree n.
(wild) gean
chest n. kist; buist; (human)
cheest; get it off your ~
redd yir crap; teem yir
crap
chew v. chaw
chewing-gum n. chuddy
chicken n. chucken; chucknie;
~ soup with leek cock-
a-leekie; ~-hearted adj.
hen-hertit
chickweed n. chuckenwort;
chucknart
chiefly adv. feckly
child n. bairn; chiel(d);
chill(ie); chyl(li)e; geet;
tsil; (small) eeshan (M2);
(young) etsleel (B1); littlin;
little een; wean; (beginning
to walk) g(y)angrel; with ~
wi chiel; ~ in the offing
troot i the waal; ~hood
n. bairnheid
chill n., v. geel; ~ed adj.
chilpit; stervin o caal,
stervin wi the caal; ~y adj.
airish; caaldrife
chimney n. chim(b)lay;
chumlay; lum; ~-corner
n. ingle-neuk

china *adj.*, *n.* cheena
chink *n.* bore
chinless *adj.* soo-moo't
chinwagging *n.* chirr-wirrin (s)
chipping *n.* (granite) chuckie-steen
chives *n.* size
choice *n.* wale
choir *n.* kyre; kire
choke *v.* smucht; (on food) worry
cholic *n.* belly-thraw
choose *v.* chyse; wale; wyle
chop *v.* chap
christen *v.* kirsen; ~ing *n.* kirsenin
Christmas *n.* Chrissenmas (M3); Eel; Yeel; ~ pudding *n.* dumplin
chubby *adj.* pluffy
chuckle *v.* keckle
chummy *adj.* chuff
chunk *n.* skelp; (of bread etc) whang
church *n.* kirk; at ~ kirkit; ~-gallery laft; ~yard *n.* kirkyaird
Church of Scotland *pr. n.* the Aul Kirk
churl *n.* carl; nabble, nabal; ~ish *adj.* nabble, nabal; ~ish man tike
churn *v.* (butter) kirn
chute *n.* (conveying corn to elevator) shakkin-spoot
cigarette end *n.* tabbie (Abdn.)

cinder *n.* shunner
circumspect *adj.* douce
circumstances, in any *phr.* on ony precunnances
cirrus clouds *n. pl.* (high) mackerels' backs an meers' tails
city *n.* ceety
civil *adj.* ceevil
clack *v.* chack
clad *adj.* cled
clairvoyant *adj.* fey
clamber *v.* rink
clamour *n.*, *v.* yammer
clasp *n.* hasp
clatter *n.* reemis(h)
claw *n.* claa; clook; faach, fauch (B1); seize with the ~s cleek; ~ed *v. pt.* clew
clean *v.* dicht; (a byre) muck
clear *adj.* clair; *v.* (out) redd (oot); (your throat) pyocher, redd yir throat; (up) redd up; (of weather) upple; ~ed away *ppl.* (of snow) cassen
clench *v.* steek; ~ed fists steek-it nieves
clever *adj.* clivver; fell; heidie; lang-heidit
click *v.* chack
cliff *n.* scaar, scaur
climb *v.* clim, *pt.* clam(b), clum; sclim; speel, speil; ~er *n.* climmer
clinch *v.* (settle) clench
cloak *n.* clyock

clock *n.* knock; **wall ~ with pendulum** wag-at-the-wa, waggity-wa

clod *n.* (of earth) knibloch

clog *v.* clag

close *v.* dit; steek; **~ by** *adv. prep.* aside; **~ together** *adv.* curduddoch (J); **close up** *adv.* close-tee

clot *v.* lapper

cloth *n.* claith; cloot; (very thin) flinrikin; (made of hards) harden; (sackcloth) harn

clothe *v.* claithe; clead; **~d** *ppl.* claithed; clootit; (badly) sair clootit

clothes *n. pl.* claes; clyes; cleadin; duds; graith; (second best) scuddlin claes; toggery; **~ peg** pin

cloud *n.* clood; clud (K); (small clouds flying before the wind) pack-merchants

cloudberry *n.* aiv(e)rin

clover *n.* clivver. *cf.* **clever**

clown *n.* cloon

club-foot *n.* clog-fit

clumsy *adj.* gaakit, gawkit; **~ person** hoffin; howfin; hurb

cluster *n.* dossie

clutch *n.* (of eggs) settin; lachter; *v.* claught; clootch

coal *n.* kwile; (live) eyzle

coal-dust *n.* coal-coom

coarse *adj.* coorse; grofe; orra (of a beard) gosky

coat *n.* kwite, kwyte; (dreadnought) fer-nothing; (old-fashioned) surtoo, surtout

coating *n.* (thin) yim

coax *v.* tice (wi)

coaxing *ppl., adj.* fraiky

cobbler *n.* sooter, souter; **~'s wax** rosit

cobblestone *n.* causey; cassie

cobweb *n.* moosewob; wob; **covered in ~s** wobby

cod *n.* (of medium size) sprag

coddle *v.* peppen

coffin *n.* kist; **to put in a ~** *v.* kist

cohabitee *n.* bidie-in

coin *n.* (of little value) doit; bod(d)le (J); plack

coir yarn *n.* sparty tow

cold *adj.* caal(d); caaldrife; (as ice) jeel; (of weather only) fresh; (bitter) stervation; (of the wind) snell; *n.* caal; (extreme) jeel

colewort *n.* kail, kale

collapse *v.* (with drink, exhaustion, illness) fooner

collar *n.* (of iron, as instrument of punishment) jougs

collecting-box *n.* (offertory plate at church door) brod; (with long handle, passed round church) ladle

collection *n.* rickmatick; (of
small objects) smyteral
colourful *adj.* (highly) kennelt
colt *n.* cout, cowt
comb *n., v.* kaim, kame
come away *imp.* c'wa
come to *v.* (recover) cower;
weer tee
comely *adj.* gatefarrin
comfort *n.* easedom; ~able
adj. bien; ~less *adj.* bienless
command *v.* comman
common *adj.* cowmon; *n.*
(small) loan; (village green)
loaning (s)
commoners *n. pl.* cowmonality
common-sense *n.* gumption;
mense, minse; rum(mil)
gumption; rumigumshun
commotion *n.* frother; stramash;
tirravee
communicant *n.* commeenicant
Communion *n.* (formerly) the
Sacrament
company *n.* (musical or
convivial) core
compared with *prep.* byes;
forbye; till
compel *v.* gar
complain *v.* compleen; crowp;
peek (peevishly) girn; peenge;
yarp; ~ing feebly goranichy
(B1); ~t *n.* compleent,
complint
completely *adv.* fair; freely;
reet an crap

comrade *n.* billie
conceited *adj.* bigsie; concaited;
ful (o himsel)
concern *n.* concairn; *in phr.*
the whole ~ the hail rickmatick; ~ing *prep.* anent
condescending *adj.* skichent
condition *n.* condeeshun;
precunnance; in good ~
clair; clear
conduct *v.* conduck
cone (fir etc) *n.* yowe, yowie
confident *adj.* croose, crouse;
brisk and ~ croose i the
craw
confidential *adj.* hishty-wishty;
in a ~ tone laich-in
confound *v.* confoon; dag;
deg; denum; ~ed *ppl.*
denummt; ~ it dag it;
dozen't
confus|e *v.* dammer; ~ed
adj. (of things) throwder;
throw-ither; (of people)
daivert; doilt, dylt;
(mentally) dottelt; raivelt;
adv. throw-ither; a ~d
situation a raivelt roast
(M3); ~ion *n.* (state of)
kirn; mixter-maxter;
snorl; (noisy) hurry-burry
congeal *v.* jeel; lapper
congregated *v. pt.* congregat
connect *v.* conneck; *ppl.*
conneckit

consciousness, recover *phr.*
  come alist
considerable *adj.* gey
consideration, under *phr.*
  throwhan
consort (with) *v.* colleague (wi)
constipat|ion *n.* dry-darn; ~ed
  adj. corkit
constitution *n.* constiteetion
constrained *adj.* hudden
  doon; hudden in aboot
constrict *v.* hank
contempt *excls. of* footers;
  tchach; tchoot; *terms of* (used
  of a person) scadden; scoot;
  skate; splewin; (for someone
  of dirty habits) sklype; (for
  fellow of low character)
  slung; (for worthless type)
  slype; (puny, worthless
  type) tarlich; (foul-mouthed,
  vulgar type) tink
contemptible *adj.* dirten
contend *v.* conten
contest *n.* (esp. curling) bonspiel
continual *adj.* conteenwal
continue *v.* conteena (B1), *pt.*
  conteenit; hud; (go straight
  ahead) hud stracht on
contradict *v.* conter; cwanter;
  ~ory *adj.* contermin't
contraption *n.* whigmaleerie
contrary *adj.* contermashious;
  contermin't; contrair;
  cwanterkine
contribute *v.* contreebit

control, beyond *phr.* oot o han;
  nae tae hud nor bin'; lose ~
  of oneself hiv a jamaica
controversial *adj.* kittle;
  kittlesome
convenience *n.* convainience
conversation *n.* a blether;
  collieshangie (M3); newse;
  spik; (low, muttered) toot-
  moot; ~ lozenges *n. pl.*
  readin sweeties
convers|e *v.* collogue; ~ing
  intimately corrieneuchin
convey *v.* convoy
convince *v.* goy (B1)
convolvulus *n.* creepin-eevie.
  cf. slow
cook *v.* keuk, kyeuk
cool *adj.* cweel, kweel
coop up *v.* criv up
copse *n.* shaw (J)
copy down *v.* tak aff
coracle *n.* currack
cord *n.* (used to pull cleaning-
  rag through a rifle) pul-
  throwe
corker *n.* beezer; binder;
  bummer
cormorant *n.* scrath
corn *n.* corn; oats; ~ chest
  cornkist; bruise-box;
  ~ husk sheelock; ~bin
  bing; ~flower blaewort;
  ~ marigold gweel;
  ~ spurrey yarr

corner *n.* neuk; (esp. of the eye and mouth) wick; **having ~s** neukit

corps *n.* core

corpse *n.* corp

correct *v.* correck

corresponding (to) *ppl., adj.* confeerin (tae)

corrugated iron *n.* sheet iron; tin-can

corsets *n. pl.* steys

cosset *v.* ten like a bee on a brod

cost *in phr.* ~ **them a lot** pyke their pooch

cosy *adj.* cosh

cottage *n.* (for farmservants) bothy; (two-roomed) but-an-ben; **farm ~** cottarhoose; ~**r** *n.* (in tied farm cottage) cottar

cotton-wool *n.* caddis. *cf.* **fluff**

cough *n.* hoast; (deep-seated) kirk-yaird hoast; (catarrhal) pyocher; blocher; (whooping) kink-hoast; *v.* (bark) bouch; bowff; clocher; pyooch; (huskily) craighle

could *v. pt.* cud; cwid; *neg.* cudna; cwidna

coulter *n.* (iron cutter at front of plough) couter

count *v.* coont

countenance *n.* coontenance

counter *n.* (shop) coonter

counterweight *n.* conterwecht

country *n.* kwintra; kwintry

couple *n., v.* kipple

courage *n.* spunk

course *n.* coorse; **of ~** of coorse; an coorse (A2)

court *n., v.* coort

courteous *adj.* mensefu; genteel

cover *n.* hap; (thin) scriffon; striffin; *v.* hap; *ppl.* happit; (over) hap up

cow *n.* coo, *pl.* kye; nowt; (suckling calves) sooker; (name for a cow) Crummie; ~**-dung** *n.* sharn; (liquid) **sharn bree;** ~**shed** *n.* byre; (division between stalls) traivis, trevis

coward *n.* coord(ie); coof; ~**'s blow** *n.* coordie-lick; ~**ly** *adj.* coordie

cower *v.* coor; coorie, coory; corrie; crulge (doon)

cowrie shell *n.* (small) kysie; calfie's mooie; Johnny Groatie

coy *adj.* skeigh

crab *n.* partan; (small, greenish, found in shore pools) grindie; grindie tocher (B)

crack *n.* (audible) knack; ~**ed** *ppl.* crackit

crafty *adj.* sneck-drawin (A2)

crag *n.* heuch

cram *v.* pang; stech

crash *n.* reemis(h)

cravat *n.* graavit, grauvit

crave *v.* green efter; lowe for (M3); mang for (G)

crazed *adj.* dylt, doilt

crazy *adj.* gyte; **drive him ~** raise him wull

creak *v.* jirg

cream *n.* ream; crame (S); **~ pot** *n.* stoopie (BI)

crease *n.* lirk, lurk; *v.* crunkle; *ppl.* crunkelt; gruggelt

creat|e *v.* creeat; **~ure** *n.* craitur, cratur

credit *v.* crydit; **~or** *n.* craver

crept *v. pt.* crap; creepit

crested *adj.* (of birds) tappit

crevice *n.* bore

criminal *n.* ranegill

cringe *v.* creenge

crinkle *v.* crunkle

cripple *n.* laimiter; *v.* hirple; hurkle; **~d** *ppl.* crochle; crochly; hypal (BI)

crisis *n.* creesis; bit; **in a ~** at the bit

critic *n.* creetick

critic|ise *v.* creeticise; misca; redd up (some een); tak (some een) throw han; **~ism** *n.* (severe) kail throw the reek; **~al** *adj.* lang-nebbit

croak *n., v.* crowp; craik

crockery *n.* lame

croft *n.* craft; haudin; placie

crooked *adj.* neukit; (off centre) agee

crop *n., v.* (of land) crap; *n.* (of bird) crap

cross *adj.* crabbit; cankert

cross-beam *n.* (in rafters) baak, bauk; spur-baak, -bauk

crouch *v.* coorie, coory; corrie; croolge (M3); crulge (doon); **in ~ing position** doon on yir hunkers

crow *n.* craw; corbie; (hooded) hoodie(-craa); **~berry** *n.* knowpert

crowd *n.* bing; helm; (small) boorach(ie), bourach; (noisy) clamjamfrey, clanjamfry; crood; (confused, noisy); currieboram; mardle, mairdle, merdle; mengyie; (confused) smarrach; swarrach; *v.* crood; **~ed** *adj.* thrang

crown *n.* croon; (of a woman's cap) cockernony: *v.* croon

cruel *adj.* ill; ull

crumb *n.* crumlock

crumbl|e *v.* mirl; murle; **~y** *adj.* bruckle; crummochie

crunch *n.* crinch

crush *v.* pran

crusty *adj.* nibawa

crutch *n.* oxter-staff, oxter-stav; **~es** *n. pl.* dooble-legs

cry *v.* (weep) greet, *pt.* grat; **~-baby** *n.* bubbly-bairn;

cried his head off roared
an grat

cry *v.* (call out) scrie, scry;
(esp. when dancing) hooch;
(scream) walloch; (cry out)
yammer, yaummer

cuckoo *n.* gowk. *cf.* **fool**

cud *n.* kweed

cuddle *v.* delt

cultivate *v.* tak in; ~d (of land)
cultivet

cup *n.* (of tea) shallie (o tay)
(old term)

cupboard *n.* aamrie, aumrie;
(lower half of aumrie) cavie
(κ); cubbirt; (wall-)press;

curative *adj.* cowerin

curb *v.* pit the haims on

curdle *v.* yirn

curds *n. pl.* curds; ~ **and whey**
croods an fy; yirnt milk

curio|sity *n.* keeriosity;
(inquisitiveness) ill-,
ullfashence; (a curiosity)
n. ferly; furliemageerum (m3);
unco; ~**us** *adj.* keerious

curled up *phr.* crulgt up;
hunkert up; hushlt up

curlew *n.* whaap, whaup

curling stones *n. pl.*
channelsteens

curl papers *n. pl.* (hair in)
curlie wurlies

currant *n.* curran; ~ **bun**
curran bap; **flowering** ~
son-afore-the-father

curry favour *phr.* hud in wi;
treesh; *ppl.* in-huddin

curse *v.* (swear) ban

curt *adj.* nippit

curtail *v.* pit the haims on

curtsey *n.* beck; *v.* bob

cut *n.* gaw (*eg*, girssgaw);
v. cut, *pt.* cuttit; clip; shore;
sned; (nip off) stoo

D

daddie *n.* deddie

daffodil *n.* daffie

dagger *n.* dirk

dainty *adj.* denty; *n.* (delicacy)
flagarie

dairy *n.* dyrie, diry

daisy *n.* gowan

dally (with) *v.* tig (wi)

dam *n.* dem

damage *n.* scaith; *v.* (suffer)
get the flacht

damn *n.* (euphemism) dang

damp *adj.* (of the weather)
mochie; saft(-like)

danc|e *n.* dunce; dince (s);
hooch (s); (slow Highland)
strathspey; (Highland)
walloch; *v.* dunce; caper;
wallop (κ); ~**ing** *n.*
wallopin (κ)

dandle *v.* (a child) diddle (B)
dangerous *adj.* fell; mischancy;
(from supernatural causes)
uncanny
dangle *v.* dauchle; wingle
dare *v.* daar, daur; ~ **not**
daarna; dursna; *pt.* used as
pr. durstna
dark *adj.* mark; mirk(y);
dairk (J); dauk (K); (very)
pitch-dark; pick-mark; **as**
~ **as pitch** as mark's pick;
pitch-~ *n.* pick-mirk; ~**ness**
n. mark; mirk(ness); ~**en**
v. (at dusk) glowm (M3)
darling *n.* dawtie
dart *n.* dert
dash *n.* blash (M3); *v.* (hurry)
skelp; (noisily) blatter; (down)
ding, *pt.* dang, dung;
(about) flee aboot; **at a** ~
at a spinner
dashing *adj.* swashy
daub *v.* clart; skaik; sclarry (J)
daughter *n.* daachter (A2);
dochter (A1); dother
daughter-in-law *n.* gweed-
dother etc
David *pr. n.* Daavit
dawdle *v.* dachle; dackle
dawn *n.* daw; skreek o day;
v. daw
day *in phr.* ~**'s work** darg;
~ **labourer** darger; **every** ~
daily-day
daze *v.* dozen

deacon *n.* deykon, dykon
dead *adj.* deed, deid (stretched
out) streekit; ~**ly** *adj.* deidly;
fell
deaf *adj.* deef, deif; ~**en** *v.* deeve,
deave
deal *n.* cowp; dale; niffer;
transack; *v.* dale, *pt.* deelt
(wi); ~ **with** sort; tak throw
han; ~**er** *n.* (itinerant)
cadger; (in horses, cattle)
cowper; ~**ings** *n. pl.*
transackins (M3); trockins
dear *adj.* (expensive) daar
death *n.* daith; deeth (A2),
deith (J); dede (K); the
hinder-, hinner-en; ~**-throw**
n. deid-thraw; ~**-watch**
beetle *n.* chackie-mull
deceased *ppl.* worn awa
deceitful *adj.* forty-faal
deceive *v.* mislippen; fugle (B1)
decent *adj.* dacent, daicent;
dassint; douce
deck out *v.* prink up/oot
declining *adj.* backgaein
decrease *n.* dooncome
decry *v.* deroge; misca
defame *v.* ca for aathing;
misca; (vilipend) wilipen
defeat *n.* defait; *v.* bleck;
bauchle (B1); defait, *ppl.*
defait
defecate *v.* cack; kich; drate
(*pr., pt., ppl.* dritten)
defend *v.* fend; haad aff (O) (M3)

defer *v.* defar
deformed *ppl.*, *adj.* mishachlt
defraud *v.* snype
deft *adj.* nacky
degrad|e *v.* degraad; ~ing *ppls.* degraadin, degraadit
dehorn *v.* dodd
dehydrated *ppl.* druchtit
dejected *adj.* doon i the moo; disjaskit; blue
deliberate *adj.*, deleebrate; *adv.* deleebrately; designtly
delicacy *n.* flagerie
delighted *adj.* knichtit (M3); trickit (S)
delve *v.* dell
dement|ed *ppl.* demintit; ~ia *n.* dottledom
demolish *v.* ca doon
demon *n.* deevilock
denial *n.* na-say
dent *v.* cloor, clour
deny *v.* na-say
depart *v.* depairt; skedaddle; ~ing *adj.* wa-gaan, -gaun; ~ure *n.* wa-gaan, -gaun
depend (on); *v.* lippen (tae, till); ~able *adj.* lippenable; siccar
depressed *adj.* doon; dumpitch
deprive (of) *v.* hain o; runt (o)
describe *v.* descrive, descryve
desert *v.* forhooie; ~ed *adj.*, *ppl.* forhooiet; pervoot
deserts *n. pl.* sairin
deserving *adj.* wordy

desir|e *n.* (slight) inklin; *v.* sik, seek; ~ous *adj.* keerious
desk *n.* dask
desperate *adj.* sair made
despise *v.* think lichtfu o
destitute *adj.* nace; but hoose an haa
destr|oy *v.* connach; misaacre, missaucre; ~uction *n.* crockaneetion; gowf(f); wrack
detain *v.* deteen
devil *n.* deevil; deil; fient; sorra
Devil, the *pr. n.* Aul Nick; Clootie; Cloots; the Earl o Hell; Hornie; Nicky Cloots; Spunkie
devilish *adj.* deevilitch
devious *adj.* forty-faal
devour *v.* (greedily) gluff
dew *n.* dyow
dexterous *adj.* nacky
dialect *n.* leid
diarrhoea *n.* skitter(s); (suffering from) lowss
didn't *interrog.* didnin?
die *v.* dee, *pt.* deet; slip the timmers.
difference *n.* odds
difficult *adj.* ill; ull; (of a person) crank; (of a task) kittle(some); (of words) lang-nebbit, -nibbit; ~y *n.* diffeekwalty (accent second syllable); fyke; snorl

dig *v.* cast; dell; howk; **dug** *ppl.*
cas(s)en; dellt; howkit

digest *v.* disjeest

dignity *n.* deegnity

dilatory *adj.* dreich (K)

diligent *adj.* eident

diminish *v.* dwine

din *n.* reemis(h), remis)h)

dinner *n.* dainner, denner;
provide ~ *v.* denner

diphtheria *n.* diphthairy

direction *n.* airt; **in all ~s** aa
the airts

dirt *n.* clort; muck; **~y** *adj.*
clorty; barkit; fool; muckit;
yirdit; *v.* fyle; daidle (s);
~ied *ppl.* dirten

disagreeable *adj.* (of weather)
drabbly

disappoint *v.* disappynt;
begeck; miscomfit (BI); *ppl.*,
adj. nicket; hingin-luggit
~ment *n.* begeck; hertscaad

disbelieve *v.* misdoot

discharge *v.* (any missile) fire

discomfit *v.* pit oot

disconsolate *adj.* doon-i-the-
moo; disjaskit

discord *n.* dispeace

discount *n.* discoont; (returned
to the buyer) luckpenny

discourage *v.* dachle; dackle (C)

discourse *n.* collieshangie;
discoorse; say-awa

discuss *v.* tak throw-han; dip

disdainful *adj.* sanshach

disembowel *v.* (deer carcase)
gralloch

disfurnish *v.* displenish

disgust *n.* scunner; *v.* backset;
scunner; (nauseate)
skaichen, skaiken; (feel
disgust) ug; (*excl. of*) feech,
feich; **~ed with** scunnert
o/wi; skaikent; uggit

disgusting *adj.* fusome;
ugsome; scunnerfu;
scunnersome

dish *n.* (for serving) ashet;
dirty ~es *n. pl.* gibbles;
~-cloth *n.* dish-cloot

dishevel *v.* toosle, toozle, tousle;
~led *adj.* hudd(e)ry

dishonesty *n.* oonhonesty

dislike to, take a *phr.* tak an
ull-wull at; tak an ug at

dislocate *v.* lith

dismal *adj.* darksome; dern;
oorie

dismember *v.* lith

dismiss *v.* skail, skale

disorder *v.* groogle; **~ed** *ppl.*
agee; ill-shooken up; oot o
reel; (in the mind) fey; **~ly**
adj. ramshackle; **in a ~ly**
way ower the bows

disparage *v.* deroge

disperse *v. tr., intr.* skail, skale

display *n.* (fine) brevity,
braivity; *v.* kythe

displease *v.* miscomfit;
   looked ~d *phr.* his face wis
   trippin him
disposed to, well *phr.* weel
   affeckit tae
displeased *adj.* nae ower sair
   suited aboot
disputatious *adj.* din-raisin
dissatisfied, to be (with)
   v. ail (at)
distaff *n.* rock (cleft stick for
   wool for spinning)
distant *adj.* oot-by
distinct *adj.* clair
distorted *adj.* bogjavelt;
   bogshaivelt
distrain *v.* (for debt) reest
distress *n.* *(excl. of)* feech;
   v. vex
district *n.* districk; (*thirled* to
   a mill or in which anyone
   carries on business) sucken
distrust *v.* mislippen
disturbance *n.* reerie; strush(ie);
   stushie; stramash
ditch *n.* dutch (G, MI); sheuch;
   stank
dither *v.* dibber-dabber; swither
diversion *n.* (entertainment)
   divert
divested (of) *ppl.* runtit (O)
divide *v.* pairt; (in two) haaver
do *v. inf.* tae dee; adee; dae (S, J)
   (*pr. tense*: A, ye, we, they
   daev; he, she, it daes; *imp.*
   dee/dae); ~ not so badly dee

awa; ~ without dee wintin;
   much to ~ muckle adee
dock plant *n.* docken
doctor *n.* doctor; physeeshun
document *n.* dockiment
dodge *n.* ginkum: ginkmen (BI);
   v. jink; jook, jouk, jowk
doer *n.* deester (often contempt.)
doesn't *v. neg.* disna; *interrog.*
   disna, disnin
dog *n.* fulp; tike, tyke; doag
   (J); (bitch) bick, bik
doll *n.* dall
dolt *n.* snot
domicile *n.* doomsil
done *ppl.* deen, dune; daen
   (S). *See* fatigued
donkey *n.* cuddy
don't *v. neg.* dinna; *interrog.*
   divnin
doomed *adj.* (to death/
   calamity) fey
doormat *n.* bass
doorpost *n.* (door)cheek
doorstep *n.* doorstane (K)
dotage *n.* (in one's) dytit,
   doitit; donnert
double *adj.* dooble; twa-faul
double-jointed *adj.* dooble-
   jyntit
doubt *n.* doot; *v.* doot,
   misdoot
doubtful *adj.* dootfu
doughball *n.* twenty-minute-
   sweemer (B)
doughty *adj.* douchtie

dovecot *n.* doocot
down *adv.* doon; ~ **with** *phr.*
hoot awa wi; ~ **yonder**
adv. doonby
downcast *adj.* blue (A1);
disjaskit; dowie
down-draught *n.* (in chimney)
flan
downfall *n.* dooncome; doonfa
downpour *n.* doorpoor
downright *adv.* doonricht;
evendoon
dowry *n.* tocher. *cf.* **doonsittin**
doze (off) *v.* dover (ower);
snotter (aff)
dozen *n.* dizzen
drag *v.* trail
draggle *v.* trachel, trachle,
trauchle
drain *n.* (small open) stripe;
(in cowshed) greep; (in
street gutter) syre; (for
liquid discharge) strang-
hole; *v.* (boiled solids)
bree; (to last drop)
dreep; ~-**cover** *n.* brander
dram *n.* skite; spot; tootie; (in
the morning) mornin
draught *n.* dracht; (of air)
drucht; (of wine etc) waucht;
~-**board** *n.* dambrod; ~s *n. pl.*
(the game) draachts
draw *v.* draa, *ppl.* draan; (on a
pipe) lunt
dread *n., v.* dreed, dreid
dregs *n. pl.* quinkins

drench *v.* drook; *ppl., adj.*
drookit; ~**ing** *n.* steepin
dress *n.* (loose) slip; *v.* busk;
rig; (for a journey) buckle;
turse; (to go out) rank;
(smartly) trig
dressed *ppl.* cled; ~ **up** *ppl.*
trickit up; triggit oot;
(showily) cockit up
dressing-down *n.* dixie;
hanlin; owergae; sedarin
drib|ble *v.* dreeble; ~**let**
n. (small quantity of liquid)
jibble (contempt. term)
drift *n.* (snow) wraith; (dense)
blin-drift; smore-drift
drill *n.* (furrow with ridge on
top) dreel
drink *n.* dracht; drap(pie); (of
spirits) donal(ie); (small
quantity) lab(b)ach; (of
warming liquor) heater
drip *n.* dreep; *v.* dreep; sype
dripping *n.* dreepin;
~ **enclosure** (for sheep)
dreepin-penn
drizzl|e *v.* muggle; ~**y** *adj.*
saft(-like)
drive *n.* gurr; *v.* ca, caa;
(animals) gird; (poultry) hish;
(drive in) yark in
drizzl|e *n.* sma weet; smirr;
~**y** *adj.* dribbly; (with fog)
muggly
drone *v.* bum

drop *n.* (sometimes of alcohol) drap; dooncome; *v.* drap; (an acquaintance) purvoy
dross *n.* drush
drought *n.* drooth, drouth; drucht
drove *v. pt.* dreeve
drown *v.* droon, *ppl.* droont
drowsy, become *adj. & v.* drow
drubbing *n.* nizzin
drudge *n.* (kitchen) scudge
drug *n., v.* drog
druggist *n.* droggist
Drumlithie *pr. n.* (nicknamed) Skite
drummer *n.* (town) drumster
drunk(en) *adj.* foo, fou; drucken; (very) bleezin; mortal; as foo's a buckie; greetin foo; (incapably) styterin foo; (wildly) fleein; ~enness *n.* druckenness
dry *adj.* (sapless) foggy; (used of cows which have stopped giving milk) eel; yeld; *v.* (stooks) win; ~ out *v.* skurken; ~ up *v.* gizzen; ~er *n.* (of grain) dryster
duck *n.* deuk, dyeuk; *v.* jook, jouk
due *adj.* dyow
dull *adj.* dreich; ducksie (A)
dullard *n.* blunk
dulse *n.* (edible seaweed) dilse
dumbfounded *ppl.* dumfoonert
dumbstruck *ppl.* dusht

dun *n.* craver; *v.* crave
dung *n.* muck; sharn; (liquid) sharn-bree; (on the hindquarters of cattle or sheep) knapdarloch
dungarees *n. pl.* dungers
dunghill *n.* midden; **moisture from** ~ midden-bree; **top of the** ~ midden-tap
duplicitous *adj.* dooble
dusk *n.* gloaming; glowmin
dust *n.* dist; stue, styoo; (flying) stoor, stour; ~cart *n.* aiss-cairt
duster *n.* dister
dusty *adj.* stoorie, stourie; styooie
duty *n.* dyowty
dwarf *n.* ablach; drochle; drochlum (M3); knurlin
dwell *v.* dwaal, dwall; won (K)
dwelling-house *n.* dwallin-hoose; firehoose
dyer *n.* dy(e)ster
dying (for) *ppl.* mangin (for); ~ to *ppl.* mangin tae

E

each *adj.* ilk; ilka; ilky; ulkie
eager *adj.* attlin; ettlin; fain; gleg; verty; yivvery; **to be** ~ *v.* ettle; fidge (B1)
ear *n.* lug
earl *n.* yarl; yirl

earl|y *adj., adv.* airly; air; ear;
~**y up** vertie; ~**ier** *adj.* earer

earn *v.* airn; win

earnest *n.* (given on striking a
bargain) arles; **in dead ~** in
gnappin earnest (B1)

earrings *n. pl.* lug-babs

earth *n.* airth; (also the earth)
yird; **covered in ~** yirdit;
~**-nut** *n.* arnut; ~**enware** *n.*
lame; (shards) lames, lems

earwig *n.* forkie-(tail);
hornygoloch

ease *n.* easedom

Easter *n.* Pase, Pess; Pesch

easy *adj., adv.* easy; aisy (s);
no ~ job nae mowse job;
take it ~ hud doon the deece;
lat the theats slack; ~**-going**
adj. easy-osy; eedle-oddle;
easymin't; ~ **person** sug

eat *v.* aet; ett; ~**en** *ppl.* aeten,
etten; (voraciously) gaap;
(noisily, greedily) hamsh,
humsh; ~ **up** hing in; ~**ables**
n. pl. ettables

eaves *n. pl.* easin, eezen(s)

eccentric *n.* antic

edict *n.* edick

edify *v.* edifee; ~**ing** *ppl.*
edifeein

educate *v.* eddicat

education *n.* eddicashun

eerie *adj.* oorie

effect *n.* effeck

egg *n.* aig; (state of egg with
young bird partially formed)
gorbelt; *v.* (someone on) eik
him up (A2); eek on (M3)

egg shells *n. pl.* egg shallies

eight *adj.* acht, aucht; aicht,
echt; ~**een** *adj.* achteen;
aichteen, echteen; ~**y** *adj.*
achty; aichty, echty

either *adj., conj., pron.* edder;
edderan (can be used at end
of sentence as in Eng.

elbow *n.* elbick, elbock, elbuck;
v. joundie

elder *n.* (of the Church) eller;
elyer

elder-tree *n.* boortree, bourtree;
elyer

elevated *ppl., adj.* liftit

eleven *adj.* aleyven; eleeven,
eleiven

else *adv.* anse

elude *v.* jink

embarrassed *ppl., adj.* affrontit;
deeply ~ black affrontit

ember *n.* emmer; eyzle

embrace *n.* bosie; *v.* oxter

emotion *n.* grytehertedness;
~**al** *adj.* (showing emotion)
great-hertit

empty *adj., v.* teem; toom
(G1, J, M)

enamel *adj.* nammle

enamoured of *adj.* browdent
upo

enclose *v.* criv

enclosure *n.* close, closs; (for poultry) crive; ree; riv

encouragement *n.* hairtnin, hertnin; cuttins (*usually in the neg., eg,* nae/sma cuttins)

end *n.* en; eyn; hinner-en; hint; (of yarn) thrum; *v.* en, eyn, *ppl.* eynt; **at the ~ of** i the tail o; **~ of harvest, of the year** the backeyn; **make ~s meet** get eyns tae rug thegidder

endearment (term of) (for children) *n.* chowter; smowt

endeavour *v.* mint

endless *adj.* eynless

end-ridge *n.* en-, eynrig

endure *v.* dree; thole

energetic *adj.* fersell

energy *n.* birr; spunk; virr; (great) rake; *adj.* (lacking) fen(d)less; fushenless; thowless

engage *v.* (a farmhand) fee

engine *n.* engeen; ingine

English *adj.* suddron, soothkwintra

enlist *v.* list

enough *adj.* aneuch; aneu; enew

entangle *v.* insnorl; raivel; *ppl., adj.* insnorlt; raivelt

entertain *v.* divert; enterteen; **~ment** *n.* a divert; enterteenment

enthralled *adj.* thirlt

enthusiasm *n.* (fit of) feerich

entice *v.* goy; moyen; tryst; tyce

entitle *v.* enteetle

entrails *n. pl.* (animal) harigals; monyfaalds, monyfaulds

entrance *n.* (at ground-floor level) low door; **~-hall** *n.* trance

entrap *v.* insnorl

equal *adj., adv.* (shares) eeksy-peeksy, -picksy; *n.* marra, marrow; *v.* peer wi; **~ with** upsides wi

equipped *ppl., adj.* riggit oot

err *v.* eer

errand *n.* eeran; **on a special ~ , specially** *phr.* ance eeran

escapade *n.* ploy

escape *v.* win oot

escort *v.* convoy

Eskimo *n.* Yakki (deriv. from Yaqui (B)

especially *adv.* espeeshully; **on a special errand** eence eeran

estate manager *n.* grun offisher

evasive behaviour *n.* hunkerslidin

even *adv.* aiven, ayven; eyven; **get ~ with** get clear wi; win tee wi; (on level pegging) peel

evening *n.* even; een; eenin (from twilight to bedtime) forenicht; **in the ~** at even, at een

ever *adv.* iver, ivver

everlasting *adj.* iverlaistin
every *adj.* ilk; ilka; ilky; ulkie;
  ~body *pron.* aabody;
  ~one *pron.* aabody; **~one**
  else aa ither body; **~thing**
  n. aathin(g); **~where** *adv.*
  aawye; aa gate/gait
evil *adj.* coorse; ill; *n.* ill;
  ~-doer *n.* ill-deer
eviscerate *v.* (of deer) gralloch
ewe *n.* yowe; (from one to
  two years old) gimmer
exaggeration *n.* hose an sheen
exalt *v.* heeze
examination *n.* gyaun-ower
example *n.* spyack, spyauck;
  for ~ likein
exceedingly *adv.* byous;
  feerious; fell; terrible (*used
  intensively*)
excel *v.* ding; **~lent** *adj.* braw;
  capital
except *prep.* 'cep; 'cepin; excep;
  ~ for hud awa fae
exchange *v.* cowp; hooie; niffer;
  trock, troke
exciseman *n.* gaager, gauger,
  gager
excite *v.* flocht; kittle; raise;
  ~d *ppl., adj.* kittelt up;
  ~ment *n.* (nervous) picher;
  in a state of ~ment flochtit;
  raist; *phr.* clean aff his eggs
  (M3)
exclamations (of surprise)
  goshie; heth; jings;

loshins; loshtie (be here);
loshtiegoshtie guide's;
meggins alive; megstie me;
michty me; (blood) sang;
saal, saul; toot fie; (troth)
trogs; (of doubt, contempt)
hoots; (of impatience) tyach;
(of soothing and endearment)
weel-a-wins, -wuns; (on
lifting a weight) oopie stiff(ie)
excluded *ppl.* barrit-oot
excrement *n.* kich
excus|e *n.* affcome; **~able** *adj.*
  exkeesable
exercise *n., v.* exerceese;
  ~-book *n.* exerceese-beuk
exertion *n.* trav(a)il
exhaust *v.* jabb; **~ed** *ppl.* deen;
  foonert; forfochen; forjeskit;
  jabbit; wabbit. *See* **worn out**
exhibition *n.* exhibeetion
expans|e *n.* (of ground) sklyter;
  ~ive *adj.* (of talk) lairge
expect *v.* expeck; **~ed** *ppl.*
  expeckit
expenditure *n.* (costly) hairrial,
  herrial
expensive *adj.* daar
experience *n.* expairience;
  v. pree
expound v. expoond
expression *n.* (*eg,* of emotion)
  ootlat
extraordinary *adj.* byordnar;
  byous; exterordnar;
  ondeemas; unco

extravagance *n.* livin at haik
an manger
extrem|ely *adv.* dooms (M3);
fell; unco; ~ity *n.* hinner-en
exult *v.* craa, craw
exultant *adj.* vantie, vauntie
eye|(s) *n.* ee(n); ~ **like burning
coals** eyzly ee't; ~**lash** *n.*
brier; winker; ~**sight** *n.*
ee-sicht

F

fac|e *n.* face; phizog; ~**ial
expression** mudgeon
fact *n.* fack
fad *n.* aivis
fade *v.* scaw; ~**d** *ppl.*, *adj.*
cassen; fyaachie; scawt;
~ **away** *v.* weer awa
failed *adj.* stickit
faint *n.* dwa(a)m(ock); fant;
swarf; *v.* fant; swarf; tak
a dwam; ~**-hearted** *adj.*
chuckenhertit; henny-hertit
fair-haired *adj.* tow-heidit
fair play *phr.* fair hornie
fairy *n.* seelie wicht; ~ **court**
seelie coort
faith *n.* haith; *excl.* fegs;
haith, heth; ~**ful** *adj.* faithfu
fall *n.* (sudden and heavy)
clyte; (heavy) doosht; (with
a bump) dird; (downfall)
dooncome; (heavy) sklyte;

sklyter; (light, of rain,
snow) skiffin; *v.* fa; (with a
thud) dyst; (with a bounce)
dird; (heavily) sklyte,
sklyter; (of heavy rain,
snow) ding; (of light rain,
snow) skiff; (sound of fall
into water) plype; (of rain)
onding; ~ **asleep** *v.* win
aff asleep; (fisher term) to
catch her; ~**-out** *n.* cast-oot;
v. strive, *pt.* streeve; ~ **over**
ca ower; cowp; ~ **to** fa tee
fallow land *n.* faugh
false *adj.* faase, fause
family *n.* faimly
famished *adj.* faimished
famous *adj.* faamous
fan *n.* (agricultural) fanner
(for winnowing corn)
winnister
fancy *n.* maggot; (romantic)
noshun (O); (foolish)
whigmaleerie; ~ **cake** *n.*
fancy, funcy; ~ **work** *n.*
fineerin
far *adv.* hine; ~ **off** hine awa;
at the back o Balfuff (M3);
~ **gone** sair come at
fare *v.* faar, faur; (quite well)
turn ower; ~ **badly** misthrive
farewell *int.* faar-ye-weel
farm *n.* fairm, ferm; toon,
toun; ~**er** *n.* fairmer;
~**ing** *n.* fairmin; ~ **cottage** *n.*
cottar hoose; ~**hand** *n.*

fairm-servan; ~house *n.*
fairmhoose; firehoose;
~servant *n.* fairm servan;
(very experienced) *n.* docknell;
~stead *n.* haudin; steadin;
toon, toun; ~worker's bag
chackie; ~yard *n.* closs
farm tools (implement for
clearing ground of roots etc)
(Eng.) grubber; (for pulling
turnips) neep-click; (for
slicing turnips for fodder)
neep-hasher; (for pulling
turnips) neep-pluck; (for
hoeing turnips) neep-rinner;
(horse-hoe for weeding)
shim; (skimmer for surface
soil and weeds) skreefer;
(small rake) smiler; (for
removing turnip roots)
tailer; (for removing turnip
tops) tapner; (for twisting
straw ropes) thrawcrook,
thrawheuk; (for tilting
loose sheaves off oldstyle
reaper) tilter
farrier *n.* fairrier
farth|er *adv.* farder; farrer;
forder; (away, along)
yont; ~est *adj. adv.* farrest;
~est out farrest ootbye
farthing *n.* fardin
fascinated *adj.* fair teen on wi
fashion *v.* fack, fake
fast *adj., adv.* faist; *n., v.* fas(t)
fasten *v.* faisten; cleek; hank

fastidious *adj.* dorty;
over-~ pernickety
fat *adj.* stoot; *n.* creesh;
~ person fatty-bannocks
fatal *adj.* fattal
fate *n.* weird
father *n.* fadder; faither
(C1, F)
father-in-law *n.* gweed-fadder,
-faither
fathom *n.* faddom
fatigue *n.* harassment (A2);
v. jabb; jaap, jaup; ~d *ppl.,*
adj. deen; dylt; daivert;
forjeskit; jaapit; jabbit;
tasht; typit; wabbit
fault *n.* faat, faut; wyte
~-finding *n.* fittie-fies;
(fretful) girn; *adj.* grumlie
favour *n.* faavour; in ~ with
(esp. with God) far-ben wi;
~ed *adj.* faavourt; faart;
well-~ed (good-looking),
weelfaart; ill-~ed (ugly)
ill-faart
favourite *adj.* faavrit, fauvrit
fear *n.* fear; ferr (S)
feast *n.* (of farewell or
completion) foy
feather *n., v.* fedder; ~-duster
feather-wisker
fed up (of) *adj.* doon; scunnert
(o/wi)
feeble *adj.* dwaibly; dwebble;
dweeble; dweebly; dwobble;
dweemly-dwamly; shilpit;

thewless; **grow ~ in mind**
v. doit; **~-minded** *adj.* doitit
feed *n.* aet; **a good ~** a gweed
aet; rim-rax; *v.* mait (oot);
ppl. maitit; (from a pail)
cog; (with oats) to corn;
~ing-bag *n.* (for horses)
moo-bag; mou-bag
feel *v.* fin, *pt.* fan; **~ at home**
fin at hame
feign *v.* feignie
felloes *n. pl.* (of wheel) fillies
fell out (quarrelled) *v. pt.*
streeve
fellow *n.* chiel; billie; fallow;
folla; steel (B1); stock;
(foolish) taapie; (of low
character) slung; (mean)
tarlach; (sturdy) bumlock;
(worthless) slype
felt *v. pt.* fan
fence *n.* palin; (of furze bushes)
fundyke
fend *in phr.* **~ for yourself**
winnow o yir ain cannas
ferment *n., v.* barm
fern *n.* fairn; bracken; breckan
fester *v.* beel
fetch *v.* fesh, *pt.* feish, foosh,
fush; fess, *pt.* feese
Fetterangus *pr. n.* (nicknamed)
Fishie
fettle *in phr.* **in fine ~** in richt
bone
fever *n.* fivver

few *adj.* fyow; *n.* fyow; **a
twa-three**
fewer *adj.* fyower
fibrous *adj.* stickly
fiddl‖e (with or about) *v.* ficher;
footer; foorich; picher; **~y
job** a ficher; a footer
fidget *v.* fyke; fidge (B); fyaach
field *n.* feedle (A, A2), fiedle;
park (A); rigs; (for sowing
turnip seed) patcher;
(division of a field) wynin
fifteen *adj.* fifeteen, foifteen (A2);
~th *adj.* fifteent
fifty *adj.* fifety
fight *n., v.* fecht; pilget;
shangie; sharrie; (with
cudgels) a staffy-nevel job;
~er *n.* fechter
fill *n.* fouth; sairin; **get your
~ of** get yer sairin o; *v.* ful,
full (rhymes with *gull*),
ppl. fullt; bowdent; **~ up
completely** beamfill, -full
film *n.* (membrane) scriffan;
(thin) yim
final(ly) *adj., adv.* feenal(ly)
find *v.* fin
Findochty *pr. n.* (locally)
Finechty
fine *adj.* braw; **~-looking**
adj. (of men) buirdly; **~ly**
adv. brawlies
finery *n.* braivity; (esp. of
dress) braws; flagerie

finger *n.* finger (rhymes with singer); **the little ~** crannie; **~ tips** finger-eyns, -pynts; **~-stall** finger-steel

finicky *adj.* jinipperous

finish *n., v.* feenish; **~ed** *pt. ppl.* feenisht; throw

fir-cone *n.* (fir-)yowe; yowie

fire *n.* ingle; (blazing) inglelowe; (small, blazing, coal or peat) cutchack; (big) bevie; (flameless, of red-hot embers) greeshach (A1); **~side** *n.* ingle; ingle-cheek; (at the end of a room) *n.* fire-en; **~wood** *n.* firewid; kinlin; **~work** *n.* squeeb; (primitive, homemade) poother-deevil

fire (make up for the night) *v.* rist

first, at *phr.* erst

first rate *adj., phr.* bencape

fish *n.* (ungutted) rounder; (useless small species found in harbours) buddick; (take-home parcel of fish in the fishing industry) fry; *v.* (catch with hands in stream) guddle; **~ roe** *n.* raan; **~er-boy** *n.* fisherloon; **~er-girl** *n.* fisherquine; **~ing-line** *n.* (hand-) hanlin; **~ing-rod** *n.* waan

fist *n.* nieve, niv; **~ful** *n.* nievefu

fit *adj.* (physically) stoot; **~ for** fier (for)

fixed *ppl.* (to be depended on) solvendo

flabbergast *v.* stammygast(er); **~ed** *ppl., adj.* stammygastit, -gastert

flagged *ppl.* (of floor) flaggit

flagon *n.* stoop

flake *n.* (of snow, large) flag

flame *n.* lowe

flannel *n.* flannen

flap *n.* (excited state) flichter *v.* flaff; flaffer; wap

flash *n.* (of lightning) flacht

flattened *ppl.* (of crop) laid

flatter *v.* fraise; fleetch; **~y** *n.* (a bit of) a fraise; **given to ~y** fraisie

flax *n.* lint

flea *n.* flech; **~ridden** *adj.* flechy

fleam *n.* (for bleeding of horses) fleem

flew *v. pt.* flaa (M3)

flexible *adj.* wamfle

flick *v.* wheech

flicker *v.* blink; flicher; flichter

flight *n.* (of birds) flacht; flicht; **take ~** tak sheet

flighty *adj.* flichty; **~ person** a flee-up (M3)

flinch *v.* flench

flint and steel *phr.* flint an fleerish

flirt *v.* daff

float *n.* (for fishing) bowe

flock *n.* (of sheep) hirsel;
(of birds) flacht

flog *v.* soosh

flood *n.* (of river, stream)
spate; speet; speeth

floor *n.* fleer

flop *v.* flap

flounder *n.* fluke

flour *n.* (wheaten etc) floor

flourish *v.* fleerish; floorish

flower *n.* flooer, floor;
(artificial) gumfleer, -floor

flowering currant *n.* (blossom
appearing before the
leaves) son-afore-the-father.
(A name applied to other
plants)

fluff *n.* caddis

flukeworm *n.* (on the lung of
sheep) the hooze

flung *v. pt.* flang

flurry *n.* flocht

flutter *v.* flaff; flaffer

fly *n., v.* flee; **~-by-night**
n. flee-b-nichter

flywheel *n.* (of a spindle) whorl

foal *n.* foalie

foam *n.* faem, faim; *v.* ream

fodder *n.* fodd(e)rin

foe *n.* fae

fog *n.* (mist) haar

foggy *adj.* (fog with drizzle)
muggly

fold *n.* lirk, lurk; (of sheep)
faal(d), faul(d); *v.* faald

folk *n.* fowk (*gen.*); folk
(G, M); fock

follow *v.* folla

folly *n.* madden-dreem

fond (of) *adj.* browdent upo;
font (o)

fondle *v.* daat, dawt; delt

food *n.* mait; meat (C, J); scran
(K); **off his ~** aff o's mait;
able to take ~ mait-haill

fool *n.* coof, cuif; feel, fule;
gapus; gaak, gawk; gaakie;
gillieperous, gileepris
(hard g); gock; gowk;
gomeril; gype; haveral;
neip-heid; styoomer; sumph;
tawpie; wandocht (K)
(outstanding) dunderheid;
v. begowk; **~'s errand** feel's
eeran; Prile eeran; **~ish** *adj.*
daft; feel; feelish; fulage
(BI); gockit; gowkit; gypit;
~ishness *n.* feelness; gypery

foot *n.* fit; *v.* **to ~ it** fit it; **~ed**
fittit; **on ~** o yir fit; **~-and-
mouth** *n.* (disease) fit-an-
moo; **~ball** *n.* fitba; **~ing**
n. precunnance; **~path** *n.*
(fit-)roddie; **~step** *n.* fitstep

Footdee *pr. n.* (old fisher
district of Aberdeen) Fittie;
Futtie

for *prep.* for; tae

forbears *n. pl.* forbeers

force *n.* birr; virr; **~ful** *adj.*
fersell

ford *n.* feerd (M3); foord
foreign *adj.* fremd; fremmit
forequarter *n.* (of an animal)
  spaal, spaul
foreshadow *v.* foreshaida
foretell *v.* bode
Forfar *pr. n.* Farfar
forgave *v. pt.* forgya
forget *v.* foryet; *v. pt.* forgat;
  foryat; ~ful *adj.* forgettle
forgive *v.* forgie
fork *n.* (of a tree, in the
  road etc) glack; (used in
  farming) graip; *v.* graip
form *v.* fack (B1);
  n. (bench) furm
former *adj.* umquhile
forsake *v.* forhooie, furhooie
forth *adv.* furth; ~with *adj.*
  forfairn
fortun|e *n.* fortin; **good** ~e
  seil; **tell** ~es spay; ~e-teller
  n. (female) spay-wife; ~ate
  adj. chancy; fortnat
forward *adj.* (in direction)
  forrit; (in manner) upsettin;
  adv. forrit; *imp.* (to a horse)
  gee up!
foul *adj.* fool; foosome,
  fousome; ramsh
found *v. pt.* fan, *ppl.* fun(d).
  cf. **fin**
foundations *n. pl.* foons, founs
foundling *n.* funlin
fountain *n.* funtain; ~head
  n. funtainheid

four *adj.* fower; ~teen *adj.*
  fowerteen
fowl *n.* fool; (of the the first
  year) earock
fox *n.* tod
fragile *adj.* (feeling) aa egg
  shallies
fragment *n.* skirp
Fraserburgh *pr. n.* nicknamed
  The Broch; Faithlie
Fraserburgh native *n.* Brocher
fraud *n.* snype
freckled *adj.* ferny-ticklt
freckles *n. pl.* fern(y)-tickles
freeze *v.* jeel
freight *n.* fraacht
Frenchman *pr. n.* (jocular)
  Poddock-etter
frenzy *n.* paavie
fresh *adj.* caller
fret *v.* chirm; ~ful *adj.* cankert
Friday *n.* Freday
friend *n.* freen; ~ly (with) *adj.*
  chief (wi)
fright *n.* fleg; gast; (Abdn. City
  and coastal) fear; **took** ~
  teuk fley; ~en *v.* fleg; fley;
  frichten; (Abdn. city &
  coastal) fear; *pt. ppl.*
  fleggit; fleyt; feart
frill *n.* bord
frivol|ity *n.* (piece of) flagerie;
  ~ous *adj.* freevolous
frog *n.* poddick; puddock;
  ~spawn *n.* puddock-crood

frolic *n.* hyze; ploy; rig; splore
~**some** *adj.* daft
from *prep.* fae; (much less
common) frae (K)
front, in (of) *adv.* afore; *prep.*
afore; anent
frost *n.* freest; (hoar) rime;
v. freest; ~-**nail** *n.* pike,
pyke; sharp
frown *v.* froon; glumsh (M3);
glunsh
frugal *adj.* canny
fruit slice *n.* curran daad
fugitive *n.* (from the gallows)
rin-the-wuddie
full *adj.* fou, fu; ful, full
(rhymes with gull);
(to overflowing) beamfullt;
(after eating) bowdent
fulmar *n.* mallie (B)
fumble *v.* fummle; thrimble
fume *v.* feem
funeral *n.* beerial; fun'ral;
(refreshment) dregie
furious *adj.* feerious
furnish *v.* plenish
furniture *n.* furnitur; plenishin
furrow *n.* fur, furr; sheugh;
(open furrow between two
ridges) mids; (shallow)
scart; (set up the first
furrow when ploughing a
field) *v.* feer. *cf.* **feerin**
furth|er *See* **farther**
furtive *adj.* scoukin. *cf.* **skouk**
fury *n.* rampaage

fuss *n.* fyke; adee; (great)
mineerum; a wark;
(outcry) scronach(in);
~**y** *adj.* fashious; perjink;
(extremely) cappernyam
(B); (over-) pernickety;
make a ~ *phr.* cry bizz

G

gabble *v.* yab-yabble
gable *n.* gaivel (G); gale (M);
(top stones on gable)
tablin
gad about *v.* (often of animals)
squeerie
gadfly *n.* cleg; gleg
gaiters *n. pl.* cweetikins;
queetikins
gallery *n.* (in church) laft
gallows *n.* wuddie, wuddy;
~-**bird** *n.* rin-the-wuddie;
chait (chett)-e-wuddie
game (ball-) sappy sodgers;
(catching) leavie-oh;
(selection) a pye; (marbles
played against a door)
doorie; (playground)
jyne-on; (seashore) rocky-
on; (team game for boys)
hucky-ducky (S); (for two
with a stick) pooin the
sweer-tree; (tag) tackie,
takie; tik-an-tak

gamekeeper *n.* gamie; (the work) keeperin
gander *n.* ganner
gang *n.* gyang
gaol *n.* jile; jivvle
gap *n.* rive; (in wall or fence) slap
gape *v.* gaap, gawp
garden *n.* gairden; (on farm) yard; yaird
Gardenstown *pr. n.* (local) Gaimrie
Garioch *pr. n.* (*pro.* Geery; Gerry)
garments *n. pl.* (outer, usually untidy) bullaments
garter *n.* garten
Gartly *pr. n.* (local) Gairtly
gas *v.* (talk idly) lyaag; laig
gasbag *n.* blether; bleeter; gab
gasp *v.* glagger
gate *n.* yett, yitt
gather *v.* gaither; gedder; gether; gidder; ~er *n.* (of grain to make sheaves, usually female) gaitherer; gedderer; lifter; ~ing *n.* gedderin, gidderin
gaudy *adj.* skiry, skyrie; galliart (B1)
gaunt *adj.* chandler-chaftit
gave *v. pt.* gae (M, A2, M3); gya; gied, gid
Gavin *pr.n.* Ga'in
gawp *v.* gowp, goup; gype
generation *n.* ashun

generous *adj.* fraachty; lairdlifu; gweedwillie, gweedwullie; leebral
genial *adj.* humoursome
genius *n.* jainus
gentility *n.* genteelity
gentle *adj.* douce; lithe
gentry *n.* gintles
George *pr. n.* Dod; Geordie
get *v.* get; win; ~ **going** hing in, (*pt.* hang in); ~ **off** win aff; ~ **out** win oot; ~ **even with** win tee wi; ~ **away** swithe; ~ **on with something** hing in; ~ **over** (recover from) cower; ~ **ready** (*esp.* dress to go out) rank; ~ **up** rise, *pt.* raise, rase
gewgaw *n.* flagerie
ghastly *adj.* gash; ugsome
g(h)illie *n.* gheelie
ghost *n.* ghaist(ie); bogle, boggle (K); boodie; wreith ~ly *adj.* gowsty
ginger *n.* ginch; ~ **bread** *n.* ginch-breid
girl *n.* lassie; quine; giglet; (frivolous) hizzie; (short) cutty; (young) damishel (M3); deemie; lassickie, lassockie; quinockie; ~friend *n.* blon; laas
girthing *n.* girdin

give *v.* gie; ~ **me** (when one chooses a particular thing) chaps me; ~ **up** *v.* ring in

given that *phr.* sae be 'at

glad *adj.* gled; gledsome; blythe

glance *n.* glaff (K); glent; glaik, gleck; skance; went; twig; *v.* twig

Glasgow *pr. n.* Glaisga

glass *adj.*, *n.* gless; tass(ie)

gleam *n.* flacht; glaik; glim; glisk; leam; sheen

glen *n.* cleuch

glide *v.* snoove

glimpse *n.* glimsh (A2); glint (M); went

glitter *v.* (gaudily) skire

globe flower *n.* lucken-gowan

gloomy *adj.* dowf; drumly

glossy *adj.* sleekit

glove *n.* glive (A2); (without separate division for the four fingers) doddy-mitten

glow *n.*, *v.* glowe; lowe

glum *adj.* disjaskit; doon-i-the-moo; dowie; blue (A1)

gluttonous *adj.* gutsy

gnarled *adj.* gurly

gnaw *v.* gnaave, gnauve

go *v.* dyae (M3); gae; gang; ging; gyang (A, A1); gaan, gaun (coastal); (reach a place) win; ~ **away** *imp.* g'wa; *v.* win awa; ~ **off something** tak a scunner till; ~ **on** hud awa; ~ **over** owergae; ~ **your way** gang yir gait; ~ **up and down** dyst; **as you ~ by** i the byg(y)aan

goad *n.* (for driving horses or cattle or directing corn to the scythe or binder) gaad, gad; **one who uses a ~** gaadsman

goal *n.* (in children's games) dell

gobble *v.* yowff doon

goblet *n.* tass(ie)

God *pr. n.* Gweed; (*euph.*) dyod; nyod; od; often **good** in expletives, *eg*, good be here; good almeggins (*prob. euph. for*) God Almighty; ~ **grant** Gweed sen; ~ **knows** Gweed kens; ~ **preserve us** Gweed preserve's, Gweed keep's aa

godly *adj.* gweedlie

going *ppl.* gaan, gaun; gyaan, gyaun; ~ **about** *ppl.* agyaan; ~ **on** *ppl.* agyaan; ~**s-on** *n. pl.* ongaans, ongauns

gold *n.* gowd; ~**en** *adj.* gowden

golf *n.* gowf; ~**er** *n.* gowfer

gone *pt. ppl.* geen, gane

good *adj.*, *n.* gweed, guid; geed (F); (very) capital; ~~**for-nothing** *n.* ranagant; hurb; wallydraigle; warridrag; ~~**hearted** *adj.* gweedwully; ~~**humoured**

adj. canty; ~ies *n. pl.* chit-chow; galshachs, galshochs; perlyaag; ~-looking *adj.* weel-faart; ~-natured *adj.* gweed-naturt; ~night *int.* gweednicht; ~will *n.* gweed-wull

goodness *n.* gweedness; *excl.* gwestie, gweeshtie, gweeshtens; ~ knows *excl.* Gweed kens; for ~ sake for ony faavour!

gooseberry *n.* grozart

gore *v.* stick, *ppl.* stickit

gorge *v.* stech

gosh *excl.* goshie; jings

gossamer *n.* slammach

gossip *n.* claik; clash; (chat) crack; (person) kimmer; claik; sclave; *v.* claik; clash; crack; sclave; sclaver

got *v. pt.* gat; gowt

Gourdon *pr. n.* Gurdon

gown *n.* goon, goun

grab *v.* glammach, glammoch; mitten

gradual(ly) *adj. (adv.)* gradiwal

grain *n.* (freed from husks) shillans; (threshed) thrash; (particle) sinacle (B1); (mixed) mashlach; ~-loft *n.* corn-laft; ~ prices *n. pl.* (fixed for the year) fiars

grand *adj.* gran; (very smart) fantoosh; ~child *n.* oe (M);

oy (K), *pl.* oe(s); ~father *n.* deydie (B); granda; granfadder, -faither; gutcher (M); lucky daddy (A2); ~mother *n.* granmidder, -mither; grunny; lucky minnie

grasp *v.* glammach, glammoch; lat glammoch at; fist (B1); ~ing *adj.* nabble, nabal; rivin

grass *n.* girse, girss; (coarse) sprot; (near the sea) bent; (long, left standing in winter) fog; (long, thin) ling (J); (any tall, thin, withered stalk) windle-strae; (crested dogstail) windlestrae; ~land *n.* green ~y *adj.* girssy

grate *v.* jirg

grave *n.* graif, greff; (earth) the mools; ~stone *n.* lair-steen, -stane

gravel *n.* graivel; (compacted) chad; ~ly *adj.* chaddy

grazing *n.* foggage; *ppl.* girsin

grease *n.* creesh

great *adj.* gryte; muckle; meikle; (considerable) gey

greedy *adj.* gutsy; ~ person guts; (mean) hungry

green *n.* (village) loaning (S);

greenish *adj.* greenichtie

grey *adj.* hyaave; (turning) grizzelt; (streaked with) lyart

griddle *n.* (circular iron plate with bow handle for baking) girdle

gridiron *n.* brander

grief *n.* dool

grievances, expressed their *phr.* shook their craps

grim *adj.* door, dour

grimace *n.* murjin, murgeon, mudgeon

grindstone *n.* grinsteen

grip *n.* clacht; purchase; *v.* grup; **in the ~ of** i the throws o

gristle *n.* girsle

groan *n., v.* grain; groanach (M3)

groom *n.* (in charge of horse) strapper; shalt-loon

grope *v.* grape; glamp; **~ about** glamp aboot

ground *n.* grun(d); (large piece of wasteland) gleebrie; gliberal (B1); **~ed** *ppl.* grunt

groundsel *n.* grunsel

group *n.* boorach(ie)

grow *v.* growe; sproot

growl *n., v.* gurl; gurr; wurr

grub *n.* (of cranefly, eating germinating grain) tory; *v.* (of birds) dorb

gruel *n.* stoorum

gruesome *adj.* gash

gruff *adj.* strunge

grumbl|e *v.* grummle; girn; mump; **~ing** *adj.* grumlie; nyattery

grunt *v.* grumph; gruntle

guano *n.* (fertiliser) gwana

guarantor *n.* cautioner

guard *n., v.* guaird, gaird

guernsey *n.* (seaman's jersey) gansey; ganjie

guess *n.* guiss; *v.* jaloose, jalouse

guffaw *n.* gaff, gauff; guffa

guidance *n.* guideship

guide *n.* (example) spyaack; *v.* gye

guinea *n.* yalla geordie

gull *v.* gow

gullet *n.* weazen, weazon; wizzen.

gulp *n.* howp

gumboil *n.* gumbyle, gumbile

gums *n. pl.* geems

gunpowder *n.* gunpoother

gush *v.* jurr (K); stoor, stour (M3)

gusset *n.* gushet

gust *n.* (of wind) flan; gast (M3); (sudden) howder

H

habit *n.* haibit

hack *v.* hagger

hackle *n.* (flax-comb) heckle

had *v. pt.* haed; hed; hid; **~ not** haedna, hidna

haddock *n.* haddie; (split open, salted, sun-dried) speldin; (dried without being split) widdie

haft *n.* (of knife) heft

hag *n.* (withered) runt

haggard *adj.* chandler-chaftit

hailstones *n. pl.* hailstanes, -steens

hair *n.* (haircut) snod-in-aboot; (cut with a bowl) *adj.* bowel-crappit; ~y nep

hairpins *n. pl.* oots-an-ins

half *adj.*, *n.* haaf; ~-holiday *n.* haafie; ~penny *n.* maik; ~pennyworth *n.* maikst; ~ share *n.* haaver; ~way *adv.* hauflins; mids; haufroads; a ~way point the mids; ~wit *n.* haveral

hall *n.* ha

halt *n.* devall; devalvement; hult; *v.* devall; hult; **call a ~ pin in e pin**

halter *n.* helter

halve *v.* haaver

hammer *n.* haimmer, hemmer; (heavy) mell; *v.* haimmer; mell; (lightly) chap

hams *n. pl.* (currie)hunkers

hand *n.* han; leef, leif (ᴋ); *v.* rax; ~'s breadth *n.* hanbreed; spang; ~cart *n.* hurlbarra; hurlie; ~cuffs *n. pl.* darbies (Eng.); ~ful *n.* hanfae; (what two cupped hands can hold) gobbinfae; gowpenfu; (of unthreshed corn/hay) ripp; ~kerchief *n.* hankie; hunkie; naipkin; nepkin; ~less *adj.* ha(u)nless, smeerless; ~line *n.* (for catching cod) ripper; ripper; ~loom *n.* han-leem; ~shake *n.* hanshak; ~writing *n.* vreet; vreetin; in ~ *phr.* behan

handle *n.* hannle; lug; *v.* hannle (carelessly) toosht; ~bars *n. pl.* (of a bike) gyes

handsel *n.*, *v.* hansel

handsome *adj.* weel-faart, -faurt

hang *v. tr.*, *intr.* hing; ~ing *n.* hingin; ~man *n.* hangie

happ|y *adj.* *(now poetic)* seel; seely; seelfu; ~iness *n.* seel; seelfuness

harangue *n.* lay-aff

harbour *n.* hairbour, herbour

hard *adj.* (difficult) ill; ull; ~ against hard-tee, -tae; ~ at work i the tag; ~ on (*eg*, clothes) sair on; ~-pressed sair dung, sair made; ~ship *n.* hard; ~ struggle a sair fecht; ~ to please dorty, fashious; ~ up deft; grippit; sair aff; ~-working hard-vrocht

hare *n.* baad, bawd; maakin, mawkin; myaakin

harebell *n.* blawart (ᴋ)

harelip *n.* hare-shard

harm *n.* hairm; skaith; *v.* hairm; **~less** *adj.* hairmless; ulless-gweedless

harness *n.* graith; taikle; (for attaching harness at front of cart shaft) foreslings; (part of britchin, for attachment to rear of cart) hin-slings; (fitment on cartshaft) slider; **~ed** *ppl.* (of a horse) drachtit

harp *n.* herp

harrow *n.* harra

harry *v.* hairry, herry

Harry *pr. n.* Hairry

harsh *adj.* maroonjus

harum-scarum *adj.* reid-wud

harvest *n., v.* hairst; (opening of) moo o hairst; (field) hairst park; *v.* win, *pt.* wun; **~ home** *n.* meal an ale

has *v.* haes, his; **~ not** haesna, hisna

hash *n.* (of potatoes and salted fish) hairy-tatties

hasp *n.* hesp

hast|e, hasten *v.* hist; swithe; bang; **in ~e** like to redd fire; **~y** *adj.* ramsh; suddent

hat *n.* (deerstalker type worn by gillies and grieves) pickiesay; **top ~** lum-hat; **keep it under your ~** keep yir thoom on't

haughty *adj.* heich-heidit

haunch *n.* hinch

haunt *n.* howff; *v.* boodie (к)

have *v.* hae; hiv; **~ not** haena, hinna; *pt.* haed, hid, *pt. ppl.* haen, hin

hawk *v.* (clear throat) haach; (carry goods for sale) haak; **~er** *n.* haaker

hay *n.* hey; (built into a stack) *ppl.* stackit; (gathered row of hay) winraa; **~cock** *n.* cole; (large) tramp-cole; **~-gatherer** *n.* tummlin-tam; **~maker** *n.* hey-makker; **~-shed** *n.* heyhoose (s); **~stack** *n.* hey-ruck; hey-soo; (small) hooick

haze *n.* gull

head *n.* heid; knowe; napper; pow; riggin; (*joc.*) heidpiece; **~ache** *n.* sair heid; **~first** *adv.* heelster-heid; **~ for** *v.* ca for; heelster-gowdie; hyster-gowdie; **~long** *adv.* bellyflaucht; **~master** *n.* heid(maister); **~ over heels** heels ower gowdie; **~-stall** *n.* heid-stall; **~strong** *adj.* heidie; ramshackle

heal *v.* haill; hell (м3); **~th** *n.* heal

healthy *adj,* hale; hale an fere; (and active) kneef

heap *n.* bunkart (к); dossie; hullock; hape (s); (large) kyarn; (loose heap or stack)

rickle; (of small objects)
smatterie

hear *v.* hear, *pt.* hard; ~**ing**
n. (audience) audiscence

hearsay *n.* said-say

heart *n.* hairt, hert; ~**burn**
n. hertscaad; watter-brash

hearth *n.* ingle; chimbly-chik;
hairth (J)

heat *v.* het; *pt.* het; plot (M3)

heathen *n.* haythen

heather *n.* hedder

heav|e *v.* haive; heeze; ~**ing of
a boat** cowpin

heaven *n.* hivven; heeven (C)

heavy *adj.* wachty

hedgehog *n.* hedger

heed of, take *v.* reck; tak tent

heifer *n.* quake, quaik

height *n.* heicht, hicht; ~**en** *v.*
heichen, hichen

held *v. pt.* heeld, *ppl.* hudden

hell *n.* the ill pairt; the ull place

hello *int.* ay, ay

helper *n.* hilpinder

helping *n.* sairin

hempen *adj.* himpen

hen *n.* hen; chucken, chuckney;
(free-range) gaan-aboot
hen; (not exceeding a year
old) yearock; ~**-pecked** *adj.*
hudden-doon; ~**-run** *n.* ree;
~**wife** *n.* hennie

herdsman *n.* herd

heretic *n.* heretick

heron *n.* lang sandy

herring *n.* herrin; heerin;
~ **fever** herrin fivver

herself *pron.* (also **by herself**)
hersel; herleen

hesitate *v.* dachle; dackle;
swither

hiccup(s) *n.* esk; the hippick;
v. esk; yist; **get ~s** tak the
esk

hide *v.* hod, *pt.* hid, *ppl.*
hodden; *v. tr.* scog

hidebound *ppl.* (of cattle)
hidebun

hidey-hole *n.* hidholie

hiding *n.* sackful o sair beens

higgledy-piggledy *adv., n.*
ringum-tringum (M3)

high *adj.* heich, hich;
(of wind) reevin

highland *adj.* hielan(t)

Highlander *n.* Hielander;
(sometimes disparaging)
teuchter

highspirited *adj.* gallus; hallach
(M3); hallyrackit

hill *n.* ben; hull

hillock *n.* hullock; knowe;
(small) knablich (A2);
top of a ~ knowe-heid

himself *pron.* himsel; **by ~**
himsel; himleen

hind|er *v.* hinner; ~**rance**
n. hinner

hindsight *n.* hinsicht

hint *n.* sleumin; *v.* mint at

hip flask *n.* hipper

hip-joint(s), suffering from aching *adj.* hippit; hip-grippit

hired-hand *n.* fee't man

hiring fair *n.* ƒeein-fair; feeinmairket

his *adj.* his; 's

hit *v.* hit, *pt.* hat

hoard *n.* clossach; hushie; *v.* hain

hoar-frost *n.* rime

hoarse *adj.* hairse; roopy, roupy

hobble *v.* fuffle; hirple

hobnail *n.* tacket; ~ed boots tackety beets

hoe *n., v.* hyow(e); *v.* (turnips) single

hoist *v.* hyste

hold *n.* had, hud, haud; hid (s); purchase; *v.* hud, hid (s); ~ your tongue hud yir tongue

hole *n.* bore; (from which peat has been cut) peat-delf; peat-hagg

hollow *adj.* boss; halla; howe; (of a sound) dowf; *n.* howe; sheuch; (small, scooped out of ground for use in game of marbles) kyp(i)e; ~-backed *adj.* howe-backit

holm *n.* howm (J)

home *n.* hame; beil; doonsit (BI); (belonging to) hamel(t); ~ farm hame-fairm; away from ~ fae hame; feel at ~ fin at hame; get ~ wun hame; ~ oriented hamedrauchtit; ~sick *adj.* hamesick; ~spun *adj., n.* hamespun; hodden; grey ~spun hodden grey; ~wards *adv.* hameward; hamewith; hameworth; ~ly *adj.* hamel(t); haimal(t); hameower

honest *adj., adv.* (fair-) furth-the-gate

honey *n.* hinny

hoof *n.* hiv

hook *n.* heuk, hyeuck; (used on fishmarket floor) lowrie

hoop *n.* (child's) gird

hop *v.* hap

hope *v.* howp

hornless *adj.* doddit; hummel, hummle; hummel-doddie

horrible *adj.* ugsome

horrify *v.* horrifee

horse *n.* (small) garron; (walking in furrow) furrer; fur-beast; (landside) lanner; (disease affecting legs) grease; ~-hoe *n.* (small plough for weeding) shim; ~-trough *n.* horse-troch

hot *adj.* het; (very) plottin; ~ foot *adv.* het fit; ~ and steaming *phr.* het an reekin; ~ water bottle *n.* pig

hotel *n.* hottle

hound *n., v.* hun

hour *n.* oor; ~-glass *n.* sangless; ~ly *adv.* oorly

house *n.* hoose; dwallin(-hoose);
(the laird's) the Hoose,
the Big Hoose, the Place;
(temporary, for shepherds)
sheilin; (removal) flittin;
~ful *n.* hoosefae, hoosefu;
~-room *n.* hooseroom;
~wife *n.* hizzie; **~wifery** *n.*
hizzieskep; hoose-wifeskip
how *adv.* fat rodd; fit wye;
foo; hoo; **~ are you?** fit
like?; **~ever** *adv.* fooivver;
hooever; hoosomever;
hoosomediver
howl *v.* yowl
hubbub *n.* frother; gilgal (hard *g*)
huddle *n., v.* bourach
hullabaloo *n.* heelabalow
hum *v.* bum; **~ and haw** *phr.*
hum an hae
humbl|e *adj.* hoomble; **~ing**
adj. heemlin; **~e-bee** *n.*
foggie-bee
humid *adj.* blobbie-like
humiliate *v.* mortifee; *ppl.*
mortifeet
humour *n.* eemur; teen; **fit of
ill ~** *n.* tig
hump *n., v.* humph
hunchback *n.* shooder-e-win;
~ed *adj.* humphie-backit
hundred *adj., n.* hunner;
~weight *n.* hunnerwecht
hunger *n.* hunger (*ng* as in
singer)

hungry *adj.* hungert; (very)
yamph; yap; **~-looking**
yappy; **~ for** yivvery
hurdle *n.* (for penning sheep,
used as a gate) flake
hurricane *n.* heerican
hurry *v.* hash; **~ back** *imp.*
hist ye back; **~ off** *v.* scoot,
scout; skirt
hurt *n.* (severe) michief;
v. mischieve; (severely)
missaucre; (severely, fatally)
pran
husband *n.* man; goodman
(A2); gweedman; *v.* hain
hush *int.* wisht!
hush-hush *adj.* hishty-wishty
husk *n.* (corn) sheelock
hussy *n.* hizzie
hypocrite *n.* heepocreet;
heepocrat

I

I *pers. pron.* A; Aw; I
ice *n.* slidder (M3)
ice-cream *n.* (between two
wafers) slider
icicle *n.* ice-tangle; shochle
idea *n.* adaya; noshun
identify *v.* identifee
idiot *n.* eediot; feel; gapus
idle *adj.* orra; **~ness** *n.* idlety;
idleseat, idleset; sweirty; **~r**

n. vaig (ᴋ); ~ **capers** *n. pl.*
idelties

if *conj.* gin; gif (ʙɪ); *conj.* gin
(ᴍ2); **what** ~ fat gin

I'll *pron. with v.* Aw'se; I'se

ill *adj.* ailin; nae weel; sick, seek
(s); ull; **to be** ~ *v.* ail; *ppl., adj.*
ailin; **~ness** *n.* (a fit of) drow

ill (bad(ly) *used as prefix*
~-**fated** *adj.* unweirdy;
weirdless; ~-**humour** *n.* bung;
~-**humoured** *adj.* cankert;
~-**natured** *adj.* ill-gruntit;
ill-naturt; nabble;
~-**tempered** *adj.* nyattery;
~-**treatment** *n.* ill-eesage;
~-**use** *v.* ill-, ull-eese; ~-**will**
n. ull-wull

ill-at-ease *phr.* aff his/her eggs

illegitimate child *phr.* dykesider

image *n.* eemage

imagin|e *v.* imaagine; imaigin;
jaloose, jalouse; ~**ation**
n. imaiginashun

immediately *adv.* immed(i)antly;
instanter; in a bicker

imp *n.* buckie; deevilock

implements *n. pl.* leems

impolite *adj.* oonceevil; ill-
farrant; ill-mennert

impossible *adj.* oonpossible

improve *v.* impruv; ~**ment** *n.*
impreevement

impudent *adj.* impident; (of the
tongue) ill-hung; ~ **person**
smatchet

in *prep.* i

inadequate *adj.* (of a person)
feckless

incalculable *adj.* menseless

incapable *adj.* feckless

incidental *adj.* overly; ~**ly** *adv.*
in the bygyaan, bygaun

incline *n.* brae; ~**d** *adj.* (of a
person) fain

incompetent *adj.* feckless

inconsequential *adj.* sma drink

inconvenience *v.* disconvene;
pit aboot

indeed *adv.* awat; deed; fairly;
faith

indigestion *n.* belly-rive

induce *v.* gow (ower)

induct *v.* induck

indulged *ppl., adj.* beamfullt

industrious *adj.* eident

infect *v.* smit; ~**ious** *adj.*
smittin

infested *adj.* hotchin

inflamed *ppl., adj.* (by cold)
frostit

influence *n.* enfluence; moyen;
v. enfluence; **through your ~**
in the leethe o ye

influenza *n.* inflooensie

infuriate *v.* raise

infuse *v.* mask

ingenious *adj.* jinipp(e)rous;
nacky

inhalation *n.* (of air) gluff

inherit *v.* heir; fa heir till;
~ance *n.* heirskip
inhibited *adj.* hudden-doon
injur|e *v.* mischieve; missaucre;
~y *n.* a mischief; scaith
injustice *n.* oonjustice
inlet *n.* (narrow & rocky)
gwite
inn *n.* chynge-hoose
innards *n. pl.* puddins
innermost *adj.* benmaist
inner workings *n. pl.*
intimmers
innocent *adj.* sakeless
innovatory *adj.* new-fanglelt
inquir|e *v.* inquar; ~y *n.*
inquary
inquisitive *adj.* ill-, ull-fashent;
~ness *n.* ill-, ull-fashence
inside *adv.* ben; in-by(e); *prep.*
ben
insinuate *v.* mint at
insipid *adj.* saarless, saurless;
warsh; wersh
insist *v.* threep
instinct *n.* enstinck
instruct *v.* (someone in) wise
instrument *n.* enstrument
intelligen|ce *n.* smeddum;
~t *adj.* lang-heidit
inten|d *v.* ettle, *ppl.* ettlin; mint;
~t(ion) *n.* ettle; mint
inter *v.* beery; yird; ~ment
n. beerial
intercept *v.* kep

interdict *n.* enterdick
interesting *adj.* interaistin
interfere *v.* enterfere
intestines *n. pl.* intimmers;
monyfaalds; puddins
intimate (with) *adj.* chief (wi);
pack; thick; thrang (wi);
(esp. in favour with God)
far ben (wi); *v.* intimat;
forquant
intimidate *v.* coonjer
into *prep.* intil
intoxicate *v.* deleer; ~d *ppl.*
foo, fou; glorious. *See*
drunk
invade *v.* invaad
inventory *n.* inveetor
Inverurie *pr. n.* In'rurie
invit|e *v.* bid; inveet; seek;
~ation *n.* biddin; inveet
inward *adv.* benward
iron *n.* airn
irregular *adj.* (in appearance)
shammelt
irresponsible *adj.* haaf-hung-tee
irrit|ation *n.* aggravation;
~able *adj.* sanshach; short-i-
the-trot
Isabella *pr. n.* Beldie
island *n.* inch
it *pron.* it; 't; hit
itch *n., v.* yock; ~y *adj.* yockie
ivy *n.* eevie

J

jabber *v.* yammer
jacket *n.* jaicket; (woman's loose) vrapper
Jacobite *pr. n.* Jaicobite
jade *n.* (woman) jaad, jaud; bizzar (J)
jail *n.* jile; jivvle; *v.* jile
jalopy *n.* shan-dre-dan
jam *n.* jeely; ~ jars jeely pigs
James *pr. n.* Jamie; Jeems(ie)
Janet *pr. n.* Jinse
janitor *n.* jannie
January *n.* Janwar; Janiwar
jar *n.* (earthenware) pig
jasmine *n.* jassamine
jaundice *n.* the jandies
jaunt *n., v.* jant; ~y *adj.* jinkie
jaw *n.* jaa, jaw; ~s *n. pl.* chowks; (projecting lower jaw) gange
jeer *n.* fleer (J); *v.* jamph; lant
jelly *n.* jeely; (table) shogglywullie; ~fish *n.* (stinging) scalder; (harmless) slivverydoctor (B)
jeopardy *n.* jipperty
jerk *v.* (gently) tit; (strongly) yark; (repeatedly) joggle
jersey *n.* maasie (G); (seaman's) gansey; ganjie
jest *v.* daff; fun
Jew's harp *n.* trump
job *n.* jot; a wark; (troublesome, fiddly) footer; (involving much detail) scutterie jobbie; a ~ of work a jot wark
jocular *adj.* vokie; vyokie
jog *n., v.* cadge
joggle *v.* joogle
John *pr. n.* Jock
join *v.* jyne; (together, esp. roughly in sewing) ranter
joiner *n.* jyner; vricht; (nickname) hack-a-thraw
joint *n.* jynt; (segment) lith
joist *n.* jeest; jyst
jok|e *n.* (funny story) bar; (at some one's expense) rise; (make fun of) tak the rise o; *v.* fun; ~ing *ppl.* (*normally used in the neg.*) no ~ing matter nae jeesty; nae mowse; nae a mowse concairn
jolly *adj.* jelly
jolt *v.* daad, daud; shog; (severely) junny; *n.* cadgin; junny
jot *phr.* I don't care a ~ I carna a fushach (*liter.* a bundle)
journey *n.* traivel
jovial *adj.* joco
judder *v.* jow
judge *n.* joodge; *v.* jeedge
jug *n.* joog; stoop, stoup; stowp; (whisky) jorum
juic|e *n.* bree; ~y *adj.* sappy
jumble *n., v.* jummle
June *pr. n.* Jeen

juniper *n.* etnach
junk *n.* rottacks; ~food
   n. galshachs, galshochs;
   perlyaag
just *adv.* jist; joost (A2); ~ after
   prep. (of time) the back o;
   ~ like *prep.* siclikes; ~ now
   adv. phr. enoo, eenoo; eynoo;
   eyvnoo; iv noo; iv now
justice *n.* joostice

K

kail stalk *n.* kail runt
keen *adj.* gleg, glegsome;
   keerious; ~ on on for
keep *v.* kep; *v. pt.* keepit;
   ~ away hud oot ower;
   ~ clear of hud redd o; haud
   aff o; ~ going haud gyaan;
   ~ in with hud in wi; ~ mum
   keep yir thoom on't; ~ up
   keep tee; ~er *n.* (of farm at
   weekends) catcher; toondie,
   toondy; toonkeeper
kennel *n.* cooch; ~-attendant
   n. dog-dirder
kettle *n.* byler (R); a different
   ~ of fish a different Maggie
   Rennie (B)
kill *v.* fell
kiln *n.* kil
kilted *ppl., adj.* kiltit
kind *adj.* couthie; douce;
   kine; *n.* (nature, sort) kine;

kinkind, -kine; all ~s of
aa (kin)kine o; ~-hearted
adj. kyne-hertit; ~ness
n. couthieness
kindl|e *v.* kennle; ~ing *n.*
   kinlin; kennlin
kindly *adj.* couthie
king *n.* keeng; ~dom *n.*
   keengdom
kinsman *n.* freen(d); frien(d)
kipper *n.* speldin
kiss *n.* smack (K); smeerich;
   smoorich
kitchen *n.* kitchie; but-the-
   hoose; ~-maid *n.* kitchie-
   deem
kite *n.* (plaything) draigon;
   (bird) gled; gleed
kitten *n.* kit(t)lin
knave *n.* (in cards) munsie
knick-knacks *n. pl.* trokes
knife *n.* futtle; whittle; (large)
   gullie
knight *n.* knicht
knit *v.* shank; wyve; ~ting *n.*
   wyvin; ~ting-needle *n.*
   (wyvin-)weer; wire; ~ting-
   wool *n.* worsit
knob *n.* knag
knock *v.* ca; chap; knack;
   knap; (sharply) knype;
   (about) cadge; ~ at/on
   gang rap; ~ down ca doon;
   ~ over ca ower
knoll *n.* knap, knowe

knot-hole *n.* navus-bore
know *v.* ken; wat; wot; I ~ awyte; I ken; *neg.* kenna; dinna ken; watna; *pt.* kent *neg.* kentna; watna; **~ledge** *n.* ken

L

labour *n.* laabour, lawbour; (day's work) darg
labouring *n.* dargin
lack *n., v.* wint
lad *n.* callant; loon, loun
ladle out *v.* lave (BI)
lady *n.* leddy; **~'s man** *n.* a bit o a lad
lag *v.* trytle
lain *ppl.* lyen
lamb *n.* (little) lammie; (male with only one descended testicle) rig-lamb; (pet brought up on the bottle and summoned by the call, *sick*) sick lamb
lament *v.* croon; willieway
laminate *v.* skelve (BI)
lamp-lighter *n.* leerie
lancet *n.* fleem
land *n.* lan; (exchanged) excamb; (low-lying, beside river) haagh, haugh; ~ **(on)** *v.* licht (on); **~mark** *n.* prop; **~owner** *n.* laird; **~side** *adj.* (side of plough next the unploughed land) lanside; **~ward** *adj.* lanwarth
lane *n.* (narrow) wynd
language *n.* leid
languor *n.* langer
languish *v.* dwine
lanky person *n.* stilpert
lantern *n.* (han-)booet; booit; lantren; **~-jawed** *adj.* lantren-chaftit
lap *v.* lab; lapper; lerb
lapwing *n.* pee-weet (M, R); peesie (-weep) (S); teuchat, teuchit
larch *n.* larick
large *adj.* bookit, boukit; muckle; meikle; (something of prodigious size) *n.* a bosker
lark (about) *v.* hollach (aboot)
lash *n.* whang
last *adj., n., v.* laist, lest; hinmaist; ~ **out** *v.* (of people) store the kin
latch *n.* sneck
late *adv.* ahin
laudanum *n.* lodomy
laugh *n., v.* laach, lauch, *pt.* leuch; (loudly) gaff, gauff; (heartily) bicker; **to be ~ed at** laachen at; **how I ~ed fit I leuch; ~ter** *n.* laachter, lauchter
launch *v.* lench
Laurencekirk *pr. n.* Lowrenkirk, Lowrie

lavatory *n.* wattery
law *n.* laa, law; ~ful *adj.*
  laafu, lawfu
lawn *n.* green; laan
Lawrence *pr. n.* Lowrin
lawyer *n.* laavyer, lawvyer
lay *v.* plank; ~ hold of *v.*
  claaght, claught; ~-off *n.*
  lat-aff
laz|iness *n.* sweirty; ~y *adj.*
  latchie; sweer(t), sweir(t)
lea *n.* (unploughed land) ley;
  ~-corn ley-corn
lead *n.* leid; ~en *adj.* leiden;
  v. ledd (K); ~er *n.* heidbum-
  mer; heid-dooster
leaf *n.* (of potato/turnip etc)
  shaw; (of cabbage/kail)
  n. blade
lean-to *n.* lean-tee; too-fa
leap *v.* lowp, *pt.* lowpit; lape,
  pt. lap
learn *v.* lairn; leern; ~ed *adj.*
  leernt; ~ing *n.* lairnin;
  leernin; lear
lease *n.* (of a farm) tack;
  ~d farm tack; ~ of life tack
  o life; *v.* set
leather *n.* ledder; ~ strap *n.*
  (formerly used by
  schoolteachers for
  punishment) tag; tawse
  v. (thrash) ledder
leave *n.* (of absence) afflat;
  v. lea, ley (A1); lave (s);
  pt. leeft; (one home for

another) flit; (in the lurch)
  lanter; take one's ~ weer awa
lectern *n.* laiteran; lettrin
left, turn *imper.* (instruction
  to a plough horse in
  Buchan) hi
leftovers *n. pl.* orrals
leg *n.* hoch (M3); shank; loamin;
  (animal/human) spaul; (*joc.*)
  skink; pull my ~ draa ma leg,
  hae a hyze wi me; ~less *adj.*
  shankless
leisure *n.* leasure, leesure
lemonade *n.* ale. (also used of
  other aerated waters)
lend *v.* len, *pt.* lennit
length *n.* lenth; linth; at full ~
  phr. flaughtbred; at long ~
  length o lang
lest *conj.* for fear
let *v.* lat; lit; lut; *pt.* lat; leet;
  loot; *ppl.* latten, lutten;
  ~ alone latten be; ~ it be
  known that lat licht that
let *v.* (land, property) set
let-down *n.* begunk; snipe,
  snype
lethargic *adj.* oonfersell;
  smeerless; thowless
letter-be *n.* (the one who
  feeds in the straw in rope-
  twisting) latter-oot
liar *n.* leear
liberal *adj.* fraachty, frauchty;
  leebral; (extravagantly)
  lordlifu; *n.* leebral

library *n.* leeberary

licence *n.* leeshens, leeshins

lichen *n.* fog

lick *n.* (of fluid) lerb

lie *n.* lee; (big) whapper;
v. lee, *ppl., n.* leein; **without
a word of a** ~ onleet; *v.* (in
bed etc) lig (*lit.*)

lift *n.* (in a vehicle) hurl; (up)
hyste; *v.* heeze; luft; (up)
heft; (with effort) heist,
hyste

light *adj., n.* licht; *v.* licht,
kennle; **indirect** ~ borrat
licht; **make** ~ **of** lichtlifie;
~-**fingered** *adj.* tarry-fingered;
~-**headed** *adj.* cairriet; litchie;
~**house** *n.* lichthoose; ~**ning**
n. lichtnin; (streak of)
flacht o fire

like|d *v. pt.* liket, likit; ~**ly** *adv.*
lickly; belike; **most** ~
likest; ~**ned** (**to**) *ppl.*
lickent wi

liking for *n.* broo o; noshun o

limp *adj.* (from weakness)
waffle; *n.* hirple; *v.* hirple;
clench (A2); crochle;

line *n.* (fishing snood made of
horse hair) tippen

linger *v.* dachle, dauchle

lingo *n.* linga

linnet *n.* lintie

liquid *n.* bree

liquor *n.* (from Eng. naphtha)
naftie, naphtie

listen *v.* hearken

listless *adj.* oonfersell;
smeerless; heepochon-
dreech (B1)

litany *n.* leetiny

literary *adj.* leeterary

litter *n.* (brood) cleckin

little *adj.* sma; wee; *n.* bittie;
suppie; thochtie; tickie;
toushtie

liv|e *v.* won (K); (at an
address) bide, *pt.* bade,
bed(d); stop; ~**elong** *adj.* (of
the day) leelang; ~**ing being**
n. leevin

live|lihood *n.* liveliheid;
throw-beerin; ~**ly** *adj.*
croose; lichtsome; ~**stock**
n. beas'

load *n.* lade, laid; (two or more
cartloads, barrowloads)
fraacht, fraucht; draacht,
draucht

loaf *v.* sorn

loathsome *adj.* scunnerfu;
scunnersome

lobster *n.* (fisher term) labster

loch *n.* (small) lochan

lock *n.* (of hair) tait

loft *n.* laft

loiter *v.* lyter

London *pr. n.* Lunnon

long *adj.* lang; ~ **ago** lang syne;
than an awa; **the** ~ **and the
short of it** the reet an the
rise o't; ~-**gone** lang-geen,

-gane; **~-legged** lang-leggit;
~-legged person stilpert

long (for) *v.* green (efter);
mang (for)

look *n.* leuk; scance; vizzy;
(evil) scook, scouk;
backward ~ vizzy backart;
v. leuk; scance; ~ **after**
v. notice; tak aboot; ~ **for**
v. sik, seek; ~ **out** *v.* (search
and find) rank oot; **on the**
~-out for on the haik for

loosen *v.* lowssen

lop *v.* sned

loquacious *adj.* crackie

Lord *excl.* lod; losh; loshins;
loshtie; ~ **guide us** loshtiegoshtie guide's

lordship *n.* lairdskip

lorry *n.* larry

lose *v.* loss; tine, tyne,
pt. ppl. tint

loss *n.* (by cheating) snipe,
snype

lost *ppl.* tint; (astray) wull;
get ~ flee up; **got** ~ gaed
wull

lot *n.* (situation) billet; (large
amount) hantle; hullock; **~s**
of hullocks o; hantles o; **the**
whole ~ the hale jing-bang;
hale apotheck, hypotheck;
hale rickmatick

loth *adj.* erf; sweer(t), sweir(t)

lots *n. pl.* kavils; **drew** ~ ceest
kavils

loud *adj.* lood; squallachy

lous|e *n.* loose; **~y** *adj.* loosie

lout *n.* fang; fleep; flype;
(rough) gillieperous,
gileepris (hard *g*)

love *n.* luve; *v.* loo, loe

lovely *adj.* bonnie, bonny

low *adj.* low, laigh; lyaach;
~-lying ground laigh;
~land *adj.* lallan; **~lands**
n. pl. laalands, lawlands

lower *adj.* nether; *v.* laichen;
~ **your voice** laichen yir
wird (M3)

loyal *adj.* leal

lucky *adj.* chancy; licky

lug *v.* humph

lumbago *n.* lumbaga

lumber *n.* rottacks

lump *n.* (large, of cheese, beef
etc) clite; kneevlick; knyte;
fang; (also used as mild
insult) knibloch; **~y** *adj.* (of
porridge) knottit

lunatic *n.* madder, maddie

lunge *v.* brainge (*cf.* **breenge**),
flist; **make a sudden** ~ mak
a flist at

lungs *n. pl.* (human or
animal) lichts

lure *v.* moyen; goy

M

Macduff native *pr. n.* Duffer
mad *adj.* gyte; wid; wud;
   (raging) red-wud (ᴋ); reed-
   wud; ~**den** *v.* raise; ~**ness**
   n. madden-drim, -dreem;
   (sudden) wudden-dream
madam *n.* muddim
maggot *n.* maive
magic *n.* glamour; glamourie
magnet *n.* lodesteen, lode-
   stane
magpie *n.* pye; pyot
mainpin *n.* docknail
maintain *v.* menteen; (assert)
   haud oot
majesty *n.* maijesty
majority, the *n.* the feck
make *v.* mak; fack (ʙɪ); fake;
   (cause, compel) gar;
   ~ **known** lat licht; ~ **no**
   difference mak nae odds;
   ~ **off** skedaddle; ~**r** *n.*
   makker; **makings (of)**
   makkins (o)
malcontent *n.* (female)
   peekin-eevie
malefactor *n.* ill-deer
mallet *n.* mell
malt *n.* maat, maut
maltreat *v.* ill-eese; ill-guide
man *n.* maan; maanie; carl;
   chiel; (little) mannikie;
   (little, old) carlie; (strong)
   bumlock; gurk; (form

of address) min; ~**hood**
   n. manheed; ~**ly** *adj.*
   beerdly; buirdly; byoordly
manage *v.* tak aboot; ~**r** *n.*
   (of farm) grieve; (of an
   estate) grun offisher
manger *n.* foresta
manipulate *v.* maneeplate
manner *n.* menner; **in what ~?**
   fat gate?; ~**s** *n. pl.* haivins;
   mainners; menners; ~**ed** *adj.*
   mennert; **well-~ed** weel-
   mennert; **ill-~ed** ill-mennert
mantelpiece (shelf) *n.* chumla(y);
   chumla-heid
manual *adj.* maniwal
manure *n.* muck; (on the
   surface) tapdress; ~**-barrow**
   n. muck-barra; ~ **distributor**
   n. (horse-drawn) bone davy
many *adj.* mony; ~ **a one**
   mony een
marble *n.* (glass) bool; (game
   of ~s played against door)
   doorie
March *n.* Mairch
march *n., v.* mairch, merch
mare *n.* mear, meer
Margaret *pr. n.* Marget
market *n.* mairket, mercat;
   (agric.) mart; mairt
marking substance *n.* (for
   sheep) keel

marriage *n.* mairrage,
  mairritch; (paraphernalia)
  bucklins (A2)
married woman *n.* kimmer
marrowbone *n.* marra-been
marry *v.* mairry; mairry on
  (tae), *ppl.* mairrit; wad, *pt.*
  waddit; buckle wi
marsh *n.* stank
Martinmas *pr. n.* Martimas
marvel *n.* mervel ~**lous** *adj.*
  mervellous
mash *v.* chap; ~**ed potatoes**
  chappit tatties
masquerade *v.* guise
mass *n.* (great crowd)
  mengyie; (seething) hotter
master *n., v.* maister
match (equal) marra, marrow;
  not ~**ing** marless; **well-~ed**
  weel yokit; *v.* peer wi
match(-stick) *n.* spunk
matted *adj.* (of grass) foggagy
matter *n.* maitter; **doesn't** ~
  maksna, disna mak; **no** ~
  deil-ma-care
maximus *n.* (gravest error in
  Latin prose composition)
  maxie
May *n.* Mey
me *pron.* ma
meadow *n.* ley
meal, a *n.* brose
meal-chest *n.* girnal; (farmservant's) meal-kist; meal-
  bunk (s); mealer (s)

mealy-mouthed *adj.* mealy-
  moo't, -mou't
mean *adj.* dirten; (shabby)
  wheetie; (unsporting) skicy;
  (tight-fisted) close han't;
  grippy; hungry; nar; near
  (the been); near-beg(y)aan;
  ~**ness** *n.* near-beg(y)aanness;
  near-begaunness; **having
  the appearance of** ~**ness**
  wheety-like; ~ **person**
  n. hunger; a hungry Angus
meander *v.* (of a stream)
  wimple
means *n.* moyen
meant *pt. ppl.* meent
measles *n. pl.* the mirrles
measure *n., v.* miser, missour;
  mizzer, mizzor; ~**ment** *n.*
  mizzerment
measures (grain: 6 bolls)
  chalder; (fourth part of
  a boll) firlit; (fourth part
  of a peck) lippie, leepie;
  (liquid, equal to Eng. pint)
  mutchkin
meat pie *n.* (turnover) braddie;
  bridie
meddle *v.* mell; middle
medicine *n.* feesick; pheesic
meet *v.* (by chance) kep; ~**ing**
  n. (arranged) tryst
melancholy *adj.* darksome;
  dowf; dumpitch; oorlich
mellow *adj.* maamie, maumie,
  mawmie

membrane *n.* scriffan

memorial *n.* prop

memory *n.* (recollection) myn (A1)

men *n. pl.* mannies; mennies; men; chiels

mend *v.* men; sort; (patch) cloot; (by coarse darning or sewing) ranter

mentally disturbed *phr.* haein a sklate aff

mention *v.* moo-ban (B1); *in phr.* not to ~ forbyes

mercy *n.* leenity; merciment

merry *adj.* blithe(some), blythe; mirky

mess *n.* kirn; queeger; soss; splyaacher (M3); (disgusting) sotter; (wet or dirty) slorach; (scattered) splutrich (B1); ~ about *v.* kirn; picher; (at domestic work) scuddle; scutter

messenger *n.* (sent ahead of bridegroom to summon bride) sen

mettle *n.* smeddum; spunk

middle *n.* mids; (of the house) mid-hoose; (of the night) riggin o the nicht

midge *n.* midgie; midgeck

mid-ridge *n.* mid-rig

midst *n.* mids

midwife *n.* howdie

might *n.* micht; *v.* micht; mith; ~ not *v. neg.* minna; mithna; mithnin

mignonette *n.* meeninit

migraine *n.* megreem

mildew *n.* mildyow

milk *n.* (jet from a cow's teat) strin; *v.* (draw the last milk from a cow) drib; ~-cow *n.* milker; preparation of ~ milkness; ~-strainer *n.* search

mill *n.* mull; (stone hand-mill) quern; ~er *n.* mullart, mullert

million *n.* meellyin; ~aire *n.* meelyinaire

mind *n., v.* myn

minister *n.* minister, meenister, minaister (A2)

minnow *n.* minnon, bandie

minute *n.* meenit

mire *n.* (bog) lair; (mud) dubs; gutters

mirror *n.* gless

mischief *n.* ill-tricks; mischeef; (a bit of) protick; ~-maker *n.* buckie

mischievous *adj.* ill-trickit; ~ boy nickum; silly-made-up

miser *n.* hunger (*ng as in singer*); a hungry Angus; ~ly *adj.* nar; near-begaun, -beg(y)aan

miserable *adj.* meesrable; oorlich

misfortune *n.* mislippenment

mishap *n.* mishanter; scavie (B1)

mismanage *v.* mislippen
misshapen *ppl., adj.* mishachelt
missie *n.* teacher (s)
missionary *n.* missioner
mist *n.* haar; rack (ʀ); (thin, cold) gull; (in a billow) folm
mistake *n.* mistak; misteuk (ʀ); **~n** *pt. ppl.* misteen, -taen; **if I'm not ~n** or it chates me; **be ~n** misdoot yirsel
misty *adj.* mochie
mix *v.* kirn; mell; **~ture** *n.* mixter; mixter-maxter; queeger; **~-up** *n.* quigger
moan *n., v.* main
mob *n.* kinallie
mock *v.* geck; jamph; scowff; **~ery** *n.* jamphin
moderate *adj.* (in price) canny
moderately *adv.* middlin
moderation in all things *phr.* there's a mids i the sea
modern *adj.* modren
moist *adj.* sappy
mole *n.* mowdie(warp), mowdiewart; **~catcher** *n.* molie
moment *n.* mamen; **in a ~** in a fuff (ᴍ3)
Monday *n.* Monanday
money *n.* bawbees; siller; tin (ᴀ); (just enough to pay one's way) rin-watter; (unexpected) fun siller

monkfish *n.* (Buchan) caithick; (Moray Firth) oof
monologue *n.* say-awa
monument *n.* moniment
mood *n.* teen; bin; tift (ʀ); **bad ~** ill teen; **in the ~ for** on for; **~y** *adj.* maggotive
moon *n.* meen, mune; **~light** *n., v.* meenlicht, munelicht
moor *n.* meer, muir; (peat moor) moss; **~cock** *n.* muir-cock; **~land** *n.* muirlan
mooring-pot *n.* paal
mope *v.* mump
more *adj.* mair; mae (ʀ); **~ than** *prep.* passin
morose *adj.* strunge
morsel *n.* glammach, glammoch
mortgage *n.* wadset
moss *n.* fog; (alpine club) stag-moss; **~-covered** *adj.* foggit; **~y** *adj.* foggy; (stuffing wall crags with ~) foggin e was
most *adj., n.* most; the feck; **~ly** *adv.* maistly; feckly
moth *n.* moch; **~-balls** *n. pl* moch-baas; **~-eaten** *adj.* moch-aeten; mochie
mother *n.* midder; mither; mammy; (pet name) minnie; **~-in-law** *n.* gweed-mither
mould *n.* moold; (a mould for ball, spoon etc) caam, caum;

~-**board** *n.* cleathin; ~**y** *adj.*
foostie; fooshtie; foostit

mount *v.* munt; ~**ed** (**on**) *ppl.*
cockit (on)

mountain *n.* ben; muntin;
~-**ash** *n.* rowan; rodden;
rantree; (berry) rodden

mourn *v.* murn; ~**ing clothes**
n. pl. murnins

mouse *n.* moose

moustache *n.* mowser

mouth *n.* gab; maa, maw;
moo, mou; ~**ful** *n.*
moofae, moufu; gnap;
(large) rive; (of food or
drink) howpie; ~-**organ**
n. moothie, mouthie

move *n.* meeve; (jolting)
hotter; *v.* meeve; muv (B1);
gee, jee; (hurriedly) fudder;
(quickly and noisily)
bicker; binner; (with
rocking motion) jow; (with
friction) hirstle, hurshle,
hursle; hushle; (awkwardly
or jerkily) hodge, hotch;
hotter (smoothly) snoove;
make a wrong ~ gie a
vrang hotter; **on the** ~ on
the ca; ~ **house** flit; ~**d** *adj.*
(emotionally) affeckit;
(deeply) sair affeckit;
~**ment** *n.* meevment; (quick)
binner; (jolting) hotter

mow *v.* maw

mucus *n.* (nasal) sno(ch)tter(s)

mud *n.* dubs; clort; glaar,
glaur; gutters; lair; slabber;
(alluvial, left in tidal rivers)
sleek; slich; ~**dy** *adj.* clarty;
dubby; dubbit; lairy; (of
water) drumly; plytery;
~-**spattered person** *n.* drablich

muddle *n.* queeger; ~**d** *adj.*
throw-idder; throwder;
(mentally confused) raivelt

muggy *adj.* mochie

multitude *n.* multiteed

multure *n.* (miller's fee)
moolter, moulter; mooter,
mouter

mumble *v.* mum; mummle

mummer *n.* guiser; guizard (J)

mumming, to go *v.* guise

murder *n., v.* muther

murmur *n.* chirm; myowte;
v. chirm; (plaintively)
chunner

museum *n.* musaium

mush *n.* spyooterie

music *n.* meesic; ~**al tones**
airels

mussel *n.* (shelled) sheelter (B)

must *v.* maan, maun; *neg.*
maana, mauna; beet, *pt.* beed

mute *n.* (from dumb) dummie

my *poss. pron.* ma;
~ **goodness** *excl.* my cert;
my certie; ~**self** *pron.* (also

by ~self) masel; masellie;
ma nainsel

N

nag *n*. (horse) naig(ie); nyag
naked *adj*. nakit; nyaakit; stark
napkin *n*. nepkin
nappy *n*. hippen
narrative *n*. say-awa
narrow *adj*. nairra, nerra
nasty *adj*. naisty
national *adj*. naitional
native wit *phr.* mither wit
natty *adj*. jinipperous
natural *adj*. naitral; ~ herbage
  natur-girss
Nature, nature *n*. Natur,
  natur, naitur
nauseated (by) *ppl.*, *adj*.
  ska(i)kent (wi)
near *adj*. nar
nearly *adv*. near; nearhan;
  naarhan; geylies
neat *adj*. nait; nacket; snod;
  ~ person nackety
necessary *adj*. necessar
necessity *n*. needcessity
neck *n*. (twisted) geck-(gyke-)
  neck; *adj*. gyke-neckit
need *n*. needcessity; *v*. need;
  neg. needsna, *pt*. nott,
  pt. neg. nottna
ne'er-do-well *n*. neer-dee-
  weel; wuddiefu

neglect *v*. mislippen; negleat
  ~ful *adj*. tentless
neigh *n*. (of horses) nicher
neighbour *n*. neebour; neeper,
  neiper; ~ly *adj*. neiper-like
neither *conj*., *pron.*, *adj*. naider;
  naither, nether; nedder;
  nedderin
nephew *n*. neffy
nervous *adj*. nervish
nest *n*. (of wild bees) bike
nestling *n*. cheeper; gorbal;
  gorblin; gog (s)
never *adv*. niver, nivver; ne'er;
  ~theless *adv*. natheless;
  still-an-on
new *adj*. nyow(e); (quite)
  spleet-new; ~ly *adv*. new;
  newlans, -lins
New Year's Eve *n*. Hogmanay
Newburgh *pr. n*. (near Ellon)
  Neebra
news-starved *adj*. news-gizzent
next *adj*. neest, neist; neesht
niggard|ly *adj*. near-beg(y)aan;
  near-begaun; *adj.*, *adv*.
  scuddy; ~liness *n*.
  near-beg(y)aanness;
  near-begaunness
night *n*. nicht; last ~ the
  streen; yestreen; overtaken
  by ~ nicht-boon, -boun;
  ~cap *n*. nicht-mutch
nimble *adj*. swack, swak;
  swippert, swuppert; swyppert
nitwit *n*. gapus

no *adj.* nae: *eg,* nae wark;
~ **one** nae een; *adv.* na;
~, **thank you** na, thenk ye;
~**body** *pron.* naebody; nae een;
~**where** *adv.* naewye
nobbly *adj.* knablick
nois|e *n.* (loud) dirdum;
dundeerie; min(n)eer;
mineerum; ~**y** *adj.* raachle,
rauchle
nominated *v. pt.* nominat
none *pron.* nane, neen; ~ **at**
all neen ava
nonsense *n.* blethers; blickers;
buff; havers; stite, styte;
talk ~ haver; **stuff and** ~ buff
and nonsense
noose *n.* mink
northern *adj.* norlan; ~ **lights,**
the *pr. n.* the merry dancers
Norway *pr. n.* Noroway (A2)
nose *n.* cooter, couter; neb,
nib; niz; nob; snoot, snout;
with a dripping ~ *phr.*
wattery-nibbit; ~**bleed** *n.*
bleedy cooter
not *adv.* nae, *eg,* she's nae
gaan; no, *eg,* she's no gaen
(A, C1, G1, K, S); the Deil,
eg, the Deil he did; fient a,
eg, ~ **one** deil een; fient een;
~ **likely** fient afears; ~ **a bit,**
~ **at all** damn the bit; damn
the fear; damn the lenth; deil
a nip; fie na; fient hait; (*plus*

adj.) eg, ~ **at all pleased** nae
neen pleast
notch *n.* gneck; hack; nick
nothing *n.* naething; nocht;
noth; (said) naither eechie
nor ochie; **a mere** ~ *n.*
wanwurth; ~ **at all** fient hait
notion *n.* noshun; (foolish) gee;
to take a ~ *phr.* tae tak a tig
nought *n.* nocht
now *adv.* noo; **just** ~ aenoo;
eenoo, eynoo; eyvnoo;
ivnoo; ~ **and then** fyles;
noo an than; noo an aan;
noos an aans; ~**adays** *adv.*
nooadays
nowhere *adv.* naegait (M3);
naewye
nuisance *n.* badderation; bucker;
scutter; (child) tirment;
a mott i yir ee
number *n.* nummer; a wheen;
a curn; a puckle; (large
number) a gweed curn;
dose; hantle; spreeth
numskull *n.* gapus

O

oak *n.* aik
oat|s *n.* aits; corn; ~ **ball**
(given to children during
baking) sooie; ~**cakes**
n. pl. (ait)cyaaks, kyacks;
bannocks (S); (in a round)

kyaak o breid; (taken as
dessert in bowl of milk)
breid; (crumbled into
milk) murly-tuck, snap-an-
rattle; (buttered by thumb)
thoombpiece; ~ **husks** *n. pl.*
(fermented, boiled, used
for sowans) sids; **~meal**
n. aitmeal, meal; (quantity
received from the mill at
one time) maillyer; (when
boiled thicker than gruel,
with butter and honey)
brochan; (~ or peasemeal
mixed with boiling water
or milk) brose; (mixed
cold with water) crowdy;
(with boiled milk) knotty
tams; (pudding) mealie
puddin; (pancakes) saatie-,
sautie-bannocks; (cooked
with onion, dripping &
seasoning) skirlie; **~en** *adj.*
aiten

oath *n.* aith; charge
obedient *adj.* obaidient
object *n., v.* objeck
oblige *v.* obleege; **~d** *ppl.*
behudden; obleeged; (not
obliged) onbehudden
obscene *adj.* fouty
obstacle *n.* bunkert
obstinate *adj.* stockit; thraan,
thrawn
occasional *adj.* antrin; **~ly**
adv. fyles

occupy *v.* occupee
October *n.* Jocktober
odd *adj.* (incidental, unmatched)
orra; **~-job man/boy** (on
farm) orraman, orraloon;
(peculiar) unco; **~s and
ends** trokes; **~ity** *n.* ferlie;
(~ person) antic; (untidy
person) track
odour *n.* waff
of *prep.* o
off *adv, prep.* aff
offence *in phr.* take ~ at
someone tak the gee wi
offend *v.* miscomfit; offen
officer *n.* offisher
official *adj., n.* offeecial
officiate *v.* offeeshyat
often *adv.* af(f)en; aft; aften
oh *excl.* och
oh yes *excl.* hoot ty
oil *n.* ile; eelie (M3); **~-cake**
n. ile-cake; ~ **lamp** *n.* ily
(-lamp); (old-fashioned)
cruisie, crusie; **~-skin** *adj.*
n. ile-skin; **~y** *adj.* eely
ointment *n.* eyntment; saa,
saw
old *adj.* aal(d), aul(d);
(very) tike-aal; **~er** *adj.*
aaler, auler; **~est** *adj.*
aalest, aulest; ~ **age** *n.* eild;
eld (C1); **-fashioned** *adj.*
aal-farran(t)
ominous *adj.* forbodin

on *prep.* on; o; **on to** *prep.*
on o

once *adv.* eence; ance (C, G1);
~ **upon a time** eence on a
day; **at** ~ in a fup

one *adj.* ae; *n.* (numeral) een;
the ~ (contrasted with the
other) the teen; the taen (s);
~ **way or another** *phr.* tye
wye or e tidder (M3)

on-goings *n. pl.* ong(y)auns

onion *n.* ingan

only *adv.* jist; nocht bit

onslaught *n.* dirdin

ooze *n.* glaar, glaur

open *adj., v.* apen; ~ **air** the
furth; **in the** ~ **air** thereoot;
~**ing** *n.* slap

opinion *n.* opeenion; opingan;
(high) notion; ~**ative** *adj.*
heidie; noshunate;

opportunity, at every *phr.* at
aa hans

oppose *v.* conter

opposite *adj.* conter; **in the** ~
direction i the conter airt;
prep. anent; fornent;

ordain *v.* ordeen

ordeal *n.* throw-come

order, out of *prep. phr.* agley

ordinary *adj.* ordinar

ornament *n.* (showy) furligorum; (fantastic and useless)
whigmaleerie; (architect-
ural ornamentation) furli-
mafaals

ostentatious *adj.* vantie, vauntie

other *adj., n., pron.* idder; ither;
odder; **the** ~ (contrasted
with the one) the tither

otherwise *adv.* itherweese

ought *v.* ocht; *neg.* ochtna

ounce *n.* unce

our *pron.* oor; wir

ours *pron.* oors

ourselves *pron.* (also **by** ~)
oorsels; wirsels

out *adv.* oot; ~ **of** oot o;
(bed, a cart etc) ootower;
~ **of favour with** oot wi;
~ **of things** oot amint (s);
~ **of the way** ootby; ~**break**
n. ootbrak; ~**cast** *n.* ootlin;
~**cry** *n.* (querulous) scronach
(A2); ~**do** *v.* cow(e); ootding,
pt. ootdang; ~**field**
n. ootfeedle; ~**fit** *n.* rig-oot;
~**going** *n.* (departure at
end of season) ootgang;
~**house** *n.* oothoose; ~**ing**
n. ootin; ~**lay** *n.* ootlay,
ootlie; ~**let** *n.* ootlat; (at
spring) stroop; ~**line(s)**
n. pl. rinnins; ~**most** *adj.*
ootmaist; ~**side** *adv.* ootby;
thereoot; the furth; ~**spoken**
adj. tonguebetroosht;
~**standing thing of its kind**
n. beezer; binder; ~**ward(ly)**
adj., adv. ootwith, -wuth

over *adv.* ower; (past) by;
by wi't; ~ **against** *prep.*

fornent; **all** ~ aa behan;
~**all** *n.* vrapper; rapper;
~**boiled** *ppl.* (of potatoes)
throw the bree; bylt
tae spooterie; ~**burden** *v.*
(yourself) forfecht yirsel;
~**cast** *adj.* lowrin; owercassen;
~**come** *adj.* (by emotion)
greathertit; ~**come** *v.* ding;
~**do** *v.* forfecht yirsel;
~**flow** *v.* jibble ower; ream
(ower); ~**head** *adj., adv.*
owerheid; ~**heated** *ppl.*
stecht; ~**joyed** *ppl., adj.*
liftit; ~**lay** *v.* owerlay;
~**look** *v.* owerleuk; ~**night**
adv. owernicht;
~**-particular** *adj.* jinipperous;
~**run (with)** *adj.* hotchin (wi);
~**seer** *n.* (of farm) grieve;
owersman; ~**take** *v.*
owertak; ~**turn** *v. tr.*
(turn upside down) folm;
tr., intr. cowp; whummle
(J); ~**turned** *ppl.* (sheep)
cowpit; ~**wrought** *adj.*
wrocht-up
ow|e *v.* acht, aucht; awe; ~**ing**
awin
owl *n.* oolet (A); hoolet;
howlet (G1)
own *adj.* ain; nain; nown; **hold
your** ~ hud yir nain; **one's** ~
self yir nainsel; *v. pr.* (in
3rd pers. sing.) acht; yacht;
ppl. echt; yacht

ox *n. sing.* nowt; owse;
(fattened for market) feeder;
(killed at Martinmas for
winter use) mart; mairt;
~**en** nowt; owsen
oyster-catcher *n.* skirlie-wheeter

P

pace *n.* space
pacify *v.* peshifee
pail *n.* (wooden, for milking
or herring guts) cog(gie),
cogue
pain *n.* jip; pyne; (animal
suffering pain) pyner; (*excl.
of*) feech; **seized with** ~ (in
the hips) *pl., adj.* (hip-)
grippit
paint *n., v.* pent, pint; ~**ing the
town red** oot o yir box
palace *n.* pailace
palaver *n.* fracaw (A1);
palaiver (K)
pale *adj.* gowsty
paling *n.* palin
palm (of the hand) *n.* liv(v)
pamper *v.* pappen (M3) peppen;
~**ed** *ppl., adj.* (of farm
animals) fence-fed
pane *n.* peen
panic *n.* pavie
pant *v.* blyaav; pech; (with
heat or exertion) fob
paper *n.* pepper

Papist *n.* Paapist
parapet *n.* (of a bridge) lanstell
parched *ppl., adj.* gizzent
parent *n.* paarent
parish *n.* pairis; paroch(ine) (ᴋ)
parlour *n.* the room; (in a but-an-ben) ben-the-hoose; horn-en
part *n.* pairt; trail; (small) tait; (very small) nimp; nippock(ie); *v.* pairt; sinder, sinner; (the hair, or sheep's wool) shed
particle *n.* hait; sinacle (ʙɪ); styme; (small) mott
particular *adj.* parteeclar; particklar; (very) pernickety; **~ly** *adv.* freely; particklarly; **~ly fine** freely fine
parting *n.* pairtin
partner *n.* pairtner
partridge *n.* pairtrick (ᴍ, ᴄ); paitrick (ѕ, ᴍɪ)
party *n.* pairty; shine; splore; (for women) henshine
pass *v.* win (won) by; (something to someone) rax; **~ over** rax ower by; (through or over) owergae; **~ the time away** fite the idle pin; **~ away** weer awa
passage *n.* closs; pass; throwgang; (in a house) trance

passing, in the *phr.* i the bygaein; i the bygaan
past *n.* bygane(s); *prep.* by
pasture *n.* pastur
pat *v.* (fondle) clap
patch *v.* cloot; **~ed** clootit
path *n.* roddie; waakie
patron *n.* paatron; **~age** *n.* paatronage; **~ise** *v.* paatroneese
pattern *n.* pattren
pause *n., v.* devall
pavement *n.* planestanes, -steens (ᴋ)
pay *n., v.* pey; **~ment** *n.* peymen
peace *n.* quaitness
peak *n.* snoot; **~ed** *adj.* (of a cap) snootit
pearl *n.* pairl
pea|s *n. pl.* piz; **~-shooter** *n.* pluffer
pease meal *n.* piz-meal; pizzers
peat *n.* (individual) cloddie; (pile of) stack; **~ bucket** peat backet; **~-cutting** mossin; **~ dust** drush; **~-moss** peat-fog
peck *n., v.* (of birds) dorb; pick; **fourth of a ~ measure** lippie
peculiar *adj.* unco
peddle wares *v.* cadge
peep *v.* keek; teet; **~-bo** keek-a-bo; teet-a-bo

peevish *adj.* girnie; nibawa; nyattery; orpiet (A2); ~ **person** wittrel, witterel

pelt *v.* clod; daad, daud

pen *n.* (for cattle) pumphel

penholder *n.* penner

peony rose *n.* peeny

people *n. pl.* fock, folk, fowk

perched (on) *ppl.* cockit (on)

perfect *adj.* perfit

perhaps *adv.* ablins; aiblins; mebbe

periwinkle *n.* buckie; wulk

perjur|y, commit *v.* manswear; ~**ed** mansworn

perplexed *adj.* hobbelt

persevere *v.* ca awa; hing in; stick in

person *n.* bodie; leevin; wicht; (insignificant or child) sheemachan

persuade *v.* gow (ower); perswaad

pertain *v.* perteen

pert girl *n.* clip; (person) smatchet

perverse *adj.* camsteerie; contermin't; ill-gatit, ill-gettit

pester *v.* (with entreaties) deeve, deave

pet *v.* daat; dawt; *n.* daatie; tae-ee

Peter *pr. n. dim.* Patie

Peterhead *pr. n.* (nickname) the Blue Toon; ~ **native** *pr. n.* Bluemogganer

petrol *n.* peetrol

petticoat *n.* kwite; quyte; *in pl.* cotts; (made of wincey) winceys

pew *n.* (square, with door) pumphel

pewter *n.* pyowter

phlegm *n.* clorach; haach

physical *adj.* feesickle; ~**ly** *adv.* body-bulk

physician *n.* physeeshun

piano *n.* peanny

pick *v.* pyke

Pict *n.* Picht

picture *n.* picter, pictur

piece *n.* (large) daad, daud; fordel (B1); knyte; (very small) nimp; nippock(ie)

pierce *v.* prob (incl. piercing of cow's stomach to release gas)

pig *n.* grumphie; (fisher words to overcome taboo) grunter; Sandy Campbell; ~**nut** *n.* arnut; ~**sty** *n.* swine's hoose

pigeon *n.* doo; ~-**toed** *adj.* pirn-taed

pilfer *v.* pilk

pill *n.* peel

pillow *n.* pilla

pimp|le *n.* plook; ~**ly** *adj.* plooky

pin *n.* preen; (or knob) knag; *v.* preen; ~-**headed** *adj.* preenheidit

pinafore *n.* peenie; (loose) slip

pincers *n. pl.* turkis

pinch of *phr.* (of salt) a starn o;
a tickie o

pinched *adj.* wainished-like

pine *v.* dwine

pine torch *n.* fir

pinnacle *n.* toopachin, toopican

pipe (for smoking) *n.* bowl;
lunter (short tobacco pipe)
cutty; (chain of tin pipe-lid)
rackle; (stem) stapple

pique *n.* the pet; be ~d at tak
a pyke at

pit *n.* pot

pitch-dark *n.* pick-mirk

pitcher *n.* craggin; pig;
(wooden) stoop(ie)

pith *n.* fushen, fushon

pitifu *adj.* peetifu

Pitsligo *pr. n.* (nickname) Kyack

pity *n.* peety; *v.* meen for; peety

place *n.* staa; *v.* plank

plague *n.* pleege

plaice *n.* plashie; plash fluke

plaid *n.* faik; fayich; fyaaak

plain *adj.* (blunt) aff-han;
(simple) ha(i)mal(t)

plank *n.* (of wood) deal; plunk

plant *v.* (seedlings or tubers) set;
~ation *n.* plantin

plaster *n.* plaister

plate *n.* plett

platter (wooden) *n.* trencher

playground *n.* playgreen;
playgrun;

plaything *n.* plaik, playak

plead *v.* prig

please *v.* suit; ~d *adj.* pleast;
plaised (s, cɪ); ~d with teen
wi; not best ~d with nae
sair suitit wi

pleas|ant *adj.* couthie; leesome;
lichtsome; pleesint, plizzant;
~ure *n.* pleesur(e)

plentiful *adj.* raffy

plenty (of) *n.* rowth, routh (o)

pliable *adj.* weffle

plight *n.* plicht; pilget (Bɪ);
plisky (Bɪ)

plod *v.* lowder; stowff

plough *n.* pleuch (A, Mɪ);
ploo; (projecting wing
on sock) ploo-feathers;
(~-handles) ploo-stilts;
v. ear (A2); pleugh; ploo;
(shallow furrows) ebbploo;
brak-fur; (fallow land)
fauch; ~ed land *n.* red-lan;
~ing *n.* earin (A2); plooin;
~ing marker *n.* prop; ~man
n. plooman; plyooman (M3);
~share *n.* sock

plover *n.* plivver

plug-hole *n.* jaa-hole

plum pudding *n.* dumplin;
(boiled in a cloth) clootie
dumplin

plump *adj.* sonsy

plunder *n.* herry; *v.* reive;
spulyie; (bird's nest) harry;
herry

plunge *n.* plunch; *v. tr.* (into
   boiling water) plot; ~ **churn**
   n. plump churn
pocket *n.* pooch, pouch; pock
   (J); (back) airse-pooch;
   (inside) oxter-pooch;
   v. pooch
poet *n.* makar
point *n., v.* point, pynt; **on the**
   ~ of *prep. phr.* aweers o; on
   the weers o
poison *n.* pooshan, pooshin;
   pyshon; **~ous** *adj.*
   pooshinous
poke *v.* dab; pirl; powk
pole *n.* stang
polecat *n.* foumart
police *n.* pleece; pollis (J);
   ~man *n.* bobby
polish *n.* (black) blake
polite *adj.* ceevil; weel-mennert
politic *adj.* canny
politic|ian *n.* politeeshun; **~s**
   n. poleetics;
pond *n.* (for watering cattle)
   coble; stank
pony *n.* shalt(ie); shelt(ie); shult;
   (suffering from stringhalt)
   cleekit shalt
pool *n.* peel; pot; (shallow) hole
poor *adj.* peer, puir
pope *n.* pape
porridge *n.* porritch; potti(t)ch
   (taking *pl. v.*); parritch (J)
Portessie *pr. n.* the Sloch

portion *n.* pairt; trail; (small)
   tait
position *n.* poseetion;
   (posture) powster
possess *v.* acht, aucht; **~ion**
   n. acht, aucht
postman *n.* postie
postpone *v.* pit aff
pot *n.* pat; **went to ~** gaed
   worth
potato *n.* tattie; pitaatie (BI);
   ~ digger tattie-howker;
   ~ tool deevil; **~ foliage**
   tattie-shaw; **~ harvest**
   tattiehowkin, -liftin (J);
   ~-masher tattie-chapper;
   (pit for storage) tattie-clamp
potter *v.* plowter; plyter; scutter
poultice *n.* pultice; steepit loaf
poultry disease *n.* gyaaps
pound *n.* (sterling) poond;
   pown; pund; (in weight)
   pun; pund
pounded oats *n.* bruised corn
pour *v.* poor; **~ing rain** *phr.*
   poorin haill waater
poverty *n.* poortith
powder *n.* pooder; poother,
   pouther; **~y** *adj.* pouthery
power *n.* pooer; **~ful** *adj.*
   pooerfae
practical joke *adj., n.* hyze; rig
practise *v.* practeese
praise *n.* reeze; roose (O); *v.* reeze
pram *n.* coach
pranks, mad *n.* madden-dreem

prate *v.* gab; gange

prattle *n.* gab; *v.* gash; ~r *n.* a gab

prayers *n. pl.* gweed-words

precentor *n.* prizintor

precise *adj.* perjink; preceese; *adv.* preceesely

predicament *n.* frap; hobble

prefer *v.* prefar; ~ence *n.* prefairrance

pregnant *adj.* muckle-bookit, -boukit; in the faimly wye (A2); *v.* make ~ bairn; nick

prejudice *n.* prejudeece

pre-occupied *adj.* sair exerceesed wi/aboot

present *n.* praisent; (bought at a fair) fairin(g)

presentable *adj.* gatefarrin

presently *adv.* belyve

preside *v.* (at a Presbyterian Church court) moderate

press *v.* birse, birze; ~ on *v.* kneip on; ~-stud *n.* dome

pressure *n.* (esp. from a crowd) birse; hard pressed sair made

preten|d *v.* mak on; ~ce *n.* mak-on; ~tious *adj.* upsettin

pretty *adj.* bonnie, bonny; protty; a ~ penny a protty penny; ~ well *adv.* geylies

prey *v.* (of people) sorn on. *cf.* sponge

prick *n.* brod (K); *v.* brob; job; pirk; ~ed *pt. ppl.* brobbit; ~ly *adj.* jobby

prim *adj.* mim; mim-like; mim-moo't, -mou't; perjink; primpit

prime *n.* potestatur, pottiestattur

prince *n.* prence

principle *n.* prenciple; having strong ~s weel-prenciplt

print *n., v.* prent

privilege *n.* preevilege

probably *adv.* belike

problem *n.* tribble; tribbler

proceed *v.* wag on/awa

proclaim *v.* scrie, scry

procrastinating *ppl., adj.* aff-pittin

prod *v.* brod; prob

prodigious *adj.* prodeegious

profit *n.* (high) rug

progress *n.* fordal, fordle; make ~ get fordelt wi

project *n.* projeck

promoter *n.* deester

proof *n.* preef, pruif

properly *adv.* the richt gate

prophesy *v.* bode (K); prophesee

protect *v.* proteck

protest *v.* oot-cry

proud *adj.* poochle; prood; pridefu (J); vogie (K)

prove *v.* pruv; skeel

provided that *conj.* sae-be

provisions *n. pl.* proveesions
provoking *adj.* angersome
prudent *adj.* canny
prune *v.* cowe; sned
prying *adj.* lang-nebbit, -nibbit
public, general *n.* cowmanality
pucker up *v.* groogle *eg,*
    groogle yir broos
puddle *n.* hole
puff *n.* fuff; (of wind) waff
puffed up *ppl., adj.* (of a person)
    ful, full
pull *v.* poo, pu; tit; yark;
    (forcibly) rive; *ppl.* rivven
pullet *n.* yearock
pulpit *n.* poopit
punch *n.* plowt
punctual *adj.* punctwal
punish *v.* (thrash) aam; creesh;
    ledder; lick; soosh; ~**ment**
    n. (thrashing) licken; licks;
    be ~**ed** get yir dreels
puny *adj.* nochtie; shilpit
pupil *n.* scholar
puppy *n.* fulpie; whelpie
purple *adj.* purpie
purr *n.* (of a cat) three-
    threids-an-a-thrum; *v.* spin
    his/her thrums
purse *n.* mailin; (stocking used
    as purse) moggan
push *n.* howder; *v.* shiv(e);
    putt; (push to) birse tee;
    ~ **past** birse by
pusillanimous *adj.* bauch
    (-hertit)

Puss *pr. n.* Bauldrins;
    Bawdrons
put *v.* pit, *pt.* pat; ~ **away** pit
    past; ~ **by**, ~ **aside** *pt. ppl.*
    pat tee; ~ **down** *v.* plank;
    ~ **out** *pt. ppl.* pitten, putten
    oot; ~ **together** *v.* ranter
puzzle *v.* bleck; paal, paul

Q

quaff *v.* scoof; skowf
quake *v.* quak; shak; trimmle
quandary *n.* swither
quantity *n.* a curn; sowd;
    wheen; (large) gweed
    curn; feck; hantle;
    (small) bittock; pick;
    starn(ie); tait; tooshtie;
    tweeshtichen (M3); (very
    small) skirlie; (small, of
    liquor) skite; tootie; (tiny)
    stime, styme
quarrel *n.* cast-oot; faa oot;
    scashle; sharrie; split;
    strush(ie); throw-the-muir;
    tirr-wirr; tulzie; *v.* scashle;
    strive, *pt.* streeve, *ppl.*
    striven; threep; ~**some** *adj.*
    camsteerie; din-raisin
quarter *n.* (of oatcake round)
    corter, korter; (of a year)
    raith
quart measure *n.* (with
    knobbed lid) tappit hen

queer *adj.* unco

quench *v.* (thirst) slack; slock, sloke; sl(y)ocken

querulous *adj.* crowpy; girny; orpiet (A2)

question *n.* queyston (M3); quisson; *v.* back-speir

quibbles *n. pl.* fittie-fies

quick *adj.* faist; slippy; ~-tempered *adj.* short-i-the-trot

quiet *adj.* quait; douce; be ~ hud yir tongue; hud yir wheesht; ~ly *adv.* quaitly; laich in; ~ness *n.* quaitness

quit *v.* quat

quite *adv.* (completely) fair; *excl.* fairly

quiver *v.* chiver; trimmle; all of a ~ o the quivvy (M3)

quiz *v.* backspeir

quoth *v.* quo

R

rabbit *n.* rubbit; ribbit (s); (used on board ship to avoid taboo word) mappie; (Russian) Roosian

rack *n.* (for fodder) haik

radish *n.* (wild) runch

rafter *n.* couple, cupple; kebar (K)

rag *n.* (thin cloth) flinrikin; (worthless) peltin-pyock; *chf. in pl.* duds; ~s and tatters tatterwallops

rage *n., v.* rampa(u)ge; in a ~ in a bung

ragged *adj.* duddie; raggit(y); tatterwallopy; ~ person tatterwallop; ~ robin raggit robin

raging *ppl., adj.* ragie; witriffe

ragweed *n.* weepies (J)

ragwort *n.* tansy

rain *n.* reyn; (light, good for crops) growin shoorie; (a heavy fall) onding; spleeter o weet; (fine) smirr; smoocherin; *v.* (slightly) spirk; spit; ~bow *n.* (broken) a teeth in the sky; ~y *adj.* drappie; weety

raise *v.* heeze; heist; hichen

rake *n.* (small, farm) smiler; *v.* raik

ramble (conversational) *n.* lat-aff

range *v.* (roam) reenge

rank *adj.* (of grass) foggagy

ransack *v.* raffle; rink (M3); rype

rascal *n.* a bit o a lad; limmer; scypal, skypal; (child) nickum; rogie

rash *adj.* ramsh

raspberry *n.* risp; sivven

rat *n.* rottan

rather *adv.* gey; geylies; (*after the adj.*) kin'; liefer; raither;

redder; some; ~ **cold** some caal; caal kin'; ~ **as if** some like

rattle *v.* tirl; **death** ~ *phr.* the daith glagger

ravenous *adj.* yamph

ravine *n.* cleuch; den; glack

ray *n.* (of sun) blink

razor *n.* rassor

reach *v.* (a place) mak; win

ready *adj.* redd

real *adj.* rale; ~**ly** *adj.* ralely

reap *v.* cut; shear; ~**er** *n.* raiper

reason *n.*, *v.* rizzon; ~**able** *adj.* rizzonable

rebound *v.* skite

rebuke *n.* owergae; *v.* gie (fowk) up their fit. *See* **scold**

recall *v.* reca

recently *adv.* newlins

recipe *n.* recaipt

reck *v.* (care) raik

reckon *v.* rackon

recline *v.* (*lit.*) lig

recognis|e *v.* ken; **fail to** ~ *v.* misken; ~**able** *adj.* (easily) kenspeckle

reconsider *v.* fell-think

recover *v.* weer tee; (one's health or spirits) cantle; (from) cower

recuperate *v.* cower; recreet

red *adj.* red, reid; ~-**cheeked** *adj.* reid-chikkit; ~-**combed** *adj.* reid-kaimed; ~**currant** *n.* rizzar; ~-**headed** *adj.* reidheidit; ~-**hot** *adj.* reid-het

reed *n.* sprot

reel *n.* (on which yarn or thread is wound) pirn; ~ **off** *v.* leet aff

refer *v.* refar

refill *n.* fully-up

refusal *n.* na-say

refuse *n.* orrals; *v.* refeese; na-say

regard *n.*, *v.* regaird

register *v.* (for proclamation of banns of marriage) beuk

regret about, express *v.* remorse

regretful *adj.* meanfu

regular *adj.* reglar

rein *n.* rine, ryne

related *adj.* sib

relationship *n.* sibness

relax *v.* rist; hud doon the deece; lat the theats slack; (assuage) *v.* swadge

reliable *adj.* lippenable; siccar

relief *n.* easedom

religion *n.* releegion

religious *adj.* releegious

relish, with *phr.* gustfu

reluctant *adj.* sweir(t)

remain *v.* bide;

remainder *n.* the lave

remains *n. pl* hinner-en

remark *n.* (quick-witted) upcome; ~**able** *adj.* unco

remedy *n.* remeid

remember *v.* mynd; myn

remind *v.* mynd; myn

remov|e *v.* remuv; (move house) flit; ~**al** *n.* flittin; (from a tenancy) ootgang

renegade *n.* ranegill

renewal *n.* (replacement) retour

rennet *n.* yirnin

rent *n.* rint

repent *v.* remorse

replacement *n.* retour

replete *adj.* (after food) bowdent; ful; ful up; stappit; weel-sairt

report *n., v.* repoort

reprimand *n.* owergaan, -gaun; owergae

reproof *n.* (severe) owergaan, -gaun; throw-the-bows. See **rebuke, reprimand**

reprove *v.* repree

require *v.* requar, requair

reserved *adj.* poochle; puchal

resident *n.* residenter

resin *n.* rosit; ~**ous** *adj.* firry; rositie

respect *n., v.* respeck; ~**able** *adj.* douce; wice-like; (of appearance) gatefarrin; ~**ful** *adj.* mensefu

responsible *in phr.* **to be ~ for it** tae be the deed o't

rest *n.* (remainder) the lave

rest *n.* rist; flap; *v.* rist; hud doon the deece; lat the theats slack; draa bridle; ~**ing-place** *n.* ludgement; ~**ive** *adj.* reistin; ~**less** *adj.* ristless; (of a horse) tittersome

restraint *n.* haud-again

restrict *v.* pit the haims on

retailer *n.* merchan

retch *v.* cowk, kowk; reetch

retort *v.* rebat

retrospective *n.* vizzy backart

reveal *v.* kythe

revel *n.* carrant; splore

reverse *n.* revarse; (of a horse etc) **into ~** intae the britchin

rheumatism *n.* the rheumaticks

rhododendron *n.* rhoddie

ribbon-ends *n. pl.* fattrels

rib-grass *n.* carl-doddie

rich *adj.* foggit; walthy; weel-geddert

riches *n. pl.* graith

rick *n.* ruck; (large, of hay or corn) moo; (small, of corn or hay) hooick; scroo; ~**-yard** *n.* stack-yaird

ricochet *v.* skite

rid *adj.* redd: *v.* redd; **get ~ of** wun redd o

riddance *n.* reddance; **good ~** gweed reddance; **off you**

go and good ~ mirra-hine; merry-hyne

ridge *n.* rig; riggin; (on which plough is turned) fleed; (side) side-rig

ridiculous *adj.* rideeclous

riff-raff *n.* raff; scruff; warriedrags, towrags an swypins o the pier

rifle *v.* rype

right *adj., n., v.* richt; **do the ~ thing** dee the richt gate; **~ turn** *phr.* (command to plough-horse in Buchan) wish; **no ~ to** nae eeran tae

righteous *adj.* richteous

rigid *adj.* strait

rigmarole *n.* la(m)gamachie; linglairy (B1)

ring *n., v.* (of a tolling bell) jow

rinse *n., v.* sloosh; sweel

ripple *v. intr.* bicker; pirl

rising *adj.* upwith

risky *adj.* oonchancie

rivet *v.* clink

road *n.* rodd; (narrow) roddie; **to take the ~** *phr.* tae rodd

roam *v.* raik, rake; reenge; (often of animals) squeerie

roar *v.* rair; (of cattle) rowst, roust; rowt (G1)

roast *v.* birsel, birstle; roast; *ppl.* roasin, roassin; **~ing hot** roassin

Robert *pr. n.* (familiar form) Rob(bie)

rock (prominent) *n.* bumlock

rocking-chair *n.* (made from a barrel) bowie-cheer (M3)

rod *n.* (for stirring porridge) spurkle; spurtle; theevil; (in chimney for hanging pots over the fire) swey; (fishing) waan

rode *v. pt.* rade; redd (M3)

roe *n.* raan

rogue *n.* widdiefu; (term of endearment for a child) rogie; **~ry** *n.* joukerie-pawk(e)rie

roll *n.* (morning) buttery-rowie; buttery; rowie; (floury) bap; *v.* rowe; wammle

romp *n.* daffin; rivin (K); splore

roof *n.* reef; riggin; **~top** *n.* riggin-crap

room *n.* (*obs. in gen. sense*) chaumer; (best) the room; (where farm-servants slept in Banff and Buchan) chaumer; (outer room in two-roomed cottage, kitchen) but (-the-hoose); (inner room, parlour) ben (-the-hoose)

roost *n., v.* reest

root *n.* reet

rope *n.* raip, rape; tow; (round eaves of a stack) eave raip; (ball of straw-rope) edderin; *v.* (twist ropes round a stack) edder; (used to lash a load on to a cart) girdin; (for hanging nappies) hippen-towie; (double ropes for skipping) lundies; **~-twister** *n.* thrawcruik; tweezlock; twiner

rose *v. pt.* rase

rough *adj.* roch; reuch (J); grofe; (unmannerly) menseless; **~ in manners** roch an richt; **~ character** *n.* ranegill; **~-and ready** *adj.* hull-run; **~-cast** *v.* (a wall with mortar) (sneck-)harl; **~ casting** *n.* harlin

round *adj., adv., prep.* roon; **~-shouldered** *adj.* roon-shoodert; (very) humphie-backit

rouse *v.* (to anger) roose

route *n.* gate

routine, the old *phr.* the aal stot

row *n.* (rumpus) reerie; sta(r)-shie; stushie; **make a ~** kick up a reerie

row *n.* (line) gyang; raa, raw

rowan tree *n.* rantree; rodden tree

rub *v.* faach, fauch (B1)

rubbish *n.* pelt; perlyaag

ruffian *n.* rochian

ruin *n.* gowf(f); (cause of) herrial; **to be ~ed** tae gae tae the gowff

rule *n., v.* rowle; **~r** *n.* rowler

rumble *v.* rummle; (of the stomach) womle

rummage *v.* reemish; rink, rank

rumour *n.* raiverie (M2), reverie (B1); caa'd aboot clype

rump *n.* rumple

rumpus *n.* fracaa (M3); ran-dan; rammie; reerie

run *v.* rin; skelp; (off quickly) skice, skyce; skite; skirt (A); uptail; (in excited or aimless fashion) fudder; (awkwardly) gunge aboot; **~ny** *adj.* rin-awa; **~ny jam** elbuck jam

rush *n.* (plant) rash; sprot; *v.* (forward impetuously) breenge; (of the wind) souch

Russian *adj.* Rooshian

rust *n., v.* roost, roust; *ppl., adj.* roostin; roostit; **~y** *adj.* roosty

rustle *n., v.* reesle, reeshle; hirs(t)le; (of grain indicating ripeness) buzzle

S

Sabbath *n.* Saabath, Sawbath
sabre *n.* saabre
sack *n.* saick, seck; **~cloth and ashes** harn bags an shunners
sacred *adj.* saacret
sacrifice *v.* secrifeese
sad *adj.* (of people) dowie; wae; (of situations) doolsome; waesome
saddle *n.* saiddle, seddle; **~r** *n.* saiddler
safe *adj.* saff; (to deal with) chancy
sag *v.* seg
sagging *adj.* seggit
sago pudding *n.* (nicknamed) birdies' eenies; puddock's eggs
saint *n.* sant; **~ly** *adj.* santly
sake, for any *phr.* for ony skaas (M3)
salary *n.* sailary
sallow *adj.* hyaave
salmon *n.* reidfish (to avoid word taboo at sea)
salt *n.* saat, saut; **worth his ~** wirth saat till his kail; *v.* (fish) roose; **~-box** *n.* saat-backet, saut-backet; **~-brick** *n.* (for cattle) saat-lick, saut-lick; **~er** *n.* saater, sauter; **~y** *adj.* saatie, sautie
salve *n.* saa, saw

same *adj.* samen; **all the ~** aa ae claith; **~ to you** sae faa ye
sample *n.* swatch
sanctify *v.* santifee
sand *n.* saan; **~-eel** *n.* sile; sunnel; **~piper** *n.* kitty-neddie
sane *adj.* aa come; aa there
sapless *adj.* foggy
saps *n. pl.* flannen broth
Satan *pr. n.* Saatan, Sawtan
sate *v.* sair
satiate *v.* sair; stech; *ppl.* sick sairt
satisf|y *v.* saitisfee; (esp. with food or drink) sair; **~ied** *adj.* weel sairt
Saturday *n.* Saiterday, Setterday
saucy *adj.* sanshach; snisty
saunter *v.* anter; pammer, paumer; staiver
savour *n.* saar
saw *v. pt.* saa; **~dust** *n.* saadist
saxifrage *n.* fou
scab *n.* scur(l); **~bed** *adj.* scabbit; scabby; **~by** *adj.* scabbit
scald *v.* scaad, scaud; plot; (slightly) scam, scaum
scamp *n.* fang; wuddiefu
scamper *v.* scour
scan *v.* scance
scandal *n.* ill-win; **~-monger** *n.* sclave
scarcely *adv.* jimp

scare *n.* gliff (B1); *v.* fley

scarecrow *n.* bockie, bokie; scarecraa, scarecraw; tattieboodie (A); tattie-bootie (C); tattie-doodle (S); tattie-dulie (J)

scarf *n.* graavit, grauvit

scatter *v.* spairge; *intr.* squatter

scavenge *v.* scran

scheme *n.* protick (M3); *n., v.* skaim, skem

school *n.* skweel, squeel; skale (S); schule (J); ~master *n.* dominie; ~ pupil *n.* scholar; (attendance officer) wheeper-in

scientific *adj.* scienteefic

scissors *n. pl.* sheers

scivvy *n.* sciffie (S)

scoff *v.* scowff

scold *v.* ban; banter; caird; coonjer; flyte, *pt.* flate; get on tae; gie intae trouble; shore (severely) bully-rag; rally on; scaal, scaul; seeg (G); tongue; ~ing *n.* bark-an-bowff; dreels; driffle; ragin; scaal, scaul; sedarin; sortin; (severe) dixie; kail-throw-the-reek; owergaan, -gaun; (mild) ragie;

scoop *n.* (metal for use with herring) sheil

scope *v.* scooth; scowth; scouth

scorch *v.* birstle; plot; scam, scaum; ~ing *ppl.* birstlin

score off (someone) *v.* hae a rive aff

scoundrel *n.* scoon(e)ral; (*joc.*) bleck

scour *v.* scoor; scunge (M3)

scowl *n., v.* glower; glumsh (M3), glunch; scool; scouk

scraggy *adj.* shargert; ~ person sharger

scrape *v.* screeve; scryaap (M3)

scratch *n.* scart; scrat; (large) screeve; *v.* claa; faach, fauch (B1); scart; scrat; screeve; ~ing-post *n.* claain-post

scream *v.* skirl; skelloch; skwaal; scryach (M3); scraich; skyalloch; yelloch

screech *v.* scraach, scrauch; skraich

scrimmage *n.* bicker; shangie

scrounge *v.* cadge; mooch; (of people and dogs) skweenge; ~r *n.* moocher

scrubbing-board *n.* scoorin-buird

scum *n.* scummins

scurry *v.* bicker; skyce, skice

scythe *n.* robsorbie (from make of scythe); ~ handle sned

sea anemone *n.* pap

seagull *n.* (Buckie) gow; (M1) maa, maw; (Fraserburgh) myaave; (Gardenstown) pule, pyool; (Peterhead) scurry; (M1) scurry-waster;

(A1, R) sea-goo; (M1) seamaa; (M3) seamyow

search *v.* rake

season *n., v.* sizzon; *v.* (food) hire; ~ing *n.* kitchie

seat *n.* sate: **take a** ~ sit doon; lean yirsel doon; loot ye doon

seaweed *n.* (with thick stalks, broad fronds) carlers; (coloured) dallies' clysies; (dulse) dilse; (a species) tangles

second *adj.* siccond; ~ **day's broth** *phr.* yavil-broth; ~ **thoughts, to have** *v.* fell-think; forthink (M3); ~-**year crop** *n.* yavil

secret *n.* saicret; **divulging a** ~ lattin oot the pooder; ~ly *adv.* stown-wyes

secure *adj.* siccar

sedge *n.* seg(g)s

see *v.* see; *pt.* saa; *neg.* saana; ~ **to** *v.* sort; ~ **through a dodge** *phr.* twig

seed *n.* sid

seek *v.* sik

seemly *adj.* wice-like

seep *v.* sype

see-saw *n., v.* coup-the-ladle

seething *adj.* hotchin

segment *n.* lith

seize *v.* cleek; mitten; nab

select *v.* seleck, wale; wyle; ~ion *n.* wale; wylin

self *n.* sel; **his old** ~ his aal eeswal (A1); ~-**important** *adj.* puchal, puchil (A2); ~ish *adj.* hame-draughtit; ~ishness *n.* selfitness; ~-**righteous** *adj.* unco-gweed

send *v.* sen

senna *n.* sinna

sens|e *n.* sinse; ~eless *adj.* glaikit; ~ible *adj.* wycelike; ~itive *adj.* (of an issue) kittle, kittlesome; (of a person) thin-skinnt

sent *ppl.* putten

separat|e *v.* sinder; sinner; (used in curling) split; ~ion *n.* sin(d)rin

sergeant *n.* sairgint

serious *adj.* sairious

servant *n.* servan

serve *v.* sair; ser; (a cow) bul(l); ~d **her right** sairt her richt

serving *n.* sairin

set *in phr.* **all** ~ riggit oot; ~ **off** get roadit; ~back *n.* backset; snipe, snype

settle *n.* deece, deese; *v.* sattle; ~ **down in a chair** *v.* clap doon

settlement *n.* (usually at marriage) doon-sittin

seven *adj.* saiven; seiven; seyven; siven; ~teen *adj.* saiventeen; seiventeen; seyventeen; ~ty *adj.* saiventy; seiventy; seyventy

several *adj.* (a) twa-three;
a curn; a wheen

sew *v.* shoo, shew; ~ing *n.*
shooin, shewin;
~ing-machine *n.* shewin-
machine

shabby *adj.* orra; scabbit;
(mean) wheetie

shaddow *n.* shadda

shaft *n.* (of barrow, cart)
tram; (of scythe) sned

shak|e *n., v.* shak; shog;
shoggle; shoogle; (roughly)
cadge; (wave) wag; **no
great ~es** nae great dell; nae
gryte shot; ~er *n.* (in a mill)
shakker; ~y *adj.* dwaibly;
shakky; shoggly; shoogly;
(from weakness) waffle

shall *v.* sall; ~ **not** s(h)anna

shallow *adj.* shalla

shamble *v.* baachle, bauchle

shanks' pony *n.* shanks' meer;
waaker's bus

shape *v.* fack (B1); ~d *ppl.*
shapit

shard *n.* (of earthenware) lame

share *n.* skair; ~ **out** *n.* pairtin;
pairt-oot (s); *v.* pairt; **badly
~d out** ill-pairtit

shark *n.* (basking) muldoan,
muldoon

sharp *adj.* (of mind) gleg;
glegsome; (of tongue) ill-
hung; (of the wind) snell;
~en *v.* sharp

shatter *v.* chatter

shaved *v. pt., ppl.* shaven

sheaf *n.* shafe, shaif; shave;
(last sheaf on top of a
stack) heid(in)-shafe; **two
sheaves = one thrave**

shear *v.* shear, *pt.* shore

shed *n.* lean-tee

sheep *n.* (female) yowe;
(young, before first
shearing) hog(g); (having
died a natural death)
braxy; (disease) braxy;
(fluke worm on lung) the
hooze; (hurdle for penning)
flake; ~-dog *n.* shaggie;
~-fold *n.* bucht; fank; faul(d)

shelf *n.* skelf; skelve (B1);
on the ~ *phr.* (of a single
woman) sattit an set by

shell *n.* shall; ~ **sand** shall san;
v. sheel; ~y *adj.* shally

shelter *n.* biel(d); leethe; lythe;
scoog, scoug; *v. tr.* scog,
skug (K); ~ed *adj.* bieldy;
lown; lythe

sheriff *n.* shirra

sherry *n.* shirry

shiftiness *n.* hunker-slidin

shiftless *adj.* fen(d)less

shilling *n.* shullin

shimmering *adj.* niddry

shine *n., v.* shine; (gaudily)
skyre

shingle *n.* chingle

shirt *n.* sark; sarkit

shiver *v.* chitter

shock *n.* astonisher; an
astonishment; begeck; gliff;
gluff; stammygaster; (fright)
gast; *v.* begeck; stammygaster;
~ed *ppl., adj.* dumfoonert;
stammygastert

shock *n.* stook; **put into ~s**
v. stook

shoe *n.* shee; *pl.* sheen, shune;
shoon; **old ~** baachle,
bauchle; ~-**lace** *n.* baachle-,
bauchle-ban; lacer; pynt, pint;
~**maker** *n.* sooter, souter;
~**maker's awl** *n.* ellieson;
eshin; ~**maker's last** sooter's
deevil

shoot *n., v.* sheet; (project from
the mouth) pluff

shop *n.* chop; shop; (small)
shoppie; ~-**assistant** *n.*
coonter-lowper; ~-**keeper**
n. merchan; ~**ping** *n.*
messages; **do the ~ping** go
the messages

short *adj.* (and stocky)
laichybraid; **~ of** scrimp o;
~**comings** *n. pl.* short-
comes; ~-**tempered** *adj.*
capernicious

should *v.* sid; shud; sud;
shouldn't sudna

shoulder *n., v.* shooder,
shouder; shoother, shouther;
(one higher than the other)
shoother-the-win; (often

of an animal) spaal, spaul;
~ joint *n.* shooderheid

shout(ing) *n.* gollar; **~ (for)**
v. cry (on); (incoherently)
gollar

shove *v.* putt; shiv; shive

shovel *n., v.* sheel; shool;
shiffle (M3)

show *n.* (fine) braivity,
brevity; *v.* kythe (B1); shaw;
~ off *n.* (of a person)
palaiver; *v.* cock; ~**y** *adj.*
skiry, skyrie

shower *n.* scrow (M3); shooer;
(sharp) blatter; (heavy)
spleeter o weet; (putting
a stop to work) lowsin-
shooer; (passing) scuff o
rain; (slight) shoorie

shrewd *adj.* lang-heidit; fell (J);
pawky; ~**ness** *n.* smeddum

shriek *v.* scraich; skelloch;
skry; walloch

shrill *adj.* squallachty

shrink *v. intr.* crine; skurken
(with age) creep doon; *v. tr.*
nirl, *ppl.* nirlt

shrivel *v. intr.* crine; gizzen,
ppl. gizzent; *v. tr.* nirl, *ppl.*
nirlt; skurken; wizzen(t)

shroud *n.* shrood

Shrove Tuesday *pr. n.* Faster's
Eve(n), (Een); Fasten's Eve

shrunken *ppl., adj.* gizzent;
nirlt; skurkent; wizzent

shudder *v.* grue, groo

shuffle *v.* fuffle; scooshle;
scushle; sclaap, sclaup;
shaachle, shauchle, shochle
shut *v.* (the mouth) dit; (the
door, ones eyes) steek;
~ the door caa the door
tee; ~ out bar oot, *ppl.*
barrit oot; ~ up (in a room)
chaumert up
shy *adj.* baach, bauch(-hertit)
sick *adj.* sick; seek (s); (of)
scunnert wi/o
sickly *adj.* gowsty; paewae;
peelie-wally; pyewae;
~-looking *adj.* fauchie
sideboard *n.* sideboord
side-by-side *adv.*
cheekie-for-chowie
side ridge *n.* siderig
sideways *adv.* sidelins;
sidiewyes
side with *v.* pairt-tak
sieve *n.* riddel; sey; (with solid
base) blin sieve; wecht
sigh *n.*, *v.* sich; sooch, soogh,
souch, sough; sugh
sight *n.* sicht; a welcome ~ a
sicht for sair een
signature *n.* signaatur
significance, of *phr.* nae sma
drink
silence *n.* seelence; ~d *ppl.*
dusht
silent *adj.* seelent
silly *adj.* daupit; feel; gypit
silver *n.* siller. *cf.* money

simmer *v.* hotter
simple *adj.* haimal(t);
(feebleminded) saft; ~ton
n. nosy-wax (B1)
since *adv.* seen; sin; syne;
prep. seen; sin; *conj.* sin;
~ then sinseen; sinsyne
sincere *adj.* aefaal(d,) aefaul(d)
sing *v.* (of birds) chirm; (in
low tone without words)
diddle; (with a loud drone)
bum; ~-song (of speech)
adj. sing-sang
singe *v.* scam, scaum; (of
food) sing, *pt. ppl.* sung
sink *n.* jaa-hole, jaw-hole;
v. (in bog or mud) lair
sip *n.* sup(pie); bleb; *v.*
(a small amount) blibber;
(noisily) slubber; (take
food or liquid esp. with a
spoon) sup
sister *n.* (*chf.* child's word) titty
sit *v.* (down) lean doon; reest;
(down with a bump) dyst;
~ down! *imp.* dowp doon;
faal yer fit; lean yirsel doon;
loot ye doon; ~ on the fence
haud the cat an play wi the
kittlen (M3)
site *n.* stance; seet
sitting *n.* (of eggs) laachter,
lauchter; ~-room *n.* the
room
situated *ppl.* sitiwat

situation *n.* (lot) billet;
powster; seetivation

six *adj.* sax; **~pence** *n.*
saxpence; **~teen** *adj.*
saxteen; **~th** *adj.* saxth; **~ty**
adj. saxty

skeleton *n.* atomie (A2)

skid *n., v.* skite

skilful *adj.* kittle; nacky;
skeely

skill *n.* skeel

skim *v.* skum

skimmer *n.* (for surface soil
and weeds) skreefer

skin *n.* bark; peelin; scud;
v. bark; flae; peel; **~ned**
barkit; **by the ~ of his teeth**
by the briers o his een

skulk *v.* scook, scouk

skull *n.* harn pan; riggin

sky *n.* lift; welkin (K, MI);
~lark *n.* lav(e)rock; livrock

slab *n.* skelp

slake *v.* (thirst) slack; slock;
sl(y)ocken

slander *n.* ill-win; *v.* misca

slant *v.* sklent, sklint

slap *n.* sclaffert; skeek; (on the
hand with a leather belt)
the scud

slate *n.* sklate; sclait; **~ pencil**
n. skaalie; skaillie; skylie;
~r *n.* sklater

slattern *n.* trail

slaughter *n.* slaachter,
slauchter; **~-house**
n. slauchter-hoose

slaver *n., v.* slaiver; sliv(v)er

sledge *n.* sled; (heavy, used on
farms) puddick, puddock

sleek *adj.* sleekit

sleep *in phr.* **lose ~ over** brak
yir nicht's rist aboot

sleight *n.* sleicht

slender *adj.* jimp; sclinner

slept *v. pt.* sleepit; **over~**
sleepit in

slice *n.* (of bread) sheave;
(thin) skelf; *v.* hash

slid *v. pt.* sled (M3); sleed (S)

slide *n.* (children's) rone; (on
ice) skip; *v.* (suddenly) skite

slight *adj., n., v.* slicht

slim *adj.* sclinner

slime *n.* (from fish, ill-smelling)
goor

slip *n.* skite; *v.* skite;
(awkwardly) sklyte, sklyter;
(move quickly) snoove; **let ~**
v. slip; **~pery** *adj.* skitie;
sliddery

slipper *n.* carpet; saftie

sloe *n.* slae

slop *n.* slabber

slope *n.* brae; **situated on a ~**
braeset; *v.* sklent, sklint

sloven *n.* trail; **~ly** *adj.*
strushel; struchlach (BI)

slow *adj.* slaa, slaw; latchie;
(of motion) dreich;

~ **person** creepin-eevie.
(*cf.* **convolvulus**); ~**-coach**
n. warridrag; ~**ly!** *imp.*
heely!
sluggish *adj.* smeerless
sluice *v.* sloosh
slush *n.* sklush; snaa-,
snawbree; slabber; *v.* sklush
slut *n.* limmer
sly *adj.* 1(*chf.* re humour)
pawky; 2 slee; sleekit;
sneck-drawin (A2) ~**ly**
adv. sleely
smack *n.* lick; skelp; snipe;
(on the hand) pandie;
~ **your bottom** scone yir doke
small *adj.* jimp; sma; wee;
n. (person) picht; ~**-holding**
n. huddin; placie
smart *adj.* smert; (grand)
fantoosh
smear *v.* clart; clort; sclairt
(on) sclarry (J); skaik, *ppl.*
skaikit; (with tongue, *liter.*)
sklaik
smell *n.* guff; (sharp,
disagreeable) kneggum; (of
fumes) yowder; *v.* smell
about (like a dog) snowk
smiling *adj.* mirky
smithereens *n. pl.* (tae)
crockaneeshun; (in)
leems (M3)
smock *n.* (for working) vrapper
smok|e *n., v.* rik, reek; **belch**
of ~ reek-book, -bouk; (of

a pipe) feuch; lunt; ~**y**
adj. reekie; smeeky (G1);
smuchty
smooth *adj.* smeeth; (and
glossy) sleekit; *v.* (porridge)
mees
smother *v.* smore; scomfish
(A1); scunfice (M3)
smoulder *v.* smuchter
smudge *n.* smad; smird
smut *n.* smad; smird; ~**ty** *adj.*
fouty
snack *n.* (portable) piece
snap *v.* (with the teeth) gnap;
~**py** *adj.* nibawa; snappus (A2)
snare *n.* girn
snarl *v.* girn
sneak *v.* sneck; ~**y** *adj.* sleekit;
thiefie
sneer *n., v.* jamph
sneeze *v.* neeze
sniff *n.* snifter; *v.* snifter;
snuff; (noisily) snocher
sniffle *v.* sneevle
snigger *v.* snicher
snipe *n.* girn-bleater (Abdnsh.)
snivel *v.* sneevil
snod *adj.* tidy
snood *n.* (of horsehair, made
by fishermen) tippen
snooze *v.* snotter
snore *v.* snocher
snotty-nosed *adj.* bibbly-nibbit
snout *n.* snoot
snow *n.* snaa, snaw; snaave;
snyaave; (slight squally

shower) fluffert; (heavy fall)
onding; (driving) blin-drift,
yowden drift; (melted)
snaa-, snaw-bree; *v*. (in
big flakes) flag; ~-**flake**
n. (large) flag; ~-**white** *adj*.
snaa-fite; ~**y** *adj*. snaavie (s)
snuff *n*. sneeshin
snuffle *v*. snotter; (like a dog)
snowk
so *adv*. as; sae; that; ~ **much**
as much; **it was ~ cold that**
it wis as caal (that caal)
soaked *ppl., adj.* sypit
soap *n*. saip
sob *v*. sab; (deeply) swult
sock *n*. hose; moggan; (with
legs cut off) fit-sock; fittock
sod *n*. fell
soft *adj*. saft; lithe; (spongy,
eg, of rotten vegetables)
fossy; fosy, fozie; ~ **drink**
n. ale; dazzle; ~**ness** *n*.
saftness
soil *n*. yird; (shallow) ebb
land; (thin, poor) scaap,
scaup; *v*. fool; fyle; suddle
soirée *n*. siree
sold *v. pt., ppl.* selt; saal, saul
solder *n., v.* sooder, souder
soldier *n*. sodger
solid *adj*. (of build) stieve
sombre *adj*. dreich
some *adj*. a curn; a fyow; a
puckle; a nummer; a wheen;
~**body**, ~**one** *pron*. some-

een, some-ane; ~**times**
adv. fyles; ~**what** *adj*. gey
son *n*. sin; ~-**in-law** *n*. gweed-
sin
song *n*. sang; (farmworker's)
bothy ballad, cornkister;
(silly) strood, stroud,
strowd
soon *adv*. seen; ~**er** *adv*.
seener; sheener, shuner (s)
soot *n*. sitt; (on pots) brook;
~**y** *adj*. (of pots) brookie;
coomie
sore *adj*. sair; *n*. gaw; sair;
~**ly** *adv*. sair
sorrel *n*. soorocks
sorrow *n*. dool; sorra; ~**ful**
adj. dool; dowie; sorrafu;
wae; waesome
sorry *adj*. vexed; ill-peyt for;
wae for; sorra
sort *n*. kinkind, -kine; **out of**
~**s** oot o reel
sought *ppl.* socht. *cf.* **seek**
soul *n*. saal, saul; sowl
sound *n*. soon(d); myowte;
v. soon(d); soun(d)
soup *n*. (made with offal)
womble-bree
sour *adj*. soor; (of disposition)
sturken; (to the taste) ramsh;
~**ness** *n*. soorness
south *adj., n.* sooth; ~**ern**
adj. southron; suddron;
sooth-kwintra

southernwood *n.* sudderinwid
sow *n.* soo
sow *v.* saw (s), *pt.* sew; shaw,
  pt. shew; shaave, shauv, *pt.*
  shew, *ppl.* shaaven, shauven
sow|er *n.* sawer; **~ing machine**
  n. broadcast
spacious *adj.* spaacious,
  spawcious
spade *n.* spaad, spad, spaud;
  (two-handed for cutting
  turfs, peats) flaaghter-,
  flaughter-spaad
span *n.*, *v.* spang
spanking *n.* buttock-mail
spare *adj.* (of figure) sober;
  v. spar, *ppl.* spart; **~ room**
  n. spence
spare *n.* a fordle
spark *n.* spirk; (from wood
  fire) flaesick;
sparrow *n.* (house) spurdie;
  spurgie (O); sparry (J)
spate *n.* speet; speeth
spatter *v.* spairge
spavin *n.* the spavie (horse
  disease)
spawn *v.* spen
speak *v.* spik; (angrily/
  fretfully) nyatter, rally on;
  (ill of) misca; (again) rebat
special(ly) *adj.*, *(adv.)*
  speeshal(ly)
speckle *v.* spraikle; **~d** *ppl.*
  spraiklt; *adj.* mirly; (of
  cattle and sheep) brookit

spectacle *n.* (a sight) moniment
  ~s *n. pl.* glesses
speech *n.* (of an area) spik
speed *n.* binner; lick; nip;
  v. fudder; **at high ~** at a
  gweed lick; at the iverleevin
  gallop; at howdie haste;
  full ~ ful teer; **at an**
  extraordinary ~ at an
  ondeemous binner
spelling-book *n.* spell-beuk,
  -buik
spend *v.* spen; waar, waur; wair,
  ware; weer; (of time) hud
spider *n.* ettercap; nettercap;
  wyver; **~'s web** moosewob;
  webs of a small ~ slammach
spike *n.* (of a railing etc) pyke;
  tine, *ppl.* pykit
spill *v. tr.* jilp; owercowp;
  tr., intr. skail, skale, skel;
  splyte; spull; **~ over**
  v. jibble ower; **~ings** *n. pl.*
  spleeters; spullins; skaillies
spindl|e *n.* spinnle; **~y legs**
  spinnle shanks
spinning-bee *n.* rockin
spinning-wheel *n.* wheel
spirit *n.* speerit; (mettle) gurr;
  smeddum; **~ed** *adj.* gallus;
  hallyrackit; mettlesome;
  ~less *adj.* saarless, saurless;
  ~ual *adj.* speeritool
spit out *v.* splew
spite of, in *prep. phr.* mager,
  mauger; i mauger o (A)

splash *n.* blash; jilp; skirp; splatch; *v.* skite; skirp; spairge; spark; sperk, spirk; spurk (J); splyter; **~ about** *v. intr.* jilp; (in mud or water) plowter; **~es** *n. pl.* spleeters

splatter *v.* daad, daud

splay-footed *adj.* skew-fittit; skyow-fittit

spleen *n.* melt; milt

splendid *adj.* (first rate) bencape; (*excl.*) capital; **~ly** *adv.* brawly

splendour *n.* braivity

splinter *n.* skelb; skelf

splints, put in *phr.* scob

split *v.* rive

splutter *v.* splooter, splouter

splodge *n.* splairge

spoil *v.* blad, blaud; connach; spile, spyle; **~t** *ppl.* bladdit, blaudit; (completely) connacht; geen tae potterlow; **~ed** *adj.* (of children) beamfullt; connacht; (of a person) dorty

spoke *v. pt.* spak; **~sman** *n.* forspeaker

sponge *v.* cadge; sorn; **~r** *n.* cadger

sponge-cake *n.* (in paper cup) sair-heidie

spongy *adj.* fozie

spontaneous *adj.* aff-han

spoon *n., v.* speen

sport *v.* daff

spot *n.* spat; (splash) spirk; **~ted** *adj.* fleckit; mirly

spout *n.* spoot; (of teapot etc) stroop; *v.* (talk volubly) lay-aff

sprawl *v.* sprachle, sprauchle

spring *n.* spang; (elastic force) sprent; *v.* spang

sprout *n.* (Brussels) sproot; *v.* sproot; (of grain) breer; **~ing** *n.* (of new grain) braird; breer

spruce *adj.* jinipperous; spree

spue *v.* splew

sputter *v.* hotter

squall *v.* (scream) skwaal

square *adj., n., v.* squaar, squarr

squat *v.* (on the haunches) hunker

squeal *v.* skwyle, squile; squallach

squeamish *adj.* cackie-stammackit; **be ~** *v.* womle

squeeze *v.* birse, birze

squelch *v.* plowter; plyter

squint *adj.* gley; *n.* cockle-ee; gley; **eye with a ~** gleyed ee

squire *n.* laird

squirt *n., v.* scoosh; skite

stack *n.* ruck; (steaming) het ruck; (thatched for winter) thackit ruck; (badly built & porous) wattert ruck; (foundation) ruck-foon; (support for off-centre stack) ruck-post; (stack

ladder) ruck-ledder;
(rectangle of hay/straw)
soo; ~-yard *n.* corn-yard
staff *n.* (walking) rung; staffie;
~-in-hand *adj.* staffy-nevel
stagger *v.* stacher, staucher;
staamer, staumer; styte,
stoit; styter, stoiter; stot;
stotter
stake-fence *n.* palin
stale *adj.* wachy
stalk *n.* (of kail or cabbage)
castock; runt; *v.* stilp
stall *n.* sta(a)
stallion *n.* staig
stalwart *adj.* beerdly, buirdly
stammer *v.* habber, hubber;
mant; **stamp around** *v.*
(noisily) haamer; pammer;
paut
stampede *v. intr.* (of cattle to
avoid insect bites) prick
stand *v.* stan
staple *n.* stepple
star *n.* starn(ie)
starch *n.* stairch; stiffen;
v. stairch
stare *v.* glower; gowp, goup;
gype
starling *n.* stirlin; stirrie
start *n.* aff-go; stairt, stert; *v.* set
tee; stairt; weer in (work)
get yokit; ~ing-time *n.* (at
work) yokin-time
starvation *n.* stairvation

starve *v.* stairve, sterve;
knap (B1)
stash *n.* hushie
state *n.* (of excitement)
feerich; **in a ~** in a feerich
stately *adj.* (would be) pensy
statue *n.* staito (A2)
staunch *adj.* stanch; stainch,
stench; stinch
stay *n.* stey; *v.* bide, *ppl.*
bidden; stey; (at an
address) stop
steading *n.* steadin; toon,
toun
steal *v.* chore (Abdn., Cant);
nab; rype; stale, stail; stow;
ppl. stowen
stealth, by *adv.* stown-wyes
steam *n.* stame; ~-driven
threshing-machine
stamemull, stem-mull
steep *adj.* stey; steepy
steeple *n.* toopachin; toopican
steer *n. sing. and pl.* nowt
steering-rod *n.* stang
step *n.* stap; **a ~ forward** *phr.*
a muckle stank luppen (M3)
stick *n.* (for walking) rung;
v. stap; stick, *pt.* stack,
ppl. stucken; ~y *adj.* clorty
stickleback *n.* (or minnow)
bandy
stiff *adj.* satteral
stifling *adj.* smuchty
still *adj.* (of weather) lown;
adv. aye

stilt *n.* stilpert
sting *n.* stang; job; *v.* job;
~**ing nettles** jobby nickles
stingy *adj.* grippy; nar; near
stint *n.* stent
stipend *n.* steepin
stir *n.* steer(och); stur; *v.* gee;
jee; kirn; pirl; steer; stur
stitch *n.* steek; *v.* (coarsely)
ranter; steek
stock *v.* (a farm) plenish;
take ~ tak taik
stocking *n.* hose; (sometimes
used as a purse) moggan;
(being knitted) shank;
footless ~ moggan; **shoes
and ~s** hose an sheen
stole *v. pt.* staw
stomach *n.* kite, kyte; stamach,
stam(m)ack; wame; wime,
wyme; (of a calf) yirnin;
v. stammack; ~-**ache** *n.*
bellythraw
stomp *v.* stodge; stowff
stone *n., v.* steen, stane; ~'**s
throw** steen-cast; ~-**chat**
n. steen-chackert; ~**crop**
n. fou;
stony *adj.* steeny, stany
Stonehaven *pr. n.* (to outsiders)
Steenhive; (locally) Stonie
stood *v. pt.* steed
stool *n.* steel, steil; creepie;
(square-shaped) buffet steel;
(with short legs) cutty steel

stoop *v.* lout
stop *v.* stap; gae fae; hud fae
store *n., v.* fordal, fordle
stormy *adj.* (of weather)
cankert; gurlie, gurly
story *n.* (tall tale) binder; (old
and stale) caal kail het; (long,
about nothing) lab(b)ach (R);
(drawn out) lagamachie;
linglairy (B I)
stout *adj.* brosie; stoot, stout
straight *adj., adv.* eyven;
stracht, straucht; **off the ~**
prep. phr. agley; agee;
~**en** *v.* strachen; straichen;
stracht, straucht; ~**en your
tie** set yir tie eyven; ~**away**
adv. instanter; strachtwye,
strauchtwye; ~**forward** *adj.*
(honest) fair-furth-the-gate;
stracht-oot-the-gate
strain *v.* (milk through a
sieve) sey
strainer *n.* (of milk) seyer
strange *adj.* keerious; unca,
unco; (unknown) frem(d);
~**r** *n.* ootlin; unco man; *pl.*
the fremt; unco fowk
strangle *v.* worry
strap *n.* (leather for punishment
in school) tawse; ~**s** *n. pl.*
(buckled leather, worn
below the knee by
farm-hands) nicky-tams;
waal-tams

straw *n.* strae; (loose, *eg,* on field after harvest) strab; (bundle of) win(d)lin; **the last ~** the croonin shafe; *v.* (one's boots) strae (T), stra (R) yir beets; **~berry** *n.* straaberry; **~-rope** *n.* (ball of) clew, cloo

stray *v.* rake

streak *n.* spraing; straik

stream *n.* burn; (small) strype; stoor, stour

street *n.* causey; (narrow) wynd; **~-sweeper** *n.* scaffy

strength *n.* strenth, strinth; **on the ~ of** *phr.* in the leethe o; in the lythe o

stretch *v.* rax; streek; streetch

strewn *ppl.* sprent

strict *adj.* streck, strick

stride *v.* lamp; spang; sten(d) (A2)

strife *n.* sturt (C)

strike *v.* cloor, clour; clowt, clout; gird; strick, strik; (sharply) knype; wap

string *n.* twine; tow; (of a fiddle) thairm

strip (off) *v.* tirr; **~ped naked** tirrt nyaakit

stripling *n.* callant

strive *v.* strive, *pt.* streeve

strode *v. pt.* strade

stroke *n.* straik, strake; (blow) daad, daud; (on the palm) paamie; sclaff; sclaffert; (sharp) wap; (of good luck) raise-o-the-win; *v. pt.* strack

stroll *n.* taik; *v.* danner, dauner; dander, daunder

strong *adj.* baul (B1); beerdly; buirdly; fere; kibble; stoot; strang; (of wind) reevin; **~ly** *adv.* starkly; **~hold** *n.* haald, hauld

strove *v. pt.* streeve, struve

struck *v. pt.* strack; *ppl.* strucken

struggle *n.* pilget; tyaave, tyauve; (hard) sair fecht; sair tyaave; ae pot an row; *v.* tyaave, tyauve, *pt.* tyeuve; strive, *pt.* streeve; waachle, wauchle; warsle, warstle; witter (K)

stub *v.* (the toe etc) stob

stubble *n.* stibble

stubborn *adj.* thraan, thrawn; stockit (M3); **~ness** *n.* gee

stucco *adj., n.* stookie

stuck *v. pt.* stack; *ppl.* stucken

stud *n.* tacket; **~ded boots** tackitie beets

student *n.* colleeginer (A1); (first year) bajan(ella)

stuff *v.* stap; (full) pang; **~ed full** stappit fu

stumble *n., v.* hyter; styter, stoiter; stotter; (of a horse) snapper

stultified *ppl.* dytlifiet

stump *n.* (for chopping wood)
hack-stock; *v.* stowff
stun *v.* da(i)ver
stunted *adj.* crynt; scrunt; (in
growth) settril; shargart;
~ **person** sharger
stupid *adj.* bleat; daupit; dylt,
doilt; dytit, doitit; donnert;
feel; gaakit, gawkit; gapus;
glaikit; gypit; ~ **fellow** stirk
(*See* **fool**); ~**ity** *n.* feelness;
gaakitness, gawkitness;
gypery;
stupify *v.* daver; dozen
sturdy *adj.* buirdly; fere; kibble
stutter *v.* habber, hubber; mant
subject *n.*, *v.* subjeck
substance *n.* graith
such *adj.* sic; siccan; ~ **and** ~
sic an sic; ~**-like** *adj.* siclike
suck *v.* sook; ~**er** *n.* (of tree)
sooker; ~**ling calf** *n.* sookin
caafie
sudden *adj.* suddent (C); ~**ly**
adv. suddent; in/on a
suddenty; ~**ness** *n.* suddenty
sue *v.* soosh
suffocate *v.* scom-, skumfish;
scunfice (M3); smore
sugar *n.* succar
suit *n.*, *v.* shoot; sheet, shuit;
v. set (M3); ~**able** *adj.* suitin
sulk *v.* mump; funk (B1);
~**y** *adj.* sturken; **look** ~**y**
v. glumph

sullen *adj.* drumly; maroonjus;
scoukin; ~**ness** *n.* gee;
soorness
sully *v.* fyle; suddle
sum *n.* soom; (large) sowd;
(small) triffle; trifflie
summer *n.* simmer
summit *n.* toopachin; toopican
sumptuous *adj.* lordlifu
sun *n.* sin; ~**burned** *adj.*
sinbrunt; din-skinnt;
~**set** *n.* sindoon; ~**shine** *n.*
sinsheen
sunder *v.* sinder; sinner
sundry *adj.* sinry
sunk down *adj.* seggit
superannuated *ppl.*
sooperanniwat
superior *adj.* (of attitude)
skichent
supernatural, the *n.* feart
things
superstit|ion *n.* supper-
steeshun; a fret; ~**ious**
beliefs *adj.* & *n. pl.* feart
things
supervisor *n.* owersman
supper *n.* sipper
supple *adj.* soople, souple;
swack, swak; **make** ~
swacken
support *n.* stey; ~**er** *n.*
uphaader
sure *adj.* seer; sure; shair (S);
~**ly** *adv.* seer; seerly; surely;
shairly (S); fairly

surface *n.* (of water) screef;
screeth; scriff

surfeit *n.* forleithy (B1)

surl|y *adj.* strunge; **~iness** *n.*
soorness

surmise *n.* sleumin

surpass *v.* cow(e)

surprise *n.* astonisher; (*excl. of*)
goshie; govie-dick(s); jings;
loshins; loshtie (be here);
loshtie-goshtie-guide's;
meggins alive; megstie me;
michty me; serve's

surround *v.* ring

survive *v.* (as a race and *fig.* as
an individual) store the kin
(*chf. used in neg.*)

suspect *v.* jaloose, jalouse;
suspeck

suspense *n.* tig-tire; **in ~**
in captire

suspicious (of) *adj.* ill-thochtit

swagger *v.* cock

swallow *n., v.* swally; (quick(ly))
scoof, scouf; (bird) *n.* swalla

swarm *n.* hobble; smarrach;
swarrach; *v.* heeze

swathe *n.* (cut by scythesman)
bout

sway *v.* swey; swye; swig (J);
(influence) swye

swear (-word) *n.* sweer, sweir;
v. sweer; ban; (vehemently)
sweer blue lowes (B)

sweat *n.* swat; (state of sudden
heat) feem; *v.* swat (*pt.* swat,
swattit); swate (A2); swite,
swyte

swede *n.* swad; Swaddish neep

sweep *v.* soop (K); swipe, swype

sweet *n.* (round) sweetie-boolie;
pl. galshachs, galshochs;
smachrie; **~heart** *n.* lad; jo
(J, M3); **~-seller** *n.* (female)
sweetie-wife

swell *v. tr. & intr.* swall; hive,
ppl. hoven

swept clean *ppl. & adj.*
besom-ticht

swerve *v.* jee; jink; jouk

swift(ly) *adj., adv.* swith; swyth

swig *n., v.* scoof, scouf; waach,
wauch; *n.* teethfu; *v.* wowff

swill *v.* sweel

swim *v.* sweem; soom (C, K);
~mer *n.* sweemer

swindle *v.* swick; **~r** *n.* swick

swing *n., v. tr. & intr.* showd;
sweeng; swey; **~-boats** *n. pl.*
(at the carnival) showdin-
boats

swingle-tree *n.* sweengle-tree

swirl *v.* sweel

swish *v.* sweesh

swivel *v.* sweevle

swollen *ppl.* flozent; **~-headed**
adj. swall-heidit; swaleheidit (S)

swoon *n., v.* swarf

sword *n.* soord; swoord; soward

sympath|ise *v.* mak mean for; *neg.* mak nae mean for; sympatheese; **~etic** *adj.* sympatheesin

Synod *n.* seenit

syrup *n.* seerup

T

table *n.* brod; buird

tackle *n.* taikle

tag *n.* (game) tackie; takie; tik an tak

tail-board *n.* (of cart) back-door

tailcoat *n.* claw-haimmer coat

tail end *n.* tail-eyn

tailor *n.* tyler; tylie; tailyer; (intinerant) whip-the-cat

take *v.* tak, *pt.* teuk, *ppl.* teen; taen (s); **~ care of** tak aboot; **~ it easy** lat the theats slack; **~ out** *v.* oot wi *eg,* he oots wi his siller

talk *n.* blether; jaa, jaw; tauk; (abusive) ill-jaw; (idle, silly) clashmaclavers, clish-ma-claver; gypery; (intimate) collogue; (low, muttered) toot-moot; (foolish) yaam; yaum (R); *v.* gash; jaa, jaw; (nonsense) blether; haver; (idly and at length) laag; lyaag; laig; (volubly) lay-aff; (excitedly) (yab-) yabber; *adj.* (given to unwholesome talk) kyaard-tonguet; **~ing about** on aboot; **~ative** *adj.* crackie; gabby; **~ing-to** *n.* dixie; hanlin; sedarin

tall *adj.* (and agile) strappin; (tall person) *n.* traleel; (lanky, ill-shaped person) trypal

tangle *n., v.* snorl; (of objects) wumple; **~d** *ppl., adj.* raivelt; snorlt

tanned *adj.* din-skinnt

tantalise *v.* tantaleese

tap *v.* chap; tig; (a hobnail) chat

tapioca *n.* (nicknamed) puddock's eggs

tardy *adj.* latchie; dreich (K)

tare *n.* teer

tart *adj.* satteral

tassle *n.* tossil; toshil

tast|e *n.* gou; *v.* pree; **~eless** *adj.* saarless, saurless; wersh; **~y** *adj.* fine(-tastit)

taught *ppl.* taacht, taucht

tavern *n.* cheenge-hoose; chynge-hoose

tax *n.* cess

tea *n.* tay; (sly cup) fly-cup; fly; (made in the cup) tinkie's maskin; **~pot** *n.* taypot; (earthenware) trackie **~spoon** *n.* tayspeen; **~spoonful** *n.* tayspenfae teach *v.* lairn; leern; teach; ~er *n.* (male) dominie; (female) missie (s)

team-picker *n.* (in games) chyser

tear *n., v.* rive; (rip) teer; ~-stained *adj.* grutten; begrutten

tease *n.* tarraneese; *v.* tarraneese; *tr.* banter

tease out *v.* tase oot (s)

teat *v.* tit; pap; blind ~ blin tit

ted|ium *n.* langer; langsomeness; ~ious *adj.* langsome

teeming with *phr.* hobblin wi (M3)

teeth *n. pl.* chowdlers

teetotum *n.* tottum, totum

tell all *phr.* teem yir crap

tell-tale *n.* clipe, clype

temper *n.* birse; dander; teen; bad ~ ill teen; in a ~ in a bung

temperamental *adj.* cappernyam

temples *n. pl.* (of the head) haffets

tempt *v.* temp; ~ing *adj.* tempin, timpin

tend *v.* ten; *ppl.* tennit

tenement *n.* land

tent *n.* tint

term *n.* (at school) raith

tern *n.* (Arctic) tarick

terrif|y *v.* terrifee; ~ied *ppl.* terrifeet

test *v.* skeel (M3)

testament *n.* tasment; tastement; tesment

test|y *adj.* nippit; ~ily *adv.* nippit-like

tether *v.* tedder (M3); ~-peg *n.* backie; baikie

than *conj., quasi-prep.* nor

thank *v.* thank; thenk (s)

that *adj., pron.* aat; thon; yon; *conj.* at

thatch *v.* thack; theek (J); (by means of stob or stake) stob; (rope-thatch with a cloo) swap; ~ed thackit; stobbit

thaw *v.* thow; ~ing *ppl.* (of weather) fresh

the *def. art.* e; the

themselves *pron.* (also by themselves) theirsels

then *adv.* syne; than

therapeutic *adj.* cowerin

thereupon *adv.* syne

these *adj., pron.* aat; thase; thir; thon; yon; thae (s, j, c)

thick *adj.* (of water) drumly; ~ with (a person) thrang wi

thief *n.* reiver

thigh *n.* (lower part of human thigh) hoch, hough

thimble *n.* thummle

thin *adj.* (of a person) skinny; wainisht-like; ~ legs spurtleshanks; ~-legged *adj.* spurgie-hocht; ~ person *n.* skinnymalink

thing *n.* (the very) the verra dunt;
~**ummybob** *n.* thingumboob;
thingumenderry

thirst *n.* drouth; thrist; ~**y** *adj.*
droothy, drouthy; thristy

thirty *adj.* thretty

thistle *n.* thrissle, thristle

Thomas *pr. n.* Tam

thorn *n.* stob

thorough *adj.* thoara (M3);
~**ly** *adv.* freely

those *adj.* (or these) aat; thir;
thon; yon; thae (S, J, C, M3)

thought *n., v., pt., ppl.* thocht;
~**less** *adj.* thochtless

thousand *n.* thoosan(d)

thrash *v.* aam, aum; ledder; lick;
creesh; soosh; thrash, *pt.*
threesh; ~**ing** *n.* buttock
mail; howder; ledderin;
lickin; limerin; peelin

thread *n.* threid; (unbleached)
whitet-, whitie-broons;
losing the ~ of his thought
aff his stotter

threat *n.* threet; ~**en** *v.*
thraten; threet; threeten;
~**ening** *adj.* threetnin;
(of weather) cankert;
gurlie, gurly; lowrin;
(supernaturally) uncanny

threshing-mill *n.* thrashin-mull

threshold *n.* doorcheek

threw *v. pt.* ceest

thrill *v.* thirl

thrived *v. pt.* thrave; thruve

throat *n.* cra(i)g; gizzen (M3);
hawse (K); thrapple; witters;
clear the ~ haach; haachle

throb *n., v.* stoond, stound

throng *n.* thrang

throttle *v.* thrapple

through *adv., prep.* ben; throw

throw *n.* (heavy) doosht;
v. cast; fung; haive; thraw;
(with a bump) dyst; (down
with a thud) doosht; (of
rope or fishing line only)
shyve; ~ **off** *v.* (a coat) cast;
~**n** *ppl.* (*eg,* from a horse)
cassen

thrush *n.* mavis (M)

thud *n.* dird

thumb *n.* thoom(b); ~**-rope**
n. thoom-raip

thump *n., v.* dird; dunt

thunder *n.* thunner; ~ **clap**
thunner-stane

Thursday *n.* Fiersday

thwarted *ppl.* stickit

tickl|e *v.* kittle; ~**ish,** ~**y** *adj.*
kittlie, kittly

tidy *adj., v.* snod; trig; ~ **up**
v. snod

tie *v.* (tightly) hank; **tiers**
(used for tying) tials

tight *adj.* ticht; ~**-fisted** *adj.*
grippy; near (the been);
~**-fitting** *adj.* nippit; ~**en**
v. tichen;

tile hat *n.* (black) lum hat

till *conj.* ontill, oontill

timber *n.* timmer; **seasoned** ~ wun-timmer

time *n.* time; **in** ~ *phr.* (musically) timeous; **in course of** ~ come time; ~ **off** *n.* afflat; ~-**serving** *adj.* time-sairin

timid *adj.* bauch(-hertit); scaur; skeigh

timorous *adj.* arch (*ch* gutteral)

tin *n.* mill, mull; ~**ful** *n.* mulfa

tingle *v.* dirl; thirl

tinker *n.* caird; cyaard; gate-ganger; kyaard; tinkie; tinkler

tinware *n.* fite iron

tipple *n.* bleb

tipsy *adj.* chippit; foo, fou, fu; far on; sprung; weel on

tiptoe *v.* tice on yir taes

tired *adj.* weariet; **very** ~ forfochen; sair awa wi't; sair come at; typit; wabbit; ~**ness** *n.* tire

titbit *n.* eattock; cheery-pyke

tithe *n.*, *v.* teind

title *n.* teetle

tittle-tattle *n.* claik; clash; **an item of** ~ a claiver

to *prep.* tae; (usually before a vowel) till; tull

toad *n.* ted; ~**stool** *n.* puddocksteel

toast *v.* birsel, birstle

tobacco *n.* tobaacca; (unconsumed in pipe) dottle; ~ **pouch** spleuchan; splochan; splyoochan (M3)

today *adv.*, *n.* the day

toddler *n.* g(y)angrel

todo *n.* adee

toe *n.* tae

together *adv.* thegidder; thegither

toilet *n.* wattery

told *ppl.* bidden; *v. pt., ppl.* taal, taul; telt

toler|ate *v.* bide; thole; tolerat; ~**ance** *n.* merciment

toll (of a bell) *n. v.* jow

tombstone *n.* teemsteen

Tomintoul *pr. n.* Tamintowl

tomorrow *adv.* the morn; ~ **night** the morn's nicht

tongs *n. pl.* t(y)angs; (hinged wire-tightener in fencing) taings

tongue-tied *ppl., adj.* tongue-tackit

tontine *n.* tamteen

too *adv.* an aa; as weel; tee; tae (s)

took *v. pt.* teuk; tyeuk

tool *n.* teel; wark-leem, -loom

toothache *n.* teethache

toothless *adj.* teethless

tootle *v.* (on a wind instrument) tweetle

top *n.* tap; (spinning) peerie; pirn (card with pin passing through, resembling a teetotum) tipperteen; *v.* tap ~ **man or woman** tapster; **over the** ~ (in behaviour) throw the bows; ~**most** *adj.* eemaist; ~**sy-turvy** *adv.* tapsalteerie

torch *n.* (paraffin torch used at sea) bubbly

tore *v. pt.* rave; reeve, *ppl.* riven *cf.* **rive**

torment *v.* tarraneese; tirment

torture *v.* (as a martyr) martyreese

totter *v.* styter; (from old age) tite, tyte

touch *v.* fin; (lightly in passing) scuff; **to the** ~ tae the fin (M3); ~**ed** *ppl.* (emotionally) affeckit; ~**y** *adj.* kittle

tough *adj.* teuch, tyeuch

tousle *v.* tossle; toosle, tousle; ~**d** *adj.* toosy, tousy

towel *n.* tool

tower *n., v.* toor, tour; ~**ing** *ppl., adj.* toorin, tourin

town *n.* toon, toun; ~**-dweller** *n.* toonser

toy *n.* plyaak; plaik

trace *n.* (for a horse) theat; **kick over the** ~**s** kick ower the theats; (the slightest ~) sinacle (B1)

tractor *n.* (Field Marshall diesel) pom-pom

train *v.* (animals to go in traces; children M3) track

tramp *n.* gangrel; trump; (with quarters on farm in exchange for work) quarterer; *v.* haik; londer

transact *v.* transack; ~**ion** *n.* transack

trash *n.* pelt; trag; trock, troke

travel *n., v.* traivel; ~**ler** *n.* gyaanaboot boddy, *pl.* folkies; ~**ling people** *n. pl.* tinkies

treacle *n.* traikle; trykle; ~ **toffee** *n.* claggum; claggieleerum

tread *v.* treid (J)

treat *n.* cheery-pyke; gallshach, galshoch; trait, trett; *v.* (harshly) ool; **harshly** ~**ed** *ppl.* oolt

treble *v.* threeple

trek *v.* haik

tremble *v.* chitter; trummle

trench *n.* sheugh

trencher *n.* truncher

trestle *n.* mason's mear

trice, in a *phr.* in a bicker; in a whup

trick *n.* aivis; begeck; gaa, gaw; ginkum; ginkmen (B1); jink; plisky; prot(t)ick; rig; (of the weather) widder-gaa; *v.* begeck; begowk;

to play a ~ on tae hae a
hyze wi; tae play a rig; tak
the rise o; ~ery *n.* joukerie-
pawkery; ~y *adj.* (of a task)
fykie; kittle; kittlesome; quirky
trickle *v.* pink; treetle
trifle *n.* triffle; trifflie;
(worthless) quinkins
trifling *adj.* nochtie, noughtie
trim *adj.* jinipperous
trip *v.* hyter
triple *adj.* threeple
triplet *n.* threeplet
trollop *n.* limmer
trot *v.* tite, tyte; treetle
troth *excl.* trogs
trouble *n.* baachle; fash,
dispeace; trebble, tribble;
~some thing tribbler; *v.* fash;
don't ~ yourself dinna fash
yir thoom/yir heid; make ~
raise din; mak dispeace;
~-maker *n.* din-raiser;
~-making *adj.* din-raisin;
~some *adj.* fashious; (of a
job) fykie
trough *n.* troch
trouser|s *n. pl.* breeks, briks;
troosers; (of thick cotton)
moleskins; ~ braces *n. pl.*
galluses; ~ fly *n.* spaver;
~ed *ppl.* breekit
trousseau *n.* providin
trout *n.* troot
trowel *n.* trool

truant *n.* fugie (rhymes with
budgie); *v.* true (the skweel)
~ officer *n.* catcher (s)
truce *n.* (in games) parley,
after the cry *parleys-on*
truck *n.* (dealings) troke
trudge *n., v.* haik; londer;
lowder; traik; trail
trump *v.* trumph
trust *n.* lippenance; *v.* lippen
tae; troo; ~worthy *adj.*
lippenable
truth *n., int.* trowth; ~ful *adj.*
trowthfu
try *v.* sey
trysting-tree *n.* covin-tree
tuck in *v.* fang in; hing in
tuck up *v.* (skirts, sleeves etc) kilt
Tuesday *n.* Tyesday
tufted *adj.* foggagy
tug *n., v.* rug; tit; yark
tumble *n.* tummle; keelupper
(from upturned keel);
v. sclyter, tummle; ~down
adj. tummle-doon
tumbler *n.* (glass) tummler
tumult *n.* shirrameer;
shirramineer
tune *n.* teen; (lively, on the
bagpipes) port; (lively) rant;
spring
turd *n.* toldie (Abdn.)
turf, a *n.* a divot; truff; (piece
of) fell
turkey-cock *n.* bubbly(jock)

turmoil *n.* dirdum(dree)

turn *n.* (to play etc) shottie;
v. (over) fommle; wammle;
wommle; w(h)ummle; (of a
river) wumple; (inside out)
flype; (sudden) jink; twine;
~ **and twist** weemple an
wample

turncoat *n.* turnkwite

turnip *n.* neep; **~-slicer** neep-
hasher; **~-lantern** neepie-
lantrin; **~-hoeing** neep-rinnin;
~ **and potato soup** lefts an
richts; ~ **watch** neep waatch

turnover *n.* owerturn

turret *n.* toopachin; toopican

Turriff *pr. n.* Turra

twelve *adj.* twal; **~-month
period** *n.* towmon(d);
twalmont(h)

twenty *adj.* twinty

twice *adv.* twise

twilight *n.* gloam; gloamin;
gloomin; glowmin (M3)

twine *n.* (strong) tow

twinge of rheumatism *n.* chang

twirl *n., v.* birl

twist *n.* crook; thraw; *v.* kinsh;
thraw, *ppl.* thrawn; twine;
~ed *ppl.* warplt; **~ing** *adj.*
thrawart

twitch *v.* tit

two *adj.* twa; twae; **~-faced**
adj. dooble; **~-handed** *adj.*
twa-han; **just the ~ of them**
theirsels twa

type *n.* teep

tyrannise *v.* tirraneese

tyrant *n.* tirran

U

udder *n.* aidder; ether

ugly *adj.* ill-, ull-faart

umbrage *n.* umrage

umbrella *n.* umberella

un- *prefix* on-; oon-

unaware *adj.* onwuttin

unbaptised *ppl., adj.*
oonbapteest

unbeholden *adj.* onbehauden

uncanny *adj.* eldritch;
oonchancie

uncaring *adj.* ooncarin

unceasing(ly) *adj., (adv.)*
oondevallin

uncivil *adj.* oonceevil

uncommon *adj.* ooncommon

uncontrollable *adj.* oot o han;
naither tae haad nor bin

uncouth *adj.* hull-run

uncover *v.* tirr

undamaged *adj.* clear

undecided *adj.* i the deid-
thraw; **to be ~** *v.* swither

under *prep.* oonder; ooner;
~-cattleman *n.* little
bailie; **~clothes** *n. pl.*
nether duds; **~ground**

adj., adv. oondergrun;
~**most** *adj.* naithmaist;
~**pants** *n. pl.* (long) draars;
draavers ~**shirt** *n.* semmit;
seemit; linder; linner;
sarket, sarkit; ~**stand** *v.*
oonerstan, *pt.*, *ppl.*
oonersteed; winnerstan;
~**take** *v.* tak in han; ~**taking**
n. oonertakkin

undigested *adj.* ondisjeestit
undoubtedly *adv.* oondootitly
undress *v.* tirr
undulate *v.* wammle
unearthly *adj.* eldritch;
oonchancie; ooncanny
uneducated *adj.* onedicat
unending *adj.* oonendin
uneven *adj.* shammelt
unexpected *adj.* oonexpeckit
unfair *adj.* (used by children)
skicy
unfamiliar *adj.* unca, unco
unfeeling *adj.* onfeelin
unfortunate *adj.* misfortnat;
unweirdy
unfrequented *adj.* lown
ungenerous *adj.* ill-willie;
(used by children) skycie
ungrateful *adj.* peyed-thankless;
pickthank; pykethank
unhappy *adj.* oonhappy
unheeding *adj.* onheedin
unintelligent *adj.* preen-heidit
unkempt *adj.* hudd(e)ry

unkind *adj.* ill; ull; ~**ly** **done**
ull-deen
unknown *adj.* oonkent; unco
unlawful *adj.* oonlawfu
unless *conj.* onless, oonless
unload *v.* unlade; (a catch of
fish) liver
unmannerly *adj.* menseless
unmethodical *adj.* ramshackle
unmindful (of) *adj.* onmynit (o)
unnatural *adj.* oonnaitral
unpleasant *adj.* (in behaviour)
ill-, ull-farrant
unprincipled *adj.* oonprenciplt
unquenched *adj.* oonslockent
unreasonable *adj.* oot o theat;
oonrizzonable
unrighteous *adj.* oonrichteous
unroof *v.* tirr
unruly *adj.* (of children) royd,
royt
unsatisfied *adj.* (of food and
drink) ill-sairt
unsettled *adj.* (of weather)
tittersome
unsociable *adj.* saachen,
sauchen
unsought *ppl., adj.* unsocht
unspecified *ppl., adj.*
onspeshifiet
unsporting *adj.* skycie
unstable *adj.* oonstable
unsteady *adj.* (of a table etc)
shoogly; (of person) stitery
unstretched *ppl., adj.* onstreekit

untidy *adj.* strushal, strushel; ill-shaken up, ill-shooken up; struchlach (BI); throw-idder; throwder; ~ **person** eeshich (BI); ticket; track; wallydraigle

until *conj.* or; ontil, oontill

untiring *adj.* ontirin

untroubled *adj.* oonfasht

unwashed *ppl., adj.* oonwaashen

unwell *adj.* oonweel; oot o reel; paewae; **to be ~** *v.* ail

unwilling *adj.* oonwullin; sweer(t), sweir(t)

unworked *adj.* (of land) unvrocht

unyoke *v.* lowse

up *adv.* up; hup

upbringing *n.* upfessin, -feshin

uphold *v.* uphud

upland *adj.* upthrow

upon *prep.* upo

upper hand *phr.* wheep han

uppermost *adj.* eemaist;

upper part of field eemaist wynin

uproar *n.* carrant; collieshangie; dirdum(dree); gilgal (hard *g*) (BI); kickup; rammy; reerie; remishin; rippit; shirram(in)eer; stramash; stushie

uprooted *ppl., adj.* (by the wind) win-casten

upset *v. tr.* kittle; vex; (overturn) cowp; (a plan) cowp the creels; whommle

upwardly mobile *phr.* uppish

upwards *adv.* upwuth

urine *n.* strang; (stale, used as detergent) maister; ~ **jar** maister-pig

urinate *v.* pish

urination *n.* rin-oot

us *pron.* hiz; huz

usage *n.* eesage

use *n.* eese (*pro.* eece); **full ~ of** *phr.* weelins; *v.* eese (*pro.* eeze); ~**d to it** eest wi't

useful *adj.* eesefu; essfu

useless *adj.* eeseless; feckless; ~ **person** footer

usual *adj., adv.* eeswal(ly)

utmost *adj.* itmaist

utter *v.* moo-ban

uvular "r" *n.* (sounded in throat) burr; hurl in the throat; *v.* to use the uvular "r" burr

V

vacant *adj.* vaacant, vawcant

vacillate *v.* swither

vagabond *n.* vaigabon

vagrant *n.* gangrel; gyangrel; (contempt. Abdn.) minker; trump

vain *adj.* full; vantie, vauntie

valentine *n.* valinteen

valley *n.* strath; (narrow) glen; howe

valu|e *n.* vailye; (something of little value) wanwurth; (something of no value) tinkler's curse; ~able *adj.* vailyable

vanish *v.* vainish

vapour *n.* vaapour, vawpour; yoam, yowm

variable *adj.* immis (B1)

vegetation *n.* growthe

vehicle *n.* viackle; (old and rickety) shan-dre-dan

venomous *adj.* veeperate

venture *v.* ventur, *ppl.* vintrin

very *adj., adv.* fair; fell; foo; gey; verra; unco

vessel *n.* veshel; (drinking) pintstowp, -stoup

vest *n.* seemit; semmit,

vestige *n.* sinacle

vetch *n.* (tufted) fidgick; **wild peas** fidgick piz

veterinary surgeon *n.* ferrier

vibrate *v.* dirl; tirl

vibration *n.* dirl; tirl

vicious *adj.* veeperate; veeshus

view *n.* (range of vision) scance; vizzie; (mental attitude) opingan; vyowe

vigil *n.* (over the sick) onwyte

vigour *n.* fushen, fushon; **lacking ~** fushenless; **~ously** *adv.* ful teer; teeth an nail

vilify *v.* (vilipend) wilipen

village *n.* clachan; toon, toun; (with parish church) kirkton; ~ **green** *n.* loaning(s)

vindictive *adj.* vengefu

violence *n.* (to person or property) bangstrie

violent *adv.* veelent

violin *n.* fiddle

viper *n.* veeper

virago *n.* randy

vision *n.* veesion

visit *n.* veesit; *v.* (briefly) ca in by; cry in by; ~or *n.* veesitor; (the first to meet a marriage party or call on New Year's Day) first-fit

vituperative *adj.* veeperate

vivid *adj.* vive

voice *n.* vice, vyce

voluble *adj.* lairge

vomit *n.* splewin; *v.* byock (B1); kowk (A); puke (B1); spue; splew; spoot

vouch *v.* vooch

vow *v.* voo

vulgar *adj.* grofe; groff

W

waddle *v.* shochle; waachle, wauchle

wade *v.* wide, wyde

wager *n., v.* waager, wauger

wages *n. pl.* waages, wauges;
(farmhand's) fee; (in
advance) sub
wagon *n.* (two-wheeled, open)
bogie
wail *v.* croon; walloch
waistcoat *n.* waskit; weskit;
(sleeved) shaftit weskit;
shafter; (under-jacket) fecket
wait *v.* bide; wyte *pt.* wat
(M3); wytit; *imp.* heely; ~ **a**
moment hoaver a blinkie
wakeful *adj.* waakrife, waukrife
waken *v.* waaken, wauken
walk *n.* waak(ie), wauk; traivel
(s); (stroll) taik; (long,
wearisome) trail; *v.* waak,
wauk; leg it, shank it; traivel;
(about) chowp aboot;
(noisily) clamp; (awkwardly)
fuffle; (unsteadily) hyter;
(hand-in-hand, arm-in-arm)
link; (clumsily) haamer;
(aimlessly) pammer; (in mud
or water) plyper; (slowly)
stodge; (with a spring) stot;
(with heavy, swinging gait);
slewie (B1); (in a stomping
way) stumpart, stumper;
(in flat-footed way) sclap;
sclaup; ~**er** *n.* waaker,
wauker; ~**ing-stick** *n.* rung;
~**way** *n.* waakie
wall *n.* wa; (of stone) dyke;
(dry-stone) dry steen dyke;
(built of sods) feal dyke;

~ **clock** *n.* (with pendulum)
wag-at-the-wa; waggitie-wa;
~-**cupboard** *n.* press; ~-**eyes**
n. pl. ringel-een
wallop *n.* forfeffis; ringle;
skeegin
wallow *v.* (in mud) slocher
wand *n.* gad, gaad; waan
wander *v.* anter; hake; rake;
staiver; stravaig; wanner;
(in speech) raivel; ~**er** *n.*
gate-ganger
want *n., v.* wint; wunt
wares *n. pl.* gibbles; waares
warm *adj.* waarm; (of good
growing weather) forcie;
v. (before the fire) beek;
bek; byke
warped *ppl., adj.* gizzent
warrant *v.* warn; ~**y** *n.*
warrandice
was *v. pt.* wis, *neg.* wisna
wash *n.* waash; (quick) cat's
dicht; *v.* waash, *pt.* weesh(t);
ppl. waashen
washing-line *n.* claes tow
waste *n.* waistry; wastry;
wastrifeness; ~ **away** *v.*
dwine
water *n.* watter; **dash of** ~
jaw; ~-**closet** *n.* wattery;
~**fall** *n.* linn; watterfa;
~-**glass** *n.* (for preserving
eggs) wattergless; ~-**hen** *n.*
beltie (G1); ~ **sprite** *n.*
kelpie; ~ **tap** *n.* stroop;

~ing-can *n.* rooser; ~y *adj.* (of flavour) waable, wauble

wave *n.* waav; (at sea) jaa, jaw; *v.* wag

way *adv.* wye; wa; wan; **come a~ in** come yir was ben; *n.* gate; wye; **to be in the ~ in** the road; **out of the ~!** oot o the road!; **in the ~ of** (doing etc) the weers o (M3); **in what ~?** fat road?

weak *adj.* feckless; fen(d)less; saft; thowless; waffle; waik; wyke; ~**-minded person** *n.* saftie; ~**ly** *adj.* sober; ~**ness** *n.* waikness; wykeness

wealth *n.* gear; **accumulate ~** *v.* fog, ~y *adj.* walthy

wean *v.* speen; spen

wear *n., v.* weer; ~ **yourself out** ca yirsel deen

wear|y *v.* jaap, jaup; ~**ied** *ppl.* dylt; wabbit; weariet; ~**isome** *adj.* dreich; langsome

weasel *n.* futrat, futtrat; ~y **person** futtrat

weather *n.* wadder; widder; wither; (~ good for crops) *adj.* forcie; (~ good for growth) *adj.* growthie; ~**-beaten** *adj.* din-skinnt. *cf.* **sunburned**

weave *v.* wyve

weaver *n.* wabster

weaving *n.* wyvin

web *n.* (spider's) moosewob; (of small spiders) slammach; (woven fabric) wab

wed *v.* wad, *pt.* waddit; mairry; ~**ding** *n.* mairritch, mairrage; waddin

weed *n.* wide, wyde

week *n.* wik; ook, ouk; ~**-end** wik-en; **a ~ today** this day ook/wik

weep *v.* greet; sab

weigh *v.* wye, *pt.* wyt; ~**ed down** (with) *ppl.* wechen doon (wi); doun-presst (wi); ~**t** *n.* wacht, waucht; wecht; (for fastening horse in stall) sinker; ~**ty** *adj.* wachty, wauchty; wechty; ~**ing machine** *n.* (steelyard type) steilert

weird *adj.* ooncanny; ~**o** *n.* wully-goo

weld *v.* (by hammering) clink

we'll *pron. with v.* we's

well *adj.* weel; *adv.* brawlies; brawly; brulies; weel; *int.* aweel; weel; wale (s); ~**-bred** *adj.* genteel; mensefu; ~**-built** *adj.* kibble; ~**-favoured** *adj.* weel-faart, -faurt; ~**-fed** *adj.* brosy; sair-maitit; ~**-intentioned** *adj.* weel-mynit ~**-known** *adj.* weel-kent; (by sight) kenspeckle; ~**-loved** *adj.*

leal-loved; ~-**mannered** *adj.*
weel-mennert; mensefu;
~-**matched** *adj.* (of people)
weel-yokit; ~-**off** *adj.*
bien; foggit; geddert;
weel-geddert; ~-**to-do.**
See well-off
well *n.* waal
wellington boots *n. pl..* waldies
went *v. pt.* gaed, geed; gid
wept *v. pt.* grat; *ppl.* grutten;
(noisily) roared an grat
we're *pron. with v.* we's
were *v. pt.* war; wur; *pt.*
neg. warna
west *adj., adv.* wast; ~**ern**
adj. waster; ~**ward** *adv.*
wastlins; wastward
wet *adj.* wat; weet; plytery;
(of weather) drabbly;
v. drabble; weet, *pt. perf.,*
ppl. wutten
wether *n.* (castrated ram)
wedder
wetting *n.* steepin
wettish *adj.* weetichtie
whack *n., v.* skelp
whale *n.* whaal, whaul
what *adj., pron.* fat, faat;
fit; fut; ~ **a**, ~ **a lot of** fat a;
whotten a; ~ **sort of** fatna;
~-**do-you-call-it** *n.* fat-
ye-ca't; ~**ever** *adv., conj.*
fativver
wheedling *ppl., adj.* fraiky

wheel *v.* (~ a barrow) rowe;
~-**barrow** *n.* hurl-barra (M3)
wheeze *v.* clocher; whazzle;
wheezle
whelk *n.* wulk
whelp *n.* fulp
when *adv., conj., pron.* fan,
faan; fin
where *adv.* faar, faur; whaar,
whaur; ~ **else** *interrog. adv.*
faar idder; ~**ever** *adv., conj.*
farivver; ~**as** *conj.* forbyes
whether *conj.* fidder; fudder;
futher; gin
whey *n.* fy
which *pron.,* fulk; whilk; *rel.*
pron. whilk; fit (s); ful; ~ **of**
you ful o ye
whiff *n.* gluff; waff
while *conj., n., v.* fyle; (little)
fylie; filockie; wee; whilie;
whylock; **stay a** ~ bide-a-wee
whim *n.* gee; maggot; tig;
full of ~**s** maggotive
whimper *n.* girn
whin *n.* fun, funn; ~ **mill** fun
mull
whine *v.* peenge; yammer
whinny *n.* nicher
whip *n., v.* fup; wheep; whup;
~-**hand** *n.* fup-han; ~**per-in**
n. dog-dirder
whirl *v.* furl; whurl; ~**y** *adj.*
furly
whirr *n.* birr; *v.* binner
whisk away *v.* wheech

whisker|s *n. pl.* fuskers; **~ed**
ppl. fuskert
whisky *n.* fusky; whusky; the
cratur; **small ~ bottle** cutter
whisper *v.* fusper; **~ing** *n.*
fusperin; toot-moot (B1)
whist *n.* whust
whistle *n.* fustle; (of the wind)
sough; (whistling sound)
wheeber; *v.* fustle; sough;
wheeble; wheeple; (in a low
tone) sowff
whit, not a *phr.* dag the bit
white *adj.* fite
whither *adv.* whaur awa
whitlow *n.* futlie (beelin)
Whitsunday *n.* Wutsunday
whittle *v.* fite; futtle
whizz *v.* wheech; wheek
who *pron.* fa, faa; wha (G1)
whole *adj., n.* hail(l), hale;
~sale *adj.* hale-wheel;
~some *adj.* halesome
whom *pron.* wham
whooping cough *n.* kinkhoast
whore *n.* hooer, hure
whorl *n.* (flywheel on spindle)
forl
whose *pron.* whase (G1),
whause
why *adv.* fat for; fit wye;
foo; hoo
wicked *adj.* ill; ull; wicket
wide-awake *adj.* vertie (M3)
widow *n.* weeda; widda;
widdie (J)

wife *n.* goodwife (A2);
gweedwife; kimmer; wife
wight *n.* wicht
wild *adj., adv.* wil; wudden;
wull; maroonjus; (high-
spirited) gallus; (giddy)
halycut (K); (to madness)
witriffe; (of children) royd,
royt; (unfrequented) bosky;
~cat *n.* wullcat; **~-like** *adj.*
wull-like; **~ mustard** *n.*
skellach
will *n.* (testament) tasment;
tastement; tesment; wull;
v. wull, *neg.* winna; wunna
William *pr. n.* Weelum; Wull(ie)
willing *adj.* redd; wullin
willow *n.* saach, sauch;
(abounding in willows)
sauchy; **~ wand;** saach-
waan, widdie-waan
wind *n.* win; (gust) flan;
(sudden gust) howder; (off
the sea) oot-win; (high)
reevin win; **~bag** *n.* gab;
~fall *n.* capshun; fun siller;
~ instrument *n.* tooteroo;
~pipe *n.* weazen, weazon;
wizzen; **break ~** pump; let
off; **~y** *adv.* winny
wind *v.* (a rope) kinsh; (of a
river) wimple
window *n.* windae; windy (J);
winnock (A1); wunda (M3);
wundockie (M3); **~-catch** *n.*

windae-sneck; ~ **pane** lozen;
~-**sill** *n.* sole

wing *n.* weeng

wink *v.* blink

winnow *v.* winny; ~**ing machine** *n.* fan; fanner

wipe *n.* dicht; dirrum-dicht; *v.* dicht

wire *n.* weer; ~-**tightening lever** peer-man

wise *adj.* wice, wyce

wish *n.*, *v.* wiss; wuss; ~**bone** *n.* thocht-been

wisp *n.* wusp

wit *n.* wut; *pl.* wuts

witch *n.* carlin(e)

with *prep.* wi

wither *v.* widder; ~**ed** *ppl.* (of flowers) wallant

without *prep.*, *conj.* athoot; wi-oot; withoot; withouten; on (used with *pt. ppl.*); ~ **being** on-been; ~ **having** on-hed; ~ **doing** on-deen etc, **to do ~ them** tae eese wuntin em

witness *n.* wutness

wizened *adj.* foggie; gizzent

wobbl|e *v.* waable, wauble; ~**y** *adj.* (of objects) shoogly; (of people) waable, wauble

woe *n.* wae; *excl.* waly; ~-**is-me** wae's me; ~-**begone** *adj.* hinginluggit; ~**ful** *adj.* waefu

wolf *n.* wowff

woman *n.* umman; wife; wifie; *pl.* weemen; (married) kimmer; (old) carlin(e); (big, fat) frow; (*derog.*) besom (of doubtful character) kiltimmer; (of ill repute) runk; (loose, loose-tongued) randy; (dirty, untidy) trail; (loose) vyaig; (worthless) baggerel; cutty

womb *n.* wyme

won *v. pt.* wan

wonder *n.* ferlie; winner; *v.* winner; wonner, *ppl.* winrin; (at) ferlie (ᴋ); **no ~** sma winner; deil a muckle winner (ᴍ3); ~**ful** *adj.* winnerfu

wood *n.* (substance) timmer; wid; (trees) wid; wud; (small) widdie; shaw (ᴊ); ~**en** *adj.* timmer; widden; ~**louse** *n.* slater; ~ **pigeon** *n.* cushie-doo; ~**shaving** *n.* flaesick, flezick; spell; ~-**turner** *n.* (maker of caaps) caaper, cauper

wool *n.* oo; woo; (knitting) worsit; ~-**bag** *n.* worsit-bag; ~**ly** *adj.* ooie

word *n.* wird; ~**s** *n. pl.* langidge

work *n.* wark; trava(i)l; (day's work) darg; (messy or difficult) scutter; *v.* darg; wirk, *pt. reg.*, also vrocht, wrocht; (in a flurried way) foorich; (messily) kirn, plowter, plyter; (clumsily) haamer; (at pressure) hash; (vigorously) link at, timmer on/up; (at domestic chores) scudge, skudge; (awkwardly) scutter; (ineffectually) tooter; (strenuously) tyaave, tyauve; (hard) yark; **start ~** yoke, yoke intae; **set to ~** wire intae; **stop ~** lowse; **at ~** *prep. phr.* ayoke; **~er** *n.* wirker; **~-house** *n.* peer(s)hoose; warkhoose; **~ing period** yokin

world *n.* wardle; warl(d); wordle; **~ly** *adv.* war(l)dly; **~ly-wise** *adj.* warly-wise

worm *n.* wirm; **~wood** *n.* wormit

worn *adj.* (weel-) tasht

worn out *ppl., adj.* caad deen; forfochen; forjeskit; foonert; (with hard work) fochen-deen; puggled; sair awa wi't; sair come at

worr|y *v.* wirry; **~ied** *adj.* pit/ pitten oot; vext

worse *adj.* waar, waur; **the ~ for wear** waar o (or i) the weer

worst *adj., n.* warst

worsted *adj., n.* wirsit, worsit; (fine, from spun wool) fingerin

worth *n.* wirth; **~ his salt** *phr.* wirth saut till his kail; **for all his ~** hail teer; **~less** *adj.* orra; weirdless; **~less thing** *n.* wa-cast; **~y** *adj.* wordy; *n.* woorthy

would *v.* wad, wid, wud; **~ not** wadna, widna, wudna

wound *n.* hagger; sair; *v. pt.* wun

woven *ppl.* wivven

wraith *n.* wreith

wrangle *n.* dibber-dabber; tirr-wirr

wrap *n.* hap-waarm; *v.* vrap; wap; wip; wup

wrath *n.* wraith

wreath *n.* (of snow) vreath

wreck *n.* wrack

wren *n.* vran

wrestl|e *v. liter.* shak a fa; *fig.* vrastle; warsle, warstle **~ing bout** *n.* shak-a-fa

wretch *n.* vratch; wratch

wright *n.* vricht; jyner

wring *v.* vring

wrinkled *ppl.* runklt, wrunkelt

wrist-bone *n.* shacklebane, -been

writ|e *v.* screeve, screive; scrive; vreet *pt.* vrat; vrote; *ppl.* vrutten; **~er** *n.* vreeter

writing *n.* vreet; (long piece of) screed; **~-desk** *n.* vreetin-dask; **~-paper** *n.* vreetin-paper

writhe *v.* wammle

wrong *adj.*, *n.* vrang; wrang
wrote *v. pt.* vrat; vrote
wrought *v. pt.* vrocht

Y

yank *v.* yark
yard *n.* (unit of measurement)
yaird, yerd; **~stick** *n.* ell-wan;
farm~ *n.* closs
yarn *n.* (woollen) worsit;
(ends of) thrums
yawl *n.* yole; (used for catching
cod by hand-line) ripper-yole
yawn *n.*, *v.* gant
year *n.* ear; year; towmond;
twalmont(h); **last ~** fernyear;
was-a-year; **~ before last**
fernyear was-a-year
yearn (for) *v.* mang for; green
(efter) (Bɪ)
yeast *n.* barm
yell *n.*, *v.* skraich; skirl; yall
yellow *adj.* yalla; **~ish grey**
fyaachie; **~-hammer** *n.*
yaldie; yeldrin; yirlin;
~ iris *n.* seg; **~ turnip** *n.*
yalla
yelp *v.* yalp

yeoman farmer *n.* bonnet
laird
yes *adv.* ay; ty; yea
yesterday *n.*, *adv.* (esp.
evening) the streen,
yestreen
yet *conj.* still an on; yit
yield *v.* ring in
Y-junction *n.* split-the-win
yokel *n.* countra geordie
yonder *adv.* thonner; yonner;
yont
you *pron.* ee; ye; *pl.* (in
vocative case) you eens; **~'ll**
pron. with v. ye'll; ye's; **~r**
poss. pron. yer; yir
youngster *n.* ted; **~s** *n. pl.*
yunkers
yourself *pron.* yersel; yirsel;
by ~ yirsel
youth *n.* (abstract term)
youthheid; (young man)
halflin; birkie; (talented)
lad o pairts; (smart young
man or girl) swankie
Yule *n.* Eel; Yeel; (12-day
pagan celebration after
winter solstice)

Luath Press Limited

committed to publishing well written books worth reading

LUATH PRESS takes its name from Robert Burns, whose little collie
Luath (*Gael.*, swift or nimble) tripped up Jean Armour at a wedding
and gave him the chance to speak to the woman who was to be his wife
and the abiding love of his life. Burns called one of the 'Twa Dogs'
Luath after Cuchullin's hunting dog in Ossian's *Fingal*.
Luath Press was established in 1981 in the heart of
Burns country, and is now based a few steps up
the road from Burns' first lodgings on
Edinburgh's Royal Mile. Luath offers you
distinctive writing with a hint of
unexpected pleasures.
Most bookshops in the UK, the US, Canada,
Australia, New Zealand and parts of Europe,
either carry our books in stock or can order them
for you. To order direct from us, please send a £sterling
cheque, postal order, international money order or your
credit card details (number, address of cardholder and
expiry date) to us at the address below. Please add post
and packing as follows: UK – £1.00 per delivery address;
overseas surface mail – £2.50 per delivery address; overseas airmail –
£3.50 for the first book to each delivery address, plus £1.00 for each
additional book by airmail to the same address. If your order is a gift,
we will happily enclose your card or message at no extra charge.

Luath Press Limited
543/2 Castlehill
The Royal Mile
Edinburgh EH1 2ND
Scotland
Telephone: +44 (0)131 225 4326 (24 hours)
email: sales@luath. co.uk
Website: www. luath.co.uk